Items should be returned on or before the last date
shown below. Items not already requested by other
borrowers may be renewed in person, in writing or by
telephone. To renew, please quote the number on the
barcode label. To renew online a PIN is required.
This can be requested at your local library.
Renew online @ **www.dublincitypubliclibraries.ie**
Fines charged for overdue items will include postage
incurred in recovery. Damage to or loss of items will
be charged to the borrower.

Leabharlanna Poiblí Chathair Bhaile Átha Cliath
Dublin City Public Libraries

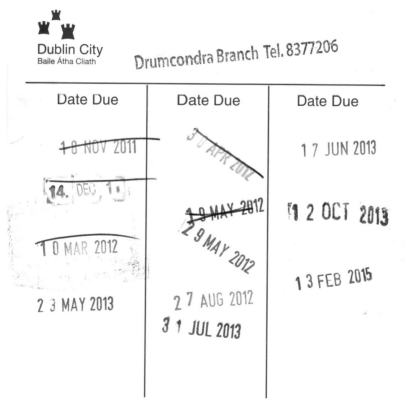

Dublin City
Baile Átha Cliath

Drumcondra Branch Tel. 8377206

Date Due	Date Due	Date Due
18 NOV 2011	30 APR 2012	1 7 JUN 2013
14. DEC 1.	1 9 MAY 2012	1 2 OCT 2013
1 0 MAR 2012	2 9 MAY 2012	
		1 3 FEB 2015
2 3 MAY 2013	2 7 AUG 2012	
	3 1 JUL 2013	

A CITY IN WARTIME

Dublin 1914–18

A CITY IN WARTIME

Dublin 1914–18

PÁDRAIG YEATES

Gill & Macmillan

Gill & Macmillan
Hume Avenue, Park West, Dublin 12
with associated companies throughout the world
www.gillmacmillan.ie

© Pádraig Yeates 2011
978 0 7171 4972 8

Index compiled by Helen Litton
Cartography by Design Image
Typography design by Make Communication
Print origination by Síofra Murphy
Printed and bound by ScandBook, Sweden

This book is typeset in Minion 10.5/13 pt.

A CIP catalogue record for this book is available from the
British Library.

5 4 3 2 1

To my father, Patrick (Jack) Yeates, and mother,
Annie (née Dowling) Yeates, who played as children
in the ruins of the Easter Rising...

CONTENTS

ACKNOWLEDGEMENTS

This book grew out of one written more than a decade ago called *Lockout: Dublin, 1913*. Over the years I often wondered what happened to many of the actors in that titanic struggle, not least the citizens of the city, and why Dublin was such a different place by the time the first Dáil assembled in the Mansion House on 21 January 1919. This book is the result.

The advent of the war was the real turning point in twentieth-century Irish history, as it was in that of every country in Europe. Elements within the Unionist, Nationalist and Labour camps had created the potential for a political explosion of quite serious domestic proportions by 1914; but the power of that explosion was increased exponentially by the advent of a world war. Dublin was the detonator and therefore deserves special study.

As with *Lockout*, the newspapers of the day, primarily the *Irish Independent* and the *Irish Times*, provided the narrative motor for this book. I delved down various byways as my attention was drawn to them by the newsmen (and handful of newswomen) of the day. I am glad to see that much of the academic snobbery surrounding reliance on newspapers as a historical source has evaporated over the years. They certainly have agendas, sometimes pursued quite shamelessly, but they have the great advantage of operating in a public arena where their version of events is open to scrutiny and challenge.

I owe my own preconceptions of events during those years in large part to family recollections and traditions. I was privileged to know quite a number of people who lived through the era, and I deeply regret that I never recorded their reminiscences when I had the chance.

I wish to acknowledge the advice and assistance I received from Mary Clarke, Maire Kennedy and their colleagues in the Dublin Civic Archives; Catriona Crowe and the staff of the National Archives; Commandant Victor Lang and Hugh Beckett of the Bureau of Military History; Brendan Byrne and the Irish Labour History Society; Jack McGinly of SIPTU; the staff of the Berkeley Library, TCD; Gerry Kavanagh and his colleagues at the National Library of Ireland; the staff of the National Photographic Archive; John Johnston-Kehoe; Mary Jones; Michael Lee for photographs and documents relating to his great-grandfather Edward Lee and family; Breandán Mac Gearailt; Mícheál Ó Móráin and Brigid Ashe for information on Thomas Ashe and for permission to use pictures; Theresa Moriarty; Eve Morrison; Ed Penrose; Peter Rigney; my editor, Séamas Ó Brógáin; from Gill & Macmillan, Deirdre Rennison Kunz for putting up with last-minute changes to copy, Jen Patton for pursuing some of my more arcane requests for pictures, Ciara O'Connor and

Fergal Tobin. Fergal is part-parent of this book, as he proposed the original *Lockout* project and agreed to acknowledge its offspring.

Finally, I wish to thank my son Simon for his support and Geraldine Regan for her encouragement over many years.

Any errors are my own, and, as far as possible, I have tried to acknowledge and recruit my prejudices and predilections constructively to the task of writing this book.

ABBREVIATIONS

ANZAC	Australian and New Zealand Army Corps
AOH	Ancient Order of Hibernians
DMP	Dublin Metropolitan Police
DSER	Dublin and South-Eastern Railway
DUTC	Dublin United Tramways Company
GSWR	Great Southern and Western Railway
INTO	Irish National Teachers' Organisation
IRB	Irish Republican Brotherhood
ITGWU	Irish Transport and General Workers' Union
ITUC	Irish Trades Union Congress
ITUC&LP	Irish Trades Union Congress and Labour Party
KC	King's counsel
MGWR	Midland Great Western Railway
NSPCC	National Society for the Prevention of Cruelty to Children
RDS	Royal Dublin Society
RIC	Royal Irish Constabulary
TCD	Trinity College, Dublin
UIL	United Irish League
WNHA	Women's National Health Association

A note on place-names
Because various streets and buildings have been renamed since 1914, the first reference to each gives both titles, for example 'Royal Barracks (now Collins Barracks)'; 'Sackville Street (now O'Connell Street)'. Subsequent references use whichever name is most appropriate in the text.

A note on money
The pound (£) was divided into twenty shillings (s) and the shilling into twelve pence (d). Intermediate amounts were written in a combination of denominations, e.g. 3s 6d; £2 10s. Some relatively small amounts in pounds might be written entirely in shillings, e.g. 42s (£2 2s).

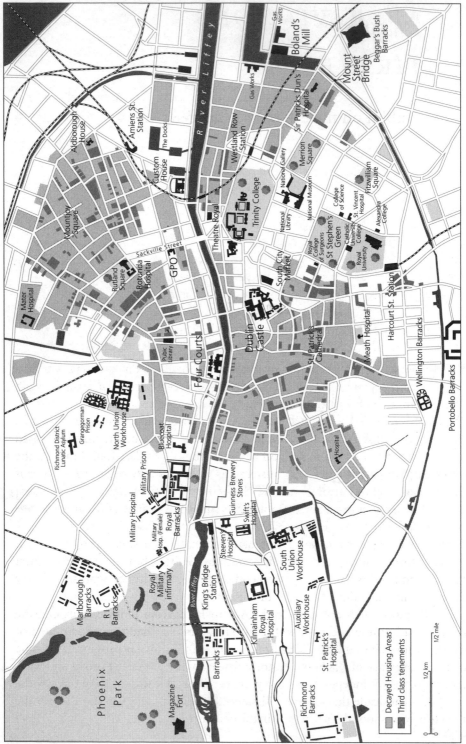

Dublin 1914–16

Gas Works

Boland's Mill

Beggar's Bush Barracks

Mount Street Bridge

River Liffey

Sir Patrick Dun's Hospital

The Docks

Amiens St. Station

Custom House

Aldborough House

Gas Works

Westland Row Station

National Gallery

Merrion Square

Fitzwilliam Square

College of Science

Mountjoy Square

St. Vincent Hospital

Alexandra College

National Museum

National Library

Sackville Street

Rutland Square

Rotunda Hospital

GPO

Theatre Royal

Trinity College

South City Market

Royal College of Surgeons

St Stephen's Green

Catholic University College

Royal University

Harcourt St. Station

Mater Hospital

Four Courts

Public Library

Dublin Castle

St Patrick's Cathedral

Meath Hospital

Wellington Barracks

Portobello Barracks

Grangegorman Prison

Richmond District Lunatic Asylum

North Union Workhouse

Bluecoat Hospital

Hospital

Military Prison

Military Hospital

Guinness Brewery Stores

Swift's Hospital

Military Hosp. (Female)

Royal Barracks

Steeven's Hospital

South Union Workhouse

River Liffey

King's Bridge Station

Royal Military Infirmary

Marlborough Barracks

R.I.C. Barracks

Royal Barracks

Phoenix Park

Magazine Fort

Kilmainham Royal Hospital

Auxiliary Workhouse

St. Patrick's Hospital

Richmond Barracks

Barracks

Decayed Housing Areas

Third class tenements

½ km

½ mile

| FIRST BLOOD

Dublin on the eve of the First World War

The First World War came early to Dublin. From 9:30 a.m. on Sunday 26 July 1914, companies of Irish Volunteers from the city's north side began assembling in Father Mathew Park, Fairview, for a march.

It had been posted as a routine martial excursion for Ireland's recently formed amateur nationalist militia, the third in as many weeks. But by the time ranks had been dressed and the men moved off at 10:30 the north-siders found that all the south-side companies had been mustered as well, and they began to wonder if something special was up. If it was, the authorities were taken unawares, and there was only a token posse of the Dublin Metropolitan Police to accompany the Volunteers.

All over Europe armies were mobilising after the assassination of Archduke Franz Ferdinand of Austria in Sarajevo a month earlier; but the honour of first blood would fall this day to these weekend soldiers, a handful of Scottish infantry and, above all, the ordinary citizens of Dublin.

The archduke, heir apparent to the Austro-Hungarian Empire, had been the victim of bad timing and poor traffic management. The bad timing consisted of paying a state visit to the capital city of the empire's South Slav province of Bosnia on the anniversary of the Serbs' historic defeat by the Turks at Kosovo and their subsequent loss of independence 360 years before; and it was a wrong turn by the Archduke's cavalcade that gave the dissident Serbian student Gavrilo Princip the opportunity to shoot the town's distinguished visitor.

By contrast, what was about to happen in the capital city of Britain's Irish province was the product of superb timing and organisation. The men, between two and three thousand strong, first realised there was something different about their route march when they saw groups of cyclists posted at junctions directing them towards the fishing village of Howth, nine miles north of the city, a favourite excursion spot for day-trippers. It was a long march for citizen-soldiers, and they sang military songs, such as 'Clare's Dragoons,' 'Step Together' and the soon to be ubiquitous 'Soldier's Song' to keep their spirits up between the showers that spliced the summer sunshine.

As the men approached the village a gap in the trees gave them a glimpse of the sea and a yacht tacking off Lambay Island, five miles to the north. Some jokingly called to each other, 'She must be the boat bringing us the guns.'

By 12:30 p.m. the long column of Volunteers filled Harbour Road, but the men were not allowed to fall out. When the yacht they had seen off Lambay entered the harbour the lead companies were sent up the East Pier at the double to clear it of civilians while the rear companies blocked all access to that end of the harbour. By 1 p.m. hundreds of German Mauser rifles were being passed up from the deck of the *Asgard* into eager outstretched hands. Thousands of rounds of ammunition had already been spirited away in five motor cars.

One unusual aspect of the operation, little commented on at the time, was that the unloading and distribution of the weapons was not carried out by the Volunteers but by members of Fianna Éireann, the republican boy-scout organisation whose members, despite their years, were better organised and drilled than their elders.

The small detachment of Royal Irish Constabulary resident in the village was powerless to intervene, and when a more enterprising Coastguard patrol put out from the far side of the harbour to approach the gun-runners they quickly withdrew when Volunteers levelled rifles in their direction.

The harbourmaster, W. T. Protherow, was made of sterner stuff. Having hastily donned his uniform, he rushed down the pier, to be met by 'a living wall' of men. He demanded to be let through, regardless of threats to 'put a lump of lead in his head' and turned away defeated only when his RIC escort, making a more realistic assessment of the situation, refused to clear the way.

To cheers from crowds of local people, the ebullient Volunteers marched back towards Dublin. One of the organisers, Michael O'Rahilly (also known by his invented title 'the O'Rahilly'), captured the mood and could be forgiven the hyperbole when he wrote: 'For the first time in a century one thousand Irishmen with guns on their shoulders marched on Dublin town.'

The telegraph wires to Howth had been cut, and the Coastguard had to send a man by bicycle to Baldoyle to raise the alarm. The first, totally inadequate contingent of police arrived by tram to intercept the Volunteers at Kilbarrack. The constables took one look at the opposition and boarded the next tram back to the city. At the village of Raheny, more than half way back to Dublin, the Volunteers encountered a larger contingent of police. Far from attempting to obstruct the march or seize the weapons, however, the police cheered them on, and the marchers, allowed a badly needed break, showed off their new rifles to the equally enthusiastic constables. According to some press reports, the two groups joined in a rendition of 'A Nation Once Again' before the march resumed.

This was not as strange or unusual as it might appear. Nationalist Ireland believed itself on the brink of home rule. When the nationalist leaders John Redmond and John Dillon had arrived at Buckingham Palace for talks with the British government and Unionist leaders a few days earlier, members of the Irish Guards regiment had cheered; and on Saturday a detachment of Royal Dublin Fusiliers at summer camp in Youghal marched down the Main Street on their return from the rifle range also singing 'A Nation Once Again.' True, the conference at Buckingham Palace had broken down, but most nationalists still believed that their unionist fellow-countrymen would eventually be won over to the goal of self-government. Many of them felt grateful to Ulster unionists for founding their own armed militia, the Ulster Volunteers (later the Ulster Volunteer Force), and creating a precedent that nationalists could emulate.

The previous April, under cover of night, the Ulstermen had brought in thousands of weapons and millions of rounds of ammunition with impunity in order to resist home rule by force. Now the Irish Volunteers had carried out an almost identical operation in broad daylight; and if their feebler financial resources could stretch only to nine hundred rifles, it was certain that more would come. Most importantly, the Howth gun-running was a statement of intent that would stiffen the resolve of the Liberal government to face down militant unionism.

But the government did not see it that way at all. It wanted to keep guns out of Ireland, and in 1913 a royal proclamation had been issued that banned the continued importation of weapons. Firearms, mainly intended for Ulster, had been seized with amazing regularity *en route* through the ferry ports to the north. That very weekend some 55,000 rounds of ammunition, thought to be intended for the Ulster Volunteers, had been seized in Birmingham, the home of British small arms manufacturing and the power base of England's leading unionist political dynasty, the Chamberlains.

When the Assistant Commissioner of the DMP, William Vesey Harrel, received word of the Howth episode he telephoned the Under-Secretary for Ireland, Sir James Dougherty. Dougherty arranged to meet Harrel at Dublin Castle to discuss the situation. Harrel failed to show up, and Dougherty began to fret—with good reason. The under-secretary was a member of a fast-vanishing breed of radical Ulster Presbyterian liberals committed to the cause of home rule. Harrel was also an Ulsterman but from a vehemently unionist tradition.

Dougherty sent a note belatedly to Harrel's headquarters, advising him that 'forcible disarmament of the men on the march into Dublin with these arms should not, in the circumstances, be attempted.' Harrel was not in his office to receive the warning: he was busy gathering policemen to block the Howth Road where it debouched near the Volunteers' rendezvous that morning in Fairview. He had sent for urgent military reinforcements, and two tramloads of the King's Own Scottish Borderers arrived in the nick of time to block the Volunteer column as it reached Fairview. The Volunteers swung smartly right into the Crescent and onto the adjoining Malahide Road to avoid the military, but Harrel was equally quick and sealed off the new escape route. He then demanded the surrender of the guns.

A tense confrontation ensued. Darrell Figgis, a Dublin journalist and writer who had helped organise the gun-running, invited Harrel to step into a front garden to discuss the problem. Figgis argued that parades through Irish towns by paramilitary bodies were commonplace and that only the previous Sunday a similar march had been held through Belfast by the Ulster Volunteers. He accepted that the gun-running was illegal, and that he was guilty, and he offered to surrender himself into police custody. It was a creative compromise, and a potential face-saver for the authorities, but Harrel would have none of it. When he was informed that Volunteers were taking advantage of the lull to spirit guns away through open fields towards the city, he ordered the first rank of policemen to seize the rifles. They made a half-hearted attempt to carry out this order before the Volunteers drove them back with rifle butts, hurleys and home-made truncheons. According to Figgis, the police were so unenthusiastic that when they inadvertently captured him in a scuffle he was thrust back into the Volunteer ranks with an injunction 'to keep to the thinking and leave the fighting alone.' The second line of police refused point blank to assist their heavily outnumbered colleagues. According to most reports, they even cheered the Volunteers.

Harrel, who had held the 160-strong military contingent in reserve, now ordered them forward with fixed bayonets, but with little effect. Some nineteen Mausers were seized, but the soldiers lost two of their own Lee-Enfields. One member of the Volunteers, Captain Michael J. Judge, who found himself fighting for his country less than a mile from his home in Clonliffe Avenue, collapsed after being bayoneted by a soldier through the left arm and chest. A few ranks back Joseph Lawless, a young Volunteer from Saucerstown, near Swords, climbed onto the coping of a low wall to see Judge, his company commander, fall. He drew his revolver, and when another officer tried to grab it Lawless accidentally discharged it.[1] The melee came to an abrupt halt. The two sides drew apart, with honours even: three Volunteers, two soldiers and one constable had been injured.

Perhaps the most telling tale of the changing balance of forces was in the manner of their removal. The injured constable had to make his own way to hospital, assisted by colleagues, on a tram; the two soldiers had to wait for an army ambulance; but the Volunteers were driven post-haste by private motor car to the Mater Hospital.[2]

Now began the long retreat of the King's Own Scottish Borderers to the Royal Barracks (now Collins Barracks) at the other side of the city. Their distinctive headgear advertised their place of origin, and even in the relatively respectable lower middle-class suburb of Fairview the 'crowd groaned, hissed and hooted the soldiers … and told them to go back to their own country.' The 'lady spectators were even more intensely indignant and outspoken than the men,' according to the *Irish Independent*. Words were supplemented by occasional missiles as the soldiers neared the inner-city slums, and there was a bayonet charge on the North Strand, where civilians fled down side streets or into local shops. By the time the contingent reached Sackville Street (O'Connell Street) it had acquired a taunting tail of about two hundred Dubliners, mostly young men and boys. As the *Freeman's Journal* noted afterwards, further trouble could have been avoided if there had been a police presence, but after the melee at Fairview the DMP had left the soldiers to their own devices.

The soldiers turned again on their tormentors, almost on the spot of the previous year's 'Bloody Sunday,' when hundreds of civilians had fallen victims to DMP batons during labour disturbances. The soldiers now lashed out with equal lack of discrimination at passers-by. And worse was to follow.

When the contingent reached the north quays and the narrower confines of Bachelor's Walk, the crowd swelled and grew closer. Stones flew, one soldier was kicked to the ground and another stunned by a flower pot thrown from a house as a new mob poured down Liffey Street to threaten the unit's flank. It was at this point, by the Ha'penny Bridge, that the rear ranks turned and fired two volleys. Whether they acted on impulse or on the order of an officer was never properly established, but the fusillade left three people dead and eighty-five wounded, at least thirty of them seriously. The three dead were Mary Duffy, a 56-year-old widow who had a son in the Royal Dublin Fusiliers, Patrick Quinn, a coal porter and father of six, and James Brennan, a seventeen-year-old messenger.

That night all troops were confined to barracks, and one soldier with a Scottish accent who was foolish enough to venture out in civvies was thrown in the Liffey. The Lord Lieutenant, Lord Aberdeen, wanted to visit the injured in hospital but his officials refused to allow him risk his person, given the mood in the city.[3]

Dublin was plunged into mourning, and there was a huge turn-out the following Wednesday for the funerals. The crowds were reminiscent of those that followed the procession of labour martyrs during the Great Lock-out a few months earlier. Businesses closed and, as if to reprimand the futility of Assistant Commissioner Harrel's activities, the procession was headed by Volunteers equipped with their recently acquired Howth Mausers. Besides the principal mourners, who included Mary Duffy's son, Private Thomas Tighe, in dress uniform, was the whole spectrum of nationalist Ireland. The Lord Mayor, Lorcan Sherlock, led the city's aldermen and councillors, followed by contingents of the United Irish League, the National Foresters in their Robert Emmet uniforms, trade unions, the Volunteers' female auxiliary, Cumann na mBan, Fianna Éireann, and groups as disparate as two hundred students from the College of Science and sixty Christian Brothers.

The procession wended its way from the Pro-Cathedral in Marlborough Street to the scene of the crime at Bachelor's Walk before proceeding to Glasnevin Cemetery. The crowd was packed so closely as it approached the Ha'penny Bridge that it could barely move. 'The assembled thousands became overwhelmed with grief ... Hundreds wept and sobbed aloud,' the *Freeman's Journal* reported. People walked up the south quays in a parallel procession; others leaned out of office windows, climbed lamp-posts and even clambered onto the roof of the Mater Hospital to catch a glimpse of the procession passing by. There were no political speeches, but the *Freeman's Journal*, mouthpiece of moderate nationalists and the Irish Party, took comfort in the fact that 'mingled with the sorrow for the dead, was a feeling of pride in the splendid discipline and manly bearing of the Volunteers.'[4]

Even as the crowds gathered by the Liffeyside to mourn their fellow-citizens, Austrian gunboats had begun to bombard the Serbian capital, Belgrade, in the opening salvoes of what would become the First World War. Within the week the United Kingdom would be at war with the Austro-Hungarian Empire and its powerful ally Germany. The enormity of these events would quickly overshadow Dublin's street brawl; but Princip's opportunist shots and Darrell Figgis's well-planned arms delivery were both indications that Europe's young generation of militant nationalists, for all their ragamuffin uniforms and inexperience, were going to be more effective in obtaining their objectives than the bemedalled and titled rulers of the vast imperial prisons in which so many small and competing nationalities languished.

————

Dublin was already trying to recover from the traumatic social upheaval of the previous year. Between August 1913 and February 1914 the city had experienced the greatest industrial conflict in Irish history. More than four hundred employers had banded together to lock out fifteen thousand workers and to smash the nascent syndicalist Irish Transport and General Workers' Union. Another ten thousand workers had been laid off as a result of the dispute, which saw a third of the city's population on the bread line. It bore hardest of all on the enormous underclass of casual labourers, hawkers, street dealers and beggars, who had no union and precious little Christian charity to fall back on.[5]

The Great Lock-out of 1913 had been far more than an industrial dispute: it had been a political contest, a public debate played out as street theatre—much of it bloody—about the type of society people wanted under home rule. On one side had been the new Irish ruling class in waiting, Catholic, conservative and grasping; on the other had been a loose coalition of socialists, suffragists, trade unionists and radical nationalists who had varying visions of a more democratic, outward-looking and secular society. It was also the first occasion—and the last for many decades— when an urban protest movement dominated the Irish political landscape.

Memories of the lock-out and the ferocious police baton charges that accompanied it were still fresh in the public memory when more civilian blood was shed on Bachelor's Walk in July 1914.[6]

———

On the day the Volunteers began their dramatic march to Howth the most exciting event envisaged in the city had been an experimental run by a fleet of eight motor buses between O'Connell Bridge and the Point Depot at the end of the North Wall. Motorised transport had first made an impact during the lock-out, when employers found that one lorry could do the work of nine horse-drawn carts. Lorries were also much better at breaking through strike pickets.

Ironically, the debut of motorised buses would ultimately sound the death knell of the city's tram system. It was the refusal of Dublin United Tramways Company to recognise the right of the ITGWU to represent its employees that sparked the lock-out. The chairman of the DUTC, William Martin Murphy, was Ireland's richest Catholic entrepreneur.

Many Dubliners, particularly the more respectable sort, wished to put the events of the previous year behind them. The great event of the summer of 1914 had been the Civic Exhibition, held in the grounds of the magnificent King's Inns in Henrietta Street, designed by James Gandon. The exhibition featured examples of model housing schemes, garden cities, garden suburbs, model cottages, municipal displays, historical art and archaeology, industry and commerce, public health and food, child welfare, bee-keeping and much more. It showed Dubliners all these aspects of modern urban living that their city lacked and that might banish evil memories. The central theme of the exhibition was town planning, and the Lord Lieutenant, John Gordon, Earl of Aberdeen, offered a prize of £500 for the best plan for housing Dublin's 25,882 families then living in tenements. At the opening ceremony on Tuesday 14 July a telegram from King George V, read by Lord Aberdeen, expressed 'the hope that it might result in an improvement in the housing conditions of Ireland.'

In a veiled reference to the lock-out, the earl's wife, Ishbel, explained that

the housing and town planning section had its origin in the widespread feeling which arose out of the sad events of last winter, which made the whole country feel that the time had come when all classes and sections of the community must join to see that this reproach to the city of Dublin should be swept away.

Unfortunately, the city's 100,000 slum-dwellers were not present to hear her. The admission charge to the opening ceremony was 2s, equivalent to more than half a week's rent for many of them. But a reduced rate of 6d was available on Wednesdays, when half-day closing might allow shop assistants to attend, and on Saturdays for other employees fortunate enough to work a 5½-day week.[7]

The exhibition was extremely popular with the better-off members of society, attracting eighty thousand paying visitors.[8] Katharine Tynan recalled:

> People could entertain their friends in the Dining Club—it was quite the thing to give luncheon and dinner parties there—there was a splendid dancing hall with room for the exclusive and the unexclusive … illuminated gardens, with all the fun of the fair, a cinema theatre, all sorts of amusements, as well as instructive habits.[9]

While there was a consensus on the need to tackle Dublin's housing problem, at least in official circles, the question was how. The neglect of successive British administrations had been aggravated by the lackadaisical and hamfisted manner in which the Chief Secretary for Ireland, Augustine Birrell, and his Cabinet colleagues in London handled the lock-out. Events during those dreadful months provided one of the best arguments yet for home rule. But would an Irish parliament and executive prove any better? The Irish Party had been thrown into disarray by the industrial warfare in Dublin and had been unable to take a position vis-à-vis capital and labour; neither had the corporation (city council), which had been deeply divided by the dispute.

Some nationalists had been embarrassed by the lock-out. They perceived Dublin as the premier local authority in the country, even if Belfast had overtaken it in wealth and population. The corporation was held up as a model for the new home rule parliament; but many Dubliners regarded the 'Corpo' as a byword for corruption, dominated as it was by the same sort of small business interests and career politicians who filled the ranks of the Irish Party.[10]

The inquiry was conducted by the Local Government Board, the body responsible for ensuring that local authorities lived up to their obligations. The initiative had been prompted by the Church Street tragedy of 2 September 1913, one week into the lock-out. Numbers 66 and 67 had collapsed that evening, killing seven people, including two children, aged four and five; another eight tenants were seriously injured. The number of deaths would have been much higher if all the tenants had been at home, or if a party for several hundred children in the Father Mathew Hall opposite the houses had ended early, as the rubble from the collapsing buildings had tumbled into the street.

Housing was an emotive issue in Dublin. The tenements may have been a cause of shame for some and a health threat to all, but they were also the largest source of unearned income for the city's middle classes. Landlords included such pillars of society as the chairman of Dublin United Tramways Company and president of the Dublin Chamber of Commerce, William Martin Murphy, and George Plunkett, papal count and father of the 1916 leader Joseph Plunkett. Their power was reflected in the presence of seventeen slum landlords—unionist and nationalist—on the corporation.[11] This lobby resisted every effort by city officials and progressive councillors, mainly Labour representatives, to increase the expenditure on slum clearance. They were so successful that in the decade before 1914 domestic rates (a local tax on house property) were lower in Dublin than at any time in the previous century. Consequently, the corporation's slum clearance schemes were drastically underfunded.

Even the cost of acquiring properties for slum clearance was prohibitive, as landlords were entitled to compensation equivalent to ten years' rental income.[12] The most significant social housing initiatives were undertaken by private bodies, such as the Iveagh Trust and the Dublin Artisans' Dwellings Company. However, these projects were self-financing, which meant they provided accommodation to slightly better-off working-class families that could afford rents of 5s a week. Some 70 per cent of tenement dwellers paid rents of 3s 6d or less.

The inevitable result was that Dublin had the worst housing of any city in the United Kingdom. In 1913 there were 25,822 families living in tenements, four out of five of them in a single room and 1,560 in cellars. There were 1,300 derelict sites in the city, eleven of them in Church Street before the collapse. The sheer size of the problem made enforcement of the housing by-laws impossible. Even after the Church Street disaster only twenty-six dwellings in the city were closed as insanitary, and not a single prosecution was begun for overcrowding, compared with 689 cases taken against women living in these tenements for prostitution. Church Street, which contained by no means the worst houses, had an average of five people to a room. In total almost 23 per cent of the city population lived in one-room tenements, compared with 13 per cent in Glasgow and 0.03 per cent in Belfast. A report prepared by officials of the Housing Committee stated:

These figures speak for themselves. There are many tenement houses with … between 40 and 50 souls. We have visited one house that we found to be occupied by 98 persons, another by 74 and a third by 73.

The entrance to all tenement houses is by a common door off either a street, lane or alley, and in most cases the door is never shut, day or night. The passages and stairs are common, and the rooms all open directly either off the passages or landings … Generally, the only water supply is … a single tap … in the yard.

Toilets, or 'closets', were either in the yard or, worse still, in the basement, so that residents might have to come down three or four storeys to use them. Access to the toilets was open 'to anyone who likes to come in off the streets, and is, of course, common to both sexes.' The buildings were dilapidated and 'in a filthy condition, and in nearly every case human excreta is to be found scattered about the yards and on the floors of the closets, and in some cases, even in the passages of the house itself.'

Such drawbacks did not prevent yards, stairways and even closets being used for casual sex. Understandably, many tenement residents, especially women, used the yard closets only for slopping out chamber pots. The officials concluded that 'we cannot conceive how any self-respecting male or female could be expected to use accommodation such as we have seen.' Yet, in spite of all the handicaps, the report paid tribute to the efforts made 'by many of the occupants to keep their rooms tidy, and the walls are often decorated with pictures.'[13]

The poor sanitation was aggravated by an inadequate drainage system, incapable of removing the raw sewage and resulting in a sickly-sweet aroma hanging over large areas of the city. Not surprisingly, all sorts of health problems flowed from this infrastructural deficit. Death rates for Dublin, which included the much healthier environs of Rathmines, Pembroke, Clontarf, Blackrock, Kingstown (Dún Laoghaire) and Howth, remained consistently above those for Belfast and for British cities. In 1913 the rate of 23.1 per thousand compared with 18.4 in Belfast, 14.3 in London and 12.8 in Bristol. In the first quarter of 1914, when the effects of the lock-out were at their height, the death rate rose to 25.9 per thousand and the child mortality rate rose by almost 50 per cent. The general filth and overcrowding ensured that child mortality rates were the worst in Europe. Every year infectious and communicable diseases, such as tuberculosis, diarrhoea, whooping cough and sexually transmitted diseases (then known as venereal disease) accounted for more than a third of all deaths in Dublin.[14]

Whatever about the ratepayers, the blindness of employers to the problem was hard to understand. There was a consensus that bad housing was a major contributory factor to the labour troubles of 1913. 'Decently housed men would never have fallen such a complete prey to mob oratory,' bewailed the *Irish Builder*, and it was widely accepted that one reason that the general secretary of the ITGWU, Jim Larkin, made few inroads into firms such as Guinness's and the railway companies was that they provided decent housing for employees. The Chief Secretary, Augustine Birrell, vowed after reading the inquiry's findings that 'this report cannot be allowed to rest, as so many other reports have done'; but he was soon to be overwhelmed by other events.[15]

The findings of the inquiry and the five months of violent industrial conflict in the city had caused few in the ranks of the city's middle-class establishment to change their views. Father Tom Finlay, regarded as a very progressively minded Jesuit, had told the Catholic Commercial Club in 1901 that 'religion must be the dominant influence in every sphere of life,' but in 1914 he had no difficulty in rejecting the notion that an increase in the wages of unskilled labourers would help alleviate their suffering and stabilise social relations in the city. 'If it paid the

employers of Dublin to give higher wages they would give them,' he told the
Statistical and Social Inquiry Society in March. However,

> the public were not given to acts of generosity of this kind on a large scale.
> They thought charity was charity and business was business, and the law of
> business, as they understood it, was always to purchase in the cheapest
> market.[16]

Unfortunately the Local Government Board report, published in January 1914, was
too comprehensive and too honest for its own good. It criticised the city's Chief
Medical Officer, Sir Charles Cameron, for granting rebates in rates to councillors
who owned slum property and who made false claims for renovation. The council
rallied to Cameron's defence and pointed to his long record of public service, both
voluntary and paid, from the 1860s.

Within two weeks an alliance stretching from William Martin Murphy's *Irish
Independent* to Arthur Griffith's *Sinn Féin* was united in condemnation of the
report. In May the nationalist majority on the corporation produced a detailed
critique of the inquiry's findings that not alone questioned its methods but claimed
that the Local Government Board was responsible for the housing problem through
its own inactivity and was now using it to justify interference with the autonomy
of the city fathers. Above all, the inquiry's recommendations were damned as
expensive, impractical and a classic example of 'Britain's malign interference in
Irish affairs.'[17]

Dubliners were divided by religion as well as class. There were more than 92,000
Protestants in the city and county, the largest concentration outside Belfast. While
they had not been a majority in the city since the early eighteenth century, they
had dominated its political, social and economic life well into the nineteenth, and
the residue of their historic primacy still left its mark in the twentieth. By 1911
Protestants formed less than 17 per cent of the city's population but remained a
majority of those engaged in banking, senior business management and many of
the higher professions. Catholics now formed a slight majority in the junior ranks
of the law, medicine and accountancy. Even in such areas as the appointment of
Justices of the Peace, where nationalist political influence with the Liberal
government might have been expected to have made inroads, almost two-thirds
of Dublin JPs were Protestants, compared with 42 per cent in Ireland as a whole.[18]

The dominance of Protestants was most marked in the higher reaches of social
and economic life. All the directors of the Bank of Ireland were Protestants, and all
but two of them signed a public letter sent by southern Unionists to the government

in November 1913 warning of the dire economic consequences of home rule. This might explain why the bank had few customers among the rising Catholic middle class in the provinces, but it was still a power to be reckoned with in the capital. The larger manufacturing, engineering and railway companies were also largely the preserve of the old Protestant commercial elite.[19]

Of course the majority of Dublin Protestants were not wealthy, but they were not poor either. Martin Maguire, historian of the city's Protestant working class, puts the number of male Protestant workers at less than six thousand in the early 1900s, with another four thousand in the county. There were as many relatively prosperous Protestant white-collar workers and shopkeepers. The only unskilled occupation where Protestants outnumbered Catholics was soldiering; and the British garrison added 3,100 working-class Protestant males to the population on the eve of the First World War.[20]

Inevitably, the majority Catholic populace saw their Protestant counterparts as privileged. As a child growing up in the city, the future republican activist Christopher ('Todd') Andrews felt that

> Dublin at the turn of the century … was divided into two classes: the rulers and the ruled. The rulers were mainly Protestants, the Catholics the ruled. The Catholics at whatever income level they had attained were second-class citizens.

Protestants were 'as remote from us as if they had been blacks and we whites,' Andrews recalled.[21] His own family ran a dairy in Summerhill and could afford to send him to university. Idealistic and ambitious, Andrews was one of a new generation of nationalists who grew up with a heightened awareness of what a difference religion could make in the higher reaches of society, and he resented it deeply. It is not surprising, therefore, that he drew attention to the gulf between the two main religious communities in Dublin; but there was one important way in which they differed from their counterparts in the North that went largely unremarked: they were not segregated in rival ghettoes. Working-class Dublin Protestants lived cheek by hungry jowl with working-class Catholics and endured the same hardships and insecurity. Andrews reflected a widely held perception when he wrote that 'there were many poor Protestants in Dublin but never destitute Protestants.'[22] Even allowing for a certain exaggeration, the autobiographies of Seán O'Casey testify otherwise, and poor Protestants who encountered such agencies as the Church of Ireland relief scheme in Ringsend could testify that the charity of their social superiors was as hard-faced and tight-fisted as that of the Catholic middle classes and clergy.

Both denominations used the workhouse as the benchmark for awarding food and money. The Ringsend establishment paid 10d for an eight-hour day chopping wood. It was run by the Church Army, an Anglican response to the

Salvation Army. The title of the institution—the Church Army Labour Homes for Criminals, Inebriates, Tramps and Deserving Unemployed—was a mission statement in itself.

This lack of social solidarity within Dublin's Protestant community was the result of a long process of gradual decline dating, ironically, from the series of economic problems that followed the Act of Union in 1801. Until well after Catholic Emancipation in 1829 there had been a strong sense of community among the city's embattled Protestant minority, and Dublin had been a byword for Protestant militancy since the seventeenth century, its skilled artisans providing the rank and file of the Orange militia to protect local liberties. There was sectarian rioting in Dublin as late as the First Home Rule Crisis of the mid-1880s, when shots were fired from the Conservative Working Men's Club in York Street on nationalist rioters.[23]

But the skilled artisan became an endangered species as traditional manufacturing declined. Skilled occupations such as weaving gave way to unskilled or semi-skilled employment in the brewing and confectionery industries, where some of the jobs were filled by Catholic women workers as well as men. W. and R. Jacob, which became one of Dublin's largest employers of female labour, bought out an ailing coach-making concern to build its factory in Bishop Street. That the Jacob family were Quakers simply underlined the fact that religious considerations played second fiddle in the new industrial economy.[24] One consequence was that skilled Protestant workers comprised a disproportionately high share of Dubliners emigrating in the nineteenth and early twentieth centuries.

The one significant area of growth in employment for skilled workers was provided by the railway and tram works at Inchicore; but local Protestant craft workers often lacked the necessary skills to find jobs there, and instead positions were filled by craftsmen from Britain. Far from subscribing to Dublin's Protestant working-class traditions, British craftsmen often married local Catholic women. Although 42 per cent of skilled workers in Inchicore were Protestant by 1913, it was a Labour Party stronghold during the lock-out, and the workers were impervious to the appeal of unionism. William Partridge, one of the Labour councillors for New Kilmainham, was the son of an English train driver who had married the daughter of a Catholic farmer while working in Athlone. Partridge was brought up as a Catholic, and he proved a devout one. During the lock-out he corresponded at length with the Archbishop of Dublin, William Walsh, explaining the workers' case to him.[25]

If lack of suitable employment led skilled Protestant workers to emigrate on a large scale, unlike their departing Catholic counterparts there was no steady stream of rural co-religionists to make good the numbers. Contrary to the popular image, Protestants were a predominantly urban phenomenon in early twentieth-century Ireland. The Anglo-Irish gentry and Protestant farmers accounted for no more than a third of the total, but their high social and political status tended to dominate the image of Protestants in the South.

The dwindling population of Dublin co-religionists led to increasing numbers of Protestants marrying Catholics. The existence of the mainly Protestant British garrison did not help maintain numbers either. A third of the grooms at Protestant weddings in the years before the First World War were soldiers, who took their brides with them when they were posted back to Britain, or overseas. This meant that increasing numbers of male Dublin Protestants had to seek a wife from among the Catholic community. After the Papal *Ne Temere* decree in 1908 children in a mixed marriage were usually reared as Catholics, adding further to the erosion of the Protestant working-class community. One famous example was the marriage of the Catholic socialist James Connolly of the King's Liverpool Regiment to the Protestant domestic servant Lillie Reynolds. Their children were reared as Catholics, and Lillie converted at her husband's request while he was awaiting execution in 1916.

Not that marriage between Protestants guaranteed prosperity or security. When Seán O'Casey's sister Bella married Nicholas Beaver, a Protestant member of the same regiment as Connolly, she had to give up her job as a teacher in St Mary's Church of Ireland Primary School. It proved the first step on the road to destitution.

While some oases of privilege survived, there is little in the history of Dublin working-class Protestantism in early twentieth-century Dublin to sustain the image of a labour aristocracy. Their main vehicle of organised cultural and political expression, the Conservative Working Men's Club, was given over to billiards and 'prodigious drinking.' More uplifting activities, such as lectures on 'The life and times of Lord Beaconsfield' or 'The difficulties, disadvantages and dangers of home rule,' had to be abandoned for lack of interest.

———

Middle-class Protestantism proved more robust. As late as 1900 the richest of the Dublin city constituencies, St Stephen's Green, was represented by a Unionist MP, James Campbell. He lost the seat partly because middle-class Protestants, like their Catholic counterparts, were involved in a widespread flight to the suburbs, where the air was cleaner and the rates lower. The mere fact that Protestants were over-represented in the higher strata of society meant that they had a strong presence in the new townships of Pembroke and Rathmines, as well as in Kingstown. They had no difficulty retaining political control of Rathmines and Kingstown right up to 1914, and they lost Pembroke to the nationalists in large part because of ratepayers' discontent with the inefficiency of local services and the presence of a substantial settled population of skilled workers in the area that preferred to vote for Labour and nationalist candidates. The Unionists were displaced by Labour as the second-largest party on Dublin Corporation only in 1913.

South County Dublin was represented in the House of Commons by Unionists as late as 1910. The incumbent was no less a figure than Walter Long, a former Tory

Chief Secretary for Ireland and the leader of the Unionists in the House of Commons between 1906 and 1910. Long was succeeded as Unionist leader by Edward Carson, another Dublin MP, who held one of the two safe seats for the University of Dublin (Trinity College).

The unionists had held on to the South County Dublin seat with the help of loyal upper and middle-class Catholics. When the seat eventually fell to the nationalists in the second election of 1910 the successful candidate was William Cotton, a leading figure in the business community whose patriotism was broad enough to allow him to support motions for loyal addresses to the monarch at Dublin Corporation meetings. He owed his membership of the corporation not alone to the middle-class voters of the city's South-East ward but to a strong working-class vote in Ringsend supplied by loyal employees of the Alliance and Dublin Consumers' Gas Company, of which he was chairman.

If many nationalists were suspicious of Cotton's conservative views, unionists were often equally suspicious of their own candidates when they expressed moderate views. Long's predecessor in South Dublin, Sir Horace Plunkett, lost the seat in 1900 when militant Protestants put up an independent unionist candidate, so splitting the vote, alienating loyal middle-class Catholics and letting a nationalist candidate in.

In 1904 a by-election in the St Stephen's Green division (constituency) of Dublin caused by the death of the incumbent nationalist MP revealed how deep the divisions in unionist ranks ran, but it was also a harbinger of the future. Senior figures within the Unionist Party were not inclined to contest the seat, especially as the new nationalist-backed 'independent' candidate, Laurence Waldron, was a stockbroker and former unionist who would be a moderating influence in the House of Commons. Several leading business figures, including Sir William Goulding,[26] chairman of the Great Southern and Western Railway, and Lord Iveagh, head of the Guinness dynasty, resigned from the Unionist Representative Association in protest at a grass-roots revolt that led to the association supporting the candidacy of Norris Godard, a Crown solicitor. It was a foolish nomination, as Godard could stand only by relinquishing his lucrative government post, which he declined to do. The former Unionist MP for the constituency, James Campbell KC, was available to stand and had the added advantage of being wealthy enough to finance his own campaign, but the Unionist Representative Association would not have him.

There followed an unseemly row about the rival candidacies of another lawyer, C. L. Matheson, and Michael McCarthy, a colourful renegade nationalist from Cork who was popular with militant unionists because of his books denouncing the evils of Catholicism. Matheson secured the nomination but, as expected, was defeated by Waldron.

This was the last significant revolt by militant lower-class unionists against their social superiors in Dublin. From then on Dublin Unionist electoral strategy sought to maximise potential support by promoting a number of front organisations in local elections, such as the Business Party, the Unionist Municipal Reform Party and the Dublin Citizens' Association. Their main platform was securing for ratepayers better value for money from local authorities. This oblique attempt to woo middle-class Catholic voters enjoyed little success, but it was an indication that behind the increasingly hysterical southern unionist rhetoric towards the Home Rule Crisis of 1912–14 Dublin's middle-class unionist community was tentatively searching for an accommodation with the middle-class nationalist majority. When Carson transferred the seat of unionist power in Ireland to Belfast there was relatively little resistance in the capital.[27]

1913 witnessed the last hurrah for southern unionism with a rally at the Theatre Royal in November. The stage was 'a cave of Union Jacks,' including the largest one ever made; but the speeches of Carson, Campbell and the Conservative Party leader Bonar Law were overshadowed by the events of the lock-out. In 1914 the reality of partition was accepted by many Dublin unionists, particularly by business leaders such as Goulding and Sir Robert Gardner of the city's leading accountancy firm, Craig Gardner.[28] Both men had been close allies of William Martin Murphy during the lock-out, and that struggle had shown Dublin's business leaders, Protestant and Catholic alike, that far more united than divided them. It was Gardner who moved the vote of thanks to Murphy on his victory over the workers at the annual general meeting of the Dublin Chamber of Commerce in January 1914.

Besides, many of the unionist old guard were dying out and the younger generation sometimes took a more sanguine view of the future. At the annual general meeting of the Dublin Unionist Association in March 1914 it was necessary to elect a new president as the incumbent, the Earl of Pembroke and Montgomery, had recently died. His son and heir, Captain Sidney Herbert of the Royal Horse Guards, was elected in his place. Captain Herbert had been the unsuccessful Unionist candidate for the St Stephen's Green division in 1910. While he took comfort from the fact that the government faced 'an Ulster which is organised, which is prepared, and which is determined to resist Home Rule to its very utmost,' he declined to comment on how far Dublin unionists should be prepared to go in meeting the crisis. As a serving officer he did not think it appropriate to comment either on 'certain events which have taken place in the Army during the last ten to twelve days.' This was a clear reference to the Curragh Mutiny, when some Anglo-Irish officers at the main British army base in Ireland threatened to resign rather than take part in manoeuvres meant to overawe unionist opposition to home rule in Ulster.[29] He probably saw his own future as secure, whatever arrangements were made for devolved government in Ireland. Other participants were similarly muted in their contributions, while some leading figures, including Goulding and Gardner, did not bother to attend, sending their apologies instead.

There was no mention at the meeting of the four hundred men who had joined a surreptitious Dublin Volunteer Corps, also known as the Loyal Dublin Volunteers, who drilled weekly in the Fowler Memorial Hall in Rutland Square (now Parnell Square). Their commander was a retired colonel, Henry Master, who was also grand master of the Orange Order in the city, which comprised eleven Orange lodges, including one in Trinity College.[30] The corps had about a hundred rifles and planned to defend the middle-class townships against rampaging Catholic mobs if home rule was introduced. Some members had registered as reservists with the Ulster Volunteer Force, which promised to provide guns and ammunition for Dublin if hostilities broke out.[31]

Meanwhile the president of the Dublin Women's Unionist Club, Lady Arnott, welcomed an offer from the Women's Unionist Associations of Wales to provide temporary accommodation for the women and children of southern unionist families in the event of civil war. Almost simultaneously, Mrs Dudley Edwards told a meeting of the Women's Volunteer Corps, set up to 'advance the cause of Irish liberty,' that she hoped members 'would offer the Nationalist women and children of Belfast and Ulster the shelter of their homes in cases of dire necessity.' To a mixture of applause and cries of alarm from her audience she suggested that it might be best for the police and military to withdraw in order to allow 'the two sections of Irishmen to fight it out amongst themselves.'

Ironically, these Boudicas were probably inspired by the 'Dublin Kiddies Scheme' of Dora Montefiore during the lock-out of the previous year, whereby temporary homes for strikers' children had been offered by trade unionists in Britain. On that occasion Mrs Dudley Edwards had been one of the most vehement critics of the scheme.[32]

————

The reaction of the Catholic Church to the Montefiore scheme in 1913 showed how much the balance of social forces had changed in Dublin. Although there had been no outbreaks of sectarian rioting in the city since the 1880s, low-intensity warfare had continued through other means. The main vehicles of conflict were charitable organisations such as the Society for Irish Church Missions to the Roman Catholics and the Society of St Vincent de Paul. Their main weapons were child proselytism and soup kitchens for the homeless and migrant workers. The former was by far the most emotive.

The Society of St Vincent de Paul reported rescuing between 240 and 250 children 'from proselytising day schools' in the first half of 1913, as well as 19 children from other Protestant institutions, mainly orphanages. The secretary of the Society, T. J. Fallon, reported to Archbishop Walsh that the religion of some of the rescued children had been seriously subverted by exposure to the activities of the Irish

Church Mission. One eleven-year-old boy 'was so perverted that he would not repeat the words of the Hail Mary,' while a six-year-old told his parents, 'We must never pray to the Virgin Mary.' A girl kept returning to her former Protestant school because, the report said, she was 'hopelessly demoralised from bribes and feasts.'

The endemic poverty of the Dublin working class left mothers susceptible to bribes from the Irish Church Mission. They would be offered weekly cash payments, groceries or bags of coal to allow their children to attend Protestant schools, and there were self-improvement classes for the mothers themselves. Often a poverty-stricken mother would give up one child to a residential school, such as the Bird's Nest Institution in Kingstown, in return for help with rearing her other children at home.

Catholic charities, such as the Society of St Vincent de Paul, could not compete, for the simple reason that their poor were so numerous. In the first half of 1913 the society was able to raise only £130 for its anti-proselytism campaign, of which £50 came from the Jesuits and £30 from Archbishop Walsh. In contrast, the Bird's Nest Institution had an annual income of more than £4,400 and the Protestant ragged schools had a collective income of £14,000. In these circumstances the Society of St Vincent de Paul sometimes resorted to drastic measures, such as having children attending Protestant schools committed to industrial schools run by Catholic religious orders for minor infractions of the law. There were also Protestant industrial schools.

In one case the society investigated the placing of five Catholic children in a Protestant industrial school. It found the mother dying of cancer in a cellar in Chancery Street. The society's visitors promised 'to save the children from the worthless father' if the mother would grant them custody. She was provided with a bed in St Vincent's Hospital after signing over the care of her children to the society. When she died, the society immediately transferred four of the children to a Catholic industrial school. The youngest, a nine-month-old baby, died in unspecified circumstances shortly afterwards.

The Irish Church Mission did not endure such activities passively. The Rev. Michael Goff organised pickets to escort proselytised children from their homes to school to make sure they were not approached by St Vincent de Paul counter-proselytisers.

In October 1913 matters came to a head because of the lock-out. By then most of the workers involved in the dispute had been unemployed for more than six weeks, and extreme hardship was widespread. The churches had been slow to respond, and most middle-class Dubliners showed their hostility to the strikers and their charismatic leader, Jim Larkin, by refusing to contribute to relief funds. It was into this sectarian minefield that the British socialist and suffragist Dora Montefiore stepped with her innocent proposal for a 'Dublin Kiddies Scheme' that would provide workers' children with foster homes in England for the duration of the dispute.

Nationalists such as Mrs Dudley Edwards were outraged and were quick to point out that most of the foster-parents would inevitably be Protestants, socialists, or even atheists. (It was not clear which of these categories would constitute the greatest threat to the children's spiritual welfare.) Archbishop Walsh condemned the scheme unequivocally and said that strikers' wives who availed of the offer 'can be no longer held worthy of the name of Catholic mothers.' Mobs led by priests marched to the railway stations and docks to forcibly prevent the 'deportation' of children. Once the *Irish Independent* and *Evening Herald*—both owned by the employers' leader, William Martin Murphy—began publishing the names and addresses of the families prepared to avail of the scheme, it collapsed.

The Dublin Kiddies project was the only occasion in the five-month lock-out when the authority of Larkin was seriously challenged among his followers.[33] It was also the first great confrontation between the clergy and the champions of civil society in modern Ireland over who should determine a child's welfare, the parents or the Catholic Church. It proved an unqualified victory for the church.

The Protestant churches remained largely quiet during the controversy, but it gave many individual Protestants pause for thought. As T. D. Rudmose-Brown, professor of Romance languages at Trinity College, put it, they had been provided 'with an interesting foretaste of the joys of unfettered Home Rule to which we are hastening.' And James Campbell, one of the two Unionist MPs for the University of Dublin, told the anti-home-rule rally in the Theatre Royal, 'I honestly believe that I would have a greater chance of liberty, of personal judgement and of conscience under Jim Larkin and the Irish Transport Union, than I would under Joe Devlin.'[34]

————

'The fantastic policy ... of spending money in taking the children away for what I heard is called a holiday, can do no real good,' Archbishop Walsh told the Society of St Vincent de Paul shortly after the Dublin Kiddies Scheme collapsed.

It can have but one permanent result, and that, surely, the very reverse of a beneficent one. It will make them discontented with the poor homes to which they will sooner or later return, that is to say, those who will return at all. That surely is a result by no means to be viewed with anything but abhorrence by anyone sincerely anxious for the welfare and happiness of the poor.[35]

Dr Walsh was a humane and in many ways an enlightened church leader. He was also a friend of organised labour, at least in its more respectable guise, as represented by an older generation of leaders from the more moderate craft unions. His belief that the poor could be reconciled with their lot represented the views of many middle-class Dubliners of all religious persuasions. However, middle-class Catholics were by no means as resigned to their fate and to remaining second-class citizens in their own city.

In July 1901 the *Leader* published an article describing a wide range of occupations from which Catholics were excluded or in which they were grossly under-represented. This Dublin weekly journal was the vehicle of D. P. Moran, a gifted if somewhat vituperative journalist who encouraged the upward mobility of middle-class Catholics. His articles struck a chord, and at the end of the following year a Catholic Association was established to promote the employment and businesses of co-religionists, even to the extent of boycotting Protestant rivals. The association justified its blatantly sectarian approach by claiming it was simply doing what Protestants had been doing for generations. The association's handbook told members bluntly: 'We must fight with all our might until we have laid our hands on as much power, place and position ... as our numbers, our ability, and our unabated historical claims entitle us to demand.'

It enjoyed some initial successes, but its tactics proved counter-productive in the long run, as increasingly did wild and unfounded allegations against various organisations. In 1904 Archbishop Walsh condemned its activities and it dissolved itself. An attempted resurrection as the Catholic Defence Association did not fool Dr Walsh or his fellow-bishops, and the association's most amenable members were siphoned off to help form the Columban Knights, a new creation by the archbishop. Although initially a Dublin organisation, its aim was to create a discreet national lobby similar to the Freemasons, and in 1915 it merged with a similar northern body to form the Order of the Knights of Saint Columbanus.[36]

Such quiet, 'behind-the-scenes' stage management was the preferred option of Dr Walsh, who was by temperament shy and intellectual. One of his greatest achievements had been negotiating the creation of a National University with the Liberal government in 1907 and 1908.[37] The main offspring of this initiative was University College, Dublin, which was dominated by a Catholic ethos as well as having an institutional and academic parity with TCD that had never been attained by the old Catholic University or its successor, the Royal University.

Nationalist politics in the city were not as amenable to Dr Walsh's guiding hand and were riven by divisions. The main nationalist organisation was the United Irish League, which had begun as a rural protest movement but evolved, more by accident than design, into the Irish Party's main organisational vehicle in the constituencies. Some 70 per cent of the Dublin Corporation were members of the UIL. Publicans, small merchants, shopkeepers and builders formed the backbone of the league in the city. Clientelism provided the UIL's electoral base, and a reputation for jobbery and corruption made little impact on its electoral dominance before 1914. Like the Unionists, the UIL benefited from the restricted franchise that operated under the Local Government (Ireland) Act (1898).

The requirement that electors be householders, or lodgers who paid more than 4s a week in rent, and that they have at least a year's residence in the same premises meant that the great majority of unskilled and semi-skilled workers and their families, living in the city's tenements, had no vote. Most of these slum-dwellers paid rents of no more than 2s 6d or 3s 6d a week. With more than thirty thousand evictions a year in Dublin, the 'midnight flit' by near-destitute tenants was rife, and inclusion in the electoral register seemed an irrelevance. Nor did the seventeen thousand domestic servants—the city's largest occupational group—qualify for the franchise, despite the fact that they 'lived in' for years.

All these factors contributed to only 38,000 inhabitants out of a population of 299,000 having the vote. The electorate was therefore composed largely of the middle classes and skilled workers.

But the political resilience of the UIL was wearing thin by 1914. While the Irish Party could claim, with some justification, to have done much to transform the life of rural Ireland, the same could not be said about Dublin. The imminence of home rule and the political crisis this had provoked put unexpected pressures on local councillors whose ward-healing skills had done little to prepare them for the demands that the crisis placed on them. The leader of the Irish Party, John Redmond, emphasised unity above all else in securing home rule. Any dissent in nationalist ranks on secondary issues, such as a woman's right to vote or trade union recognition, was seen as the lowest form of treachery. This put the UIL organisation in serious danger of losing touch with a younger generation of Dubliners at a time when the city was undergoing social upheaval.

The inability of the UIL and the Irish Party to deal with urban issues was exposed by the lock-out. When the Lord Mayor, Lorcan Sherlock, proposed a motion at the corporation calling for the withdrawal of police from the city in the aftermath of baton charges on 'Bloody Sunday' that left more than five hundred people injured, the UIL councillors split. Those representing wards with a large working-class population, such as the Lord Mayor himself and Dr James McWalter (who spent the afternoon and evening of Bloody Sunday treating the injured in his surgery), voted for the motion, while the majority of UIL members voted against. It was defeated by the relatively tight margin of 26 votes to 21. The twenty nationalist councillors opposed to the withdrawal of police from the city were supported by the four unionist councillors present and by two independents representing the comfortable suburbs of Clontarf and Glasnevin. Supporters of the motion included the six Labour councillors present and four Sinn Féin members, as well as nine nationalist councillors.[38]

Whether corporation members would have voted in such numbers to have the police withdrawn from Dublin if there had been the remotest possibility of it happening is another matter. Unlike British cities, Dublin Corporation had no control over the police forces in the capital. Both the DMP and the RIC were under the direction of the British administration in Dublin Castle. The Commissioner of the DMP, Sir John Ross, and the Deputy Commissioner, William Harrel, were based in the Castle. Their force of 1,173 men was sorely stretched by the lock-out, and no fewer than 947 took sick leave as a direct result of injuries sustained during the dispute.[39] Order was maintained only with the help of the RIC and the military.

But far more damaging for the police in the long run than their physical injuries was the antagonism engendered in many working-class districts by strike-breaking activities, including the intimidation of pickets, taking notes of speeches at public meetings for Crown prosecutions, and attacks on workers' homes. In the years ahead some members of the DMP would pay a high personal price for their behaviour.

The UIL survived the lock-out intact, for two reasons. One was the defeat of the workers, who had been starved into submission; the other was the poor showing of Labour candidates in the local elections of January 1914. Of ten 'Larkinite' candidates only one was elected, for the Labour stronghold of Kilmainham. However, the results were deceptive and due to poor electoral tactics by Labour rather than lack of support. The Larkinites received 12,026 votes to the 16,627 for candidates supported by the UIL and came within 150 votes of winning seats in four constituencies.

The UIL also faced a threat from within nationalist ranks. If Labour ran ten candidates against the UIL in eight constituencies, the UIL faced challenges from rival nationalist groups in twelve. In one instance, Drumcondra, the split nationalist vote between the UIL candidate and a rival from the Ancient Order of Hibernians allowed a unionist to top the poll. An independent nationalist candidate, Laurence O'Neill, defeated the UIL nominee, Patrick Shortall, in the Rotunda ward. Shortall was a builder who had locked out his workers the previous year, while O'Neill, an auctioneer, was popular and associated loosely with the Sinn Féin group in the corporation.

———

The AOH seemed a greater threat to the UIL in 1914 than Sinn Féin or Labour, precisely because it was closely allied to the Irish Party. In fact the AOH had originated as a Catholic electoral machine in Belfast and then spread its organisational tentacles southwards. The introduction of the National Insurance Act by the British Chancellor of the Exchequer, David Lloyd George, in 1911 gave a huge boost to the Hibernians: by 1914 the AOH's insurance section had seventeen thousand members, and even trade unions vehemently opposed to the order's activities, such as Jim Larkin's ITGWU, often lodged their members' insurance contributions with their more financially adept competitor. The ubiquity of the Hibernians on the insurance front allowed *Irish Freedom*, the monthly journal funded by the secret Irish Republican Brotherhood, to poke fun at former members of Sinn Féin in Dublin who applied for jobs as insurance agents with the AOH.[40]

By 1914 the order's head office had moved to 32 Rutland Square in Dublin, where John Dillon Nugent, a native of Keady, Co. Armagh, presided as national secretary.[41] A former bailiff and insurance agent who rose to become a broker, Nugent was a city councillor for the comfortable middle-class suburb of Sandymount and had ambitions to win a parliamentary seat.

The manoeuvring for parliamentary nominations was particularly intense in Dublin, because most of the six sitting MPs were either old or in poor health. None of them had distinguished themselves during the lock-out, and they refused to take a stand collectively on the issue of union recognition. William Cotton, who had captured the Unionist seat in South County Dublin, was a business associate of the employers' leader, William Martin Murphy, and predictably hostile to the workers. So was Patrick J. Brady, a solicitor who represented the St Stephen's Green division and who owed his seat in part to his close association with lay Catholic organisations such as the Society of St Vincent de Paul. After remaining silent during the lock-out, he offered mild criticism of the employers' tactics at the 1914 annual general meeting of the Dublin Chamber of Commerce but opposed a parliamentary inquiry into the lock-out in a House of Commons debate three weeks later. As he told the chamber of commerce, he did not want the dispute 'paraded all over the world' for the benefit of 'anarchists and promoters of evil.'

Brady was doubly dammed. He had done little to reassure his overwhelmingly conservative electorate that he was the right man for the job, and in 1910 he had won the seat by the relatively small margin of eight hundred votes from his unionist rival, Lord Sidney Herbert. The fact that Brady had dabbled with Sinn Féin in his youth, before finding its policies too radical, cannot have reassured many Irish Party voters.[42]

Joseph Nannetti had represented the College Green division since 1900. He was a printer by trade who helped found the Dublin Trades Council and was the principal adviser on labour affairs to the leader of the Irish Party, John Redmond. Nannetti played no part in the events of 1913, having suffered the first of a series of strokes that rendered him an invalid. He was not expected to live long.

William Abraham was another 'labour nationalist' and former trade union activist who represented the overwhelmingly working-class Harbour division. At seventy-three he was the oldest of Dublin's representatives in the House of Commons. His chief claim to fame was that he had been the MP who formally proposed Parnell's resignation as leader of the Irish Party after the O'Shea divorce case in 1890. His Protestant faith (he was a Congregationalist) was probably the reason he had been selected for this role, but it cannot have endeared him to Dublin nationalists, who were strongly Parnellite in sentiment. He was one of that curious brand of absentee home-rule MPs whose devotion to the cause meant that they lived in London and were awarded seats by the party on the grounds of services rendered in the House of Commons rather than having a local power base. Abraham's seat was safe so long as the Irish Party organisation was strong, and his own health held out.

John Clancy, MP for North County Dublin, was a lawyer, former editor of the *Nation* and a veteran of the Land War of the 1880s. His chief claim to fame was as the proposer of the Town Tenants (Ireland) Act (1906), which gave urban tenants some of the rights already conceded to tenant farmers. However, the main beneficiaries of the act were small businesses and shopkeepers rather than Dublin's 100,000 slum-dwellers. Clancy was sixty-eight and showing signs of his age by the time of the lock-out, and his constituency organisation was in decline and unable to attract new blood.[43]

Another Land War veteran was William Field, who had wrested the St Patrick's division from William Martin Murphy in the bitter election of 1892, when the latter had emerged as one of the leading anti-Parnellites. Field, a butcher by trade, had a colourful career. He was an early and respected treasurer of the Gaelic Athletic Association; he helped found the Knights of the Plough, one of several proto-unions for rural labourers in the 1890s, and represented them briefly at the Irish Trades Union Congress. At the 1895 ITUC conference he successfully opposed a motion calling for the nationalisation of the land, on the grounds that 'socialism was all right if they had to deal with angels, and not with human nature.' A self-taught man, he wrote pamphlets on political and economic issues of the day and became a governor of the Royal Veterinary College of Ireland. He also became president of the Irish Cattle Traders' and Stockowners' Association, vice-president of the National Federation of Meat Traders of England, Scotland, Wales and the Isle of Man, and secretary of the Dublin Victuallers' Association.

These positions reflected Field's successful business career, but he still managed to retain working-class support. This was not just because of his Parnellite past but also from the use he made of his membership of such bodies as Dublin Corporation's Port and Docks Committee in 1913 to champion the rights of locked-out dockers. His maintenance of rather tenuous links with the IRB, of which he may once have been a member, kept open his lines to advanced nationalists. Described by one contemporary as 'a venerable figure with a wide brimmed hat and picturesque appearance reminiscent of Buffalo Bill,' he wrote plays and provided a bohemian contrast to his drab parliamentary colleagues.[44]

———

One figure that every nationalist of standing had to cultivate in Dublin was Archbishop William Walsh. Because of his close interest in the city's social, economic and political life he was well known to his flock. A poor horseman, he had been an early convert to the bicycle, which he preferred to his motor car because it provided him with a more intimate view of the city. The Lord Mayor, Lorcan Sherlock, enjoyed the nickname of 'the Lay Pope' because of his regular visits to the archbishop's palace to seek spiritual and political guidance.

It was through Sherlock that the archbishop almost succeeded in setting up an employer-labour conciliation board for Dublin in the summer of 1913. Unfortunately the initiative was scuttled by William Martin Murphy, who was determined to smash Jim Larkin's union and almost succeeded in the lock-out that followed. Murphy and Larkin were two of the few public figures in the city who would be impervious to Dr Walsh's political and diplomatic skills. Now the perils of irreconcilable class warfare were to be joined by the rising spectre of a new generation of radical nationalists, armed with a vaguer ideology and guns.

Dr Walsh, who had shown an uncanny knack for anticipating change and ensuring that the Catholic Church was on the right side from the Parnell era onwards, was coming to realise that the UIL was a spent force, and he had no more time for the virulent sectarianism of the AOH than he had for Larkinism. As one of the archbishop's wide network of correspondents, the moderate unionist Sir Shane Leslie, observed, Dr Walsh 'realised that without his Protestant brethren there was no united Ireland.'[45]

———

One positive result of the war with Germany was the removal of the King's Own Scottish Borderers from the city when they were shipped to France. But the memory remained, and the killings were commemorated in a ballad that rechristened the regiment the King's Own Scottish Murderers.

On Bachelor's Walk a scene took place which I'm sure had just been planned,
For the cowardly Scottish Borderers turned and fired without command.
With bayonets fixed they charged the crowd and left them in their gore,
But their deeds will be remembered in Irish hearts for ever more.[46]

Chapter 2

'THE DESOLATING CLOUDBURST OF WAR'

Dublin before the Easter Rising

D ublin barely reacted to news of the United Kingdom's formal declaration of war on Germany on Tuesday 4 August 1914. There was none of the jingoism in evidence elsewhere. Most citizens were preoccupied with the horrific events on Bachelor's Walk ten days earlier, now the subject of a Royal Commission; and they took advantage of the fine bank holiday weather to forget about the succession of conflicts that had engulfed the city over the previous twelve months.

The rapture, unionist as well as nationalist, that greeted the dramatic pledge by the leader of the Irish Party, John Redmond, in the House of Commons that the Irish Volunteers could be relied upon to defend the country, in co-operation with the Ulster Volunteers, was more in tune with feelings in London than in Dublin. Although Redmond had not consulted his colleagues beforehand, the enthusiastic reaction among the political elite suggested that his speech was not only a generous gesture but a master stroke. Militant separatists were thrown momentarily off balance, while the nationalist and unionist press alike were fulsome in their tribute. The *Freeman's Journal* described the speech as a 'momentous and historic declaration,' while the unionist *Irish Times* went further and felt that 'no Irishman—no man of Irish blood in any part of the world—will read Mr. Redmond's speech without a thrill of joy.' It urged the government to regularise the status of volunteers, north and south; and some southern unionist peers offered their services for the training of Irish Volunteer units locally. The Earl of Meath, who was His Majesty's Lieutenant for Dublin, went so far as to call for a monument to the Kaiser, in recognition of all he had done to unify Ireland.[1]

In fact several former army officers with a unionist background, including the Earl of Meath, were already working with the Irish Volunteers to improve the quality, organisational consistency and political respectability of the organisation. The one most involved was Colonel Maurice Moore, who was Inspector-General of the Volunteers. Among nine senior appointments announced on 5 August was the Earl of Fingall, who agreed to become Chief Inspector of the force in Co. Meath. The nationalist press, borne along by Redmond's oratory, enthusiastically promoted every rumour that the government and War Office would harness this new-found national unity to the war effort. But the government lacked the vision of a Redmond, or even a Fingall, and by 8 August the earl was examining horses for the army's remount department at the Royal Dublin Society's grounds, selecting those fit for service abroad. By the end of the month he had resigned from the Volunteers, because they refused to place themselves unconditionally under the control of the War Office.[2] The Earl of Meath resigned as president of the Irish Association of Volunteer Training Corps, and the false dawn of Irish unity based on support for the British war effort ended in mutual recrimination.[3]

Dubliners did not allow the high-flown political rhetoric, and hopes, to deflect them from life's social staples. The Baldoyle Races provided the highlight of the weekend, and the city's streets were unusually quiet, even for a bank holiday. The few scattered showers 'served a useful purpose in tending to lay the dust,' the *Irish Times* reported. All the papers remarked on the exceptionally good weather and urged Dubliners to conserve water, as the Roundwood reservoir was 9½ inches lower than usual for the time of year. Few seem to have paid much attention, judging by the corporation's repeated warnings in the press of water rationing.[4]

———

Besides, politics continued to demand the public's attention. On Sunday 2 August rumours spread through the city that more guns had been landed by night at Kilcoole, Co. Wicklow. The small police detachment in Bray was held at gunpoint when it tried to stop a convoy of motor lorries, charabancs and motorcycles whisking weapons through the little seaside resort to the city.[5]

There was clearly no shortage of transport and other resources available to the gun-runners. Participants included such pillars of the community as Sir Thomas Myles, medical head of the Richmond Hospital, who provided the yacht that landed the guns, and members of the younger generation of professionals attracted towards radical nationalism, such as Harry Nicholls, an engineer with Dublin Corporation's Electricity Department. Nicholls, who had taken part in the events at Howth the previous weekend, was a member of the Church of Ireland who had been radicalised by exposure to the Gaelic League and then to police batons during the

1913 Lock-out. By the summer of 1914 he was a member not only of the Irish Volunteers but also of the IRB.

Of more concern to the general public was the news that train services were being drastically curtailed to facilitate troop movements. This was quickly followed by an announcement that the Dublin Horse Show, due to begin on 25 August, had been cancelled. The show had been dogged by bad luck for several years. The 1911 opening had been blighted by a railway strike, the 1912 show by an outbreak of foot-and-mouth disease, and the 1913 show by the start of the lock-out. In 1914 the grounds were commandeered by the military to facilitate the mobilisation of reserves and the training of recruits.

The cancellation of all excursion trains in the first week of the war effectually marked the beginning of an era when the railways would fall increasingly under government control, which lasted until 1921. For the moment most operational decisions were left to the local management and boards of directors. The largest company, the Great Southern and Western Railway, was inundated with appeals for free transport. These included the Red Cross Society seeking to forward medical supplies to the Local Government Board, which itself wanted to transfer displaced Belgian refugees and to distribute 2,500 80-pound Québec cheeses to families in distress. Individuals also sought concessions, such as Lieutenant-Colonel L. G. Esmonde, who sought a free travel pass on the grounds that he was an inspector with the Irish Volunteers, whom, he asserted somewhat optimistically, were now part of the 'Imperial war effort.'

It is not clear how many requests were granted. However, as a gesture of their commitment to the war the directors of the GSWR put a first-class dining-car and sleeping-carriages at the disposal of the officers' mess of the Main Supply Depot at Kingsbridge (now Heuston Station). It was a gesture they came to regret, as they had great difficulty in ejecting their guests when the carriages were required for other duties, including the transport of wounded soldiers. The officers eventually decamped at the end of October, complaining at the lack of suitable alternative billets in the vicinity of the station.[6]

———

Of greater concern to the wider public was the rapid rise in food prices. Unlike the military, civilians had no automatic access even to basic foodstuffs. Overnight sugar shot up from 2½d a pound to as much as 6d, butter increased from 1s a pound to 1s 6d, flour from 10s a sack to 12s, and bacon from 1s 1d a pound to 1s 4d. When newspapers questioned the price increases, retailers blamed the wholesalers, who in turn blamed the creameries, the farmers and cross-channel suppliers. The latter had suspended credit facilities and were demanding cash with every order.

The sudden price increases may have been a factor in attacks on several German pork butchers' shops around the city on the night of Saturday 15 August. The most serious incidents were at the premises of Frederick Lang in Wexford Street and of George Reitz at Leonard's Corner on the South Circular Road. The mob was led by a newly enlisted soldier. Not only were both premises wrecked but Lang was arrested and interned, while his family was left impoverished. He joined eighty other 'enemy' aliens, mainly hotel waiters and shopkeepers.

The only full account of this pogrom appeared in the following issue of the *Irish Worker*.[7] It reported that the DMP stood 'idly by.' This was not quite true, for at least some of the looters were arrested and were subsequently charged. They were mainly teenage boys and girls. Several of their mothers also appeared in court for receiving stolen goods, most of it meat and sausages. The Lord Mayor and members of Dublin Corporation's committee on foodstuffs when it met the following Monday unanimously condemned the looting.[8]

This did not prevent the corporation from withdrawing the honorary freedom of the city from Dr Kuno Meyer, the prominent Celtic scholar, founder of the School of Irish Learning (later merged in the Royal Irish Academy) and a friend of the founder of the Gaelic League, Dr Douglas Hyde. Fortunately, the Germanophobe city fathers were unaware that Hyde's wife, Lucy Cometina, née Kurtz, was also German, or they would probably have disgraced themselves further.[9]

Xenophobia and fear over food prices fed off each other. When Dublin Corporation held its first meeting of the war on Monday 10 August, food prices were at the top of the agenda. It was agreed to set up a cross-party food committee to control prices. Another motion called on John Redmond to secure legislation enabling 'municipalities to deal direct with wholesale merchants and farmers with regard to such necessaries as food and fuel, as retail merchants state they are unable to deal profitably without charging the public prohibitive prices.' The legislation was never passed, and the committee had to seek the voluntary co-operation of the wholesale and retail provision trade. It should not have been difficult, given that twenty-four of the eighty councillors were either wholesalers or retailers themselves, but it was to prove a problem at times, with trade representatives frequently not bothering to turn up for meetings.[10]

An easier and more effective measure was the decision to publish recommended maximum prices for staple products, such as butter, bacon, cheese, eggs, lard, margarine and flour. This had some effect in moderating inflation, at least in the early period of the war. Not only would shortages inexorably force up prices but differentials of between 20 and 50 per cent were maintained between prestigious retailers in the principal thoroughfares, such as Sackville Street and Grafton Street, and shops in poorer districts.[11]

And although Ireland was a net producer of food during the war, prices were usually significantly higher than in Britain. Some differences could be accounted for by the fact that products such as sugar and tea had to be imported. In August

1914 sugar cost up to 41 per cent more in Dublin than it did in London. But such home-produced items as cheese and flour were also dearer, although butter was the same price in both cities. The honorary secretary of the Dublin Chamber of Commerce, R. H. Andrews, a wine merchant, explained the difference in the stronger bargaining power of the English market. This was little consolation to hard-pressed Dubliners.

It would be 1916 before any statutory controls were introduced, and for a wide range of items these became effective only from mid-1917. This meant that Dubliners experienced increases in the price of such basic food items as bread, meat and potatoes of 70 per cent, 190 per cent and 250 per cent, respectively, in the first three years of the war. Food prices and food shortages would be important factors gnawing away at support for the war in Dublin from the opening salvoes.

_____

Apart from the debate on food prices, little was said at the August meeting of Dublin Corporation to suggest that a world war had begun. The main focus of attention was the Bachelor's Walk shooting. Aldermen and councillors unanimously condemned 'the savage crime of Sunday 26th July' and called for the dismissal of 'the permanent officials of Dublin Castle who were responsible, either by direct action or by negligence for calling out the military.' Not even the unionist councillors demurred.

There were no votes for King and Country, despite John Redmond's rousing speech in the House of Commons a week earlier. In so far as the impending conflict impinged on the consciousness of corporation members at all it was very much in a resentful way: for it seemed that the British government intended excluding Irish local authorities from access to cheap loans to finance working-class housing schemes. The Housing (No. 2) Act was passed on 10 August 1914, and £4 million was made available for slum clearance by local authorities in Britain. The idea behind the legislation was to combine outdoor relief[12] for building workers made idle by the war with investment in new housing.

As the *Irish Times* pointed out, Dublin had more than its share of unemployment and had the worst slums in Europe. The Lord Mayor telegraphed Redmond and the Prime Minister, Herbert Asquith, after the corporation meeting to make them aware of Dublin's displeasure.[13] A week later, thanks partly to the lobbying efforts of P. J. Brady, MP for the St Stephen's Green division, the Housing Act was extended to Ireland.[14]

Regrettably, it proved an empty victory. Dublin Corporation was given details of the scheme only in January 1915, by which time Treasury economies to meet long-term military commitments had severely restricted access to house-building schemes. In May funding was stopped for all schemes not already approved.

Unfortunately, the secretary of the Local Government Board had not forwarded any of Dublin Corporation's requests for funds to the Treasury, nor had it been notified of the deadlines.

The City Architect, Charles McCarthy, and City Treasurer, Edmund Eyre, told the Housing Committee that the act was 'a make believe and a sham.'[15] The *Irish Builder*, mouthpiece of the industry, along with the Dublin Trades Council, condemned the city's treatment, as did a public meeting in Clanbrassil Street, where blame for the debacle was placed squarely on the Local Government Board. A special meeting of the corporation passed a motion of no confidence in the board.[16] A deputation was sent to the Chancellor of the Exchequer, Sir Reginald McKenna, to express the public's outrage. He eventually agreed to a grant of £6,000 to allow the corporation to acquire sites for building new houses in Ormond Market, beside the Four Courts, in Spitalfields, near the Coombe, and the McCaffrey Estate, adjoining the South Dublin Union, when things improved.

It was all a far cry from the high hopes entertained when the Civic Exhibition was launched. Before, to quote Lord Aberdeen, 'the desolating cloudburst of war' had caused a sharp falling off in attendances. The closing ceremony, on 31 August 1914, provided a suitable coda to Dublin's blasted hopes. After the speeches of the distinguished guests a swarm of slum-dwellers descended on the grounds and took all the furniture.[17]

They showed more prescience than the city fathers, who had no plans for meeting the crisis. During the course of the war nearly a thousand tenements had to be closed as unsafe, and 3,563 of the 4,150 families made homeless as a result had 'gone on to intensify congestion of the still standing 6,735 tenement houses.' There were funds for building only 327 new houses during the war years, in a city that would need to rehouse fifty thousand people by 1918.[18]

———

Dublin's poor would lose valuable allies in high places when the Aberdeens were evicted from the Viceregal Lodge in 1915. It all arose from Lady Ishbel's efforts to promote Britain's war effort among Irishwomen. She had launched several important social initiatives before the war, of which the most significant had been the founding of the Women's National Health Association. Even before the Civic Exhibition closed she called a meeting in the Royal Dublin Society's premises to which a wide variety of women's organisations were invited.[19] Among those who responded, besides the Women's National Health Association, were the United Irishwomen, the Irish Volunteer Aid Association,[20] the St John Ambulance Brigade and Cumann na mBan. Republican apologists subsequently explained the presence of Cumann na mBan by saying it was to avail of any opportunities for training that might arise and could be used later in the nationalist cause; but it also probably reflected the confusion in nationalist ranks about where Redmond's declaration of war in favour of the empire might be leading them.

Agnes O'Farrelly, a lecturer in education at University College, Dublin, and a leading light within the moderate wing of the Gaelic League, had presided at the inaugural meeting of Cumann na mBan in April 1914.[21] While Cumann na mBan would quickly depart the scene, a plethora of wartime women's organisations would emerge that did much useful work in providing hospital care for casualties, among other activities. Initiatives included the conversion of the State Rooms in Dublin Castle into hospital wards, the establishment of the Irish War Hospital Supply Depot at 50 Merrion Square and the mobilising of working-class women and war refugees in the provision of food parcels and clothes for soldiers at the front, including those taken prisoner.

Such activities tended to reflect the social status quo. Lady Aberdeen initiated the hospital in Dublin Castle, the Marchioness of Waterford presided over the Hospital Supply Depot and Lady Fingall chaired the Central Committee for Women's Employment, at the request of Sir Matthew Nathan, Under-Secretary for Ireland.[22]

Perhaps the most extraordinary venture was the League of Honour, set up in November 1914. This emulated a similar crusade in London to draw attention to the threat that war posed to female morality. It was feared that young married women left to their own devices, and with their husbands' separation payments to spend, might fall victim to drunkenness, or worse. The Church of Ireland Primate, Dr John Baptist Crozier, told a meeting in Dublin that the league would 'band together women and girls with the object of upholding the standards of women's duty and honour during the time of war.'[23]

As Eileen Reilly has pointed out, only women with plenty of free time and independent means could afford to engage in voluntary war work. These included those members of the burgeoning Catholic middle classes who believed, like their husbands, in Redmond's strategy that the best way of securing greater freedom for Ireland was by supporting the British war effort.

Alexandra College, which had both a unionist and a feminist ethos and had pioneered a model of secondary education that would allow women to carve out a career for themselves in the new century, supplied another important source of recruits. The 1,000-strong College Guild, which was open to present and past pupils, undertook three projects in the city. These were a hostel for Belgian refugees, a workroom for the unemployed and, no doubt mindful of the League of Honour agenda, a club for soldiers' wives. All three were relatively modest operations. The hostel was in a house belonging to the Adelaide Road Presbyterian Church at 16 Northbrook Road and accommodated fourteen refugees (out of some 2,400 Belgians who arrived in Ireland).[24] The Guild Workroom was in Westland Row and employed no more than a dozen women full-time and between twenty and thirty part-time, who produced such items as socks for the war effort. It relied heavily on public subscriptions. The social club was in Westmorland Street, and the emphasis was on enlightened entertainment with an educational bent, such as music, cookery and sewing lessons. There was less enthusiasm for 'health culture' among visiting soldiers' wives, mothers and sisters, according to guild reports. Like similar initiatives by the Women's National Health Association and the League of Honour, the organisers saw it very much as an antidote to debauchery.

Pupils and past pupils of Alexandra College undertook other initiatives. A knitting association despatched two thousand articles of clothing to the front, mainly to members of the Leinster Regiment, in which many male relatives served. Others responded to the appeal of the Irish Sandbag Committee for volunteers; and fifty-three participated in the college's nursing division, helping maintain the Irish War Hospital Supply Depot in Merrion Square. One past pupil, Norah Fitzpatrick, established a Soldiers' Recreation Room in St Stephen's Green, catering for almost three hundred soldiers. Many of the soldiers said the facilities for reading, games, writing letters, getting a cup of tea and cake for 1d, or simply a chance to talk, made it seem 'like home.' In some instances it was probably a welcome refuge from their real homes in the city.

Some past pupils of Alexandra College were recruited into clerical jobs in the civil service, including the Press Censor's Office, and an adventurous few served as nurses at the front.

However, the main vehicle for voluntary involvement by women in the war effort was the Voluntary Aid Detachments, which provided basic training in nursing, ambulance-driving and other duties that helped free men for military service. Many VADs participated in the Dublin City Branch of the British Red Cross Society, providing more than three thousand students for first aid and home nursing courses as well as producing more than 14,000 garments and supplying 891 pounds of tobacco and 78,578 cigarettes for the troops by 1917.[25]

One of the most important initiatives arose out of the involvement of two women who were members of the emerging generation of science graduates. Alice Brunton Henry joined the Women's VAD in the Royal College of Science at the beginning of the war and in 1915 was appointed quartermaster of the Irish War Hospital Supply Depot. As in most such initiatives, she operated under the presidency of an aristocratic patron, in this instance the Marchioness of Waterford. Together with Mrs W. C. Wright, a botanist at the Royal College of Science, she pioneered work in developing sphagnum mosses from bogs for use in surgical dressings. Families around the country were asked to collect, dry and send in consignments of moss to the depot. By the end of 1917 more than 300,000 dressings a year were being produced for the British Red Cross Society and the Croix-Rouge Française.[26]

As official patron of the British Red Cross Society in Ireland, Lady Aberdeen was hopeful from the beginning of the war that the local organisation might achieve international recognition, but she faced significant practical obstacles as well as opposition from unionist quarters. On 20 September she wrote to all the newspapers reporting progress in training VAD volunteers and advertising a meeting to organise new branches in Co. Dublin, where the Countess of Meath had agreed to preside.

However, the copy of the letter sent to the editor of the *Freeman's Journal* included a private note expressing concern at 'a bit of a plot to capture the Red Cross Society in Ireland and run it in such a way from London and through County Lieutenants and Deputy Lieutenants that it will be unacceptable to the Irish Volunteer people etc.' She expressed the hope that 'ultimately we may be able to have an Irish Red Cross Society directly under the War Office.'[27] Unfortunately, the note was leaked to Griffith's *Sinn Féin* and Larkin's *Irish Worker*. The British Red Cross Society in Ireland asked Lady Aberdeen to disavow the statement, which she could not do if she was to retain a shred of credibility.

This was only one of a long list of indiscretions by Lady Aberdeen, whose urge to do good was exceeded only by her capacity to cause controversy and undermine the impartiality of her husband's position as Lord Lieutenant. The Chief Secretary for Ireland, Augustine Birrell, had complained to the Prime Minister, Asquith, during the lock-out that the Aberdeens 'won't be left out of anything for a moment. It is a capital disaster their being here at this crucial time.'[28] Lady Aberdeen had also alienated such influential figures as Sir Horace Plunkett, the liberal unionist founder of the co-operative movement, trade union leaders and radical nationalists, who believed her charity works smacked of 'souperism' and had dubbed her 'Lady Microbe.' Now the prayers of Birrell and many others were being answered. Asquith wrote to Lord Aberdeen thanking him and his wife for their conspicuous service. Despite a vigorous rearguard action, the Aberdeens departed on 15 February 1915, although they would return to Ireland to visit friends from time to time.

While they may have been scorned by many unionists and lampooned by radical nationalists, the Aberdeens were among the few occupants of the Viceregal Lodge to try to help the poor and marginalised in Irish society, especially women. That Lady Aberdeen finally made a crucial blunder by campaigning for an autonomous Red Cross organisation in Ireland, even though it would be answerable to the War Office, said more about the realities of the power relationships between Dublin and London than about her own indiscretions.[29]

———

On the same day that Lady Aberdeen sent her ill-fated letter to the *Freeman's Journal*, John Redmond made a more serious error of judgement. Speaking at

Woodenbridge in his own Wicklow constituency, he exhorted a parade of five hundred Volunteers to account for themselves as men 'not only in Ireland itself, but wherever the firing line extends in defence of right, of freedom and religion in this war.'

How much thought Redmond put into his speech is not clear: apparently it was an impromptu effort, like his offer in the House of Commons in August of the Volunteers' services to defend Ireland's shores. He may have been influenced by a meeting with a representative of Field-Marshal Kitchener, Major-General Sir Bryan Mahon, shortly beforehand. He had told Mahon (who would soon lead the mainly Irish 10th Division at Gallipoli) that the Irish Volunteers would place themselves under British control only if they were not required to take the oath of allegiance or to serve abroad. Mahon told Redmond that defending Ireland's shoreline would not save the country from 'German vengeance' if Germany won a decisive victory in Europe. He seems to have made a strong impression, and on 16 September, four days before the Woodenbridge speech, Redmond told the Inspector-General of the Volunteers, Sir Maurice Moore, that he would advise Irishmen to enlist. On 18 September he issued a manifesto calling on Ireland 'to give her quota to the firing line,' but adding that the Volunteers must also maintain themselves in a state of readiness in order to defend Ireland. His brief speech at Woodenbridge was along similar lines and did not call on the Volunteers to enlist en masse. However, it was read that way by Redmond's enemies within the national movement.[30]

For the militant minority in the Irish Volunteers who had set up the organisation in November 1913 only to see it taken over by Redmond, Woodenbridge was a parting of the ways. On 3 August they had been faced with a fait accompli, and the chief of staff, Eoin MacNeill, had signed a statement, drafted by the Volunteers' secretary and Dublin City Treasurer, Laurence Kettle, warmly welcoming Redmond's gesture.[31] Now Kettle's moderating influence was brushed aside, and on 24 September a majority of the founders of the Volunteers reconstituted themselves as a Provisional Committee. They resumed formal control of the organisation, declaring that Redmond had no right to offer the services of the Volunteers to 'a Government that is not Irish' for service overseas. The Volunteers had one duty and that was to defend Ireland, not to take part in 'foreign quarrels.'[32]

In the event, the great majority of the rank and file followed Redmond into the National Volunteers—but not to France. In Dublin a relatively high proportion of the membership cleaved to the militants. As Joseph O'Brien said, it was as if

the forces of Irish political disaffection began to gather in and radiate from Dublin to an extent that the capital became sharply distinguished from the rest of Ireland for the sustained vigour with which the idea of British rule in Ireland came under attack.[33]

In many ways this was not surprising. While constitutional nationalism had secured major land reforms for rural Ireland, the capital had relatively little to show for more than a hundred years under the Union. In 1800 it was the second metropolis of the empire; in 1914 it was poorer and smaller than many British cities, excelling Belfast only in the number of theatres, variety halls and that new phenomenon, picture houses. The emergence of the Volunteers was a final expression of a slow cultural process that had been evolving for a long time.

Recent work by historians on the development of the Irish Volunteers in the provinces and their evolution into a national revolutionary militia has stressed the importance of the interaction between different political groupings and highly motivated young people, predominantly male, in promoting political radicalisation in urban centres that then spread to the rural hinterland. If this was so, Dublin must have been a veritable incubator. Not alone did traditional organisations associated with militant nationalism, such as the IRB, GAA and Gaelic League, flourish in the city but there were also women suffragists, trade unionists, socialists and even a revolutionary socialist militia, the Irish Citizen Army. Arguably, the Irish Volunteers could not have been born in any other part of Ireland but Dublin; certainly the Citizen Army could not.

How large the militant rump of the Irish Volunteers was in Dublin is difficult to say. Some estimates put the number as low as 350, while others put it at more than 2,000. Dublin Castle intelligence reports on Volunteer elections in the city suggest that 1,900 adhered to the Provisional Committee and 4,850 went with Redmond. The majority of men in the 1st and 2nd Battalions of the Dublin Brigade, based in the inner-city areas, voted to stay with the Provisional Committee, together with the Inchicore men. The highest level of support for Redmond was in the more prosperous districts. The entire Volunteer membership in Rathmines and Blackrock, along with the Grocers' Association's corps, voted for Redmond's leadership. In the other city battalions and in Kingstown significant minorities voted for the Provisional Committee.[34]

By 1915 it was clear that the militant minority was setting the pace in the city. Redmond's followers, now calling themselves the National Volunteers, were beginning to wither away. Those of a military inclination either followed Redmond's advice and enlisted to fight for the rights of small nations abroad or drifted back to the militants.[35]

———

Some idea of the gap in attitudes between young Dublin nationalists and some of their country cousins at the beginning of the war is given by the case of the unfortunate Michael J. Ashe.

At thirty-eight years of age Ashe had spent his entire adult life working with the Ordnance Survey. He normally lived with his wife in Dublin but spent some months in 1914 working in the west of Ireland. On 29 September, a week after the Woodenbridge speech, he attended a meeting of the Irish Volunteers in Loughrea, Co. Galway, and denounced Redmond for selling the Volunteers for 'a scrap of paper' promising home rule. He added that he was 'entirely against Irishmen joining the Army; their place is at home.'

He may have felt he was safe among fellow-nationalists, but within days reports of his seditious remarks had reached the ears of the RIC and of his superiors in Dublin. The local police obtained statements from witnesses, who amplified Ashe's offence. They gave details of his contacts with local Sinn Féiners and his distribution of seditious literature. One informant, Pat Treacy, a farmer from Rathruddy who regularly sold eggs to Ashe, produced copies of the *Irish Worker, Sinn Féin* and *Ireland*, which the Dublin man had left with him. Treacy told the RIC:

He asked me if I would like the Germans to win. I said I would not, why would I, and that only for the English I could not live. He said that if the Germans came to Ireland they would make me a freeholder of my farm. I asked him would he like the Germans to win, and he said he would. I said that if every man in Ireland thought as I do that they would be at the front and that he ought to be there. He said that if the Germans came in he would assist them— that England might have his body but they haven't his heart and soul.

The police report that accompanied Treacy's statement added that Ashe thought he could express his feelings as freely in Loughrea as he did in Dublin.

District Inspector McDonagh added in another report that while it had been very difficult to obtain statements about Ashe's conduct in the past, 'the reliable members of the Irish Volunteers at Loughrea have, of late, shown a disposition to aid the police in procuring evidence against pro-Germans and other extremists.' Relations were so cordial that when ten members of the Loughrea Volunteers left the town to join the British army District Inspector McDonagh organised an RIC guard of honour to see them off at the railway station.[36]

Ashe was promptly dismissed and his pension forfeit. When it was discovered that he had managed to obtain clerical work at Islandbridge Barracks (later Clancy Barracks) he was promptly sacked again, and the Post Office was also instructed not to employ him. Appeals by Ashe to the Ordnance Survey and to the Lord Lieutenant were of no avail. Nor was a letter on his behalf signed by seven MPs in September 1915. The signatories included most of the MPs for Dublin, as well as Tim Healy and William Duffy. The latter, who represented Galway in the House of Commons, was present at the Volunteer meeting where Ashe made his rash comments.

The punishment meted out to Ashe was severe, given his previous unblemished record. As he pointed out to his superiors, when colleagues had been dismissed for slackness or incompetence they usually kept their pension entitlement. What is equally surprising is the number of senior officials who were involved in the case, including Lord Aberdeen's successor as Lord Lieutenant, Lord Wimborne, the general officer commanding the forces in Ireland, Major-General Lovick Friend, the Deputy Inspector-General of the RIC and the Solicitor-General. The latter felt that Ashe could be successfully prosecuted on the grounds of the pro-German statements he had made in private but felt that the speech that actually led to his dismissal provided shakier grounds. The combination of severity, insensitivity to personal circumstances and lumbering bureaucracy did not bode well for the future of the Irish administration in the troubled times that were now approaching.

Ashe was in many ways a typical Irish civil servant of the younger generation, nationalist in outlook but conscientious in the performance of his duties. Despite his indiscretions he had a brother and three nephews serving in the British forces and had made generous contributions to office collections for a wounded soldiers' fund. Now he was disaffected, forced to move to a less salubrious address in Pimlico and placed under police surveillance.[37]

Ashe's namesake Thomas Ashe was a very different proposition. He was only twenty-nine when the war broke out, but already he was one of the leading lights of militant nationalism. He had been the principal of Corduff National School near Lusk, Co. Dublin, from 1908. He was keen on science but even more so on history. Rebel songs were taught to the children, such as 'Who Fears to Speak of '98?' and 'Boolavogue'. In geography lessons he would point at England on the map and tell the class not to mind it, as it would 'disappear one of these days.' His assistant teacher, Mary Monks, said:

> History lessons were all about Ireland … The favourite part of Irish history was when the English were defeated—at this point the children applauded: again we were all brought through the long centuries of persecution, and told the wrongs inflicted on Ireland by England. When a drill lesson would follow one of these sadder history lessons there would be flag signalling etc.; he would say 'stand erect, hold up your head, remember you are Irish soldiers and may have a chance to fight for Ireland one day.'

He told her that he hoped to 'fight and die for Ireland.'[38]

A keen musician and athlete, Ashe established the Black Raven Pipe Band in Lusk, organised local feiseanna, staged nationalist plays and persuaded a local landowner to give one of his fields over to hurling and football matches. He was a big man. One local man recalled him later as 'a powerful footballer. No one could take a ball off him, with the size of him.'[39] He regularly walked the eleven miles into

Dublin for meetings of the Irish National Teachers' Organisation, the Coiste Gnótha (executive committee) of the Gaelic League and, later, the Irish Volunteers.[40]

He first came to national prominence as a leading figure on the left of the Gaelic League, and he was publicly denounced by the president of the league, Douglas Hyde, for trying to politicise the movement. It did him no harm. When Margaret O'Farrelly, one of Hyde's supporters, proposed that the Coiste Gnótha be reduced in size to weed out the militants, Ashe was re-elected, along with such allies as Éamonn Ceannt, Michael O'Rahilly, Seán T. (also John T.) O'Kelly and Diarmuid Lynch.[41] All were to play important roles in the coming national revolution. By 1915 the influence of the militants was such that Ashe was able to successfully propose the veteran Fenian Tom Clarke as secretary of the league, although Clarke spoke no Irish.

A crucial element in the success of the militants in both the Gaelic League and the Irish Volunteers was the IRB. Its president, Denis McCullough, was a regular visitor to Corduff, as were other leading militants, such as Sir Roger Casement.[42]

Local people referred to Ashe's house, which came with the post of school principal, as 'Liberty Hall'. His views reflected the radical flux of the period. Men who would later become synonymous with conservative thought and practice, such as the future Minister for Finance Ernest Blythe, had railed against the evils of capitalism and advocated workers' co-operatives during the 1913 Lock-out.[43] Ashe's own thoughts on social and economic issues were moving in a similar radical but ill-defined direction. During the lock-out he wrote to his brother Gregory: 'We are all here on Larkin's side. He'll beat hell out of the snobbish, mean, seoinín employers yet, and more power to him.' In the same letter he added that Larkin and 'Jem Connolly are now asking their men to drill like Carson's. If we had them all drilled I know what they'd direct their rifles on very soon.'[44]

His involvement in the INTO brought him into close contact with labour movement activists, particularly James Connolly and Seán O'Casey. It is not hard to see why, given Ashe's interest in Ireland's historical development, literature, drama and even militarism. Connolly and O'Casey were closely involved in the formation of the Citizen Army. But Ashe was not a socialist; instead he advocated decent wages for workers, particularly agricultural labourers, and profit-sharing. The latter idea he owed to his Kerry roots. In an unfinished novel written in Lewes Jail after the 1916 Rising he explained:

> The fishermen in the west ... of Ireland have a peculiar custom in their division of the week's profits. One man owns the boat, nets, sails, and provides the food and all the other necessaries ... The proceeds of a week's work are divided between the crew and the boat—half going to each.[45]

Ashe showed little understanding of an urban economy; he was far better acquainted with the realities of growing up on a family farm and living in the still rural society of north Co. Dublin. His views were nevertheless too much for the parish priest, Father Byrne, a staunch supporter of the Irish Party. Byrne resented the influence of the young radical, regarding him as 'a modernist and an anti-cleric.' In fact, as Ashe's correspondence shows, his wide circle of friends included several priests as well as some De La Salle brothers in Waterford, where he had undergone his teacher training.[46] But in none of these situations had Ashe been fighting for social leadership of the community as he was in north Co. Dublin.

Meanwhile his position within the national movement was strengthened by a fund-raising trip to the United States on behalf of the Gaelic League, organised by another IRB member, Diarmuid Lynch. The trip lasted from January to October 1914, and Ashe met Casement there, who was fund-raising for the Volunteers. Like Casement, and his namesake Michael Ashe, he welcomed the prospect of a 'German-Irish entente' and said Ireland could 'rule the British Isles from College Green'. During his American stay Ashe urged the Coiste Gnótha to take a strong stand against partition, which would help him raise funds from Irish-Americans.[47] He asked, equally unsuccessfully, for newsreel film of hurling matches and Volunteer parades to be sent over. He told the secretary of the Gaelic League, Pádraig Ó Dálaigh, that he could raise $500 a showing. His instincts were sound. At the very time he was looking for films the American director John Sidney Olcott was making silent feature films in Killarney to exploit the Irish-American demand for romantic stories with a strong sentimental nationalist streak. Ashe collected $1,000 for the Irish Volunteers in America and sent it to Tom Clarke.[48]

Ashe was furious at the news of Redmond's support for the British war effort. He wrote to a friend on 24 August 1914:

> Let us reverse the pictures of Emmet on our walls. No slavish people ever did what we propose doing—defend our land and our people for the tyrant during his difficulties that he may come when they are over and enchain us again.

He added that Irish-Americans were so infuriated with Redmond that they had stopped sending funds.

Ashe returned from the United States shortly afterwards, via Belfast, where he discussed the political situation with James Connolly and Cathal O'Shannon of the ITGWU. He told them of the violent Irish-American reaction to Redmond's Woodenbridge speech.[49] Connolly soon followed Ashe to Dublin, to become acting general secretary of the ITGWU after Larkin left for America.

When Connolly set up the Irish Neutrality League the following year Ashe was one of the first to join. Meanwhile he threw himself into organising the Volunteers in north Co. Dublin and organised the only attempt at large-scale manoeuvres involving his own battalion and the north city battalions in open country.[50] It was generally agreed to be a shambles, but Ashe learnt valuable lessons, including the need to train his units as potential flying columns in the event of a rising.[51]

———

Of course neither of the Ashes was typical either in his situation or in his response to Redmond's speech at Woodenbridge. If perhaps 2,000 Dublin Volunteers remained true to the Provisional Committee leadership, more than 21,000 men volunteered for service under the Crown in the first two years of the war; and by the time the war ended 25,644 Dubliners had served in the British army.[52]

The capital had always been fertile recruiting ground for the British army. Between 1899 and 1913 there was only one year when Belfast, with a substantially larger population, contributed more men than Dublin. In some years Dublin provided double, and even treble, the Belfast figure.[53] A major reason for the disparity was the high level of unemployment in Dublin among unskilled workers, who provided a traditional source of recruits.

The 1911 census shows that there were 17,269 general labourers in the city and 2,044 factory labourers. Another 10,358 workers were employed in relatively low-skilled jobs such as messengers, porters and coal heavers. These accounted for more than 27 per cent of the male working population, or up to five times the percentage for British cities. Dublin Corporation occasionally spent money on projects such as road works to alleviate the problem but it refused to adopt the Unemployed Workmen's Act until parliamentary grants were introduced to administer it in 1906. Even then, the Corporation's Distress Committee restricted eligibility to work on relief schemes to men living in the city for at least two years.

When the Liberal government established a system of labour exchanges in 1909, Dublin absorbed 60 per cent of all available unemployment funds for Ireland. The numbers signing on regularly exceeded those in much larger British cities, such as Glasgow and Manchester, not to mention Belfast.[54]

The British Army not only provided an escape route from poverty, but offered enhanced career prospects for soldiers returning to civilian life. Rightly, or wrongly, there was a perception that Protestant and Unionist employers in Dublin looked more favourably on ex-soldiers applying for a job. Furthermore, a soldier could earn up to 7s a week as a reservist after leaving the colours. This could transform his quality of life. Ireland's leading social scientist, D.A. Chart, estimated that, in 1914, a labourer's family had a disposable income of only 3s 1d out of a weekly wage of 18s, after the essentials of rent, food, heat and light were paid for. An additional 7s made possible the renting of better accommodation and the purchase of decent clothes, food and footwear, not to mention the occasional family treat.

The defeat of Jim Larkin and the ITGWU in the 1913 Lockout undoubtedly increased unemployment amongst trade union militants blacklisted in the dispute, but there is little evidence to support the notion that hundreds joined the British Army. On the contrary, many availed of one-way boat tickets provided by TUC affiliates to seek jobs in Britain in early 1914 when the Lockout ended. Certainly, when war broke out in August 1914 there was a report in the *Dublin Evening Post* of an apocryphal 'Dockers Company' formed in the 'Pals' Battalion of the Dublin Fusiliers from blacklisted men. However this seems unlikely because the surge in military traffic caused by the outbreak of war, combined with the recall of dockers who were reservists to the colours, created an immediate labour shortage in the port. The *Post* also reported that members of the Orange Order linked Loyal Dublin Volunteers were joining up suggesting it was promoting the idea of war as a unifying force in Ireland against a common foe.[55]

But the flow of recruits from Dublin in 1914 was never as great as from British cities or Belfast.[56] The response to the initial call to arms came from the Unionist community and Catholic professionals who identified strongly with the promised Home Rule dispensation. To some extent this reflected British trends where the rate of volunteering was highest among the middle classes.[57] Subsequent working-class recruitment was very much on economic grounds as will be seen below.

Lawyers in Dublin gathered as early as 10 August at the Imperial Hotel to discuss forming a company and they would merge with similar groups to form the 7th 'Pals' Battalion of the Dublin Fusiliers.[58] The moving spirit behind the battalion was Frank Browning, one of Ireland's leading cricketers and president of the Irish Rugby Football Union. He used the Lansdowne Road grounds for organising and training a 'Volunteer Corps' that was generally open to the city's middle classes, who were even provided with a new recruiting office in Grafton Street. As the Dublin Fusiliers' nickname in the army was the 'Toughs', the 'Pals' Battalion was dubbed 'the Toffs in the Toughs'. Men too old or unfit for active service were formed into the Georgius Rex Reserve Corps, or Georgeous Wrecks as Dubliners christened them.

On Wednesday 16 September the 'Pals' Battalion received the greatest send-off of any British Army contingent from the capital.

Barristers, doctors, solicitors, stockbrokers, barbers, medical students, engineering students, arts students, businessmen who had responsible positions, civil servants and insurance agents—marched off to Kingsbridge station en route to the Curragh Camp for training, receiving a great ovation from the public and their friends as they went. From almost every window in Nassau Street, College Green and Dame Street, handkerchiefs and hands were waved to them.[59]

Their Gethsemane would come in 1915 at Gallipoli. Meanwhile the 'old sweats' of the reserve had already departed unnoticed to man the trenches on the Western Front. Many would die before the New Year dawned.[60]

———

Dissent never disappeared entirely. As early as 25 September a recruiting meeting at the Mansion House in Dublin addressed by the Prime Minister and Redmond was interrupted by hecklers. The meeting was held to coincide with the opening of the new recruitment office in Grafton Street, which would provide a more salubrious venue for respectable applicants who wished to join the colours than the existing premises in Great Brunswick Street (now Pearse Street). Once more the Earl of Meath was involved in the initiative, along with Sir Maurice Dockrell, a respected employer and a leading figure in the unionist community in the city. The incidents at the meeting were serious enough to warrant a request for a full report from the commander in chief, Field-Marshal Kitchener.[61]

The disruptive elements came primarily from the ranks of militant nationalists and the labour movement. Jim Larkin held a counter-demonstration outside the Bank of Ireland in College Green. He called on the crowd to swear 'hatred to the Empire,' while the Irish Volunteers confronted the DMP, augmented by members of the AOH in Dawson Street, outside the Mansion House meeting. By an unfortunate coincidence for the recruitment drive, one of the civilians wounded at Bachelor's Walk, forty-year-old Sylvester Pidgeon, had died earlier the same day, and the news was broadcast around the city by opponents of the war.[62]

———

While small in numbers, the Volunteers possessed a much stronger appeal than the British army for those interested in active citizenship. Skilled industrial workers, white-collar workers and members of the professions made up two-thirds of the membership. Even those recruited from lower social classes tended to be upwardly mobile individuals. The democratic structure of the Volunteers, allowing for debate, the election of officers and an opportunity to influence policy at conventions, made it infinitely more appealing than the blind obedience and lack of respect for most things Irish that recruits experienced in the British military machine.[63]

Once the initial emotional surge was over, the main appeal of the British army was to the urban unemployed and unskilled workers. A breakdown of recruitment figures for 1915 suggests that the recruitment rate in the city of Dublin was three times higher than in the county. Given the concentration of middle-class and unionist populations in the latter area, this would suggest that economic necessity continued to be the main factor driving men to join up.[64] Of course some were ex-regulars who were part of the reserve and liable to being called up in the event of war.[65] These men would have been mobilised immediately, and by mid-August 1914 the *Irish Builder* was complaining about the bulk of Dublin builders' labourers being called up as members of the reserve. At the same time large retailers were complaining about the dearth of young porters and messenger boys, who were deserting for military service. This probably reflects the poor pay and conditions of these youngsters as much as any enthusiasm for the military life.

———

There was also a significant 'pull' factor in recruitment. Unlike the Continental powers, Britain did not have conscription, and various initiatives were needed to promote enlistment. Within a week the government decided that civil servants who joined up would receive their full pay, have military service counted for pension purposes and have their jobs kept open for the duration of the war. The Local Government Board adopted a similar approach, but it was up to individual local authorities whether or not to adopt such a scheme.

Dublin Corporation implemented it with little enthusiasm and only provided half pay; even this was stopped for employees whom they felt did not require it.[66] The Dublin Port and Docks Board was another public body that released reservists for military duty on half pay.

Some large employers, such as the Dublin distilling companies and Guinness, promised to hold jobs for employees who enlisted. Guinness provided half pay, and more than 650 men from the brewery took part in the war, of whom 104 were killed. Volunteers came from all grades and included two directors of the company, Viscount Elveden and W. W. Guinness MP. In all, more than ninety Guinness employees received a commission or its equivalent.[67] Penal rates of tax on alcoholic beverages and restrictions on consumption were to have a catastrophic effect on business, and it was in the interests of brewers and distillers to encourage recruitment among surplus staff as the war progressed.

However, the patriotic instincts of other companies that were strongholds of unionist sentiment, such as the railways, conflicted with the need to maintain adequate staffing levels, because their services were in greater demand than ever. Although the largest company, the Great Southern and Western Railway, immediately offered to pay 4s a week to the wife of any man who joined up, and 5s if the couple had children, it soon became concerned at the possible effect on operations. Sir William Goulding, chairman of the GSWR and of the Railway Association, representing the other operators, sought to secure some control over the recruitment process on behalf of the industry.

The railway companies had a strong bargaining position, as they could point to their statutory obligation to provide essential services to the state, while the British government tended to see Ireland primarily as an underdeveloped recruiting ground. It was not until November 1915 that a working agreement was achieved with the Lord Lieutenant and the director-general of recruiting for Ireland, Lord Wimborne. He gave an assurance that no man would be recruited from the railway companies who was considered indispensable to their operation, and in return Goulding gave an assurance that enlistment slips would be distributed to all railway employees. The undertaking to be signed by would-be volunteers read:

I voluntarily undertake to enlist for the period of the War in the Division, Regiment or battalion I mention. I understand I will not be called upon without the previous consent of my Company.

A circular was also sent out by the GSWR to all men earning not more than £200 a year, giving the amounts it would pay to employees who joined up. Those who had a wife or children were guaranteed the equivalent of four-fifths of their basic pay, taking into account any separation allowance provided by the army. For single men or widowers the directors said they would look at claims for other dependants, such as elderly parents, on their merits.

The railway companies all gave a commitment to re-employ men in 'similar positions' to those they vacated if they were physically fit to carry out the work at the end of the war or on their discharge. The GSWR also agreed at an early stage in the war to maintain pension contributions to the Railway Clearing System Superannuation Fund in order to preserve servicemen's pension rights. Other railway companies soon followed suit.

Of more immediate concern was a resurgence in militancy among railway workers in Britain and Ireland. Their bargaining position was transformed by the war. Many of them were essential for maintaining services and too highly skilled to be replaced easily. On 5 February 1915 the National Union of Railwaymen served a pay claim on the Irish companies that had already been conceded in Britain. The smaller companies, such as the Midland Great Western Railway and the Dublin and South-Eastern Railway, were willing to negotiate, as they felt 'they made better settlements with the aid of the Union than with their men alone, that recognition is bound to come sooner or later and that the companies would do better to accept the inevitable.' The larger employers, and particularly the GSWR, which had smashed the 1911 strike by railwaymen, wanted to hold out.

In truth their situations were very different. Despite overall control by the War Office, the Irish companies still retained more autonomy than their British counterparts. One drawback to this comparative freedom was that they could not expect a subvention from the exchequer to meet increased wage costs. By the beginning of March the Irish companies conceded increases of between 1s and 1s 6d a week, compared with increases of 2s to 3s a week in Britain. While the smaller, loss-making concerns applied successfully for state subsidies to meet the cost of wage increases, the highly profitable GSWR found its application rejected. In a statement to the newspapers the secretary of the GSWR, R. Crawford, said his company had been refused a 4 per cent increase in fares because

> it had operated more efficiently than its competitors and reduced costs. It was now being penalised for its success and was having to pay the increases out of its reserves. Under these circumstances my Board think that they are acting generously and have the welfare of their employees at heart, in giving these increases when they would be fully justified, having regard to their anomalous position in not increasing their liabilities.

He stressed that these were not wage increases but 'special allowances to the staff to continue until the end of the year, should the war last so long.' He dubbed the pay increase a 'War Allowance.'[68]

The outcome reflected to a degree the changing balance of forces in the Dublin labour market. While the great surge of volunteers was dropping sharply, and was long spent before the end of 1915, the railways had already haemorrhaged more men than they could comfortably afford to lose, especially in the crafts. Sir William Goulding might express disappointment at the 'poor response' of employees to the latest recruiting drive and promise to make 'a strong appeal' at the next shareholders' meeting, on 23 March 1916, but privately he advised the military authorities against sending canvassers to recruit men directly in the works.

> It would be far better if they [the employers] urged them in every way and leave it to the Companies to say who could not be spared. You may be certain we won't retain any that can be done without.[69]

The Easter Rising was now five weeks away, and public sentiment was about to change dramatically.

———

Not that public sentiment among Dublin workers was ever that much in favour of the war. Among corporation employees who did not have to worry about job security or what their employer thought, only 169 had joined the forces by 1916. A little more than half of these were from the Paving and Cleansing Departments, where the relatively poor pay and working conditions were probably incentives.

Labourers constituted the majority of recruits in most corporation departments; the exceptions were relatively small and included the Tuberculosis Unit, from which one nurse, one clerk and one labourer joined up, and the Public Health Service, from which three sanitary officers, one disinfector and two labourers did so. In the Main Drainage (Loan) Department the two labourers were balanced by two engineers, and in the Workshops four skilled workers and three labourers volunteered. Altogether only nine corporation employees who could be construed as professionals volunteered, compared with 113 labourers. This reflected the general class bias that saw labourers disproportionately represented in the armed forces.[70]

The figures for Dublin Corporation probably reflect the general recruitment pattern and attitude to the war in the city more accurately than those in such firms as Guinness, where a paternalist corporate culture promoted loyalty to the legislative Union and the Crown.

Table 1
Dublin Corporation recruits, 1914–16

	Salaried professional	Salaried clerical	Skilled and supervisory	Labourers	Totals
Sewers	0	0	1	3	4
Engineer's staff (clerical)	0	1	0	0	1
Main Drainage	0	0	1	9	10
Main Drainage (Loan)	2	0	0	2	4
Housing (Engineers)	0	0	0	3	3
Paving	0	0	10	33	43
Dangerous Buildings	0	0	0	1	1
Waterworks	0	0	1	9	10
City Architects	0	3	0	1	4
Fire Brigade	0	0	2	0	2
Public Lighting	0	0	0	8	8
Workshops	0	0	4	3	7
Cleansing	0	0	19	23	42
Electricity Supply	3	0	2	9	14
Cattle Market	0	0	0	1	1
Food Market	0	0	0	2	2
Technical Education	0	0	0	1	1
Libraries	0	1	0	0	1
Housing	0	0	0	2	2
Tuberculosis	1	1	0	1	3
Public Health	3	0	1	2	6
Totals	9	6	41	113	169

The greatest 'pull' factor of all for most working-class recruits in Dublin was the announcement on 8 August that separation allowances would be paid to the wives of soldiers. Given the low wages and high unemployment for unskilled workers in the city, army pay was relatively attractive, especially for a married man with children. A labourer could expect to earn between 16s and 18s for a 48-hour week; in comparison, the weekly separation rate for a wife was 12s 6d, while the serving husband was receiving 1s a day as well as free board and lodging. If the couple had children the family was very much better off, with rates rising to £1 a week for a wife and three children and £1 2s if there were four children. The rates were higher again if the husband secured promotion.[71]

Table 2
Weekly separation allowances[72]

	Private and corporal	Sergeant	Warrant officer
Wife	12s 6d	15s	23s
Wife and one child	15s	18s	26s
Wife and two children	17s 6d	21s	29s
Wife and three children	20s	24s	32s
Wife and four children	22s	26s	34s

Given the high proportion of Dublin working-class families with British army connections, and the relative strength of the radical separatist tradition in the city, attitudes towards soldiers were bound to be quite complex. Even within families a situation frequently arose where different brothers served in the army and in the Volunteers, most famously in the case of the Daltons and the Malones.[73]

The veteran republican Todd Andrews later wrote of the years before the First World War that

the soldiers … with their red coats, their reviews, their trooping of the colour outside the Bank of Ireland were accepted by us as soldiers. Many of the lads around Summerhill had been at Colenso or Mafeking but they were still 'us'.[74]

His fellow-Dubliner Wilmot Irwin recollected much tenser relations. He lived in the former unionist township of Drumcondra, not far from Summerhill, and came from a lower middle-class Protestant background. At one cavalry review in Marlborough Barracks (now McKee Barracks) he recalled that 'a number of civilians omitted to uncover during the playing of the British National Anthem and sundry troopers started to knock them [their headgear] off.' On another occasion a military band performing in the Hollow in the Phoenix Park had to abandon the anthem after being 'assailed by a shower of stones from spectators.'

Both these incidents occurred well before the lock-out or the Bachelor's Walk shooting.

At the same time, Irwin recalled that the declaration of war and Redmond's support for it made 'the whole population … extremely pro-British. It seemed that militant strikes, civil clashes and gun-running episodes had been forgotten.' The 'only signs of the impending trouble were the route marches of the Irish Citizen Army … and the Irish Volunteers, both sections now carrying rifles openly in the streets.'[75]

Chapter 3 ⌒

'BLOOD, HORROR, SHRIEKS AND GROANS'

The honeymoon with the British war effort was doomed to be short-lived. For one thing, Dublin, unlike Belfast and many British cities, possessed no war industries. Those products it did manufacture, such as biscuits, beer, whiskey, and confectionery, would not budge the front line 'by even an inch.'[1] However, they could help pay for munitions that would.

The first war budget, in November 1914, showed the shape of things to come. Income tax was doubled, from 3¾ to 7½ per cent, but the threshold for liability remained at £160 a year, well above the annual income of skilled workers and most of Dublin's lower middle classes. Far more serious was the decision to increase duties on consumer items such as tea, from 5d to 8d in the pound, and to increase taxes on porter, stout and strong ales by between 17s and 19s a barrel.

The thinking behind such measures was to reduce spending on luxury items, improve public health and provide badly needed funds for war industries.[2] Whatever the impact in Britain, the implications for Ireland's drinks industry were disastrous. With the prospect of a protracted conflict, a second war budget was introduced in May 1915, which was even worse. Not only was duty on beer almost doubled for the second time in six months but the duty on whiskey, which had escaped an increase in November, was doubled from the pre-war rates. As if to add insult to injury, the light ales brewed in Britain were spared.[3]

Irish public opinion took offence at British Liberal politicians who felt that more abstemious habits were a small price to pay for victory. The *Irish Independent* proclaimed:

In Ireland the public have something more serious to consider than mere interference with their daily habits. Here we have at stake the existence of industries which are the most important in some of our largest centres, and which are the actual main stay of smaller towns.

It predicted that thousands of investors would suffer and that state intervention would be required to deal with the resultant unemployment. The new taxes represented 'prohibition without compensation.' Not only did the rest of the nationalist press agree but so did the *Irish Times*, voice of southern Unionism.[4]

On Sunday 2 May a mass meeting was held at the Nine Acres in the Phoenix Park. It was the last great demonstration of constitutional nationalism in the city, and already its patriotic credentials were being called into question. William Field, one of the longest-serving and most radical Parnellite MPs in the city, was heckled for not voting against the new legislation. He told the crowd:

> It was arranged by the head of the Party [Redmond] that we were not to vote, and I am a member of that Party and under the discipline of it. I am obliged to obey orders.[5]

What infuriated many nationalists was that previous big increases in the duty on whiskey had been introduced by the same Chancellor of the Exchequer, David Lloyd George, in 1909, when the Irish Party had tamely accepted it as part of the price for keeping the Liberals in power and securing home rule. The *Cork Free Press* wrote that no-one knew better than John Redmond

> the terrible effects Mr. Lloyd George's frightful ... taxes will have on Irish trade. His own speech is clear and irrevocable evidence that he regarded Mr. Lloyd George's proposals as fatal to Ireland ... Yet when he got the opportunity to back his words with votes he collapsed.

Such was the rancour in nationalist ranks that the *Irish Independent* reprinted this comment, despite its traditional antipathy towards the rival publication.[6]

In fact there was little that nationalist Ireland could do. The Liberal government had the support of the Tory opposition, and the military. The war had fundamentally changed the political equation in the House of Commons, something Redmond understood but the Irish nationalist voter did not.

Things would become a lot worse in August 1916, when the Output of Beer (Restriction) Act limited production to 85 per cent of the previous year's output. Distillers had production cut even more drastically, to 30 per cent of the average yearly output. The Immature Spirits (Restriction) Act (1915) had already banned the sale of any stock produced in the previous three years, and in December the

Irish distilleries were taken over by the Ministry of Munitions and converted to the production of industrial alcohol.

By then about half the work force in the brewing and distilling industries had been laid off, many of them constituents of William Field, who had been heckled in the Phoenix Park. Not surprisingly, brewers and distillers with surplus employees were among the most enthusiastic in co-operating with the Department of Recruiting in supplying men to meet the butcher's bill in Flanders.[7]

———

One of Field's old colleagues in the Irish Party had died only days before the Phoenix Park rally, opening the way for Dublin's first by-election of the war. John Nannetti, the long-serving Nationalist MP for College Green, was already incapacitated by the series of strokes he had suffered. A printer by trade and the founding father of the Dublin Trades Council, he had been Redmond's chief link with the trade unions and his adviser on labour matters. He represented the dominance of the craft unions in the labour world of the previous century and had long been out of favour with the younger generation of more militant leaders. When he died there were few of the usual tributes, and one old comrade on the trades council, Peadar Macken, described him as 'an example of what a labour man ought not to be … tied up with a party inimical to Labour.'[8]

In fact the timing of his death could not have been better from the trades council's point of view. Its new leadership had just taken over the Labour Party organisation in the city, and it quickly nominated Thomas Farren of the Stonecutters' Union to fight the election. His opponent was the secretary of the Ancient Order of Hibernians, John Dillon Nugent. A native of Keady, Co. Armagh, Nugent was a close ally of the northern nationalist leader Joe Devlin and had been associated with the strong-arm tactics used by the AOH against opponents within the nationalist movement—and outside it, such as suffragists and socialists. He had become one of the city's leading insurance brokers through the AOH's own company, the Hibernian Insurance Fund.

Devlin, who had a strong working-class base in west Belfast, liked to portray himself as a champion of labour and to remind audiences that 'whatever rights labour enjoys in Ireland, it owes them to the [British] Labour Party.'[9] He invited the Dublin Trades Council to send delegates to the convention at which Nugent was selected, but the union leaders had not forgotten Nugent's role in the 1913 lock-out, when, besides using the AOH organisation in the city to undermine them, he had joined with the Catholic clergy in inciting mobs against Dora Montefiore and her helpers when they tried to bring strikers' children to temporary homes in England.[10]

Farren had been one of the 1913 leaders, though he was not as well known as Jim Larkin or James Connolly. It was Connolly who wrote Farren's election address.

He described the selection of Nugent as 'a studied insult to the Dublin working class'[11] and Nugent himself as 'the malevolent enemy of trade unionism on every occasion, great and small, where he could exercise his influence.'[12] Farren's brief electoral address attacked the Irish Party for blocking the extension to Ireland of 'the best provisions of every social reform' passed by the House of Commons.

The Labour candidate also declared his opposition to partition, and called for votes for women.[13] The *Irish Citizen*, weekly paper of the women's suffrage movement, reciprocated by supporting Farren's campaign. On election day, 11 June, Farren obtained 1,816 votes, against 2,445 for Nugent. Most worrying from the nationalist viewpoint was the fact that only 4,261 voters out of more than 8,000 bothered to turn out.

It was a very creditable performance, considering that Farren entered the contest only seven days beforehand and that there had been no systematic canvass or organised campaign to combat the AOH and UIL machines. Nor, apart from the *Citizen*, did Farren receive a sympathetic press. Nugent's campaign accused Farren of 'Larkinism and Syndicalism combined with pro-Germanism,' as well as being opposed to the war effort and to the Catholic Church. Socialist though he might be, Farren took the opportunity of the vote of thanks to the returning officer to tell the crowd he was secretary of the largest men's confraternity in Dublin and had been a member for twenty-two years.

Nugent had a tough time from hecklers at the count, who accused him of being a bailiff and an employer of scab labour. Farren had to appeal for quiet to allow his successful opponent to conclude his election speech.[14]

While some of the Labour activists, such as William O'Brien, had worried that their anti-war stance had told against them, the attractions of the Redmondite position were fast fading. On 25 May the Liberal Prime Minister, Asquith, announced a grand wartime coalition. Among the new Tory ministers was Carson; but Redmond opted to remain outside the Cabinet. Nationalist Ireland saw it as yet another blow to the cause of home rule. The comment of the *Dundalk Examiner* was typical of a mood of deepening disillusion in nationalist ranks.

The Irish Party has been playing a certain game for ten years. The denouement has now come, and it is only too manifest that they cut a sorry figure.

Nor was the news from the front good. Dubliners had been treated to lavish if inaccurate war news from the outbreak of hostilities, including the doings of local units, such as a report of how thirteen members of the Royal Dublin Fusiliers made it back to their lines with the help of Belgian farmers. Their graphic description of the German ambush of their unit near Courtois—'they shot us down by scores'[15]—was hardly reassuring to would-be recruits or their families. But these were men of the tiny regular army, who often had few ties outside their units. It would be 1915 before the impact of the conflict hit the home front, as Kitchener's 'first 100,000' completed their training and entered the fray.

The last act of the 'Old Contemptibles' came in the spring. On 22 April 1915 the Germans launched the Second Battle of Ypres to try to capture the town. On 25 April the 2nd Battalion of the Royal Dublin Fusiliers took part in the counter-attack at Saint-Julien. Observers noted that they advanced in 'faultless order' into the morning mist, to be swept away by machine-gun fire. One detachment managed to reach the town under Captain Tobin Maunsell but was forced to withdraw for lack of support. The battalion had lost 510 members in the attack. Incredibly, the remnants of the unit raised 'three cheers for Jim Larkin' when they returned to the trenches, as if they had just attended a rally outside Liberty Hall. Undoubtedly the unit contained elements of the ITGWU, probably reservists forced to rejoin the regiment when hostilities began.

The battalion, reconstituted with reinforcements, was back in action a month later at Château du Nord, renamed by British soldiers Mouse Trap Farm. It was supposed to be recuperating when it was the target of a strong German attack on 24 May. By the time relief forces arrived it had suffered 583 casualties. The farm remained in allied hands, a heap of 'mud and rubbish,' but the battalion had practically ceased to exist, as had its sister unit, the 1st Battalion, which had lost 569 dead in the Gallipoli landings at Seddülbahir (called Sedd el-Bahr by the British army), which had taken place on 25 April.

What made the sacrifice of the Dubliners there all the more futile was that the naval crews bringing them ashore were all killed by Turkish fire from the shore, and the onslaught continued remorselessly as the boats drifted in a reddening sea. Some men drowned, weighed down by their equipment, as they leapt overboard and tried to reach the shore. Those who succeeded were caught on the underwater barbed wire the Turks had laid and were shot as they tried to struggle free.[16]

Little of the horror of war, especially as it affected Dublin units, seeped past the military censors. Of more immediate import was news that Brigadier-General Hill had put all licensed premises in Dublin off limits to soldiers—in the interests of discipline. The order included sailors and policemen, and applied also to restaurants and theatres where drink was sold. The Licensed Vintners' Association 'thoroughly agreed' with the decision, and so did most civilians.[17]

————

By the summer of 1915 the war was visibly affecting mainstream politics in the city. At the corporation's meeting on 14 July a maverick nationalist councillor, John Ryan, proposed a motion demanding that the Government of Ireland Act (1914)—which granted a measure of home rule but had been suspended for a year—be implemented 'for all Ireland on September 17th next' at the latest. Two

UIL stalwarts, Councillors William Delaney and Thomas Murty O'Beirne, quickly proposed an amendment that the corporation 'look with confidence to Mr. Redmond and the Irish Party, to select the best and speediest means and the proper moment for bringing the Home Rule settlement into operation by the summoning of the Irish Parliament.' Although the amendment was adopted, it was only by 30 votes to 22, with several nationalist councillors voting for the original motion, alongside Labour and Sinn Féin members.[18]

Even the watered-down version was too much for Redmond, who wrote back from Aghavannagh, Co. Wicklow, on 20 July expressing concern at the damage the motion could do in 'extremely critical times,' when 'a single false step might ruin the work of 35 years.' He assured Dublin Corporation that

> nothing can undo the enactment of Home Rule by the Imperial Parliament. But let us recognise the great and overshadowing fact that the war ... dominates all other issues ... [The] highest duty and most vital interest of Ireland ... is to do everything in her power to support the cause of the Allies.

Ironically, he also warned of the need to maintain 'the Volunteer Movement, and to stand ready for any emergency that might arise.' No-one could tell

> when the war may take a turn which may bring Ireland's hour; and I appeal ... to my countrymen to organise and prepare, so that, when that hour does come, they may be ready.

At the meeting of 6 September the letter was incorporated in the minutes on the proposal of the High Sheriff, Councillor Patrick Shortall, a builder who had locked his employees out in 1913, and seconded by Councillor William O'Hara, who owed his narrow victory over Labour in the 1914 municipal elections to strong clerical support.[19] Redmond would become increasingly dependent on the most conservative and unpopular elements in the UIL and AOH in the city.

Although his letter was adopted by the councillors, at the same meeting they also passed a motion 'that we declare we will not have Conscription.' It was proposed by Alderman Tom Kelly of Sinn Féin and passed by 31 votes to 7. This arose out of a conference hosted in the council chamber on Tuesday 20 July, chaired by another radical nationalist councillor, Laurence O'Neill. The conference attracted a wide audience, and even some of the establishment figures on the platform made speeches that would have been unthinkable a few months earlier. A former Lord Mayor, Alderman J. J. Farrell, said:

> In Dublin young men have been advised to go to war by the effective means of depriving them of work. In England there are millions of men fit to fight if they were only willing. The Government do not want anything from Dublin or

the South but blood and money. If the two Volunteer forces in Ireland made up their minds that there should be no conscription there would be none.

Other nationalist councillors and the maverick Irish Party MP Laurence Ginnell shared the platform with Farrell, along with James Connolly, Councillor William T. Cosgrave of Sinn Féin and members of the Catholic clergy. In fact no fewer than six Catholic clergymen, including four parish priests, wrote public letters of support for the meeting, while apologising for not being able to attend.[20] Incipient respectability was descending on a cause that had been the solitary haven of Connolly's Irish Neutrality League when war broke out. The seven members of the corporation who voted against the anti-conscription motion included the few remaining unionists and a former unionist councillor, Andrew Beattie, who now sat as an independent ratepayers' representative for the South City ward, as well as some moderate or independent nationalists who represented areas such as Drumcondra and Glasnevin, which had significant Protestant-unionist electorates. The eccentric, deeply corrupt and contrary-minded 'Labour' councillor John Saturninus Kelly also opposed the motion, fuelling rumours that he was 'on the take' from Dublin Castle.[21]

––––

In August there was more bad news from Gallipoli. As a concession to the Irish Party, Field-Marshal Kitchener had reluctantly agreed that the 10th Division, recruited almost entirely in Ireland, would be dubbed an Irish division. Its volunteers landed at Suvla Bay on 7 August, on the opposite side of the Gallipoli peninsula to the embattled forces at Seddülbahir. The objective was to take the Turks in the rear and clear the way to Istanbul.

It was another debacle. A third of the division's strength was diverted to the Seddülbahir beach-head, and command of the rest constantly changed until its commander, Lieutenant-General Bryan Mahon, resigned in protest.[22]

In less than a week the Dublin Fusiliers 'Pals' were reduced from 239 to 106. One of the field ambulance brigades working with them lost 23 out of 33 men, killed, wounded or captured in three days of intense fighting to capture the heights of Kiretch Tepe above the bay. German officers with the Turkish troops would later report that the Royal Dublin Fusiliers and Royal Munster Fusiliers who took part in the operation came close to capturing the ridge. When they failed, the defeated troops were trapped in a beach-head rarely free from enemy fire and so congested that the stretchers of the wounded were set side by side on the sand. The lack of hospital tents meant they had to lie in the sun, amid human faeces and clouds of flies. Lack of adequate supplies of fresh water was a constant problem, and the men subsisted on tinned meat that was sometimes rotten, because the cans had been punctured in transit. Meanwhile rows of British bayonets glinted on the slopes above them, marking the spot where their dead owners lay.

Altogether the 10th Division suffered more than two thousand fatalities at Gallipoli in August, 569 of them from the Royal Dublin Fusiliers. When the wounded are taken into account, the division lost half its fighting strength. An officer of the 7th Battalion wrote with unconscious irony: 'Ireland may mourn, but the Irish may hold up their heads and be proud of their Tommies.'[23]

The truth emerged slowly. Reports controlled by the War Office had given all credit for the repulse of the German attack at Saint-Julien on the western front in April to the Canadian units involved, while the Australian and New Zealand Army Corps received what little credit there was to be gleaned from the Seddülbahir landings in the same month. In August despatches also concentrated initially on the efforts of the ANZAC forces to push northwards up the peninsula to link up with the 10th Division at Suvla. Even then the coverage was significantly less than that given to the western and eastern fronts, or indeed to the crash of the Holyhead mail train near Rugby on Saturday 14 August, in which ten people died—four of them Irish women and one a Dublin Fusilier.

The torpedoing of the troopship *Royal Edward* in the Mediterranean with the loss of a thousand men shortly afterwards, and the sinking of the transatlantic liner *Arabica* off Cork in the same week, further distracted attention from the costly failures at Gallipoli. A writer to the *Irish Independent* expressed his frustration at the lack of coverage in a brief but sharp letter.

> One is ... struck by the entire absence of mention of the two Irish regiments who, at terrible losses in officers and men, made this landing good. Viz.—1st Royal Dublin Fusiliers and the 1st Royal Munster Fusiliers: The 6th and 7th Battalions of both these famous regiments are now 'somewhere' in or near the Gallipoli Peninsula, and, given an opportunity, they will no doubt emulate the deeds of their line battalions. It is to be hoped ... that they will not be officially passed over.[24]

The letter was signed 'Dubster.'[25]

On 24 August the immensity of the losses began to emerge in the Irish press, coinciding with news that the Government of Ireland Act was now likely to be suspended until after the war, or even longer. John Redmond called on nationalist Ireland to rally behind him so that the country could speak with 'one voice' and ensure that this threat was defeated. He received short shrift from the *Irish Independent*, which pointed out that 'the time to have exhibited strength was five years ago.' It put his present problems down to a 'lamentable initial weakness' in tackling opposition to home rule.

The next day's edition published a group photograph of officers taken at Portobello Barracks (now Cathal Brugha Barracks) before their departure for the

Dardanelles. Of the 25 men in the picture, 18 were listed as killed or wounded.[26] But it was only on 27 August that Dubliners began to learn of the full scale of the disaster at Gallipoli. On the same day, sections of a despatch on the landings written by the commanding officer in the military theatre of operations, General Sir Ian Hamilton, also appeared in the press. 'The young troops of the new divisions did not get on fast enough, and the first advantage of surprise was lost,' he wrote. As a result, gains made by veteran New Zealanders had to be given up.

Details of the despatch, widely circulated in British newspapers, added insult and hurt to bereaved families in Ireland. The *Irish Independent* counselled that it

> would be better for the public to suspend judgement until the facts are fully ascertained. The casualty lists, at any rate, show that the Irish troops fought bravely and suffered heavily.'[27]

It was another nail in John Redmond's political coffin. Even his request that the 10th Division be allowed to undergo its baptism of fire under the command of its own Irish commander had been ignored.

Over the coming days Irish papers published horrific stories of the carnage. Father J. Fahey, a recently ordained Catholic priest and chaplain, described the scene at Suvla.

> An inferno broke loose. It was appalling. The men were packed so closely that one bullet would wound or kill three men. There was dreadful slaughter in the boats.
>
> I could see only what was happening in my own. First the 'cox' was shot; then an oarsman fell dead across my feet; then a bullet came through the boat and grazed the puttees on my leg; then another of the men collapsed without a sound … I never expected to reach the shore alive.
>
> There was only one anxiety amongst the men—to reach the shore and rush the Turks with the bayonet.

However, the boat struck the bottom about twenty yards from the shore, and the men had to wade the rest of the way. As Father Fahey jumped into the water a bullet went through the sleeve of his jacket 'and caught a lad behind me. A [piece of] shrapnel splashed a man's brains over me,' while a shot that hit the gunwale

> almost blinded me with splinters. I got on the beach exhausted and had to lie down amongst the falling bullets to get my breath.

A soldier trying to dig a foxhole in the sand beside him was shot through the heart. Looking back, Father Fahey saw that the beach was strewn with dead and wounded. Two boats landed about 50 yards from where I was. They held 50 soldiers each but only 20 came ashore altogether. They came under fire from a maxim gun. But these 20 had their revenge; they captured the gun and bayoneted every member of the crew.[28]

The pages of the newspapers began to fill with photographs of dead and wounded Fusiliers officers. Two brothers reported wounded were Captain J. A. D. Dempsey and Lieutenant P. H. D. Dempsey. Captain Dempsey was 'very popular in musical and dramatic circles in Dublin' and had served on the entertainments committee of the battalion.

Personal details of private soldiers who were casualties were rare, but an exception was Corporal F. J. Murphy. While thousands of his comrades were being buried at Suvla, he was awarded the honour of a funeral with military honours through the streets of Dublin because he had been one of the fatalities on the Holyhead mail train the previous Saturday. Dubliners were also able to examine replicas of a dug-out and a shooting trench in the grounds of Iveagh House as part of the Royal Horticultural Society show, transferred from the RDS grounds, now under military occupation. These were reportedly the most popular attractions.[29]

The next day's *Irish Independent* published a group photograph of twenty-eight officers of the 'Pals Battalion', of whom nine had been killed and a further six wounded. The wounded included the commanding officer, Lieutenant-Colonel Downing, and Lieutenant Ernest Julian, Reid professor of law at TCD. Julian had died in fact on 8 August, three weeks before the photograph was published. Errors in news reports were compounded by censorship and slow communications. Page Dickinson described Julian as 'brilliant in his career and ... making his name as fast as man can at his own calling.'[30] It is a measure of the impact that the Dardanelles fiasco was having that Dickinson—an architect from a staunch unionist background who left Ireland in the 1920s rather than live under the Free State—felt 'unable to speak of Gallipoli: of all the horrible, ill-thought-out phases of the war that reflect discredit on those in authority, it was the worst.'[31]

Lieutenant Ewen Cameron, an officer in the 7th Battalion of the Royal Dublin Fusiliers, died without even reaching the front. The *Irish Independent* reported with brutal clarity:

He was found shot dead in a lavatory of the 10.15 a.m. train from Dublin, between Greystones and Newcastle. The door was bolted from the inside. The bullet, which had been discharged from an automatic pistol, pierced the brain.[32]

Cameron's brother Charles had served as a captain in the same regiment before perishing in a drowning accident shortly before the war broke out. Ewen had been vigorously assisting in the recruiting campaign, with the result that for the past few days he had shown serious signs of complete nervous breakdown. The news of the numerous fatalities and casualties among his fellow officers, it is said, also depressed him deeply.

Their father, Sir Charles Cameron, was deputy grand master of Ireland's Freemasons, though he was better known for the previous half-century as Dublin's chief medical officer. 'This terrible blow will [make] the little of life left to me meaningless,' he recorded in his diary that night.[33]

Another family deeply affected by events at Gallipoli was that of Edward Lee. A Methodist of modest origins from Cornahir, near Tyrrellspass, Co. Westmeath, he was known as the local man who went to Dublin and became a millionaire. He owned a string of drapery shops in Dublin and its suburbs. He had married Annie Shackleton, a member of the well-known Quaker business family, and had earlier worked for another well-known Quaker family, the Pims, at their drapery shop in South Great George's Street. In 1885 he established his own shop in Bray and the same year a second one in Kingstown. Other branches followed in Rathmines and the city centre.

Lee was renowned for two things. In 1889 he initiated a half-day holiday on Thursdays for his staff, which was later adopted by most shops in the city, and in 1913 he was almost alone among employers in Dublin in opposing the lock-out. He was certainly the most consistent and vociferous opponent of William Martin Murphy's strategy of starving the workers into submission. He joined the Industrial Peace Committee established by Tom Kettle,[34] which tried unsuccessfully to arrange a settlement to the dispute.

Lee had served as chairman of Bray Urban District Council in 1908, sponsored by Lord Powerscourt, in the Unionist interest. The first toast at the dinner held to celebrate his election was 'The King.' Two years later there was a luncheon in the Royal Marine Hotel in Kingstown to mark his handing over of the Dungar Terrace housing development, which he had built at his own expense for employees, to the urban district council. When the war came he would make his premises available for collecting fruit, fresh vegetables and game for wounded soldiers convalescing in the city's hospitals.

Life must have seemed idyllic in the summer of 1914, although Edward and Annie Lee had already known tragedy in their lives, with the deaths of five of their nine children in infancy. The surviving children lived with their parents in a big house, Bellevue, in Cross Avenue, with large grounds and tennis courts. Two of the sons, Edward and Tennyson, would follow their father into the family firm, while Robert became a doctor and Joe a barrister. A dinner was held in the Dolphin Hotel in East Essex Street, Dublin, to celebrate the calling of Joseph Bagnall Lee to the bar. Again the first toast was 'The King,' followed by 'Mr. Joseph Bagnall Lee,' 'The Irish Bar,' and 'Prosperity to Ireland.'

Joe Lee was a brilliant student at Trinity. He was senior moderator (in first place among honours graduates) in legal and political science, joint author of a book on criminal injuries and auditor of the Law Students' Debating Society. The Lord Chancellor, Sir Samuel Walker, and the Chief Secretary for Ireland, Augustine Birrell, were in the audience at King's Inns for his inaugural address on the subject of 'The Law and the Problems of Poverty.'

It was an unremarkable performance, however. Lee sought reforms in the old workhouse system and the new labour exchanges to ensure greater discrimination between the 'deserving poor,' who should be helped, and 'the loafer and semi-criminal with whom they have no option but to associate.' The greatest excitement came when suffragists in the audience heckled Birrell.

With the outbreak of war, three of the Lee sons volunteered. Joe and Tennyson were sponsored by a family friend, Lieutenant-Colonel Verschoyle T. Worship, and received commissions as officers in the 6th Battalion of the Royal Munster Fusiliers, his own unit. Robert, the doctor in the family, was commissioned in the Royal Army Medical Corps.

Joe Lee was killed within hours of landing at Suvla Bay, leading his men in the assault on the hotly disputed Kiretch Tepe ridge. Tennyson, who saw his brother's dead body being brought back into the lines, was severely wounded in the left arm. A month later and a thousand miles away their brother Robert was promoted captain for his work under fire at a field hospital in the battle for 'Hill 60' at Ypres. His companion, O. S. Watkins, a Methodist chaplain, wrote of their experiences:

> All through the night the ghastly stream poured in. I will not attempt to picture that dressing station—blood, horror, shrieks and groans. I wish I could forget it myself, and do not desire that anybody else should have to carry the burden of that memory.[35]

But the horrors of war, or at least its consequences, were beginning to make themselves visible in Dublin. On 7 September, just as the battle of Hill 60 was opening, no less than 611 war wounded arrived at the North Wall on the hospital ship *Oxfordshire* from Le Havre. Half of them were despatched, 'in a dismal downpour of rain,' to various hospitals in Dublin and the rest to Belfast, Cork and the Curragh. Members of the Automobile Association organised private transport to bring many of the wounded to local hospitals.

———

The death of yet another of Dublin's ageing nationalist MPs passed almost unnoticed in the clamour of war. William Abraham had few connections with the capital. Like Nannetti, he had been a craft union stalwart in his day, representing the Carpenters and Joiners at the British Trades Union Congress in Dublin in 1880. Like Nannetti, he was out of tune and out of touch with the younger generation of radical labour leaders. Unlike Nannetti, he had first come to prominence through his work for the Land League and had been imposed on the electorate of the Harbour division by the Irish Party machine in 1910 when local UIL branches could not agree on a candidate. Since his election he had hardly visited the city, and he even deprived the party of the bonus of a political funeral in Dublin by being buried in the Nonconformist section of St Pancras Cemetery in London.[36]

'It's the best Labour seat in Dublin, and win it we must,'[37] was William O'Brien's assessment of the Harbour division; yet Labour never contested the election. Connolly was pressed to run but refused: he was already embarked upon a course of revolutionary violence that would lead to a firing squad eight months later. He believed that the war had made elections a distraction for the working class. As early as August 1914 he had expressed the hope that 'Ireland may yet set the torch to a European conflagration that will not burn out until the last throne and the last capitalist bond and debenture will be shrivelled on the funeral pyre of the last war lord.'[38]

The president of the Dublin branch of the Railway Clerks' Association, W. B. McMahon, was prevailed upon to run instead but withdrew within twenty-four hours, pleading ill-health.[39]

In the event, the writ was not moved until 24 September, nominations closed on 28 September, and the election took place on 1 October, making it one of the shortest election campaigns on record. It was also one of the dirtiest—a three-cornered dogfight between three nationalists, Alderman J. J. Farrell, Pierce O'Mahony (better known as 'the O'Mahony') and a local publican called Alfie Byrne. Byrne cheerfully admitted that he wanted an MP's salary because he could not make a living from 'my little pub' (the Vernon Bar in Talbot Street).[40]

O'Mahony was expected to win. He was a former Parnellite MP and had been sympathetic to the workers during the 1913 Lock-out, speaking at meetings and making a substantial donation to the strike fund, whereas Byrne had been excoriated by Larkin, who famously denounced the Vernon Bar as the resort of 'slum landlords, scabs, prostitutes' bullies ... Hibs, Orangemen, Temperance humbugs ... the brothel keeper, the white slaver,' and other unpleasant characters.[41] But Byrne won comfortably, with 2,200 votes to O'Mahony's 917. The reason, besides the assiduous canvassing and constituency work for which he would become legendary, was that Byrne opposed conscription, the penal war taxes on Irish industry and the British war effort in general.

In contrast, O'Mahony was a strenuous recruiter for the British army. While Byrne shared anti-conscription platforms with Connolly, O'Mahony was addressing ever more disorderly election meetings. He vainly invoked the memory of Parnell and promised workers that a grateful British government would provide school meals for children, slum clearance and even munitions factories; but hecklers reminded him that the 'Liberals killed Parnell.' When a platform colleague of O'Mahony told them that the 'Home Rule Bill' was now an act, a wit cried back, 'But not a fact,' to loud laughter.

Farrell was never in the running. Despite his own anti-conscription stance at corporation meetings,[42] he held to the party line on the war, and was considered a somewhat risqué figure, as he had opened one of Ireland's first cinemas, the Pillar Picture House in Sackville Street, a few months earlier. A completely spurious rumour that he wanted to abolish Catholic schools was readily believed, and his two clerical sponsors were scared into disowning him on the eve of the election. They subsequently apologised sheepishly for their behaviour, but the damage had been done.[43]

Gallipoli had discredited the war effort in Dublin. The criticism of the young Irish troops by Sir Ian Hamilton, especially when it was contrasted with the favourable references by the War Office to the ANZAC forces and increasing evidence of poor logistical and operational planning, not only provided ammunition for militant nationalists but even shook the faith of Castle Catholics, such as Katherine Tynan, a confidante of the former Lord Lieutenant's wife, Lady Aberdeen.

So many of our friends had gone out in the 10th Division to perish at Suvla. For the first time came bitterness, for we felt that their lives had been thrown away and their heroism had gone unrecognised. Suvla—the burning beach ... and the blazing scrub, does not bear thinking on. Dublin was full of mourning.

On a visit to the Aberdeens she met two new war widows and a girl whose brother had died.

One got to know the look of new widows—hard bright eyes, burning for the relief of tears, a high, feverish flush in the cheeks, hands that trembled, and occasionally an uncertain movement of the young head.[44]

The *Irish Times* voiced the pious hope that

the Unionists and Nationalists who stormed the hill at Suvla have sealed a new bond of patriotism and the spirits of dead soldiers will cry trumpet-tongued against the deep damnation of internecine strife in Ireland.[45]

But the northern unionist press was having none of it. The *Northern Whig* of Belfast used figures from a Protestant chaplain to claim that the majority of the 10th Division were neither Catholic nor Irish, which was probably true after British drafts made up for casualties. However, the records show that two-thirds of those who died or were wounded during the fighting had been domiciled in Ireland.[46]

The *Northern Whig* had a more legitimate argument when it pointed out that nationalists would not be able to claim political ownership of the 10th Division much longer, because recruitment had dried up at home. Major Bryan Cooper, a former Unionist MP for South Dublin who commanded a battalion of the Connaught Rangers at Suvla Bay, described the division as 'shattered' and felt increasingly demoralised by the fact that most of the replacements were British.

By the beginning of 1916 recruitment in Dublin had fallen below four hundred, the lowest figure for the entire war. But almost seventeen thousand had already signed up, and an additional eight thousand would do so before the war ended. In total, the Dublin metropolitan area provided more than 20 per cent of Ireland's manpower to the war effort. This was by far the largest contribution outside the Belfast recruitment area, which contributed 36 per cent of recruits.[47] Dublin was always a strong traditional recruitment area for the British army, with figures almost always exceeding those for Belfast. However, this pattern was strongly reversed during the First World War. (See tables 3 and 4.)

Table 3
Recruitment to the regular army, 1899–1913

	Dublin	*Belfast*	*Ireland*
1899	1,016	795	3,987
1900	1,054	1,188	4,040
1901	1,209	748	3,778
1902	1,232	798	4,691
1903	n.a.	n.a.	n.a.
1904	869	620	3,604
1905	1,125	411	3,165
1906	764	362	2,739
1907	791	620	2,949
1908	882	801	3,265
1909	657	505	2,727
1910	505	293	2,069
1911	726	260	2,549
1912	899	286	2,756
1913	832	380	2655

Table 4
Recruitment, 1914–18

	Dublin	Belfast
1914 (Aug.–Dec.)	7,283	20,900
1915	9,612	13,734
1916	4,292	5,307
1917	3,089	4,452
1918 (Jan.–Nov.)	3,990	6,549

——

The flow of casualties from the front was an immediate reminder of the human cost of the war for everyone. By the end of 1915 there were five hundred war wounded in Dublin hospitals, often being treated side by side with other patients, such as Seán O'Casey, the future playwright, who was being cared for in St Vincent's Hospital for TB. Years later O'Casey would remember Richard Francis Tobin, a former army surgeon whose bad hearing made him wield his ear trumpet 'like a Field Marshal's baton.' Tobin's only son, Paddy, had been a captain in the 'Pals Battalion' of the Royal Dublin Fusiliers, killed on 15 August 1915. He often asked patients for news from the front, especially if they had been at Gallipoli. 'He seemed to think when he was close to them, he was closer to his son.'[48]

——

Of course the cost of the conflict was also being felt by the wider community. Inflation continued to erode incomes. The activities of German submarines and the insatiable demands of the British war machine affected the price of everything. A good example was coal, which increased from 22s a ton to 40s between the start of the war and February 1915. The risk to transport in crossing the Irish Sea and the demand from war industries in Britain meant that even hospitals treating war casualties, such as St Vincent's, were asked to reduce consumption.

Most widely affected were the ratepayers and electricity consumers. Both were mainly businesses and middle-class householders, as the poor still relied on paraffin lamps for light. The corporation's coal bill would soar from £22,000 in the year ending 31 March 1915 to a projected £53,700 in the following twelve months.[49] The Electricity Supply Committee reported that, although the city had acquired another 830 customers since the war began, mainly domestic subscribers, consumption had declined by 26,000 units, because of shortages and price rises. Some 21,000 units were accounted for by the hard-pressed middle classes, while theatres, cinemas and licensed premises consumed the rest, despite restricted opening hours and the ban on police and military personnel in public houses.[50]

The one bright spot on the horizon was the fact that the committee had stocked up on carbon electrodes for street lighting just before the war broke out. Unfortunately, replacements from the German supplier were no longer available, and Dublin would have to pay up to three times as much for poorer-quality British substitutes.[51]

The financial situation had become critical by mid-1915. If desperate measures were not adopted the respectable £9,600 profit for 1914/15 would be transformed into a loss of £23,000 by March 1916. The Electricity Supply Committee came up with two possible solutions: to meet the entire cost by putting an extra 1d on lighting and ½d on power, or to use up cash reserves and increase the rate for lighting by only ½d and for energy by a farthing (¼d). However, it noted that prices would have to remain at the new level—even if the war ended—until cash reserves were restored.

Not surprisingly, the councillors opted for the latter course, but only after deferring a decision for three months in the hope of better news from the front.[52] The corporation was also paying 50 per cent more for cement, tar, wood and asphalt than before the war, and paying up to 10 per cent more in wages, including allowances for employees at the front.[53]

At least food prices had stabilised, and bakeries in particular showed considerable restraint in passing on costs. But demand from Britain, coupled with tax on luxuries such as tea and sugar, still exerted upward pressure on prices, even for such basic items as wheat and potatoes, by the autumn of 1915.[54]

Eating out was becoming significantly dearer, as restaurants had been another luxury area to be taxed. In September the Vegetarian Café in College Street raised the price of shilling teas by a penny 'to cover the cost of everything, including the tea tax.' The Red Bank Restaurant in D'Olier Street had already increased the price of shilling lunches by the same amount, but another penny was to be charged on a 4d pot of tea and 2d on an 8d pot. However, Bewley's Cafés and Lemon and Company, the sweet manufacturers, said they would not increase prices while existing stocks lasted.[55]

––––––

There was uproar in the business community over the introduction of an excessive profits tax in the budget of September 1915. It was levied initially at 50 per cent and was to curb profiteering, particularly in armaments and clothing as well as cinemas and breweries near military bases.

The method of calculating excessive profit was to take the average return of businesses for the three years preceding the war as a base line. Unfortunately for Dublin, 1913 and 1914 had been particularly bad years, because of the lock-out and an outbreak of foot-and-mouth disease. The Dublin Chamber of Commerce and the Citizens' Association protested to the government and to John Redmond. As Sir Maurice Dockrell pointed out, 'very few firms were making a profit in Dublin in 1913.' Even companies not directly involved in the lock-out were affected, because, as Arthur Legg, whose firm made packing-cases, said, 'we had no dispute with the men but they refused to handle "tainted goods".' He put his profits for 1913 at half the usual rate.

Such considerations cut little ice with the government. Its focus was firmly on the problems of wartime Britain, including the need to assuage public anger at profiteering.

———

By now it was relatively easy to direct public anger in Dublin at the British authorities, as the controversy over fodder and milk supplies demonstrated. In the autumn of 1915 rumours began to circulate that Major-General Friend, who commanded the British forces in Ireland, intended to commandeer the first cut of hay from farms within a ten-mile radius of the city. There was widespread fear that this would lead to shortages of fodder for Dublin's five hundred dairies, on which the city depended for its milk. Any shortage of fodder would soon translate into falling milk supplies and rising prices for this vital commodity.

In fact the army was not commandeering the fodder but was paying market rates for the crop, and taking no more than it did in 1913. Most importantly, the first cut of hay was not normally fed to cattle anyway but used for horses. The army's fodder-purchasing activities did not lead to milk shortages, or price increases, but it did give ammunition to increasingly vociferous critics of the war, as did the new import duty of 33 per cent on luxury goods, such as motor cars, bicycles, films, watches, clocks and musical instruments.

Another luxury item taxed was newspapers, a burden that the press was not slow to point out fell disproportionately on Ireland, whose papers lacked the mass circulation, large advertising market and better transport infrastructure of their Fleet Street rivals that could absorb the extra costs.[56] The *Freeman's Journal* made the telling point that people in rural Ireland were far more reliant on newspapers for information than were town-dwellers. It concluded that 'no enterprise has been so hardly hit by the war … paper, metal etc. have gone up in price, and freight and insurance rates have almost doubled.' Nor could costs be recouped through price increases, while 'advertisements too have diminished.'[57] Instead the size of newspapers shrank, and with them the amount of space given to parliamentary debates, 'especially the speeches of the smaller fry among politicians.'[58] This would have implications for the Irish Party at the national and the local level. In Dublin, the coverage of council meetings shrank to a fragment of the pre-war days.

Ratepayers were caught between the nether stone of rising pay demands from corporation employees and a reduced capacity to raise revenue. A debate on increases for 1,200 civic labourers in August to compensate them for wartime inflation revolved around the fact that it would break the ceiling of £2,000 on extra expenditure provided for by the agreed ½d increase in the rates. Eventually councillors voted for increases costing £7,000, with a proviso that, as with railway workers, the pay increases would be cancelled once the war ended.[59]

In October, resigned to having to break their own guidelines on expenditure again, the councillors adopted a report recommending that £8,000 be included in the 1916 estimates for a small working-class housing estate on the Ormond Market site. However, they failed to agree a means of raising the money.[60] To clear all 14,000 slums in the city would cost £3 million, or three times the annual rateable valuation of the city. Yet Pembroke Urban District Council managed to raise £175,000 to complete 759 houses in Stella Gardens in Ringsend by September 1916. One factor behind the impressive housing record of this suburban township was undoubtedly the lower wage rates of its local authority employees; another was the relative prosperity of its ratepayers. But it also showed that progress was possible on the housing front, even in wartime, if there was the political will.[61]

Censorship added to the sense of powerlessness Dubliners felt in the crisis. Home news was restricted, and the mainstream press served up copy inspired by the War Office and obtained from the news agencies. These were sprinkled with letters and reports from individuals at the front, usually chaplains, who appeared less inhibited by the censors than other serving personnel. The poor quality of war coverage made it almost impossible to distinguish real victories from illusory ones. By the end of 1915 the only conclusions readers could safely draw were that the war was going to last a long time, that no reductions could be expected in the casualty rates and that more hardship was a certainty on the home front.

Chapter 4 ∼

'WITHOUT THE SHEDDING OF BLOOD, THERE IS NO REDEMPTION'

Meanwhile anti-war feeling was stoked steadily by the radical nationalist press. In November 1914 the *Irish Worker* and *Irish Freedom*, journals of the labour movement and the IRB, respectively, were seized. Other publications, including Arthur Griffith's *Sinn Féin* and the *Irish Volunteer*, official organ of the Volunteers, undertook to moderate their tone to avoid closure.[1]

These mosquito titles enjoyed a very small circulation: most sold between 1,000 and 4,000 copies per issue. The largest circulation belonged to *Nationality*, one of Griffith's many enterprises, which sold 8,000 copies. In contrast, the daily *Irish Independent* sold 100,000 and the *Sunday Independent* up to 70,000 copies, while a speech by John Redmond to troops at the front in 1915 had a print run of 240,000 when reproduced in pamphlet form. British army recruitment posters had a print run of anything from 500 to 40,000 copies each.[2]

Besides Griffith, the other leading figure in the production of anti-war material was James Connolly. Griffith had been a printer by trade before turning to journalism; Connolly had learnt the trade by turns between his work as a trade union activist, socialist propagandist and general rebel against the capitalist juggernaut. He saw the war as a particularly brutal manifestation of the system, and called for an equally brutal response. Unlike Griffith, he was not a free agent, and there were concerns in the ITGWU, of which he was acting general secretary during Larkin's absence in America, that his activities would bring the wrath of Dublin Castle down upon the union.

The *Irish Worker* had been printed by members of the Socialist Labour Party in Glasgow, but this had left it vulnerable to interception by the police. When Connolly proposed buying a second-hand Furnival press and running off his new publication, the *Workers' Republic*, in Liberty Hall, he fobbed off worried committee members with the explanation that the machine was 'only a little one.' They would have been deeply troubled if they could have overheard his discussions with Fred Bower and other Liverpool socialists when he went there in search of his Furnival. When Connolly told them that he felt the war provided an opportunity for revolution, Bower asked, not unnaturally, 'But is the time ripe?' Connolly replied, 'If you succeed the time is ripe, if not, then it is not ripe.'[3]

Despite the disadvantages under which anti-war propagandists such as Connolly and Griffith operated, they had two significant factors working in their favour. One was the hardship and loss the war inflicted daily on the people of the city; the other was the historic resonance that their stance against the traditional enemy struck. In contrast, constitutional nationalists could justify support for the war only on the grounds that England had changed its policy towards Ireland. This was the argument pushed by the first Irish winner of the Victoria Cross, the highest British award for bravery, Mick O'Leary from Inchigeelagh, Co. Cork, when he was heckled at recruiting meetings. He explained that England was no longer ruled by the landlord class that had oppressed the Irish but was a democracy that would treat Ireland decently. However, his father had told neighbours that if they did not join up 'the Germans will come here and will do to you what the English have been doing for the last seven hundred years.'

As the war progressed, the evidence suggested that the fundamentals of English rule, especially such intangibles as a perceived lack of respect for Irish interests or recognition for Irish sacrifices, had not changed at all.[4]

———

Another growing weapon in the nationalist arsenal was fear of conscription. By the end of May 1915 the British army had suffered 258,069 casualties, an average of 860 a day, of whom 40 per cent were listed as killed or missing in action and therefore unavailable for return to the front line.[5] There was increasing talk of conscription in Britain as the flow of volunteers failed to make good the losses. The main brake on its introduction was opposition from the British Labour Party; this led to the ironic situation where Labour politicians were among the most assiduous in addressing recruiting rallies, urging workers to enlist so that conscription would be unnecessary!

There was no such ambiguity in Dublin. No element of the labour movement actively supported the war, and most of the leadership strongly opposed it. The Irish Neutrality League was so pro-German that leading Volunteers and IRB members, such as Thomas Ashe, had no problem addressing its meetings. Another leading ally was Connolly's old friend Francis Sheehy Skeffington, joint editor with his wife, Hanna, of the *Citizen*, the suffragist weekly. Sheehy Skeffington, however, differed from his comrade in being a committed pacifist, ready to campaign and even die for the labour cause but not to kill for it.

By the summer of 1915 Sheehy Skeffington had addressed no fewer than forty anti-recruiting meetings. At one of the last, in Beresford Place on 23 May, a police note-taker recorded his speech as usual and then arrested him. On 9 June—on the same day that the British Prime Minister, H. H. Asquith, was announcing terrible casualty figures in the House of Commons—Sheehy Skeffington appeared in the Dublin Southern Police Court and was sentenced to six months' imprisonment with hard labour for interfering with recruitment. Seán Mac Diarmada, a Volunteer officer and future signatory of the 1916 Proclamation, was in the dock with him for a similar speech in Tuam but received only four months' hard labour. Presumably his speech was considered less incendiary.

Sheehy Skeffington was reported to have urged men to stay at home, even if it meant being shot for defying conscription. 'If you die at home you die defending your nation; if you die at the front you die doing the dirty work of England.' Characteristically, he accused the government of 'despotism' for refusing to grant him a jury trial. But the authorities knew that no Dublin jury would convict. He also declared, to applause from the gallery, that he would immediately begin a hunger strike, 'and long before the expiration of the sentence I will be out of prison, alive or dead.'

He not only began his hunger strike but after six days went on a thirst strike as well. The following day he was released under the Prisoners (Temporary Discharge for Ill Health) Act (1913)—popularly known as the 'Cat and Mouse Act'—previously used against suffragist hunger-strikers. He was due to return to prison in a fortnight to continue his sentence but was not rearrested.

Undoubtedly Sheehy Skeffington's high public profile and his powerful family connections—including a father-in-law who was a senior Irish Party MP and a brother-in-law who was a former MP and now a leading recruiting officer in Ireland—helped his cause.[6] But the authorities were adopting a far less rigorous approach to anti-war agitators in Ireland than in Britain, anxious to avoid creating martyrs. When Geoffrey Dunlop courted prosecution by putting his name on posters declaring that 'Warfare is murder' the police magistrate gave him three months' hard labour and immediately suspended the sentence. When Dunlop tried to read out a long statement to the court the magistrate said he did not question Dunlop's motives but drew the line at listening to ridiculous addresses.[7]

While Redmond found it increasingly difficult to keep in step with his unaccommodating British allies, militant nationalists were steadily gaining in cohesion on their march to the Republic. The split with Redmond had seen power within the Irish Volunteers return to the IRB core. The first convention of the organisation was held on 25 October 1914, in the Abbey Theatre. Eoin MacNeill was re-elected chief of staff.

After the compromises and prevarications with the Redmondites, the road seemed clear again. Richard Mulcahy, a Post Office engineer from Waterford who as an adolescent had read the *United Irishman*, yet another Griffith paper, found that membership of the Volunteers brought 'a sense of purpose and belonging he had never before known.' The meeting in the Rotunda Rink to launch the Volunteers had been

> a complete and joyous bursting open of a door, not only to the complete Dublin populace, but to the complete body of the patient, silent, suppressed Nationalist element in Ireland awakening them to their strength and inviting them to instruction.

Now that the organisation had been purged of its pro-British Redmondite elements it 'crystallised' the network of contacts already in existence through such organisations as the GAA, the Gaelic League and the IRB.[8]

A member from Lusk, John Devine, felt similarly. He had been recruited by Thomas Ashe to the Black Raven Pipe Band and the Gaelic League. He recalled: 'Loyalty was intense in the Gaelic League and Volunteers and we would think nothing of going to one another's aid. We were all one.'[9]

However, a discordant note was struck at the convention when Connolly turned up and asked for the Citizen Army to be affiliated, with two delegates. This was rejected, for fear that association with the Citizen Army might drive some supporters back into Redmond's arms. Socialism, and all forms of modernism and materialism, were seen as a threat to Irish identity and culture and the Catholic religion. For men like Mulcahy, four of whose five sisters became nuns and one of whose two brothers became a Cistercian monk, there was no desire to contaminate the movement with such associations.[10]

There were also differences of opinion within the Citizen Army about developing better relations with the Volunteers. Citizen Army men had disrupted the launch of the Volunteers at the Rotunda Rink because one of the sponsors, Laurence Kettle, was a member of a prominent nationalist farming family that used scab labour during the lock-out. Detonators were exploded and punches were thrown.[11] On 24 January 1914 Seán O'Casey wrote for the *Irish Worker* an 'Open Letter to the Workers in the Volunteers,' in which he urged them individually to 'awake from your sleep and yield allegiance to no movement that [does] not avow the ultimate destiny of the workers.'

James MacGowran, a Citizen Army member, replied, defending the Volunteers. He said that the presence of such figures as Patrick Pearse, Tom Clarke and Alderman Tom Kelly in the leadership of the Volunteers 'is sufficient guarantee that the interests of the workers shall not be trampled on.' But O'Casey was unrepentant, lampooning 'Honest Tom Kelly' and accusing Pearse of using trams during the lock-out. He constantly questioned the Volunteers' nationalism as well as their class credentials.

In May 1914 his worst fears were confirmed when the Volunteers' incoming inspector-general, Colonel Maurice Moore, said that the movement would assist the police in 'maintaining order' if the home rule crisis resulted in civil unrest. The *Irish Worker* accused the Volunteers of becoming 'a scab military institution,' and Larkin expressed fears that the Hibernians would take them over.[12]

Things came to a head at a meeting of the Army Council of the Citizen Army at which O'Casey, as secretary, proposed that another member, Constance Markievicz, should sever all links with the Volunteers, to which she was attached through Cumann na mBan. The proposal was defeated and a vote of confidence in Markievicz was passed, by a margin of one vote.[13] O'Casey resigned. He was particularly hurt by Larkin's decision to support Markievicz.

Meanwhile Tom Clarke did his best to mend bridges with the Citizen Army, agreeing to its participation in the Volunteers' parade to Wolfe Tone's grave at Bodenstown, Co. Kildare, in June 1914. After the break with Redmond, Connolly wrote that the stand taken by the Provisional Committee would send 'a thrill of joy through the heart of every true man and woman in the country.' He urged them to join the Citizen Army in a 'fight to the finish,' even though 'some of us' might end up 'on the scaffold.'[14]

Connolly's attempt to affiliate the Citizen Army to the Volunteers was in line with his declaration, made within a week of the outbreak of war, that Irishmen should welcome the Germans as allies if they landed in Ireland. While Connolly had participated assiduously in many elections, as both a candidate and election worker, he saw them as just one of many means of waging class war. As he famously declared after losing one election, workers need not wait five years for the opportunity to cast another blow against capitalism. This was why he was a syndicalist, committed to using the strength of the trade union movement to advance political and economic causes that extended well beyond the traditional preoccupations of the work-place. In January 1914, when only one 'Larkinite' candidate out of ten secured a seat in the municipal elections, Connolly appears to have become particularly embittered by the electoral process and the seeming inability of the labour movement to secure victory through it, even in what appeared the most propitious circumstances.[15]

What the war provided was a unique opportunity, not seen since the days of the United Irishmen, to adopt an alternative revolutionary strategy. But it could happen only if Connolly embraced militant nationalism. O'Casey famously noted the change in *The Story of the Irish Citizen Army*.

The Labour movement seemed to be regarded by him as a decrescent force, while the essence of Nationalism began to assume the finest elements of his nature … The vision of the suffering world's humanity was shadowed by the nearer oppression of his own people, and … the high creed of Irish Nationalism became his daily rosary, while the higher creed of international humanity that had so long bubbled from his eloquent lips was silent forever, and Irish Labour lost a Leader.'[16]

The first major manifestation of this new unity of purpose came on 1 August 1915, when armed Citizen Army men took their place alongside the Volunteers at the funeral of Jeremiah O'Donovan Rossa. It was the first great public demonstration of militant nationalism, and an estimated twenty thousand people participated, including all the Dublin units of the Redmondite National Volunteers, unarmed. It was perhaps appropriate that the last great rally of constitutional nationalism in Dublin should have been in defence of the drinks industry, while the new forces in the political arena dedicated themselves to the Fenian ideal.

Not surprisingly, very little of Pearse's brief but highly seditious speech was permitted by the censors to appear in the national newspapers.[17] Tom Clarke, who was now in charge of planning an IRB insurrection through the agency of the Volunteers, had told his protégé to make his speech 'as hot as hell,' and Pearse did not disappoint.[18] Most newspapers did manage to print at least some of the famous closing lines.

The Defenders of this Realm have worked well in secret and in the open. They think that they have pacified Ireland. They think that they have purchased half of us and intimidated the other half. They think they have foreseen everything; but the fools, the fools, the fools!—they have left us our Fenian dead, and while Ireland holds these graves, Ireland unfree shall never be at peace.[19]

It was not the words that mattered to Father Michael Curran, secretary to Archbishop Walsh, who described the funeral in his diary as 'most impressive, skilfully organised and carried out': it was 'a challenge to Dublin Castle,' and the volley over the grave 'was a defiance to England by a new generation in Ireland.'[20]

In 1913 Curran had criticised Dublin Castle for tolerating peaceful protests by strikers seeking union recognition on the same streets. He was now part of that realignment activated by the war, which set him on a convergent path with Pearse, Clarke and Connolly. He might well have concurred with the Marxist propagandist's belief, expressed in the *Rossa Souvenir*, that 'before a nation can be reduced to slavery its soul must have been cowed, intimidated or corrupted by the oppressor,' and that 'no bloodletting could be as disastrous as a cowardly acceptance of the rule of the conqueror.'[21]

Shortly before Easter 1916 the Marxist revolutionary would remind his predominantly Catholic working-class readership: 'Without the shedding of Blood, there is no redemption.'[22] By then the gap in ideology and organisational methods between the revolutionary socialist and the Fenian conspirators was closed completely, and it would indeed be sealed in blood.

————

The O'Donovan Rossa funeral took place a week before the landings at Gallipoli, where the 10th Division would experience its own Calvary. It was a year since the Great War began. An analysis of the casualties showed that the number of officers in Irish regiments killed had come to 301, a further 451 had been wounded and 102 were missing or taken prisoner. The total was 854. The Royal Dublin Fusiliers had the heaviest losses, accounting for 120, or 14 per cent of the total.[23] The regiment still held pride of place in mid-September, when losses among officers serving with Irish regiments had risen to 383 killed, 611 wounded and 119 missing or taken prisoner, a total of 1,113, of whom the Royal Dublin Fusiliers accounted for 170, or 15 per cent.[24] No breakdowns were provided for casualties other than officers, but weekly and annual casualty figures suggest that losses of other ranks were at the rate of at least ten to one for each officer in each category. A total of 3,224 men were killed in Irish regiments in 1914, and this figure trebled to 9,878 in 1915.

Worse was to come with the terrible battles on the western front in 1916, in which 13,523 men died. The figure fell to 11,823 in 1917 and to 10,654 in 1918. The total number of men from Dublin listed as dead was 4,884, by far the highest for any city or county in Ireland, comprising 16 per cent of the total. As 25,644 men altogether enlisted in Dublin, this amounts to a death rate of just over 19 per cent.[25]

While Irish regiments were haemorrhaging in France and the Mediterranean in the summer of 1915, the Irish Volunteers were holding three officer training camps. Richard Mulcahy took his annual leave to attend one at Coosan, Athlone. Commitments to other activities, such as the Gaelic League and GAA, sank into the background, but there was 'no sense of emergency' at the training camps. Similarly, the Citizen Army carried out manoeuvres at Croydon Park, the house in Marino used as the ITGWU recreational centre, or, as relations improved, in conjunction with Irish Volunteer units.

Volunteers took advantage of the shooting range erected in Croydon Park and another one in Liberty Hall, where participants were charged 1d to fire three rounds. The presence of police escorts during these exercises only added to the air of weekend soldiering, and participants ignored the ridicule they attracted from many Dubliners.

One Saturday in late 1915 the Citizen Army staged a mock night attack on Dublin Castle, followed by light refreshments at the ITGWU hall in Inchicore and 'a sing song into the early hours of Sunday morning.' The refreshments were prepared by the women's section of the Citizen Army, thus puncturing somewhat its image as an organisation that treated all members equally.

If the rising came as almost as much of a shock to most Volunteers as it did to Dubliners at large, the same cannot be said for Citizen Army members. In late 1915 each member was issued with a mobilisation number and an identity tag so that a body could be identified easily in the event of death in the coming fight.[26]

———

The Volunteers attracted the ire of the authorities and the scorn of many families who had fathers, brothers or sons at the front; but the position of the National Volunteers was growing even less tenable, as was shown by an incident on the night of 21 August 1915, when masked men armed with revolvers stole a hundred Martini-Enfield rifles from the London and North-Western Railway yard on the North Wall. The rifles had been bought by the National Volunteers and had been detained by Customs in accordance with regulations on the importation of arms introduced at the start of the war.

John Redmond and his deputy, John Dillon, complained to the Under-Secretary, Sir Matthew Nathan. So did Colonel Maurice Moore, who was convinced that the police were obstructing the investigation in order to embarrass his organisation. (In fact the police officer he suspected of such dirty tricks had retired six months earlier.) Moore was reduced to complaining lamely that it was

> very dangerous that such like people should be permitted to seize arms undetected. We always ask permission to import arms but Sinn Fein Volunteers smuggle in considerable quantities and have more arms than are permitted us.

The main suspects were Citizen Army men, who were well organised on the docks; but the authorities refused to bow to Moore's demand that Liberty Hall be raided to search for the missing weapons. Although General Friend supported Moore's application, Nathan feared it could lead to a potentially explosive incident. In fact the weapons were probably stolen by members of E Company of the 2nd Battalion of the Volunteers, whose area covered the North Wall.[27]

The investigation, which dragged on into November, at Moore's insistence, demonstrated the futility of the National Volunteers' position. They were an army without the means or the will to fight for, or against, anything. Whatever the shortcomings of the Irish Volunteers and Citizen Army as regards means, they would soon demonstrate that they had the will. What was still unclear was what, precisely, they were fighting for.

———

For the veteran socialist agitator and trade union militant James Connolly, 1916 began with an unresolved strike at the City of Dublin Steam Packet Company. The union was still recovering from the effects of defeat in 1913. Membership subscriptions rose by 1d a week, and death benefit was abolished for the families of members who joined the British army and died in the war: in response to one application Connolly wrote that mortality benefit covered only deaths in 'Civil Life' (emphasis in original).[28] As many as 2,700 ITGWU members were serving in the British army by early 1915, so the decision had obvious financial benefits for the union. Connolly justified the move on two other grounds: opposition to the imperialist conflict and the fact that army wives and widows received a pension from the War Office.

A few ITGWU men at the front were there because they had been blacklisted during the lock-out as trade union militants, but the vast majority were among the thirty thousand former soldiers who were reservists and had no choice in the matter. As a former soldier himself Connolly would have been well aware of their plight, but this did not prevent him labelling them 'apostates' in the Workers' Republic. 'For the sake of a few paltry shillings, Irish workers have sold their country in the hour of their country's greatest need and greatest hope.' It was a view that few workers shared, or even understood, in February 1916.[29]

The dispute in the City of Dublin Steam Packet Company was another legacy of 1913. On that occasion Connolly's predecessor, Jim Larkin, fought a three-month strike to secure 30s for a 60-hour week, or 6d an hour—the 'dockers' tanner.' As in 1913, the City of Dublin company refused to follow the lead of the other shipping lines, which had agreed new rates with the ITGWU in 1915. For his part Connolly was determined to exploit the growing labour shortage caused by the war to regain ground lost in the lock-out. While the other shipping companies dressed up the pay rise as a 'war bonus' to mask very real increases in wages, to between 37s and 42s a week, the City of Dublin refused to countenance any increase. Instead it tried to invoke the Munitions of War Act (1915), which outlawed strikes and lock-outs in industries essential to the war effort. The Munitions Tribunal rejected the company's application, and the strike began on 27 October.

In yet another echo of 1913, the company appealed to Dublin Castle to make a show of force, break up the pickets and have the Admiralty requisition its ships. Connolly responded with a warning that an Admiralty requisition of the ships would be regarded as an act of war. He offered to provide weapons for the pickets from the Citizen Army arsenal. William Martin Murphy backed the company and urged carriers to lock their ITGWU members out, just as they had done in 1913. However, history was not due to repeat itself. The Under-Secretary for Ireland, Sir Matthew Nathan, declined to involve the Admiralty in such a volatile situation. The carriers ignored Murphy's advice and, when their own employees threatened sympathetic strike action in support of the dockers, bought them off with a pay rise. Nor were Citizen Army members anxious to step up the dispute by lending weapons purchased with hard-earned cash to the strikers.[30]

The ITGWU strikers were soon joined by the seamen and firemen working on the City of Dublin vessels. Edward Watson, a senior director of the company and a leading figure in the unionist community and Dublin Chamber of Commerce, called on Nathan to use the Defence of the Realm Act (1914) to deport the ringleaders in the dispute. The government had already deported Irish Volunteer officers and Sinn Féin members under the act for making seditious speeches, but Nathan was of the opinion that the employer was to blame for the present crisis. He was also mindful of the politics of the ITGWU and its leader's dual role as acting general secretary of the ITGWU and commander of the Citizen Army. Ironically, he partly justified his refusal to allow the authorities to intervene on the grounds that the union 'was not merely a labour organisation.'[31] As with Colonel Maurice Moore and his complaint about missing guns for the National Volunteers, Dublin Castle felt the less involvement the better.

It was a view shared by Sir George Askwith, the industrial relations trouble-shooter who had been involved in an unsuccessful attempt to settle the 1913 Lock-out. He now headed the Committee on Production, regulating the shipbuilding and engineering industries, and the company's stance confirmed him in his poor opinion of Dublin employers. Even other Dublin employers had little time for the City of Dublin's intransigence and appealed privately to Nathan to suspend the government mail boat contracts in order to bring Watson and his fellow-directors to their senses.[32] In contrast, there was strong popular support for the strikers. More than a thousand workers turned out for a meeting called by the trades council in November 1915. The lone voice in opposition came from the renegade Labour councillor John Saturninus Kelly, who used corporation meetings to denounce the 'pro-Germans' in Liberty Hall and called for the ITGWU to be declared an illegal organisation.

By 24 February 1916, when the Board of Trade finally offered to intervene, the City of Dublin Steam Packet Company was willing to treat; but now it was Connolly's turn to overplay his hand. He turned down mediation, on the grounds that all the company had to do was pay the going rates in the port. He was probably concerned that anything less would unravel the agreements with other employers. The City of Dublin management boxed clever by conceding an increase of 5s a week to ships' crews and approaching the National Transport Workers' Federation in Britain for recruits. When the *Workers' Republic* threatened to publish the names of the 'Brit-Huns' who scabbed on fellow trade unionists, Watson demanded protection for the strike-breakers and the suppression of the paper. Nathan supplied extra police protection but continued to avoid a direct confrontation with Connolly and the Citizen Army.

The strike would drag on until 27 June 1916, when Askwith finally intervened on behalf of the Board of Trade and awarded the dockers basic pay of 37s a week and 8d an hour overtime. This brought their earnings more or less into line with other shipping companies. By this time Connolly was dead and many other labour leaders in prison, and credit for the settlement was claimed by the new member of Parliament for the constituency, Alfie Byrne.[33]

In the meantime almost three thousand building workers began what would be the biggest strike of the year. On 1 April 1,500 carpenters and bricklayers demanded an increase of 2d an hour and plasterers 1d an hour; the Building Trades Employers' Association offered between ¼d and ½d. More than 1,250 labourers, other craft workers and builders' suppliers were laid off as a result.[34]

Like the City of Dublin strike, this dispute threatened to drag on indefinitely, until the fighting in Easter Week destroyed most of the commercial area around Sackville Street and caused extensive damage elsewhere. Reconstruction now became the priority. As the *Irish Independent* commented, 'with half the principal street of Dublin in ruins it would be little short of a crime if the building trade were allowed to delay for a single day the work of reconstruction.'[35] Captain Fairbairn Downie of the Ministry of Munitions, which was at a critical stage in developing a National Shell Factory in Parkgate Street, was appointed arbitrator. At the end of May and in early June he awarded a series of increases that meant most building workers received pay increases of 1½d an hour, including 1d an hour war bonus. The bonus would cease once the 'articles of peace' had been signed. This raised average earnings from £100 14s 6d a year to £115 17s, an increase of slightly less than 15 per cent.[36]

———

Dublin Castle's reluctance to intervene in trade disputes was in marked contrast to events in Britain, where trade union militants in such areas as the Tyne and Clydeside were arrested under the Defence of the Realm Act and threatened with conscription under the Military Service Act (1916), even though they worked in protected war industries. Wholesale arrests and deportations were used to smash shop stewards' committees, because disruption to industry had serious implications for the war effort. Dublin's peripheral role proved a blessing as far as trade unions were concerned. Workers were benefiting from the compromise hammered out in Britain under which unions were compensated for greater controls imposed on industry, including a ban on strikes in essential industries, by the introduction of state arbitration bodies to handle claims for better pay and conditions.[37] As Theresa Moriarty has pointed out, 'compulsory arbitration, which trade unions feared as industrial conscription, conversely encouraged trade unionism.'[38] The mere threat of a strike would often spur state intervention in disputes, in the form of binding arbitration. Irish trade unions found they had de facto recognition in many industries, and workers flocked to them in a way they never did to the British army.

Of course there were political complications militating against a heavy hand with trade unions in Dublin, especially if they involved raids on Liberty Hall. Just before Christmas 1915 the newly elected nationalist MP for North Tipperary, Lieutenant John Esmonde, told Connolly, on behalf of the Irish Party leadership, that he must call off the docks strike. Connolly told him to 'go to hell.'[39] On 24 March 1916 the police finally raided the building, looking for copies of the *Gael*, a short-lived separatist weekly whose previous week's issue had managed to simultaneously infuriate Dublin Castle and ridicule John Redmond. They beat a hasty retreat when Connolly produced a revolver and threatened to shoot them. From then on the hall had a permanent armed Citizen Army guard.[40]

A few days later Connolly would address his last strike meeting with workers of the City of Dublin Steam Packet Company. Easter Week was approaching, and the union leader cum revolutionary socialist, who had always stressed the complementary role of trade union and political work, was now heading down a road to insurrection that diverged sharply from the political practice of a lifetime.

———

In some respects it is hard to understand Connolly's pessimism about class politics in the deepening crisis caused by the war. Labour members of Dublin Corporation now formed the second-largest block, after the United Irish League, and stood a real chance of winning parliamentary representation in some constituencies. They worked effectively with Sinn Féin councillors and some of the more radical members of the nationalist block to push a progressive agenda in such areas as housing and education.

One reason for Connolly's disillusionment with electoral politics may have been the deep antipathy that existed between him and the leading Labour councillor, P. T. Daly. Daly had been much closer to the absentee ITGWU leader Jim Larkin than Connolly had been. In fact he had been Larkin's preferred choice to deputise for him while in America. Daly was far more gregarious than Connolly, more urbane and a snappier dresser, where Connolly was often dour in manner and appearance. Connolly's 'prickly integrity' and his insistence on mastering opponents in debate on important political and ideological issues militated against the sort of horse-trading that occurred in City Hall. Daly was a fine public speaker, possibly better than Connolly, and an able tactician. However, a chequered political and financial past dogged him. A printer by trade, he had risen fast in the ranks of the trade union movement and in the IRB. His early career demonstrated the strong organic links between craft unionism and Fenianism in late nineteenth and early twentieth-century Dublin.

As a member of the IRB he made a fund-raising tour of North America in 1903 but used some £300 of the money raised to help provide for his family. While Daly's explanation of the loss was accepted, shortly after his return to Dublin he was purged from the IRB leadership by Tom Clarke. Clarke was intent on reviving the IRB's revolutionary potential and rooting out the drinking-club elements, along with any taint of corruption, financial or political. Daly, who had also served as a Sinn Féin city councillor, defected to Labour, but his past was a malign legacy. Opponents within the Labour movement would revive the rumours from time to time, and Daly's weakness for drink sometimes played into their hands.[41]

However, no-one represented the cause of workers more effectively in the council chamber. A major issue was that of wages and war bonuses for corporation employees. By early 1916 the price of many basic foodstuffs and of fuel had increased by 50 per cent, but wages lagged behind and there were widespread complaints that even the increases that had been approved, such as the 2s a week war bonus, were not being paid to many corporation workers. Unskilled and casual employees were worst affected.[42] Daly not alone championed the right of all corporation employees to the war bonus but proposed raising the minimum wage for general labourers to 25s for a 50-hour week and that of 'light labourers' to 20s.[43] He also proposed an incremental scale of 2s for every five years of service, up to a maximum of 35s.

He faced stiff opposition from a combination of nationalist, unionist and independent councillors, mindful of the ratepayers who would have to foot the bill. Alderman Andrew Beattie, a former unionist now operating under the ratepayers' standard, proposed referring the matter to the Estates and Finance Committee. He was seconded by a UIL stalwart, Sir Joseph Downes, the confectionery entrepreneur known affectionately to Dubliners as 'Lord Barmbrack'.

The amendment was carried by a slender margin of 25 to 21 in January 1916. Besides the Labour vote, Daly's supporters included several nationalist councillors, including Laurence O'Neill and the new MP for the overwhelmingly working-class Harbour division, Alfie Byrne. By contrast, Sinn Féin split, with the group's leader, the grocer and wine merchant William T. Cosgrave, putting the ratepayers' interests first and voting with the nationalist and unionist majority.[44]

Daly returned to the attack with a slightly reduced claim on 14 March. While the minimum rate demanded was still 25s a week for unskilled labourers and 20s for men doing 'light' work, the incremental scale was halved to an extra 1s a week every five years, to a maximum of 30s. This time attempts to defer a decision, though supported by the Town Clerk on financial grounds, were comfortably defeated, by 31 votes to 12. Eventually only seven members voted against the new pay scale, including unionist members, Beattie, and the Lord Mayor, the tobacco magnate James Gallagher.[45]

Daly's political skill was also demonstrated in his simultaneous campaign to include the notorious Newfoundland Street area of the north docks in the city's housing programme. 'Newfoundland' was bounded by Lower Sheriff Street, Guild Street, Lower Mayor Street and Commons Street. Nationalist councillors from more prosperous wards blocked the proposal at first but were worn down by the continuous attacks from Daly, other Labour members and some Sinn Féin councillors. A plea from the parish priest, Father James Brady, in which he described in graphic detail the appalling conditions of the area, helped swing the vote. Eventually enough nationalist councillors supported Daly's invocation of part 1 of the Housing of the Working Classes Act (1885) to begin the long process of slum clearance in Newfoundland. Again Alfie Byrne was to the fore among the nationalists realigning with Labour and Sinn Féin.[46]

————

By 1916 the effect of the war on municipal politics was making itself felt in other ways. There was an interesting trial of strength at a corporation meeting on 6 March when Alfie Byrne joined with the leader of the Sinn Féin group, William T. Cosgrave, to propose a motion condemning the increasing tax burden on Ireland. Resentment was all the worse because of the negative effect the war was having on Irish trade and industry. The main nationalist grouping around the UIL proposed an amendment, requesting the Irish Party in the House of Commons 'to resist by every means in their power any proposal for increases in tax.' There was no difference in substance between the wording of the two motions, yet the amendment supporting the Irish Party was accepted by only 23 votes to 18.[47]

Eighteen months of enduring the hardships of a war John Redmond had endorsed was fracturing nationalist unity. Barely a week later, on 14 March 1916, the former Unionist councillor Andrew Beattie was proposing a motion protesting at the failure of the government to give Ireland 'orders for Munitions of War in fair and reasonable amounts, in proportion to our increased taxation and per capita of the population as compared with the populations of England, Scotland and Wales.'[48] It was passed unanimously, although some saw it as an implicit criticism of the failure of Redmond and the Irish Party to lobby effectively for war contracts. But Dublin was shortly to make its own unique contribution to the Great War.

————

A foretaste was provided on St Patrick's Day, when the Irish Volunteers held a church parade in the city, effectually taking over College Green and the streets leading into it. The Green was a traditional parade ground for the British army as well as of the original Irish Volunteers in the eighteenth century. Every 4 November the military had fired a volley to celebrate the birthday of King William III, whose equestrian statue dominated the scene. The parades had ended in the early nineteenth century and Orange parades some time afterwards, but King William still sat astride his horse, though frequently daubed with paint, and worse. The Green also contained the old Irish Parliament building, now housing the Bank of Ireland, and so the symbolism of the Volunteers' occupation of this space was not lost on Dublin's citizens, or the occupants of the Castle.

After contingents attended mass at the Pro-Cathedral and ss Michael and John's Church in Exchange Street,[49] the Volunteers reassembled along College Green and Dame Street for inspection by their chief of staff, Dr Eoin MacNeill. Sentries with fixed bayonets prevented vehicles, including trams, from disrupting the proceedings. A car containing British officers tried to force its way through until the commandants of the 3rd and 5th Battalions, Éamon de Valera and the recently appointed Thomas Ashe, turned them back. Ashe told his men to use their bayonets if necessary.

Otherwise there were no incidents, or even speeches, but leaflets were distributed calling on Irish men to join the Volunteers and assert the nation's sovereignty at home. The newspapers estimated that between 1,600 and 2,000 men turned out, equipped with 'a very miscellaneous collection' of weapons, including about eight hundred serviceable rifles and many revolvers.[50]

In contrast, the Irish Party continued its recruitment campaign for the British army. In company with the Royal Dublin Fusiliers, John Field, the veteran Parnellite MP for St Patrick's division, told recruiting meetings at the James's Street Fountain and Dolphin's Barn that Irishmen were fighting side by side with Welsh, English and Scottish colleagues 'for freedom, fatherland and Christianity.' His audience could thank the vigilance of the Irish Party that Ireland had been spared conscription, and the onus was now on the citizenry to come forward and keep up the numbers of the Irish battalions on a voluntary basis. He suggested that the government should allow members of the Constabulary to join the colours to help make up the numbers.

A local publican and UIL councillor, John Scully, presided at the meetings, while members of the Royal Dublin Fusiliers said it would be shameful to leave '95 per cent' of the fighting to Englishmen. The *Irish Times* reported that the recruitment procession was headed by boy scouts with torches, but it did not say how many recruits stepped forward.[51]

———

The same day London was 'awash' with shamrock, and three million Irish flags were distributed in the metropolis by leading society figures and their helpers, such as Lady Sligo at the Berkeley Hotel and Lady Limerick on London Bridge. The aim was to remind British people of the Irish contribution to the war effort. In the same spirit Queen Alexandra visited the depot of the Irish Guards and presented the regiment's reserve battalion with shamrock. She was accompanied by the King, Lord Kitchener and John Redmond. King George v paid lavish tribute to the 'heroic endurance' of his Irish troops. As the *Irish Times* would acknowledge next day, the royal visit was intended to make some amends for the 'contemptuous oblivion in which the deeds of Irish troops in the western battlefields and on the Gallipoli heights were for a long time condemned to remain owing to the neglect or prejudice of officers in high command.' These were strong words for the leading organ of unionism in Ireland. Ironically, it was one of the worst offenders, Lord Kitchener, as colonel of the Irish Guards, who responded to the King's speech with a declaration that Irish soldiers would never forget their monarch's kind words and remained 'ready to respond to every call of duty.'

Newspapers reported that Redmond was allowed a few private words with the King and a handshake. That evening he attended a concert at King Edward vii's Hospital for Officers and told wounded Irish soldiers they could take consolation in the knowledge that they were fighting for 'the protection of small and weak nations against the most wicked oppression that had ever been attempted in the world's history.' It all appears to have gone down well, not least with soldiers in France, who received consignments of shamrock and pieces of green ribbon from the champion of small nations and constitutional nationalism.[52]

By now there seemed to be a significant divergence between the mentality of ordinary soldiers at the front and events at home. This was understandable, given the small amounts of leave granted to enlisted men. The difficulty experienced in obtaining leave was a recurring theme of letters from members of the Royal Dublin Fusiliers in France to Monica Roberts, founder of the Band of Helpers to the Soldiers. She lived in Stillorgan, Co. Dublin, with her father, the Rev. William Ralph Westropp Roberts, a senior fellow of Trinity College. She devoted herself to providing comforts for the Fusiliers, including handkerchiefs, shirts, boracic ointment, Vaseline, chocolates, dried fruit, trench torches, gloves, watches, playing cards, pipes, tobacco and cigarettes.[53]

One of her pen friends was Sergeant John Brooks, a regular soldier who had been in France almost from the beginning of the war. He told her in December 1915 that it was hard for NCOs to get leave, 'for they can't spare us.' But private soldiers were no better off. Private Kirwin was more than eighteen months in France before he received home leave. Other soldiers were unfortunate enough to discover that their first visit 'home' was a trip to hospital in Britain to be treated for serious injuries, or trench fever. This still counted as 'leave', and they would have to join the back of the queue when they returned to the front.[54]

Monica Roberts's own letters to the soldiers asking them what they needed were bright and caring but could become gushing on occasion, or ill-timed. 'Everyone in Ireland is very proud of all our brave Dublin Fusiliers,' she told Private J. May in a letter dated 10 July 1915.[55] It was returned: May had been killed in action a few days before.

Soldiers rarely mentioned politics, but when they did they assumed nothing had changed since the outbreak of war. There was a touching naïveté to Sergeant Brooks's comment as Christmas 1915 approached that 'things at home must be very quiet as everyone has someone out fighting for King and Country.'[56] Yet Brooks had little time for unionists, scoffing at the ignorance of things military shown by 'Carson's army', as he described former members of the Ulster Volunteer Force.

> We had to take a lot of them for to show them what work was to be done in the trenches ... as they knew nothing about soldiering ... We had to be with them night and day, which was very weary on us.[57]

The preoccupations in the trenches reflected the harshness of the conditions. Private Edward Mordaunt of B Company, 2nd Battalion, Royal Dublin Fusiliers was one of the first Irish soldiers in France. From Upper Rutland Street in the inner city, he had enlisted in February 1911 and landed in France on 25 September 1914. Recounting his experiences, he wrote:

> The worst of it was the winter out here. We were both frozen and up to our chests in water. Dear Miss Roberts I think if I was made of iron I would not stick it out as well as I am doing.[58]

A month later he was thanking her for a parcel,

> especially my favourite cigarettes Woodbines, and I need not tell you my Dear Friend that your socks are very useful, especially when I come out of the trenches ... There is nothing like a change of clean socks for a reprieve with a cigarette.[59]

Another correspondent from the same battalion, Private Joseph Clarke, had different priorities.

> The most essential part of a parcel sent to the trenches is the food stuff ... Dainties ... although very palatable are not what the fighting man really wants. The most suitable parcel is the one which contains good, solid food stuffs such as short-breads, tins of sardines, small bottle sauce, café au lait and home made cakes.[60]

While politics barely featured, support for Redmond's policy at the front seemed firm in 1915 and the spring of 1916. Writing about an impending attack on German positions in late August 1915, Edward Mordaunt said: 'For those we love I am not afraid to die tomorrow because I know it is in a *good cause*.' (Emphasis in original.)[61] Nor did another Christmas in the trenches unduly upset him.

We are having a very hard time of it now ... between rain, frost, snow and slush. It has us near dead ... but still Are We Downhearted—NO.

Like all her correspondents, he told Monica Roberts that the platoon parcels helped raise morale. In January he took up her offer of a pair of leather gloves. 'The gloves would be very useful when I go on patrol at night with a few bombs to share among the Huns.'[62]

Many soldiers were buoyed by the hope that the war would end soon. Private Harry Loughlin of the 1st Battalion, Royal Dublin Fusiliers, wrote from the Dardanelles: 'We have gained a very worthy name for ourselves and the country we were sent from and showed the fighting quality of the Irish soldier.' He concluded: 'We soon shall finish up here with victorious honours.'[63]

On 8 April 1916, a fortnight before the Easter Rising, Private Thomas Finn wrote: 'It is the weather for beating the Huns.' But he added: 'I wish myself it was over.' Ten days before the rising Sergeant Heafey of the 8th Battalion wrote that his unit expected to be in action again soon and would

> show what Irishmen are made of and keep up the credit of our Ould Country as we done in days gone by. One consolation we have, we can see by the news daily that the Hun is done for on all sides.[64]

There was no conflict between such belligerence and the politics of home rule, for the Irish Party had never opposed physical force on principle, only on pragmatic grounds. The party's support for the British war effort was based on the notion that Irishmen could fight for their country and the right of all small nations to self-determination by defending Belgium. Queen Alexandra's presentation of shamrock to the Irish Guards and William Field's addresses in James's Street and Dolphin's Barn were manifestations of this convoluted endorsement. In contrast, the Irish Volunteers' message was simplicity itself. A short pamphlet by Joseph Plunkett, distributed by Volunteers in College Green, tackled Redmond's position head on: he argued that it made as much sense for an Irishman to join the British army to defend his country as for a Belgian to defend his country by joining the German army.[65]

———

Even on St Patrick's Day casualty lists were published in the newspapers, to remind young Irish men of what awaited them if they joined up, and cinema newsreels carried even more graphic warnings.[66] As Sir Henry Robinson, vice-president of the Local Government Board, remarked, the war films showing big shells exploding in the midst of a lot of troops 'going over the top,' though interesting enough, were not the kind of thing calculated to encourage young men to leave their peaceful and comfortable homes.[67]

Indeed the news from the front and the casualty lists underlined the eminent sense of staying at home. By early 1916 *Young Ireland* went so far as to claim it was probably a good thing home rule had not been granted in 1914, as an Irish government headed by Redmond would probably have sent even more men to the front.[68]

But the Irish Volunteers' St Patrick's Day parade in Dublin was more than a riposte to the Redmondite war policy: it celebrated the ascendancy of the IRB in the Volunteer organisation, particularly in Dublin. The organisation was now being directed by a secret Military Council within the IRB. Its members dominated the headquarters staff of the Volunteers and the Dublin command structure. The commanders of all four city battalions (Ned Daly, Thomas MacDonagh, Éamon de Valera and Éamonn Ceannt) were IRB men, as was the commander of the recently formed 5th (Fingal) Battalion, Thomas Ashe. The weak link in the chain was the need to spin a conspiratorial web around the Volunteers' chief of staff, Eoin MacNeill, to make sure he had no knowledge of the planned insurrection.

MacNeill was of the view that a rising was justifiable or capable of winning popular support only if it was undertaken against the imposition of conscription. The conspirators' hope was that, faced with a *fait accompli*, he would endorse the Military Council's plan.[69]

Most IRB members, such as Richard Mulcahy, were unaware of what was being planned; yet their political conditioning, through their involvement in the Volunteers and various cultural organisations, was such that they would not be found wanting on the day. Mulcahy was typical of the emerging Volunteer officer class. The son of a civil servant in Waterford, he had gone from the Christian Brothers' school to the Post Office. In 1908 he was transferred to Dublin and in 1916 became a member of the Engineering Department. He had earlier turned down a scholarship to the College of Science after the Post Office refused him three years' leave of absence—no doubt a source of resentment. His interest in things national had led him to join the Keating Branch of the Gaelic League. Its president was Cathal Brugha; another member was Michael Collins, recently returned from England to avoid conscription.

Like Mulcahy, Collins was a member of the IRB, having been sworn in while a young emigrant in London. Mulcahy was sworn in as a member of the Teeling Circle at a regular Dublin venue for such meetings, the National Foresters' Hall, 41 Rutland Square. He recalled later that the circle was almost moribund and usually met once a month for about twenty minutes, when members paid their dues and suggested potential new recruits.

There were no matters for discussion … The members had no routine duties, nor responsibilities of any kind, nor any drilling. On one occasion an elderly member of our circle came one night with a rifle under his topcoat and explained to us the parts.[70]

Mulcahy had no difficulty reconciling membership of the IRB with a belief in the efficacy of home rule. The only specific order he ever received from the IRB was to join the Volunteers. He quickly progressed through the ranks of C Company of the 2nd Battalion, which covered the north-east quadrant of the city between Sackville Street and Fairview. By the eve of the rising he was a first lieutenant, in charge of signalling and communications, owing to his Post Office expertise. He took part in the Howth gun-running in July 1914 and remained loyal to the Volunteer Executive when the split came with Redmond. Between his summer holidays in 1915, which he spent at the officers' training camp in Athlone, and Easter 1916, Volunteer activities occupied most of his spare time.[71]

Liam Archer was another young professional with an interest in all things national. He was a civil servant and a member of the Ancient Order of Hibernians. He joined the Volunteers only after the Howth gun-running. His initial hesitation was due to the AOH advising members against joining the Volunteers, 'because the new body was not under the control of the Irish Party.' This changed after the Volunteer Executive accepted Redmond's nominees, and Archer drilled at the AOH Hall in Claude Road, Glasnevin. It was a brief involvement, because the AOH advised members to support the National Volunteers after the split over Redmond's pro-war speech at Woodenbridge. The majority of AOH members accepted this advice, but

a number, confused and disappointed, ceased membership. I was amongst the latter group and I severed my connection with the AOH at the same time.

By early 1915 he decided to rejoin the militants and soon became a section leader in F Company of the 1st Battalion. Like Mulcahy, he was an active member of the Keating Branch of the Gaelic League, but he was inducted into the IRB only shortly before the rising.[72]

Michael Staines was a shop assistant and treasurer of the Colmcille Branch of the Gaelic League. He had no time for politics or politicians, and he joined the Volunteers because it was 'non-sectarian and non-political.' Like Mulcahy, he belonged to the 2nd Battalion. He owed his rapid rise to quartermaster of the Dublin Brigade not alone to ability but to the fact that he worked in Thomas Henshaw and Company's ironmongery and engineering works at Christ Church Place, which sold revolvers and shotguns. Through his employer he could buy weapons and ammunition from gunsmiths in the city, while his brother Humphrey, a seaman, smuggled revolvers on the transatlantic liner *Baltic* to Glasgow. The brothers were inducted into the IRB at least partly to facilitate smuggling Humphrey's revolvers through the IRB's network in Britain. Staines was one of the few Volunteer officers to be given early warning of the rising. He handed in his notice to Henshaw's on 16 March to work full-time augmenting the Dublin arsenal.[73]

The man designated to command all rebel forces in the city came from a very different background to the apolitical lower middle-class activists who were coming to dominate the Volunteers. James Connolly was the son of Irish emigrants and grew up in the appalling poverty of Edinburgh's Cowgate district. A lifelong socialist, he had no qualms about his involvement in preparing for armed insurrection and had always believed the struggle for socialism was intrinsically linked with that for national freedom, although he had been scathing in his critique of the 'physical force party' in the past and the Fenians' exaltation of political violence into a principle.[74]

As we have seen, the outbreak of war and the dislodgement of old certainties that it brought led Connolly to rethink his position. He was determined not to let the conflict pass without seizing the opportunity to strike a blow for national and class freedom. One of the recurring themes of his main work, *Labour in Irish History*, is that 'only the Irish working class remain as the incorruptible inheritors of the fight for freedom in Ireland,' the only class that had stood resolutely by the struggle for independence in every generation.

In January 1916 the IRB approached Connolly, for fear he would rise prematurely and destroy the prospects for a successful insurrection. He spent three days closeted with members of the Military Council in intensive discussions, by the end of which he had agreed to throw in his lot with the physical-force party he had once despised. The alliance allowed the IRB to keep control of events; in return it gave Connolly a leading role in the direction of the national revolution. The physical-force men and the revolutionary socialist appear to have earned each other's respect.[75]

The accession of Connolly also gave the Military Council somewhere safe to meet for its final deliberations. After the abortive raid on Liberty Hall by the DMP in March, Connolly maintained a permanent Citizen Army guard on the building. While the council continued to meet from time to time in other places, such as Wynn's Hotel in nearby Lower Abbey Street, it was in Liberty Hall that the final arrangements for the rising were made; it was to Liberty Hall that senior officers in Dublin reported during the hectic hours leading up to the rising; and in Liberty Hall, while military business was being conducted upstairs, the Proclamation of the Irish Republic was being printed in the basement.

On Easter Monday morning, 24 April, when a combined force of Volunteers and Citizen Army men eventually formed up at Liberty Hall to march on the GPO, a bemused onlooker is alleged to have wandered in and asked Lieutenant Constance Markievicz[76] if they were rehearsing for a play.

'Yes,' said Markievicz.

'Is it for children?'

'No,' said Markievicz, 'this is for grown-ups.'[77]

Chapter 5

'A SCENE OF GREATER SPLENDOUR ... NEVER BEFORE WITNESSED, NOT EVEN IN THE REALMS OF CINEMATOGRAPHY'

Much emphasis has been placed on the more theatrical aspects of the rising and its 'blood sacrifice' dimension, personified by the religious predilections of the revolution's poets, Pearse, Plunkett and MacDonagh. But Eoin MacNeill accepted that the Military Council's plan was feasible when it was finally disclosed to him on the eve of the insurrection. This move coincided with the only event that linked Dublin Corporation with the drama about to be played out on the city's streets.

A British military memorandum had been given to the IRB's Military Council by Eugene Smith, a policeman who worked in the G Division (intelligence branch) of the DMP. Smith can lay claim to being the first rebel 'spy in the Castle,' long before Michael Collins reorganised the Irish Volunteers' intelligence system during the War of Independence.

The document was doctored so that it appeared to be a plan for the imminent arrest of senior members of the Irish Volunteers, Sinn Féin, the Gaelic League and, for good measure, Redmond's National Volunteers.[1] Attempts to place it in the national newspapers failed, because editors either doubted its authenticity or feared the repercussions from publishing it if it was genuine. Eventually a long-serving Sinn Féin stalwart, Alderman Tom Kelly, who was chairing a special meeting of the corporation that day to adopt the poor rate and the police rate, tried to read the document, now entitled Secret Orders to Military Officers, into the record.[2]

Dublin Castle immediately denounced it as a forgery; but the timing was impeccable. The House of Commons was in the middle of the great debate that would lead to the introduction of conscription in Britain. On 11 April, in response to a parliamentary question about the increasingly provocative activities of the Irish Volunteers, the Chief Secretary for Ireland, Augustine Birrell, assured the house that plans existed for dealing with that organisation.

MacNeill was certainly convinced of the document's authenticity and issued a countermanding order calling off a mass mobilisation of the Volunteers for Easter Sunday only after news broke that the Royal Navy had intercepted the German arms shipment meant for the rebels off the Kerry coast on 20 April. It was clear then that the crucial mobilisation of the properly armed provincial units necessary to make the seizure of Dublin a serious military proposition was no longer possible. MacNeill could see this; but members of the Military Council had invested far too much of themselves in the insurrection to call it off. To do so would leave them open to ridicule and recrimination by the whole nationalist community, as well as retribution from the authorities.[3]

The attitude of Thomas Ashe, already a senior figure within the IRB, was probably typical. He heard rumours of a countermanding order from Diarmuid Lynch, secretary of the IRB executive, while on a visit to the city.[4] Ashe ordered his men to assemble at Rathbeale Cross on Easter Sunday anyway and had them practise tactics until an order arrived definitely cancelling the rising. He told the Volunteers to 'guard your arms as you would guard your lives' and went to see Connolly at Liberty Hall. When Connolly said the rising would go ahead on Easter Monday regardless of MacNeill's order, Ashe returned to Lusk and used the IRB network, supplemented by a motorbike, to tell as many men as possible to mobilise at Knocksedan Bridge outside Swords next morning.

Only a handful turned up[5]; but the poor turn-out did not deter Ashe. The intense nationalism of the Volunteers, reinforced by the extreme religiousness of the era, made the prospect of defeat less forbidding for these men than it would have been for many of their more materially minded revolutionary contemporaries on the Continent. Ashe's last act as principal of Corduff National School had been to cut all the flowers in bloom in the garden and ask his assistant, Mary Monks, to put them on the altar in front of the Blessed Sacrament after he was gone.[6]

A local priest heard the confession of any volunteer who wanted it at Knocksedan, and most volunteers in the city who had any inkling of what was about to take place made it a priority to attend to their religious duties. Even avowed socialists such as Sergeant Frank Robbins of the Irish Citizen Army did so. As described by one of Ashe's lieutenants, Joe Lawless—the man who had accidentally fired his revolver in the confrontation with soldiers at Fairview in 1914—English propaganda sought to misrepresent them

> as anarchical, communistic, pro-German and various other things, but the fact is that the Irish nationalist gospel was based upon, not only the right of Ireland

to be free, but the absolute necessity to … pursue her destiny in accordance with her people's conception of the Divine plan.

For him the outbreak of war in Europe was 'a providential opportunity to strike for freedom.'[7]

——

An air of inevitability about the coming confrontation had been skilfully cultivated by members of the Military Council. Frank Henderson, captain of F Company of the 2nd Battalion, recalled regular talks and training exercises geared to a confrontation with the British in the city. Connolly lectured them on street fighting in early 1916, and the whole battalion mobilised one Saturday night in February when it was feared an abortive arms raid by the police on the home of Volunteers across the river in Great Brunswick Street presaged arrests throughout the city.

> Military equipment of all sorts was brought out and we waited in disciplined groups in the streets at Fairview and Ballybough … I suppose we must have been a couple of hours on the streets. That was a great test for the men themselves, because there was always the doubt before that as to how many … would turn out when it would come to the point.

Other conditioning included the commandant of the Fourth Battalion, Éamonn Ceannt, telling men that he had made his will. A couple of weeks before the rising Pearse attended a meeting of all the officers of the Dublin Brigade at Volunteer headquarters in Dawson Street. He asked them: 'Is every man here prepared to meet his God? Any man who was not in earnest should leave.' Henderson recalled: 'Only a very small number, one or two men, did not turn up after that.'[8]

In contrast, Connolly, who had a relatively small number of men (and women) to deal with, met each member of the Citizen Army individually and asked if they were willing to take part in a rising. Each member who replied in the affirmative was given a mobilisation number. On receipt of a message bearing the number they would present themselves, fully equipped, for action. The simplicity of the system helped ensure the high turn-out of Citizen Army members in the rising.

Frank Robbins, who had left his job in the Dublin Dockyard to be on stand-by for emergencies at Liberty Hall, spent his spare hours making grenades, converting shotgun cartridges for use in military weapons and ferrying weapons around the city, while the civil servant Liam Archer spent his Easter holidays on guard duty at the Keating Branch premises, 18 North Frederick Street, where some members of the Volunteer Executive were living on the run.

Archer and his comrades spent Easter Sunday night playing cards. Michael Collins joined them from the Larkfield estate of the Plunkett family, where he had helped with the accounts as well as military preparations. Archer wrote:

> His entrance was characteristic of him as I later knew him. He forced his way to a seat at the table, produced two revolvers and announced he would ensure there would be nothing crooked about this game. Not to be outdone, we all produced our weapons.[9]

Meanwhile Christopher Brady, a printer who worked for the ITGWU, was busy printing the Proclamation of the Irish Republic in the basement of Liberty Hall, assisted by the compositors Michael Molloy and Billy O'Brien. It had been a difficult job, because the press they were using was 'so dilapidated that parts had to be propped up with bricks,' wrong fonts were pressed into service, and new letters were even manufactured with sealing-wax.[10]

The proclamation, almost certainly written by Pearse and Connolly, contained significant elements from the constitution of the Irish Citizen Army, which had declared as its 'first and last principle ... the avowal that the ownership of Ireland, moral and material, is vested of right in the people of Ireland.' It also committed members to 'the principle of equal rights and opportunities for the Irish people,' which it adopted in practice with the admission of women to full membership.

The proclamation declared 'the right of the people of Ireland to the ownership of Ireland, and to the unfettered control of Irish destinies, to be sovereign and indefeasible.' It also declared that 'the Republic guarantees religious and civil liberty, equal rights and equal opportunities to all its citizens, and declares its resolve to pursue the happiness and prosperity of the whole nation and of all its parts, cherishing all the children of the nation equally.'

The Citizen Army constitution had been written by Seán O'Casey, who could thus claim to have influenced the drafting of the seminal tract of the Irish revolution that he would later lampoon in his plays.

Documents such as the constitution of the Irish Citizen Army and the Proclamation of the Irish Republic could not have been drafted, let alone adopted as political manifestos, anywhere in Ireland but Dublin. The unique milieu of radical nationalists, syndicalists, suffragists and socialists had injected revolutionary concepts into Irish political discourse that no amount of revision by the right would ever exorcise completely.[11]

About the time that Constance Markievicz was explaining to the casual eavesdropper in Liberty Hall that they were rehearsing a play 'for grown-ups,' the

Citizen Army bugler, William Oman, sounded the 'Fall in'. A group of Irish Volunteers arrived immediately afterwards to form a joint detachment with the Citizen Army for seizing the GPO. It was 11:45 a.m. Another section, composed entirely of Citizen Army personnel, including Markievicz, made its way to St Stephen's Green. Every unit was supposed to be in place by noon. The Angelus bell, ringing from the numerous Catholic steeples of the capital, provided the synchronisation signal.

Two members of the Volunteers caught by surprise decided to join the Citizen Army contingent in St Stephen's Green rather than try to reach their own unit. One was Harry Nicholls, the Dublin Corporation engineer; the other was Liam Ó Briain, lecturer in Romance languages at University College, Galway. They clambered over the railings, and as Ó Briain's feet touched the ground he felt he was standing 'in a different world to the ordinary, every day, shabbily genteel existence of dear old Dublin.'[12]

Like all great public events, the rising did indeed have some elements of street theatre about it, but it was on such a modest and parochial scale that it took a while for ordinary citizens, let alone the authorities, to realise that something more than routine paramilitary manoeuvres were taking place.

An *Irish Times* correspondent reported nothing unusual as he approached the city centre from the north side: 'the streets, to all appearances, were in their usual Bank holiday guise.' He noted that trams heading for the zoo in the Phoenix Park were packed with passengers keen to avail of half-price admission. 'Around the Nelson Pillar was the usual group of holiday idlers. Then his attention

was attracted by a slight commotion in front of the General Post Office ... A small group was gathered around a young man in the uniform of a Volunteer— either a Sinn Feiner or one of the Larkinite Citizen Army—who was standing between two pillars under the portico. This young man had a rifle with a fixed bayonet in his left hand, whilst in his right he held a bright-edged axe.

The journalist still did not realise anything was seriously amiss until he noticed other uniformed men smashing windows. The 'majority of onlookers seemed to regard the entire proceedings as a joke,' he wrote.

As he walked towards the *Irish Times* offices in D'Olier Street he noticed Volunteers taking furniture out of Mooney's pub in Lower Abbey Street to form a barricade, and similar activity was taking place at the corner of Bachelor's Walk, where the premises of M. Kelly and Son, which sold gunpowder as well as fishing tackle, were being ransacked. Crossing the bridge, he found nothing untoward in Westmorland Street, 'but from the direction of Dame Street, Parliament Street and Capel Street could be heard the ominous crackling of rifle shots.'[13] Soon, 'people in the streets were becoming somewhat excited and alarmed, and saying in a half-credulous way, that a Sinn Fein revolution had broken out.' The crowds of holiday-makers grew 'thinner and thinner,' while 'the noise of rifle shots grew louder and louder. An attack was being made on Dublin Castle—policemen had been shot down—such was the talk that passed from lip to lip.' Yet, 'despite the fusillade and the occasional patter of bullets upon the walls, people passed up and down Cork Hill with assumed indifference.'[14]

One bemused observer was sixteen-year-old Wilmot Irwin, who had accompanied his father on the tram from Glasnevin to Nelson's Pillar in Sackville Street. They walked as far as Grafton Street, window-shopping.

> I noticed ... the fine young Metropolitan Policeman on point duty at the junction of South King Street and Stephen's Green. Though I did not know it then it was Constable Michael Lahiff, 125B, aged 28 years. When I saw him he had less than twenty minutes to live. Everything seemed normal as we turned to go home. Just as we neared the end of Grafton Street a column of Citizen Army volunteers with shouldered rifles swung along towards the Green. We paid little attention to them as parades of armed and semi-uniformed men of unofficial armies were all too common.

As they returned to the Pillar they saw a convoy of lorries pass up the north side of the quays towards the Royal Barracks but still did not suspect that 'anything was amiss' until they reached the GPO and had to step out onto the road to avoid a 'shower of broken glass.' Irwin 'glimpsed a white-faced, tensed volunteer in the slouch hat of the Citizen Army smash away the panes ... as if his life depended on it, with the butt end of his rifle.' Despite the commotion, the trams were still running, and the two men made it safely home. 'My father hardly opened his mouth during the short journey to Lindsay Road,' Irwin wrote. 'I think even then he knew it was the end of an era.'[15]

In contrast, the *Irish Times* reported that as late as midnight, in spite of intensifying rifle fire,

> a number of persons of both sexes, some of them very young, were parading the principal streets ... singing and shouting, apparently much excited by the events happening around them.

No less than twelve British soldiers were reported to have died in the city's hospitals that night, compared with one 'Sinn Fein Volunteer' and four civilians, one of them a fourteen-year-old girl from Fumbally Lane, Ella Warbrooke.[16] Among the first military casualties were Private James Nolan, just arrived home on leave from service with the Royal Irish Rangers in France, and Frank Browning, sub-commandant of the Dublin Veterans' Corps.

Browning, who had initiated the 'Pals Battalion' of the Royal Dublin Fusiliers, had gone on to establish the Dublin Veterans' Corps for former soldiers and civilians too old for active service in France. Members wore an armband with the letters *GR*, for *Georgius Rex* (King George), and were promptly dubbed by wits the Gorgeous Wrecks. The unit was training in Kingstown when news of the disturbances reached it. It split in two, the main section returning to its base at Beggars' Bush Barracks in Haddington Road and Browning advancing—possibly against orders—directly towards the city centre to assist the authorities.

His men were in uniform and fully equipped but had no ammunition in their rifles when they marched down Northumberland Road into the Mount Street Bridge outpost of Éamon de Valera's 3rd Battalion. The result was a small massacre. Five members of the Dublin Veterans' Corps were killed and seven wounded. The Volunteers eventually held their fire to allow a doctor in a motor car to carry the wounded to nearby houses for treatment. Browning was among those fatally wounded.[17]

The commander of the ambush party was Lieutenant Michael Malone, whose brother William had been killed while serving as a sergeant with the 2nd Battalion of the Royal Dublin Fusiliers in the battle for Mouse Trap Farm the previous year. Malone was the best marksman in the battalion, a committed separatist and a member of the IRB.

While the attack on the Dublin Veterans' Corps has been portrayed as an unfortunate mistake, the identity of the unit was well known to Malone and his men. 'We took a special interest in the "GRs" in Dublin,' Volunteer Richard Balfe recalled later. In 1915 a detachment of Irish Volunteers had managed to obtain Veterans' Corps cap badges and insignia and presented themselves at Beggars' Bush Barracks to be armed in preparation for a display before the new Lord Lieutenant, Lord Wimborne, at Trinity College. After winning accolades for their smart drill routine they disappeared with their newly acquired weapons.[18] As far as Malone was concerned, the 'Gorgeous Wrecks' marching into view that morning were a legitimate target, though he may not have realised they had no ammunition.

Anticipating that more British soldiers would be channelled along this stretch of quiet suburban road leading into the city centre, Malone, ever the good soldier, deployed his men at posts in Northumberland Road and Lower Mount Street to create an intensive field of fire commanding the canal crossing. He himself took the most exposed position, number 25 Northumberland Road, along with James Grace, another IRB man, who had deserted from the Canadian forces to take part in the rising.

The key to the crossing was Clanwilliam House, which overlooked Mount Street Bridge from the town side of the canal. It was a large three-storey residence occupied by a widow, Mrs Wilson, and her daughter. On taking it over, Section Leader George Reynolds told his men: 'We're representatives of the Irish Republic, so I don't want you to behave like hooligans.' He set an example by raising the lower sash windows to facilitate rifle fire, rather than smashing them.

However, no amount of good manners could erase the violent nature of the venture they were engaged upon. A brutal demonstration was provided for civilians at Boland's Bakery a short distance away in Grand Canal Street. An off-duty Irish soldier returning unarmed to Beggars' Bush Barracks was shot when he responded to a call to 'clear off' by telling the Volunteers they were 'nothing but bloody traitors.' A big mill worker was cheered by local people when he carried the wounded man to Sir Patrick Dun's Hospital across the street.[19]

––––

The only leading insurrectionist who appears to have devoted much attention to the problem of creating a civil administration for the city was James Connolly. He had discussed the matter with two close friends and comrades, William O'Brien and Francis Sheehy Skeffington. O'Brien was a leading trade unionist in the city and former president of the Dublin Trades Council; Sheehy Skeffington was an ardent campaigner against all forms of social injustice. O'Brien's club foot prevented him from playing an active role in the rising, while Sheehy Skeffington was debarred by his pacifism.

It was agreed that the other members of any civilian administration would be Arthur Griffith, Alderman Tom Kelly and Councillor Seán T. O'Kelly—all members of Sinn Féin—and Sheehy Skeffington's wife, Hanna, who was a leading suffragist and social campaigner.[20] Politically it was a well-balanced coalition from the rebels' point of view, though it is not clear if the proposed Sinn Féin members were aware of the role marked out for them. In the event, only Francis Sheehy Skeffington attempted to act on his brief, with tragic consequences.

The sheer scale of the problem emerged almost as soon as the rebels seized the centre of the city and it dawned on slum-dwellers in streets close by that law and order no longer existed. Noblett's, a confectioner's shop on the corner of Sackville Street and North Earl Street, was the first to have its glass window smashed in. Before long other shops followed, including that of the jewellers Hopkins and Hopkins, Lawrence's toy shop and the cornucopia of Clery's department store. Seán O'Casey, former secretary of the Citizen Army but now a determined non-combatant because of his political differences with Connolly and other former comrades, recorded the mayhem.

The tinkle of broken glass wandered down the whole street, and people were pushing and pulling each other, till through broken windows all the treasures of India, Arabia and Samarkand were open before them ... They pulled boxes down on top of themselves, flung clothing all over the place; tried to pull new garments over their old ones; while one woman, stripped naked, was trying on camisole after camisole, ending with calm touches that smoothed out the light-blue one that satisfied her at last. All who were underdressed before, were overdressed now, and for the first time in their frosty lives the heat of good warm things encircled them.[21]

A member of Fianna Éireann, Éamonn Bulfin, watched Lawrence's from the roof of the GPO as 'all the kids brought out a lot of fireworks ... and set fire to them.' He recalled the Volunteers' own bombs on the roof of the GPO as rockets 'were shooting up in the sky. We were very nervous. There were Catherine wheels going up Sackville Street.'[22]

As overall rebel commander of the city, Connolly tried to restore order. When the looters ignored pleas from such public figures as Sheehy Skeffington and Seán T. O'Kelly to desist from 'dishonouring Ireland' by their behaviour, Connolly ordered out sections of riflemen to fire over their heads. The effect was only momentary. Even when looters were shot by Volunteers or fell victim to the increasingly deadly crossfire between the insurgents and military, the spree continued. Only when British artillery began demolishing the very buildings being robbed did the looters finally desist.

Grafton Street was spared a similar fate through a combination of volleys from the Dublin University Officers' Training Corps in Trinity College, who scattered the first forays of the looters, and the efforts of the Lord Mayor, James Gallagher, in mobilising enough respectable citizens, including shop owners and managers, to block access to the most fashionable shops in the city. Moral force succeeded where Volunteers and British army snipers failed. Quite possibly the mere semblance of order allowed this commercial oasis to exist amidst the chaos. The Lord Mayor was subsequently knighted for his efforts.

The greatest damage was not to a shop but to the warehouse of the British and Irish Steam Packet Company on the North Wall, from which looters made off with an estimated £5,000 worth of merchandise.

More than four hundred people would later be fined or imprisoned for looting during the rising, but many more escaped unscathed with their booty.[23]

Table 5
Prosecutions for offences connected with the rising

	Persons made amenable	Persons discharged	Persons imprisoned	Persons fined	Persons committed to borstal
Unlawful possession	425	27	121	277	0
Breaking into shops etc.	6	3	2	0	1

Nor was it only looters who caused problems for the rebels. James Stephens, writer, poet and registrar of the National Gallery of Ireland, was on his way home on Monday when he encountered a rebel with a revolver—'no more than a boy'—who told him, 'We have taken the city. We are expecting an attack from the military at any moment, and those people'—he indicated knots of idle onlookers clustered towards the end of the Green—'won't go home for me.'

Worse was to come later that day when Stephens saw a man shot for pulling a cart from a rebel barricade. The man, Michael Cavanagh, was a guest at the Shelbourne Hotel in St Stephen's Green and was the owner of the commandeered vehicle. He had been told he could retrieve some of his effects but took this to mean he could retrieve the cart as well. He was told to put it back or he was 'a dead man.' Instead he raised his hand 'as though he was going to make a speech … A rifle spat at him, and in two undulating movements the man sank on himself and sagged to the ground.' Some civilians carried him to the kerb, and onlookers jeered the Citizen Army men or knelt down to pray for the soul of the victim.[24]

In other places it was the civilians who sought to make order out of mayhem. At Boland's Bakery a group of determined bakers refused to leave until they had finished work. Despite being prodded with bayonets and threats of being shot, they convinced the commandant, Éamon de Valera, to allow at least some of them to remain, or else people in the area would face starvation during the fighting. As a result, food distribution was added to the Volunteers' duties at the bakery.[25]

Food supplies rapidly became the concern of all, for, as James Stephens recounted, rumour 'had to serve many Dublin people in place of bread.' Among them was Wilmot Irwin, who found by Tuesday that he had grown used to the gunfire but not to the hunger, as he sat down to 'a somewhat meagre dinner.' Local shopkeepers put up their shutters for fear the looting in the city centre would spread to the northern suburbs. However, some normality returned on Wednesday, when the British had little difficulty clearing the rebel outposts in Cabra and Phibsborough.[26]

—————

Soldiers on the south side of the city were less fortunate. Thanks to Malone's skilful deployment of his men, the bloodiest encounters of the week took place around Mount Street Bridge. On Wednesday morning thousands of soldiers from the 59th Division, a reserve force encamped astride the railway lines around London to repel any German landings in England, found themselves bound for Kingstown. Fears that rebels had seized the township were unfounded. Far from meeting any hostility, the soldiers were feted as they marched through the most loyal district in Ireland apart from Belfast. The columns were plied with tea, sandwiches and fresh fruit as they marched through south Co. Dublin.

Among those who came out to greet them were the Rev. William Roberts and his daughter Monica in Stillorgan. The Band of Helpers to the Soldiers suddenly found work to do much closer to home. There was a special welcome for Captain Frederick Dietrichsen of the Sherwood Foresters when his column reached Blackrock, for his wife, who had returned to her parents' home for the duration of the war, came out to greet him with their children.

But the reception for the 2,000-strong column would be very different when it marched into the Volunteer positions at Northumberland Road and Mount Street Bridge. Michael Malone's under-strength platoon made up in determination to deny the enemy the bridge for what it lacked in numbers and equipment. They waited until the first units had passed well into the killing zone before opening fire. Among the first to fall was Captain Dietrichsen.[27]

It took more than thirty hours of fierce fighting by the attacking column, made up largely of inexperienced recruits, to capture the rebel positions. The unit's officers had strict instructions to capture or destroy any rebel stronghold before continuing the advance. Denied any variation in their route, they formed what one Volunteer described as 'a giant human khaki-coloured caterpillar,' impossible to miss as the soldiers pushed forward.[28]

Clanwilliam House was the last building taken. By 7:30 p.m. on Thursday the Wilson residence had 'become a perfect inferno.' The sash windows that George Reynolds had insisted that his men open rather than smash had been carried away by rifle and machine-gun fire.

> The curtains and hangings were torn to ribbons; pictures from the walls, glass mirrors, chandeliers, lay on the floor shattered into pieces, the plaster had fallen from the ceiling and almost every square foot of walls inside was studded with bullets.

The rooms were filled with smoke, and sheets of flame lit the evening sky.[29]

Yet most of the Volunteers managed to escape, leaving behind five dead, including Malone and Reynolds. British casualties amounted to 234 either killed or wounded. The Sherwood Foresters' horrific casualties rendered them of limited value in the fighting ahead, and their commander, Colonel Ernest Maconchy, paid the defenders a back-handed compliment by explaining the losses as the work of 'paid mercenaries.' Another officer, Captain Arthur Lee, considered the impact all the more distressing because the battalion was community-based in Nottinghamshire and the officers and men 'all knew each other and each other's parents and relations, and to see their lifelong pals shot down beside them by their own countrymen was a shock.'

Nevertheless the regiment showed restraint in handling its prisoners. There was only one instance of military discipline breaking down. This occurred when Joe Clarke, from the contingent based in the parochial hall in Northumberland

Road, was captured with a concealed revolver. He was put against the back door of the hall, and an officer pointed his revolver at his head. He fired, but at the last moment Clarke ducked and the bullet pierced the door, narrowly missing an army doctor and the wounded soldiers he was treating in the garden outside. The doctor roundly abused his fellow-officer and ordered Clarke and the other men to be taken into custody.[30]

In another instance Volunteer Jimmy Doyle, one of the Clanwilliam House garrison, was taken prisoner by angry residents in Mount Street as he tried to flee; but before he could be handed over to the military a rival group of local people intervened and secured his release.

But the most remarkable incident of all had occurred in the middle of the fighting when a teenage girl, Louisa Nolan, ran onto Mount Street Bridge and held up her hands and called for the shooting to stop. The firing from Clanwilliam House ceased immediately, and the British followed suit. A group of doctors and nurses from Sir Patrick Dun's Hospital then came forward with a Red Cross flag to tend the wounded and remove them to safety.[31] The spontaneous ceasefire ended when a group of British soldiers tried to use the evacuation as cover to rush the bridge.[32]

De Valera has been criticised for not providing more support to Malone's unit, but the same could be said of the passivity of other commandants, such as Thomas MacDonagh, who had seized Jacob's biscuit factory in Bishop Street and remained in situ. For all their lectures and route marches, the Volunteer leadership lacked the expertise to deploy men effectively at more than section or platoon level. Besides, the confusion caused by MacNeill's countermanding order meant there were not enough Volunteers to conduct an active or coherent defence. De Valera, like MacDonagh, was reluctant to reinforce outposts such as Mount Street bridge because he was convinced that the British would ultimately launch a major assault on his main position and he would need to conserve his manpower.

On the positive side, however inadvertently, the rebel leaders' lack of aggression helped keep the number of casualties down, reducing the intensity and length of the battle for the city.

————

One of the ironies of the rising was that many of the soldiers involved in suppressing it were Irish.

If a full mobilisation of the Volunteers had taken place on Easter Sunday, as planned, the city would have been theirs for the taking. There were only four hundred British troops in 'immediate readiness' for action in the city: approximately one hundred at each of the four main barracks and a guard of six men at Dublin Castle. On Easter Monday many officers were at the races in Fairyhouse, and the general officer commanding the forces in Ireland, Major-General Friend, was spending the bank holiday weekend in London. His deputy, Colonel H. V. Cowan, had a total of 2,385 men available to him, including those at the races or on a day's leave elsewhere in the city.

Apart from the 6th Cavalry Reserve Regiment at Marlborough Barracks, every unit in the city was part of an Irish regiment. The 3rd (Special Reserve) Battalion of the Royal Irish Regiment was at Richmond Barracks, the 10th Battalion of the Royal Dublin Fusiliers was in the Royal Barracks, and the 3rd Battalion of the Royal Irish Rifles was in Portobello Barracks.[33] The first troops in action were the 5th (Royal Irish) Lancers, despatched from Marlborough Barracks to the GPO only to be scattered by rebel fire in Sackville Street, leaving behind a dead horse.

But substantial reinforcements were on their way. The military authorities suspended all civilian traffic on the GSWR line. Between 1:17 and 5:30 p.m. special trains rushed three thousand men from the Curragh to Dublin, all of them from Irish regiments.[34] The first Irish troops deployed were the men of the 3rd Battalion of the Royal Irish Regiment. Two hundred of them were quickly assembled at Richmond Barracks and easily drove in the rebel outposts at Mount Brown and the western perimeter of the South Dublin Union (now St James's Hospital) before meeting strong resistance in close-quarter fighting within the main workhouse complex.[35] The Royal Irish Regiment was joined by members of the Royal Dublin Fusiliers who had made their way across the River Liffey from the Royal Barracks to help secure Dublin Castle and contain Ceannt's men in the workhouse area.

The South Dublin Union covered 52 acres and had more than 3,200 inmates in its complex of dormitories, workshops, hospitals, churches and sheds as well as residences for the staff and open grounds. The occupants included the unemployed, the sick, the mentally ill and the elderly. In early twentieth-century Dublin nine-tenths of working-class people could expect to end their days destitute, in the South Dublin Union or its counterpart, the North Dublin Union, on the other side of the Liffey. The South Dublin Union was the larger of the two, and Commandant Éamonn Ceannt had only 120 out of the 700 men of the 4th Battalion available to defend it. Despite rapidly mounting odds, he managed to hold out to the bitter end. The main stronghold was the Night Nurses' Home, a large three-storey stone building that dominated James's Street and gave a field of fire as far as Rialto Bridge on the Grand Canal. Its military potential was pointed out by Lieutenant William Cosgrave, leader of the Sinn Féin group on Dublin Corporation. His grocery and wine shop was close by, and he knew the area intimately. His immediate superior was Cathal Brugha, who would make a legendary stand that prevented the home being captured by a British infantry attack on Thursday. Unlike Michael Malone at Mount Street, Brugha survived, though badly wounded, to become a national hero.

The fighting was mainly confined to the built-up areas, on what are now the hospital grounds. As one account put it, combat in the complex was like 'a walk through a shooting gallery,' where the wiliest combatants took off their boots and dug into blind corners to catch the unsuspecting passer-by. There were relatively few civilian casualties, and these seem to have been caused in the main by British troops, who suffered from the handicap of having to attack in an unfamiliar environment. One of the worst incidents was when a soldier threw a hand grenade into a room containing what he thought was a group of rebels but turned out to be inmates. One man was killed and most of the others severely injured. A nurse, Margaretta Keogh, was shot when two soldiers opened up at the sight of her white uniform in a hospital corridor.

The sympathy of local people seems to have swung behind the rebels. When Ceannt's garrison finally surrendered, one of the Volunteers, Peadar Doyle, recalled that 'all along the route ... we were greeted with great jubilation, particularly in the poorer districts.'[36]

Just north of the South Dublin Union a similar conflict took place, on a smaller scale, around the Mendicity Institute at Usher's Island. The Mendicity had been a forerunner of the workhouse and still dealt with the poorest of the poor. It was soon cleared of inmates by its small garrison, commanded by a nineteen-year-old former Fianna boy, Seán Heuston, promoted to commandant on Monday morning by James Connolly because there was no-one more experienced to hand. Many members of Heuston's tiny garrison of less than twenty men were as young as their commander. No-one expected them to impede the approach of the 10th Battalion of the Royal Dublin Fusiliers from the Royal Barracks for long; but they held out for two days, inflicting many casualties.

A final assault with grenades on Wednesday overwhelmed them. Heuston's second in command, Richard Balfe, another former Fianna member, was one of those hit by the grenades and lost the use of his arms and legs. Forced to surrender, Heuston's youthful garrison were roughed up by Royal Dublin Fusiliers, angered at their own losses. Balfe was too badly injured to move, and the Fusiliers threatened to bayonet or shoot him where he lay until a medical officer arrived on the scene. Balfe recalled that the officer 'claimed me as his prisoner, saying that there had been enough ... dirty work.' Balfe was removed to King George v Military Hospital (later St Bricin's Hospital) in Infirmary Road.[37]

The officer's remarks may have referred to ugly incidents in the city just across the river. The defence of the Mendicity Institute had made it hard for the military to mount any sort of determined attack on the Four Courts, and they were sustaining heavy casualties. In a rare occurrence, the North Dublin Union at Grangegorman and the adjoining Richmond Hospital were treated as neutral territory by the Volunteers and the military, thanks largely to the courageous stand of Dr Joe O'Carroll in defence of his patients. Instead of a battleground like the South Dublin Union, Grangegorman became a place of refuge for civilians in the surrounding area.[38] Unlike de Valera, the commandant of the 1st Battalion, Ned Daly, encouraged the local bakery to continue operating throughout the rising, providing bread for local people and Volunteers alike.[39] In many respects Daly and

Ceannt proved the most effective of the Volunteer commanders, making up in energy, common sense, humanity and above all determination for their lack of experience. There were ugly scenes, however, in the warren of streets behind the Four Courts when the military requirements of the insurgents involved the seizure of private property. A seventy-year-old man was shot through the eye in one altercation with the Volunteers.[40]

Liam Archer's experience was typical. After his all-night card game with Michael Collins in North Frederick Street he was told to mobilise his section at the Colmcille Hall in Blackhall Place, a regular meeting place for Volunteers, by 10 a.m. on Easter Monday. The depleted ranks created by the confusion surrounding MacNeill's countermanding order resulted in Archer being promoted to lieutenant by Daly's vice-commandant, Piaras Béaslaí, and he was taken with twenty men to the Bow Street and Mary's Lane area behind the Four Courts. They encountered some hostility there, and Béaslaí ordered Archer to fix his bayonet.

This I did and immediately a very fat dame in spotless white apron and voluminous shawl leapt in front of us and beating her ample bosom with clenched fists called on me to 'put it through me now for me son who's out in France.'

Archer declined the challenge, and Béaslaí beat a hasty retreat. Left in charge, Archer proceeded to tour the area, deploying his men and taking a plain-clothes policeman prisoner in the process. A barricade was built outside the Franciscan Church in Church Street, and there was a confrontation with the friars when Volunteers attempted to use church seats to reinforce their position. The friars appear to have won this particular skirmish. Despite it, or perhaps because of it, two priests visited the men and gave absolution to any Volunteer who requested it.

Archer tried to make life bearable for civilians by allowing people returning home from bank holiday outings through the barricades, but he discouraged sightseers and confiscated the goods of looters returning from Sackville Street and Henry Street. 'The people in the area were generally hostile for the first couple of days but later their attitude changed completely,' he said. One reason was that he made sure the fresh bread from Monks's bakery was widely distributed and not just eaten by his own men, whose home-made sandwiches barely lasted the first day. A supply of fresh tea also helped maintain the unit's morale and to avert competition with residents for scarce supplies.

In retrospect, Archer would be critical of Volunteer Headquarters for not giving enough attention to logistics, both in supplying its own forces and in looking after the civilian population. The one act of requisition Archer permitted was the seizure of blankets and a consignment of stewed figs from abandoned residential quarters in the Jameson distillery.

Archer was also critical of his own men. Their discipline was poor, and many of them left their position to look for food or to call on pals who lived nearby. Only afterwards did he realise that he should have organised sentry rosters and tours of duty.[41]

Meanwhile the decision of Daly and the British to respect the neutrality of the Richmond Hospital[42] had the bonus of ensuring medical attention for all casualties. Members of Cumann na mBan attached to Archer's unit helped provide emergency first aid and 'were outstanding in their courage and devotion.'[43] The Franciscans in Church Street also opened their doors to the wounded.

The number of casualties mounted rapidly, with Volunteers repulsing attacks from the Royal Barracks to the west and Marlborough Barracks to the north. They even took some prisoners. Among the officers captured were Lord Dunsany, the poet, and a Captain Brereton, who paid his captors the supreme compliment: 'They fought like gentlemen.'

On Friday, fighting in the North King Street area reached an even greater pitch of intensity than in the South Dublin Union. The barricades and narrow streets made progress by British troops slow, even with the support of armoured cars. Some of these had been improvised by mounting disused boilers from the Guinness brewery on a Leyland or Straker-Squire chassis, with slits for riflemen.[44] The Sherwood Foresters, who had suffered so badly earlier in the week, were once more in action, along with the North Staffordshire and South Staffordshire Regiments. All three regiments sustained heavy casualties.

Daly had deployed his men well, so that the small groups at barricades received supporting fire from other positions. Both sides burrowed through the walls of houses to outflank enemy positions, often exchanging fire at point-blank range. Inevitably there were civilian casualties among the terrified residents trapped in the crossfire. At least fifteen civilians appear to have been killed in the North King Street area, and the British military authorities later had to investigate allegations that they had been murdered by soldiers. The truth was never established, but General Sir John Maxwell, who ordered the inquiry, confided to his wife that some civilians may have been killed in cold blood. He told Kitchener:

It must be borne in mind in these cases that there was a lot of house-to-house fighting going on, wild rumours in circulation and owing to darkness, conflagrations etc., apparently a good deal of 'jumpiness.' With young soldiers and under the circumstances I wonder there was not more.[45]

——

The area around the GPO was the only place where the British were able to use their artillery with effect, gradually demolishing buildings around the rebel headquarters and forcing the garrison into the evacuation that heralded military defeat. Some of the initial artillery batteries operated from Trinity College, which had the distinction of being the main indigenous centre of resistance to the rebels.

When the rising began there were only eight collegians on duty, members of the Dublin University Officers' Training Corps. Despite its central position, the rebels made no attempt to seize the university complex, but students responded with alacrity to the summons to arms. Between members of the Officers' Training Corps, off-duty soldiers and some members of the Dublin Veterans' Corps, the garrison had increased to 44 by Monday evening and to 150 by Wednesday. The defenders concentrated initially on the eastern end of the perimeter closest to Westland Row and the railway station. The main entrance to the college in College Green was fortified, and windows suitable for firing positions were sandbagged and used for sniping.

By Tuesday regular military formations were infiltrating Trinity, cutting off the rebel headquarters in the GPO from units in the south city. By the end of the rising the college grounds accommodated a brigade of infantry, a battery of artillery and a regiment of cavalry. One college defender observed: 'The spacious quadrangles and lawns afforded excellent accommodation for the troops and it was surely a sign that Trinity had given itself wholly over to the military when one found soldiers playing football on the tennis courts.'

It was indeed an oasis of support for the British war effort. More than half the students had joined the Officers' Training Corps, and a total of 869 undergraduates gave up their studies to join the British army. As a consequence the college lost £50,000 in fees. The Officers' Training Corps was overwhelmingly Protestant and upper middle class, and the handful of Catholic members tended to come from such schools as Blackrock College and Clongowes Wood. Other staff members, including academics, white-collar and manual workers, served in the armed forces, although the latter would have been enlisted men. The strong response reflected the ethos of an institution that saw itself as an integral part of the old Protestant Ascendancy under siege. It was the only place in Ireland where recruitment levels matched those of its British counterparts. Unlike other universities, however, its members saw active service on the home front.

The 120 members of the Officers' Training Corps who defended the college in Easter Week were given silver cups and 15s each by the 'grateful citizens and traders of Dublin City.' Their officers were presented with ceremonial swords, and their commanding officer, Captain E. H. Alton, was awarded the Military Cross.[46]

———

The unarmed Dublin Metropolitan Police disappeared from the streets once the fighting began, but two were shot dead by rebels at the start of the rising and a third in Store Street station through a window. Seven were wounded, of whom two were taken prisoner. However, in Co. Meath the paramilitary Royal Irish

Constabulary was mobilised in force to deal with the most successful rebel unit of the week, Thomas Ashe's Fingal flying column.

Undismayed by the low turn-out at Knocksedan Bridge on Easter Monday, Ashe immediately set about his main task, the disruption of communications between the capital and the north-east. He took Donabate police barracks after a brief fight and Garristown without one, as the RIC there had no rifles. By Friday his small force had gained some new recruits, the most important of whom was Richard Mulcahy, who joined Ashe after sabotaging telegraph communications between Dublin and Belfast. The column attacked Ashbourne barracks as a prelude to cutting the railway line between Dublin and Mullingar. In the process Ashe went on to win the only rebel victory of 1916, when a large RIC force on its way to relieve the Ashbourne garrison was forced to surrender.

A local man, John Austin, watched the fighting from Limekiln Hill with friends, and afterwards they helped remove dead bodies from the road in a cart. Two policemen taken prisoner by the Volunteers helped. Austin recalled: 'Tom Ashe and his men were at the crossroads. They were very excited after their victory and were cheering, as men would after a football match.'

The police had twenty-seven casualties all told, including a Sergeant Shanagher, who had served in Ashbourne for a number of years and was considered 'a right bad one' by local people. He had been guiding the relief force and 'was shot right between the eyes as he left the car' leading the convoy.[47]

After disarming the policemen, Ashe paroled them before marching away. John Austin said later:

> When things had quietened down, the surviving police came down to the village and bought themselves some drink and food. They had money as the rebels had not interfered with any of their personal belongings. They were very shaken and shivering. One of them remarked to me that the rebels were great men and I replied, 'If you had won, I know what you would do.'

Irishmen who had fought for the Crown were already sensing a different attitude to their own role and that of the rebels. Lieutenant Tom Kettle's finely tuned antennae had picked up the signals. Having done his duty in Dublin and insisting on being sent to the front, he told a young family friend on the eve of departure: 'These men will go down to history as heroes and martyrs, and I will go down— if I go down at all—as a bloody British officer.'[48]

———

Irish units in the British army suffered 29 fatalities and 93 wounded, out of a military total of 103 fatalities and 397 wounded during the rising. These figures are quite low, given that the units involved were engaged longest in the fighting. This is probably due in part to their greater familiarity with the city. The unfortunate Sherwood Foresters contributed more than half the total British losses after blundering into the ambush at Mount Street Bridge. While they marched blindly into rebel fire, local clergymen and hospital staff managed to slip around the rebel positions largely unnoticed by combatants to ferry the wounded to Sir Patrick Dun's Hospital in Grand Canal Street. James Grace's sister and another Cumann na mBan member even managed to bring food through the lines for him and Malone, pushing the sandwiches through the letter-box at Northumberland Road.[49]

The total number of Dubliners who died while serving with the British army was nine, including three who were with non-Irish units: a gunner with the Royal Field Artillery, a Hussar and a member of the Royal Army Medical Corps. The most senior fatality was Colonel Henry Allat of the Royal Irish Rifles, who came out of retirement in the city to work as a draft conducting officer. He was killed in action at the South Dublin Union, as was Lieutenant Alan Rafferty of the Royal Irish Rifles. Lieutenant Gerald Neilan of the Royal Dublin Fusiliers was shot during the attack on the Mendicity Institute.

The other dead were members of the Leinster Regiment and the Royal Irish Fusiliers. The Royal Irish Fusiliers' fatalities included Sergeant-Major Patrick Brosnan, who was actually shot by his own side, as were two officers with King Edward's Horse.[50] Six Dublin members of the Royal Irish Rifles were wounded, three members of the Royal Irish Regiment and eighteen members of the Royal Dublin Fusiliers.[51]

––––

But of course the great majority of casualties were civilians, although the exact numbers are unclear, as they were not disaggregated from rebel dead and wounded. It is thought that rebels accounted at most for a third of the 180 fatalities and 614 wounded who were not members of the Crown forces. While the Volunteers and Citizen Army certainly shot some civilians, most notably looters or people actively obstructing them, it would appear that the majority were the victims of military action.

There were two reasons for this. One was the difficulty soldiers had in distinguishing civilians from rebels, as some Volunteers had little or no uniform. Lieutenant A. M. Jameson of the Leinster Regiment captured the mood in a letter home.

My corporal saw a civilian walking where a lot of Sinn Feiners were so he said he didn't know whether he was a Sinn Feiner or not, but anyhow he oughtn't to be there so he'd 'just shoot him in the foot.' So he up with his rifle and fired, and the man hopped down the street on one leg![52]

Several civilians seem to have been killed for failing to stop at military checkpoints, including a young boy on a bicycle and an old woman who was deaf.[53]

The other cause of serious civilian casualties was the decision to use artillery to clear rebels out of the city centre. Altogether 99,420 square yards of buildings were demolished as a result of bombardment and fire, primarily in the Sackville Street area, where 68,900 square yards were destroyed. Other badly affected areas included Mount Street, St Stephen's Green and Bridge Street, which all witnessed heavy fighting, as well as the Linenhall Barracks in Lisburn Street, which was set alight by Volunteers to prevent its occupation by the enemy. Unfortunately the fire quickly spread to surrounding buildings, including a wholesale pharmacy, causing the worst conflagration in the city apart from that in Sackville Street. One witness said the district was

> like a roaring furnace ... Barrels of oil were projected high in the air and exploded with a loud report ... On Thursday night it was as bright as day. A pin could be picked up by the glare.[54]

Similar scenes in Sackville Street included the destruction of the Dublin Bread Company's premises. A journalist told readers:

> The flames kissing the ball on the dome's summit are singularly impressive. Standing high above the lower plane of flame and smoke, it is thrown into relief by a background of clouds. A scene of greater splendour I have never before witnessed, not even in the realms of cinematography.[55]

While the use of artillery brought maximum force to bear on the rebel positions, especially the headquarters in the GPO, and was an important factor in hastening the decision by the leaders to end the fighting to avoid further civilian casualties, it was also an admission by the British government that it was dealing with a serious insurrection, and left it open to the charge that it was inflicting casualties on civilians to save the lives of its soldiers. It was no wonder that pictures of bombed-out Dublin streets quickly appeared in German propaganda posters, newsreels and postcards.

Dealing out death and destruction was relatively easy for the opposing forces, but coping with the casualties was more difficult and at least as dangerous. The main task of rendering first aid to soldiers, rebels and civilians alike, as well as ferrying them to hospital, fell on the St John Ambulance Brigade. It also provided drivers for the Irish Automobile Club ambulance service. Meanwhile the Dublin Fire

Brigade struggled to keep the fires under control. Both groups worked under the auspices of the Red Cross, and many St John Ambulance personnel were under the direction of the Royal Army Medical Corps, making them legitimate targets in the eyes of some Volunteers. Among the first casualties was Holden Stoddart, superintendent of the the the St John Ambulance Brigade, who was killed while assisting stretcher-bearers with a wounded soldier near the Royal City of Dublin Hospital in Baggot Street.

Fortuitously, the Dublin Fire Brigade had received a brand-new ambulance, sponsored by the cinematograph trade, in November 1915, while fire tenders dealt with ninety-three fires during the week. Some idea of the intensity of the activity is given by the fact that the owners of 196 buildings destroyed during Easter Week claimed damages of £2½ million, compared with £41,200 claimed for all other fires in the city that year and £250,000 for malicious damage during the 1913 Lock-out.[56]

The large-scale mobilisation of women for the war effort, through the Voluntary Aid Detachments and the Red Cross Society, now began to pay unexpected dividends. The War Hospital Supply Depot in Merrion Square was converted into a hospital under the direction of Dr Ella Webb, district superintendent of the St John Ambulance Brigade, within three hours of hostilities breaking out. The first amputation took place in the improvised operating theatre at 5 p.m. Several auxiliary hospitals were equipped by other divisions. Two of them, Litton Hall in Leeson Park and the High School in Harcourt Street, became fully operational.

It was the last great flowering of Dublin's voluntary Protestant middle class in action. No less than five silver medals were awarded to St John Ambulance personnel. They included three women, one of whom was Dr Webb. Twenty bronze medals were also awarded.

The only military award to a civilian went to Louisa Nolan for her heroic action in calling a ceasefire on Mount Street Bridge. She was the daughter of a retired RIC head constable, had two sisters working as nurses in England, a brother in the Royal Navy and two other brothers in the army. King George V presented her with the Military Medal at Buckingham Palace on 2 February 1917.[57]

Women also played a leading role in Red Cross mobilisation. Its offices at 29 Fitzwilliam Street were converted into a first-aid post, staffed by VAD personnel. Several Red Cross members nearby opened their homes to treat the wounded, and VADs provided the personnel to operate these *ad hoc* hospitals, which provided a hundred temporary beds. They braved gunfire in the area to carry wounded soldiers and civilians to the main hospitals. The great majority of stretcher-bearers were women. Ironically, the main obstacle to the full mobilisation of Red Cross, St John Ambulance and VAD personnel was the restrictions on movement throughout the city by the military.[58]

Several women played similar roles on the rebels' side. Cumann na mBan detachments served with units throughout the city, except Boland's Bakery, where de Valera refused them admission. They included a medical student, Brigid Lyons, and Nurse Elizabeth O'Farrell in the GPO, while Madeleine ffrench-Mullen served as a first-aid officer with the Citizen Army garrison in St Stephen's Green. Dr Kathleen Lynn, the Citizen Army's medical officer, served as senior officer at City Hall after her superior, Seán Connolly, was killed. Dr Lynn was by far the best-known woman activist involved in the rising after Constance Markievicz. It is unlikely, however, that she played a direct military role in the rising: her medical duties appear to have taken precedence.

The role of women in the rising was largely ignored until relatively recently. The official attitude was most graphically illustrated by Elizabeth O'Farrell's role in providing Patrick Pearse with an extra pair of legs during the surrender ceremony. She had volunteered to open negotiations for the rebels with the military authorities under cover of a Red Cross flag. She was with Pearse in the final negotiations with Brigadier-General William Lowe, but in the photograph her body is obscured by Pearse; only the hem of her nurse's uniform and her feet are visible below his greatcoat. The photograph would come to symbolise the largely invisible role of women in the fight for independence and in the new Irish state.

The main burden of coping with casualties naturally fell on Dublin's hospitals. All those within the combat zone experienced a flood of casualties—even the city's maternity hospitals, such as the National Maternity Hospital in Holles Street, where Nurse O'Farrell normally worked. But by far the busiest institution was Jervis Street Hospital, which treated between 600 and 700 cases, of whom 43 died; a further 38 people were brought in dead. In contrast, hospitals outside the combat zone, such as St Vincent's Hospital in St Stephen's Green, dealt with relatively few casualties.

A problem facing hospitals at the centre of the fighting was a shortage of food. At the Richmond Hospital in North Brunswick Street the recently qualified Dr John Hackett Pollock (better known later as the writer 'An Pilibín') took two students on a horse and cart adorned with a white sheet bearing a sign reading 'Richmond Hospital Supplies' to the south side of the Liffey on several occasions in search of provisions, returning safely each time.[59] Citizens in the north inner city had to do likewise and risk injury or death in pursuit of essential supplies. The high casualties there reflected not only the intensity of the fighting but also the death and injury inflicted on hapless civilians forced to seek the necessities of life amidst the carnage.

Of all the killings that occurred during the fighting the one to cause the greatest public outcry was that of Francis Sheehy Skeffington. He and his wife, Hanna, had cancelled a planned weekend excursion to Howth at Easter after Connolly suggested that they stay in the city. Connolly was probably mindful of the role he hoped the couple would play in the formation of a civilian government if the rising lasted any length of time.

As it happened, Francis Sheehy Skeffington was passing Dublin Castle shortly after the fighting broke out. Characteristically, he went to the aid of a wounded British officer lying in the street outside. 'I could not let anyone bleed to death while I could help,' he told Hanna later.

Hanna was the more nationalist-minded of the two, and she promptly organised food supplies for the GPO garrison. She showed considerable foresight, because the need for secrecy meant that most rank-and-file insurgents had brought nothing with them except the sandwiches they would need for a day's route march. When she arrived at the GPO she found her uncle, Father Eugene Sheehy, with the rebels. He said: 'My God, Hanna, what are you doing here?' She asked him the same question. He explained that he was there to offer spiritual consolation; she told him she had something more substantial to offer.[60]

Several other priests visited rebel strongholds to offer spiritual consolation to civilians and British soldiers, often at considerable risk to themselves. Archbishop Walsh showed his usual independence and political canniness by rejecting a request from Dublin Castle to condemn the rising or to call on the rebels to surrender; instead he urged his flock to remain indoors until the fighting ended.

Not content with her visit to the GPO, Hanna Sheehy Skeffington, caught up in the spirit of the moment, organised another trip, this time to the Citizen Army outpost at the College of Surgeons in St Stephen's Green, where she arrived with helpers laden with food parcels. They all sat down with the garrison to 'a glorious meal' of soup, ham and salmon, hosted by Constance Markievicz. Markievicz would recall later that, despite their many political differences, the Sheehy Skeffingtons 'instinctively took the right side' in any dispute.

It is not clear whether one of their prisoners, the City Treasurer, Laurence Kettle, took part in the repast. It was an ironic fate for the first secretary of the Volunteers, who had adhered to Redmond after the split in September 1914.[61]

Francis Sheehy Skeffington took an even more quixotic line of action than Hanna, trying to implement Connolly's plans for the establishment of some sort of civil authority by organising a civic guard to stop the looting. It says something for the powers of habit that even in these extraordinary circumstances the Sheehy Skeffingtons met on Easter Monday and Tuesday evening at the offices of the Irish Women's Franchise League over Eden Brothers in Westmorland Chambers to compare notes on their daily activities.

While Hanna continued to carry messages for the rebels and give what help she could to the wounded, Francis was busy trying to persuade civic-minded individuals, including some priests, to put on armbands and mount patrols in their districts. Many who agreed appear to have returned to the safety of their homes once he moved on in search of more vigilantes.

After meeting him for tea at five o'clock on Tuesday, Hanna walked home to care for their six-year-old son, Owen, in Rathmines, while Francis waited at Westmorland Chambers to see how many people answered his call for citizens 'to police the streets ... to prevent such spasmodic looting as has taken place.' As a feminist he had insisted on extending the invitation to members of both sexes. It made no difference: no-one turned up, and Francis eventually headed home about an hour after Hanna.[62]

As he crossed Portobello Bridge in Rathmines, some time between 6:30 and 7:30 p.m., he was arrested by a military patrol and taken to Portobello Barracks, where two other journalists, Thomas Dickson and P. J. McIntyre, were already detained, along with some civilians. McIntyre was a rather sad figure. He had produced a rabidly anti-Larkinite news-sheet called the *Toiler* during the 1913 Lock-out and was now editing one called *Searchlight*. William Martin Murphy was suspected of funding the *Toiler*, and McIntyre's latest venture, which supported the war effort from a Redmondite viewpoint, was funded by the British government. Dickson was the editor of another government-funded periodical, the *Eye Opener*, which was a loyalist mirror image of McIntyre's publication.

It was another Irishman, Captain John Bowen-Colthurst, who had arrested Dickson and McIntyre as suspected Sinn Féiners after finding them sheltering in James Kelly's pub near Portobello Bridge on the first day of the rising.[63] Kelly had been an unsuccessful self-proclaimed 'Home Rule Labour' candidate in the 1914 elections, and Bowen-Colthurst appears to have confused him with Alderman Tom Kelly, the well-known Sinn Féin figure.

On arriving at Portobello Barracks, Sheehy Skeffington was placed in a cell on his own, 'as being of a superior social position.'[64] Next day, at 10 a.m., Bowen-Colthurst took the three men out into the yard for interrogation and then had them shot by an improvised firing squad as suspected ringleaders of the rising. There was some movement in Sheehy Skeffington's leg, and a second firing party was convened to shoot him again.

Possibly realising that he may have breached the boundaries of what was permissible under military law, even during an insurrection, Bowen-Colthurst proceeded to have the Sheehy Skeffingtons' home raided for evidence to support his suspicion that the dead man had been engaged in rebel activities. The patrol was led by Colonel Henry Allat of the Royal Irish Rifles, who would soon be killed in the fighting around the South Dublin Union. The soldiers spent three hours ransacking the house in a futile search for incriminating papers. Hanna herself was imprisoned briefly.

Captain Bowen-Colthurst shot at least two other men out of hand during the rising. One was a youth named James Coade who was passing Portobello Barracks on his way home from a sodality meeting; the other was a rebel prisoner, Captain Richard O'Carroll of the Irish Volunteers. O'Carroll was a Dublin city councillor, secretary of the Bricklayers' Union and a member of the Dublin Trades Council. He was shot in the stomach for no apparent reason by Bowen-Colthurst and left unattended for some hours. It took him nine days to die of his injuries.

Bowen-Colthurst was never charged with either of these killings, and it is unlikely that he would have been charged with murdering the three journalists but for the prominence of Sheehy Skeffington, the determination of Hanna to bring the murderer to justice and the courage of another officer at Portobello Barracks, Major Sir Francis Vane.

Unable to obtain satisfaction in Dublin, Vane met Lord Kitchener in London and persuaded him to order a court-martial. Bowen-Colthurst was found guilty of murder but insane. It was to be the most publicised atrocity of the rising; and the fact that it took until June for Bowen-Colthurst to be put on trial was a significant factor in turning Irish opinion in favour of the rebels. Sinn Féin propagandists could contrast the reluctant prosecution and relatively benign outcome with the speedy expedition of the 1916 leaders by firing squad.

Chapter 6 ✌

'THESE SINN FEINERS ARE A LOT OF MURDERERS'

The initial reaction of most Dubliners to the rising was hostile. The abuse heaped by 'separation women' on the Volunteers and Citizen Army members when they surrendered is well recorded. Unfortunately, the rising coincided with the first anniversary of the attack on Saint-Julien in April 1915, where the Royal Dublin Fusiliers suffered heavy casualties.[1] Ironically, these must have included many former ITGWU members, mostly reservists.

Many of the separation women who shouted and spat at the prisoners may have been widows, sisters or mothers of the dead. Other women may simply have been angry at the dangers to which the rebels had exposed their families. In time, the separation women would come to symbolise for advanced nationalists the degradation of the Irish race and would elicit little sympathy from the British state or the loyalist community, happy enough to shed their husbands' blood but embarrassed by their vulgarity.

However, the women's reaction was by no means unusual. On the Sunday afternoon after the rising, as young Wilmot Irwin watched a cavalry column heading out along the Finglas Road to deal with Thomas Ashe and his men, a usually taciturn neighbour who worked as a salesman with a firm in the city shouted, 'They're going to shoot those bastards. They should crucify them!' At the same time a grudging admiration was emerging for the stand taken by the rebels. Irwin, a lifelong unionist who worked as a bookkeeper with an insurance broker at the time and whose brother-in-law was a British officer, admitted that Connolly's bulletin to Volunteers on the Friday of Easter Week urging them to fight on when he lay wounded under artillery bombardment in the GPO 'must have taken courage and endurance of a high order to pen.'

The petty tyrannies of martial law also took their toll on public support. Even loyal citizens needed a written permit to go about their business. Another neighbour of Irwin, a senior manager in the city, was stopped within sight of his premises in Upper Sackville Street by a private of the Royal Irish Regiment on sentry duty.

'Nobody permitted to pass here,' he declared gruffly.

'But I have a pass!' protested the manager, displaying the hastily written sheet signed by an officer giving rank and regiment. The soldier glanced at it.

'I have my orders,' he said gruffly, then seemed to soften. He glanced around as if to make sure nobody was within earshot.

'I'll tell you what I'll do, sir … I'll turn away a little piece and you make a dash for your office. It'll be all right if I fire a shot over your head?'

The manager declined the offer and went home.

As suspected rebels were arrested, sympathy began to swing further in their direction, even in such respectable districts as Glasnevin, with its sizeable Protestant and unionist population.

Many of the prisoners were themselves respectable middle-class citizens. Irwin watched a group of soldiers, accompanied by a member of the DMP, smash in a front door and drag out

an elderly man with a grizzled moustache, the father of a young family. He was hoisted none too gently on to the lorry in full view of curious neighbours. It was then I had my first revulsion of feeling. All along I had been dead against the rebels but the sight of a neighbour under the armed guard of an old Bill type of Connaught Ranger was too much for me.

'It's a damn shame to exhibit him like this!' I exclaimed hotly to a man beside me. He said nothing for a moment. He glowered at the Metropolitan policeman.

'H'm,' he muttered, 'they ran into their holes quick enough when the firing started.'

The inconstancy of public opinion, influenced in this case by a mixture of concern for a neighbour and snobbery at seeing common soldiers and policemen lording it over their betters, would prove malleable to the ideologically driven advocates of national regeneration. As Irwin himself said, the comments by the salesman about crucifying the Ashbourne men 'would have cost him his life' a few years later.[2]

———

There was, of course, one very substantial group of Dubliners deeply concerned about events at home: the men at the front. The reaction of Royal Dublin Fusiliers in the trenches mirrored the anger of their comrades on active service in Dublin. Private Christopher Fox in the Transport Section of the 2nd Battalion, Royal Dublin Fusiliers, described 'the Dublin riots' as 'disgraceful and makes us out here very uneasy.' His family lived near Linenhall Barracks, and he feared for his parents' lives. He concluded that

> these Sinn Feiners are a lot of murderers. The sooner Ireland gets rid of them the better. They have brought a nice disgrace on the Old Country. I can tell you some of the boys out here would like to catch a few of them and we would give them a rough time of it, but it's all the work of the Germans. However it all failed … I must now finish, hoping to hear in your next letter that Dublin is enjoying peace and quietness once more.

Fox was writing on the day James Connolly and Seán Mac Diarmada were executed and before news of the severity of the British military reaction to the rising was fully known. The wave of revulsion that swept Ireland in the wake of the executions and the grudging respect that even their opponents bestowed on the rebels for their stand appear to have made little impact in the trenches, at least initially. Sergeant John Brooks, a native of Co. Carlow who spent his leave in Dublin shortly after the rising, told Monica Roberts that he was warned by the police not to go out into the street in uniform. Writing to her a full month after the executions, Christopher Fox denounced 'the Sinn Feiners' work in Dublin.' He had been out in France for twenty-one months, and he put the destruction of Dublin's city centre solely down to the rebels.

> I think … it is scandalous for any civilised people to do such a thing, for when we heard it out here we would not believe it until we seen it personally and the old saying is seeing is believing. Well, I think I have said enough on the subject of Dublin, only if I had my way I would shoot every one of them.[3]

The sense of betrayal continued to rankle for many months. Sergeant Edward Heafey of the 8th Battalion told Monica Roberts in July 1917 that 'I would put every one of them out here and make sure they do some real fighting.'[4] William de Comb, a driver attached to staff headquarters, described 'those Sinn Feiners' as 'mad …'

> We have quite enough trouble without them. They want a few of us over there. We would smarten them up, no mercy. They are nothing more than traitors, don't you think Miss? I think it's simply disgraceful and I myself would deal very heavy with them.[5]

———

If soldiers coming home on leave reacted angrily at the sight of the city centre in ruins, young unionist office workers such as Irwin felt they had lost the days of their carefree youth. Making his way into town on the Wednesday after the rising, he felt that

> the sight of Lower Sackville Street with the odour of burnt wood and debris of all kinds was enough to make angels weep. All the old familiar landmarks were gone. The General Post Office, Elvery's Elephant House, the DBC Restaurant, the Metropole Hotel, the Coliseum Theatre where I had spent many enjoyable evenings, and the old Waxworks Exhibition in Henry Street, so often a haunt in winter months, were all gone in dust and debris … It was more depressing than walking through a graveyard.[6]

Young Charlie Dalton, whose older brother Emmet was serving at the front, had very different memories of Easter Week and its aftermath. At night the family had gathered as usual before going to bed to say the Rosary 'and to pray for the Volunteers.' After the fighting ended he went into the city centre to 'walk among the ruins … with a feeling of sadness, and at the same time of holiness and exultation.' He searched out places mentioned in press reports and wanted 'to meet some fellow-sympathisers, who would share my feelings but I did not know where to meet them.'

A series of requiem masses in the city would provide the means. Going to one of these in Church Street he spotted a crowd, 'mainly women, gathered around a young red haired man who began to sing "Rebel" songs, in which the crowd joined in if they knew the words.' Dalton recognised him 'as a senior school-fellow of mine, whose sympathies I had not suspected until that moment. He was Ernie O'Malley.' Both would serve on the GHQ Staff of the Volunteers during the War of Independence.[7]

———

While ruined buildings—including the Royal Hibernian Academy in Lower Abbey Street, where an estimated £40,000 worth of sculptures and paintings were lost—provided the most evocative evidence of the week's events,[8] more distressing for most Dubliners was the discovery of bodies in the rubble. Soldiers, rebels, looters and innocent civilians alike were found in buildings, laneways and back yards. The remains were taken first to the City Morgue, and more than sixty unidentified bodies were buried in pits at the rear of Dublin Castle. Business was so hectic for undertakers, particularly on the north side, that Glasnevin Cemetery allowed only one mourner per coffin. This was just as well, because an unusual feature of the proceedings was the mixture of civilian and military funerals, with Dubliners in the British army killed in action being buried alongside rebels. The aim in rationing mourners was to keep traffic moving rather than to reduce the risk of unseemly graveside rows, but some undertakers still complained of delays at military checkpoints.⁹

―――――

The British army did at least adopt emergency measures for the feeding of the civilian population. It took over the Bovril warehouse in Eustace Street to distribute concentrated meat stock,¹⁰ and Captain Fairbairn Downie of the Ministry of Munitions, who would soon be called upon to settle the dispute in the building trade, took charge of the Military Supply Depot in Parkgate Street, whence food was distributed to workhouses, hospitals and even some small traders.¹¹

In the city a number of convents used their kitchens to supplement the bakeries in meeting demand for food even while the rising was on. The Society of St Vincent de Paul provided relief in the most distressed areas once the fighting ended, but these resources were not enough to meet demand. Rich and poor alike were forced to queue for bread, and bakeries, including Kennedy's and Johnston, Mooney and O'Brien's, restricted customers to two loaves a day. The military kept order 'to prevent crushing or panic.' Citizens had little money with which to buy food of any kind. Workers had no wages, and the better off had no access to their bank accounts. The Local Government Board eventually set up thirty-one depots throughout the city for distributing free food.

By 3 May some normality began to return, with bread vans making deliveries to shops and the first vegetables appearing in greengrocers' shops. The Local Government Board commissioned Patrick Leonard, a former president of the Dublin Chamber of Commerce, to purchase £4,000 worth of cattle and sheep for slaughter in the Corporation abattoir. The meat was then sold by butchers' shops at fixed prices. The only sign of a 'food panic' was in Kingstown, where shops had remained open during the rising but stocks were low. Supplies were shipped directly to the township, and Howth was supplied from the rural hinterland.¹²

―――――

The National Relief Fund, a British state agency set up at the outbreak of the war in anticipation of the demands it would create, provided £5,000 for emergency relief in the first two weeks of May. The Lord Mayor's Fund raised another £5,000, of which £1,000 came from a concert given by the Irish tenor John McCormack in New York. Most of these funds went on providing employment on such varied projects as market gardening in Fairview, clearing derelict sites, and knitting socks for the troops. Many businesses reopened on 5 May when the military eased restrictions on movement around the city. Some companies, such as Elvery's, which had suffered serious damage to its premises in Sackville Street, managed to partly reopen for clearance sales on Monday 15 May.[13]

The restoration of gas supplies on 10 May and the resumption of tram services and theatres on 14 May were important elements in restoring a sense of normality. But things were not normal. Citizens attending the Bohemian Theatre were treated to the latest newsreels of *The Dublin Rising and the Ruins of the City*. Matinée performances only were available because of the curfew.

More subtle changes were taking place in unexpected places, such as the hospitals. At the Richmond Hospital, where Liam Archer was recovering from accidentally shooting himself in the foot, all the rebel casualties evaded arrest with the connivance of the staff. Sir Thomas Myles, medical head of the hospital, seemed to approve, although he thought the rising rash. He may have felt partly responsible, as he had used his yacht to bring guns into Kilcoole for the Volunteers some two years earlier.[14]

Among the rebel leaders there were no regrets. It seemed appropriate that the British army unit that had suffered the largest number of casualties in the fighting, the Sherwood Foresters, would provide the firing squads. The leader of the Volunteers at Ashbourne, Thomas Ashe, would later describe his time awaiting execution as 'a beautiful experience.' He told friends that he regretted the commuting of his death sentence to penal servitude for life, because he felt that never again would he be so spiritually prepared for death.

———

The city's business community thought in more mundane terms and roused itself very quickly to deal with the damage inflicted on the capital. As usual, William Martin Murphy was to the fore. He organised a meeting in the Mansion House on 4 May of merchants and businessmen affected by the destruction of the previous week. As 70 per cent of the damage was concentrated in the Lower Sackville Street area and, as Murphy candidly admitted, his own business empire was the largest casualty, it was a very focused gathering. The participants decided to seek compensation from the insurance industry, the government and Dublin Corporation for losses due to 'fire or artillery operations, as a consequence of the Sinn Fein revolt.' Murphy stressed that the committee was not interested in the causes of the insurrection 'or anything to do with the past. It was to the future they were looking.' He was loudly applauded by an audience that might have felt that the rebels were responsible for the carnage but knew they could not pay for it financially.

Other forms of retribution were another matter, and the first executions had begun the previous day. They continued until 12 May, when James Connolly and

Seán Mac Diarmada were the last insurgents to be executed after an infamous editorial calling for their deaths in Murphy's *Irish Independent*.[15]

Meanwhile, as Murphy pointed out to his audience at the Mansion House, they had all been paying taxes, rates and insurance premiums for years. Now it was payback time. A committee was set up, under the chairmanship of Sir Joseph Downes, who owned much of the block that had been destroyed between North Earl Street, Marlborough Street and Sackville Street. It included other leading businessmen and property-owners in the affected areas, such as Charles Eason, William Bewley and Sir Thomas Robinson of the Metropole Hotel. Murphy's properties included Clery's department store and the Imperial Hotel. They rejected suggestions of adding local MPs or the Lord Mayor to the committee, possibly because most of the businessmen concerned were unionists but more probably because they did not want compensation to become a political football in the House of Commons.

Confident of their own standing, they promptly telegraphed the Prime Minister, H. H. Asquith, seeking an urgent meeting.[16] Asquith went one better and visited the city on 12 May. It was not the most auspicious day: Connolly and Mac Diarmada were shot shortly before he landed. Asquith ordered an immediate end to the executions. He was horrified at rumours of civilians being deliberately shot by the military and quickly concluded from the information available that the death of Sheehy Skeffington, 'a preposterous and mischievous creature,' was nevertheless a clear case of murder. Nor was he impressed to find, on a visit to prisoners at Richmond Barracks, that many of them had not been involved in the fighting but simply rounded up as suspected sympathisers.

He appeared to be more impressed by the political analysis of Father Aloysius, the Franciscan who gave the last rites to Connolly, than by that of the military supremo, General Maxwell. Afterwards he visited the north of Ireland to assess the situation there. He returned to London convinced that the Dublin administration was a shambles, that there was no military solution to the problem and that Ireland was the 'most perplexing and damnable country' he knew.[17]

Unfortunately Asquith did not find time to meet Dublin Corporation representatives and discuss the rebuilding of the city until 6 July, and then only 'through the good offices of Mr. John Redmond, M.P.' Apart from the Lord Mayor, the delegation was restricted to those wealthier councillors who could afford the time and expense of the trip. This tipped the balance in favour of the unionist and large ratepayer lobbies. Also present were five MPs for Dublin City and County, who were not to be deterred by the lack of an invitation from the business community: Alfie Byrne, P. J. Brady, William Field, J. J. Clancy and John Dillon Nugent. Joe Devlin, MP for West Belfast, also attended.[18]

The Mayor told Asquith that Dublin needed a loan so that it could lend money to citizens whose premises had been destroyed, in addition to *ex gratia* grants. The corporation also needed funds for widening the streets and carrying out improvements. Asquith acknowledged the exceptional circumstances and was as good as his word. The Dublin Reconstruction (Emergency Provisions) Bill was introduced in August and became law in December.

Meanwhile, as early as June, the corporation approved a request from the City Architect to allow the erection of temporary buildings so that traders who wished to do so could resume business.[19]

———

The British government was anxious to see Ireland's main thoroughfare rebuilt and to erase the memory of the rising, while town planners saw it as an unrivalled opportunity to redesign the whole centre city. However, political and legal complications bedevilled the project from the start. When the bill came before the House of Commons, Sir Edward Carson—who was, after all, a representative of a Dublin constituency—raised the issue of whether compensation should be limited to property or whether civilians would be covered. Another vexed issue was whether compensation should apply only to those who had suffered at the hands of the Crown forces or to those who had suffered at the hands of the rebels as well. Tim Healy agreed that these issues had to be clarified, as did the *Irish Independent*, which argued that civilians could be compensated through the Prince of Wales Fund. It calculated that Dubliners had contributed £25,000 to the fund and were entitled to a refund. It estimated the cost of compensating civilians at a mere £6,000.

In contrast, 779 claims totalling £2.3 million had been received from property-owners by the end of June, and a further fifty claims pushed the figure over £2½ million in July. The chief fire officer, Captain Thomas Purcell, estimated the real losses at no more than £1 million.[20]

Inevitable delays saw anger against the rebels being redirected at the British government. One prominent businessman told the *Irish Times*: 'As citizens and ratepayers we are of the opinion that the Government should come to the assistance of the firms whose houses have been ruined and whose business has been swept away as a result of lack of firmness on the part of the Irish Government.'

Another, the well-known Quaker employer Charles Jacob, whose reputation for social concern had been tarnished when he locked out hundreds of women workers in 1913, added that 'life lost is as deserving of compensation as property destroyed.'[21]

The reality was very different. The amounts paid out to many of those civilians were relatively small, and some of those who sought it most, such as the families of the men killed in North King Street, would never receive compensation, because to concede their claims would be an admission of guilt by the military authorities. On the other hand, the woman with the most clear-cut claim for compensation, Hanna Sheehy Skeffington, refused it on principle when it was offered.[22]

Even where property was concerned there was a wrangle over how the burden should be shared between the imperial exchequer, insurance companies and Dublin ratepayers. As a result of the rising, rates worth £16,000 a year had been lost to a city struggling to cope with critical humanitarian demands on its resources. The final compromise, not hammered out until 1917, was that the corporation would provide thirty-year loans at low interest to any business that needed extra funds to make up a shortfall on the cost of rebuilding after the insurance companies and the exchequer made their contributions. In the meantime *ex gratia* grants of £742,928 were paid out in respect of 212 buildings damaged or destroyed and over £1 million 'in respect of stock, fittings, and other chattel losses and minor damage.' Businesses affected were also given a one-year rates holiday from the time they reopened.

Nevertheless, there were complaints about the miserly approach of the British authorities to Dublin compared with anecdotal evidence of generous grants to English businesses that were victims of Zeppelins and naval bombardments of North Sea ports, such as Scarborough and Hull. That Dublin Corporation was able to reduce both the consolidated and the police rates in March 1917 as a result of the British subsidies suggests that the government scheme was far more generous than generally conceded.[23]

Predictably, the Citizens' Association was unimpressed by the reduction in rates, and a delegation told the corporation meeting at which the new rates were struck that many businesses would go under without even greater reductions. It advocated large-scale dismissals of corporation employees, closing municipal workshops and ending subsidies for the Iveagh Market (the corporation's fruit and vegetable market) as economy measures. By contrast, Tom Foran, on behalf of the trades council, warned that any further redundancies would lead to bread riots. The councillors took heed and kept the reduction to 1s 6d in the pound, or 7½ per cent.

————

The necessities of the moment also meant that planners' dreams of civic rebirth were short-lived. Their proposals included the building of a new Catholic cathedral, complete with the large square it was thought such an important edifice required. Another square was proposed around the Custom House in a style complementing Gandon's masterpiece. This would include the removal of the railway bridge over the Liffey. The other main proposal was the development of a new central artery for the city, running from Christ Church Cathedral to the Four Courts, with Sackville Street relegated to the status of a radial road. However, none of these grandiose plans coincided with those of the city centre's property-owners, whose primary objectives were to obtain compensation and to rebuild or sell their properties as soon as possible.

Although the Dublin Reconstruction Act gave significant powers to the city architect, Charles MacCarthy, the failure to link compensation to a grand plan for Dublin, or any plan, was a fatal flaw. The delegation that had visited Asquith in London had been reconstituted as a committee to complete negotiations with the government. Nobody appeared to see a conflict of interest in such an arrangement, which resulted in the compensation scheme being administered by a commission chaired by Sir William Goulding, chairman of the Great Southern and Western Railway and a close business associate of several of the claimants, including William Martin Murphy.

Many of the claims were for five and six-figure sums, including £47,000 for Arnott's department store and £157,000 for the Alliance and Dublin Consumers' Gas Company. One of the worst casualties from the viewpoint of the Redmondites was the *Freeman's Journal*, which suffered a loss of £74,000. Despite fairly generous compensation, it would never fully recover.

In all, the commission made awards totalling more than £1 million, on top of the *ex gratia* payments already made by the government in the immediate aftermath of the rising, bringing the total to nearly £2 million. Once the money was handed over there was no pressure remaining on those businesses to co-operate with the civic planners.[24]

Leading property-owners, such as Sir Joseph Downes, resisted attempts to push back frontages, which would lose valuable development space, and even sought to rebuild with cheap imported red-brick fronts. This enraged the Stonecutters' Union as much as the planning and architectural community. One contributor to the *Irish Builder* quipped that the destructive powers of the rebels paled before those of the property-owners.

One of the few property-owners to emerge well from the debacle was the Catholic Archbishop, William Walsh. At first delighted at the proposal to build a fully fledged cathedral with a complementary square in the area of Ormond Market, a long-cherished ambition of the city's Catholics, he regretfully declined, because it would mean the eviction of tenement-dwellers and small business owners in the area.

It took until 1922 to restore most of Sackville Street (now renamed O'Connell Street) to mediocrity. In the meantime the temporary structures permitted by the corporation to enable businesses to trade did nothing to restore the boulevard to its previous glory but only added to the sense of impermanence that would prevail over the next few years. The restoration was completed just in time for the street to become the main arena for conventional fighting in the Civil War. This time it would be the turn of the other end of O'Connell Street to bear the brunt of the damage. The Custom House would be gutted by fire in the War of Independence, and the Four Courts would be the main architectural casualty of the Civil War.[25]

Unlike other local authorities, Dublin Corporation did not pass a motion condemning the rising. When it reconvened for the first time, on 10 May 1916, the events were too close to home. Dubliners had died on both sides, including a city councillor, Richard O'Carroll of the Bricklayers' Union, and several corporation employees, of whom the most prominent was Éamonn Ceannt. As well as being a signatory of the Proclamation of the Irish Republic and commander of rebel forces in the South Dublin Union, Ceannt had been a senior clerk in the City Treasurer's Department and a member of the Executive Committee of the Dublin Municipal Officers' Association, one of Ireland's earliest white-collar unions. Two councillors had received prison sentences, William Partridge, who had been a captain in the Citizen Army, and W. T. Cosgrave, who had served as Ceannt's adjutant at the South Dublin Union and had been sentenced to death. Several other members of the corporation, including Alderman Tom Kelly of Sinn Féin and Councillor P. T. Daly of the Labour Party, had been arrested in the round-up after the rising.

An example of the sheer complexity of local politics and of the personal relations of corporation members is given by the extraordinary lengths to which Alderman Patrick Corrigan went to help the imprisoned Kelly. A slum landlord and undertaker, Corrigan was a pillar of the UIL on the Corporation but was a friend of Kelly and had spoken at protest meetings over the deportation of Irish Volunteer organisers before the rising. Kelly now sent word that he had explosives stored in his business premises in South William Street. Corrigan 'got possession of a handcart, wheeled it to William Street, loaded it with explosives and brought the cargo away.' He dumped the material in small batches over time in the Liffey.[26]

Besides, the corporation was too busy coping with the consequences of the rising to carry out a political post mortem. The secretary of the Local Government Board, A. R. Barlas, had written asking it to invoke section 13 of the Local Government (Ireland) Act (1898) so that the North Dublin and South Dublin Unions could obtain overdrafts to relieve 'the destitution caused by the Sinn Fein Rebellion.' This appeal was supported by letters from the clerk of the North Dublin Union, John O'Neill, and the clerk of the South Dublin Union, J. P. Condon, who wrote of the 'exceptional distress ... in the City and County of Dublin.'

The Lord Mayor, Sir James Gallagher, proposed the necessary motion, but it was opposed by two councillors, John Ryan, the conservative nationalist representing Clontarf, and Sir Andrew Beattie, the unionist-turned-independent who now served as chairman of the Dublin Citizens' Association. Both men sought to defend the ratepayers' interest. Ryan came from one of the districts least affected by the rising. He warned his fellow-councillors that if they passed the motion 'it would only mean stampeding ourselves into very large expenditure of which they did not know the end.' He was sceptical of reports of hardship, and the proposal was unfair to the 'already heavily burdened' ratepayers when they 'were in no way accountable for the misfortune.' Although Beattie represented a ward affected by the fighting, he questioned whether there was 'any real distress.' He had heard that 'very poor children had been coming ... for relief from other wards in the city' unaffected by the fighting.

The High Sheriff, William Delaney, a nationalist councillor representing the Inns Quay ward, one of the areas worst affected by the fighting, felt that, as a victualler, he should know something of the situation on the ground. He believed 'there might be ... isolated cases of distress but ... the people would suffer nothing from postponing the matter.'

However, even a meeting from which so many of the more radical Sinn Féin and Labour councillors were absent baulked at parsimony on such an epic scale. Dr James McWalter, whose dispensary in North Earl Street had been at the centre of the storm, said that existing agencies could not cope with a crisis that was affecting between 80,000 and 100,000 people. Without the corporation's approval of extra funds the Poor Law unions could only help inmates and existing clients.

James Gately, a nationalist councillor on the Board of Guardians (governors) of the South Dublin Union, said that people were seeking relief who had never asked for it before; and the only woman councillor, the nationalist Martha Williams, said her local dispensary in Grand Canal Street dealt with nearly seven hundred cases the previous day. There were still many 'who shrunk from seeking relief ... The system was not perfect but they could not allow families to starve.' The overdraft facility was approved.[27]

Chapter 7 ~

THE 'CALAMITY OF REBELLION'

The first full meeting of Dublin Corporation after the rising took place on 5 June. It was necessary to tread sensitively, as the first item on the agenda was the potentially inflammatory series of votes of sympathy for deceased members and their relations. The choreography suggests that items were discussed well in advance.

The first vote was not contentious. The unionist alderman for Glasnevin, William Dinnage, proposed a vote of sympathy to the family of his recently deceased party colleague John Thornton, who had died of natural causes. The vote was seconded by Councillor James Cummins, a nationalist who represented the same ward.

Councillor John J. Higgins proposed and Councillor Sir Patrick Shortall seconded a vote of sympathy for Richard O'Carroll, the former Labour member and Volunteer officer killed in the rising by Captain Bowen-Colthurst. Shortall, a builder, had been knighted for his contribution to the war effort. Ironically, he had crossed swords with O'Carroll in the 1913 Lock-out, when the latter was secretary of the Bricklayers' Union and a member of the trades council strike committee.

Alderman William O'Connor proposed and Councillor Patrick Lennon seconded a vote of sympathy to Sir Thomas Esmonde MP, the head of a respected nationalist political dynasty, on the death of his 'youthful son ... through the destruction of His Majesty's ship *Invincible*.' It was the nearest Dublin Corporation would ever come to acknowledging the Battle of Jutland, one of the most decisive engagements of the First World War. The politics of this model for a home rule parliament remained resolutely parochial.

Finally, Councillor Thomas Murty O'Beirne proposed and Councillor Patrick Lennon seconded a vote extending the sympathy of the corporation's members 'to the relatives of the citizens who lost their lives during the recent rebellion.'

The Lord Mayor then referred to the 'calamity of rebellion,' which had fallen on the city 'like a thunderbolt.' He contrasted 'the steadiness of public opinion and calmness' with the 'unprecedented and almost incredible inaction of the Irish Executive.' The rateable value of the premises destroyed in the city was £33,000, which meant a loss of £16,000 a year in municipal revenue. He announced an embargo on recruitment by the corporation and called for extra financial assistance from the government, 'which had blown down the centre and most beautiful part of their city.'

Far from introducing any acrimony over the causes or progress of the rising, the corporation unanimously called for the release of Alderman Tom Kelly of Sinn Féin, chairman of the Housing Committee. Councillor Coghlan Briscoe, who was deputising for Kelly as chairman of the committee, moved the motion calling for the speedy release of this 'invaluable member' of the corporation. There were no similar calls for the release of W. T. Cosgrave or William Partridge; but then Kelly had not taken up arms against the state.

Housing continued to dominate the proceedings as Alderman Alfie Byrne proposed a motion deferred from before the rising that all the extra revenue raised from Dublin as a result of increased land valuations, income tax and duty on the licensed trade be used for slum clearance. The city had 2,288 dwellings 'fast approaching the borderline for being unfit for habitation,' on top of the 1,518 already in that category needing replacement. It was a shrewd move by Byrne. Councillor Joseph Isaacs, a well-regarded figure in the business community and the only Jewish member of the corporation, seconded the motion.

Byrne's next motion was more controversial. He proposed a 50 per cent increase in the old age pension, to 7s 6d, to relieve some of the increase in food and fuel prices since the start of the war, and he proposed a reduction in the age qualification from 70 to 65. Despite opposition from the Lord Mayor, the unionist group and the ratepayers' lobby, the motion was passed. Again the British government would be picking up the bill if it ever came to fruition.

Another proposal from Byrne was for a weekly war bonus of 3s to all officers of the corporation earning less than £100 a year. This would be an increase of 1s a week on the bonus secured by P. T. Daly for blue-collar workers before the rising. The motion, seconded by Councillor Gately, dovetailed with an earlier proposal from W. T. Cosgrave that no member of the clerical and administrative staff should be paid 'less than a labourer.'[1] The proposals reflected the fact that pay rates were rising faster for manual workers than for their white-collar colleagues, because the former were better organised in unions and better placed to exploit the labour shortage brought on by the war.

Despite sympathy for white-collar employees among corporation members, resistance to the proposal was as vociferous as usual from the ratepayers' champions. The Lord Mayor said it would be 'shameful for the Corporation to pass such a motion without knowing the cost.' The tried and trusted tactic of an amendment was proposed, to refer the matter to the Estates and Finance Committee for a report. This was defeated by 25 votes to 9. Gallagher was almost alone in voting with the unionists to oppose the pay increase.

By August the corporation had extended the 3s per week war bonus to all employees. It then faced a demand from the Amalgamated Society of Engineers for an extra 4s for craft workers, to bring them into line with an increase already conceded by the Dublin Engineers Employers' Association in the private sector. This concession led in turn to a similar claim from the Electrical Trade Union on the grounds of internal comparators.[2] These were successful, thanks largely to strong support from the Labour group and from Alfie Byrne.

In contrast, the relief provided under section 13 of the Local Government Act for those left destitute by the rising was minimal, as the figures for June 1916 (table 6) demonstrate.

Table 6
Relief paid to those left destitute by the rising, June 1916

Husband and wife	8s
One child	1s 6d
Two children	2s 6d
Three children	3s
For each child over three years of age	6d
Widow or widower	5s
Adult dependant over seventy	3s
Able-bodied single people	No relief

Two days after Dublin Corporation passed its various votes of sympathy, Field-Marshal Kitchener perished when the cruiser *Hampshire*, carrying him to Russia, sank off Orkney. It was a blow to morale in Britain but failed to elicit much interest in Dublin. Even the Unionist Central Council and the Dublin Women's Unionist Club were too preoccupied with petitions for blocking the implementation of home rule to note the passing of Ireland's premier soldier, creator of Britain's modern army and the colonel of the Irish Guards.

For nationalists of all hues Kitchener epitomised the anti-Irish bias of the British military establishment. He had facilitated the reorganisation of the UVF as the 36th

(Ulster) Division of the British army but refused to make similar arrangements for members of Redmond's National Volunteers. 'Kitchener never liked or trusted the Irish and I always believe that but for him Ireland would have been wholeheartedly in the war,' the Countess of Fingall wrote many years later. She was one of Kitchener's few female friends, but this did not prevent her recalling his many snubs to the Irish war effort, including the return of proposed colours for a suggested Irish brigade produced by the Countess of Mayo's School of Art.

> The Irish were distrusted and knew it. They distrusted in their turn ... Although thousands of Irishmen joined the Irish regiments ... their brothers who might have gone with them joined the Volunteers.[3]

Nor did the Irish Party mark his passing when it met in the Mansion House on 10 June. It could hardly avoid a vote of sympathy to Sir Thomas Esmonde on the death of his teenage son at Jutland, but it did so in silence. There were no speeches in support of the British war effort, and Redmond even used the opportunity to argue that the Easter Rising had demonstrated the need to bring forward home rule.[4]

Another indicator of the changing political climate came at the corporation meeting on 19 June, when councillors met to fill the seats left vacant by the deaths of John Thornton and Richard O'Carroll. There had been a tradition of co-opting nominees of the party of the deceased in accordance with the outcome of the last election. But on this occasion Labour and Sinn Féin councillors supported the UIL nominee, Michael Maher, dairyman and cowkeeper, to fill Thornton's seat. When Alderman William Dinnage, a unionist, protested that Maher did not even live in Glasnevin, his own candidate, Hubbard Clarke, was denounced as the director of a British company. The unionists found themselves isolated, apart from the support of a couple of ratepayer independents such as Sir Andrew Beattie, a former member of their own group, and Alderman James Moran, a nationalist and hotelier from Clontarf East who had a large unionist electorate and was a member of the Dublin Recruitment Committee for the British forces.

For unionists the outcome was worrying. In 1915 the British government had suspended elections for the duration of the war, and if a pact emerged between the UIL, Sinn Féin and Labour on how to fill vacancies, unionists could become an endangered species. Their fears were confirmed when nationalist councillors supported John Long, a Labour nominee, to replace O'Carroll. The unionists unsuccessfully proposed an independent 'businessman-rates payer' candidate for the seat.[5]

A replacement for O'Carroll was a particularly sensitive question, because the man who shot him, Captain John Bowen-Colthurst, had just been convicted of the murders of Sheehy Skeffington and his fellow-journalists after a highly publicised trial. The trial began on 6 June, lasted five days and told a dismal tale of confused command structures in which inexperienced young officers allowed themselves to be browbeaten by Bowen-Colthurst into ignoring all procedures and into complicity in the summary execution of prisoners by firing squad. The fact that most of the officers concerned, including the accused, were Irish and that the court-martial found Bowen-Colthurst guilty but insane added to the general air of disillusionment in the city.[6]

The corporation was even more exercised by the discovery of the bodies of fifteen civilians in the ruins of North King Street. Among them were those of Patrick Bealen, the 24-year-old foreman of a pub at 177 North King Street, and James Healy, a 44-year-old employee of the Jameson distillery nearby. The inquests were held immediately after the last of the 1916 leaders were executed.

Bealen had been shot six times and Healy twice. The military authorities were unable to establish which units, let alone which individuals, might have occupied this or any other house in the street when the men died. However, the position certainly registered with Major Rhodes of the Staffordshire Regiment, who gave evidence that the regiment sustained its heaviest casualties in four hours of intense fighting around the pub. Fourteen members of the regiment had been killed and thirty-three wounded. 'I am satisfied that during these operations the troops under my command showed great restraint under exceptionally difficult and trying circumstances,' he said.

The jury did not agree: they found that Bealen 'died from shock and haemorrhage, resulting from bullet wounds inflicted by a soldier, or soldiers, in whose custody he was, an unarmed and unoffending prisoner.' A similar verdict was brought in for Healy.

A specially convened meeting of the corporation condemned the deaths and those of 'other unoffending citizens' in the North King Street area. Only one independent, Alderman David Quaid, a solicitor representing Drumcondra with its large unionist electorate, voted against the motion. No unionist representative voted on the issue.[7] That a coroner's jury, selected from the ranks of the city's business community and normally sympathetic to the authorities, could bring in such verdicts was another troubling sign of the changing public mood. A precedent was being set for many similar inquests throughout the country in the years ahead.

————

It was this mood of simmering discontent that John Dillon had tried to capture when he spoke of the rising in the House of Commons on 11 May. Although Dillon represented Mayo he spent the week of the rising trapped in his Dublin home in North Great George's Street with his family, within earshot of the rifle and machine-gun fire and later the artillery.

Few constitutional nationalists living in the capital had been so out of touch with its mood than this old rural radical.[8] But he was quick to grasp the significance of the rising, and he wrote to Redmond urging him to try to stop the executions. When that failed Dillon told the House of Commons: 'It is not murderers who are being executed; it is insurgents who have fought a clean fight, a brave fight, however misguided, and it would have been a damned good thing for you if your soldiers were able to put up as good a fight as did these men in Dublin.' It was a speech that shocked colleagues in the Irish Party as well as British MPs; but then they had not seen the destruction wrought and had not caught the mood of the citizens, including members of the United Irish League who had come to Dillon's door pleading for leadership while he was unable to offer even meaningful advice. It was an anger also driven by Dillon's realisation that the life's work of constitutional nationalists was being washed away with blood and that men like himself would be 'held up to odium as traitors by the men who made this rebellion.'[9]

He did not have to wait long. On 21 May, Tim Healy made a speech that was vitriolic even by his standards. He listed the slights against the Irish regiments, the bungling of the Volunteer question, the crippling tax burden imposed on Ireland and the cutting of urgently needed housing grants for Dublin as reasons for so much disaffection. 'New crystallisations are taking place,' he told the House of Commons. 'The jobbery of the official party [Irish Party] disgusted all earnest and unselfish minds amongst the youth of Ireland.' The corruption and ineffectiveness of the constitutional movement represented by men like Dillon meant that 'all that was sober, unselfish, self-respecting and self-reliant quitted [the Irish Party] ... and joined Sinn Féin.'[10]

There were other, less exalted political casualties of the war in the city. One was Dr James McWalter, who notified the Lord Mayor in early July that he had 'received orders from the War Office to take up duty at "some place in the Mediterranean" and therefore I cannot attend the Council for some time.' McWalter had joined the Royal Army Medical Corps in June 1915 and had been congratulated by his fellow-councillors when he appeared in his lieutenant's uniform at the next corporation meeting. But now, barely noting the contents of his letter, they went on to demand an end to martial law in the city, the release of 'hundreds of citizens, men, women and boys,' suspected of having sympathy with the insurgents, and compensation for the dependants of those who had lost their lives during the rising.[11]

———

There was even sympathy to spare for members of the staff of the Town Clerk's office who sought compensation for loss of earnings because of the wartime suspension of elections under the Elections and Registration Act (1915). This meant they no longer had to prepare electoral lists and registers or oversee the electoral process. The loss of earnings ranged from £12 for junior staff to £110 for senior colleagues. The councillors approved the claim and forwarded it to the Local Government Board with hardly any debate.[12]

––––

The war effort was imposing much greater burdens on the city. As in 1915, the British military authorities requisitioned all hay crops within ten miles of Dublin for its cavalry regiments and transport corps. On this occasion, however, the move was accompanied by a government order that allowed the Army Council to fix maximum prices. While provision was made for releasing unused fodder, the process proved slow and cumbersome. As early as July the Dublin Chamber of Commerce was complaining of shortages.[13]

Even more affected than business was the city's health. The secretary of the corporation, Fred Allan, an old IRB man,[14] wrote to the military authorities 'in the strongest terms' on the matter. He told the corporation that

> during the present hot weather it is highly important that the portion of the City cleansing work which most vitally affects the public health, viz., the house to house removal of refuse must be efficiently maintained, and it would be extremely serious if, through either a deficiency of proper foodstuffs or the enforced use of inferior material, any large proportion of their stud were put out of action.

The fodder shortage remained a problem throughout the war, adding to the general air of resentment against the army. The fact that thousands of tons of hay were stored openly for the army at the docks while horses and cattle in the city starved only inflamed public opinion. On 1 August 1916, 1,400 tons of fodder, worth £11,200, were destroyed by fire, along with lorries worth £125 11s. As four ricks were set alight simultaneously, and the hay had been thoroughly pressed and dried, spontaneous combustion could be ruled out. This meant that the cost of compensation under the malicious damages legislation fell on the corporation.

Fortunately for the ratepayers, there were no further serious incidents, but complaints continued to be voiced to the military authorities about their purchasing policies. In December 1917 Colonel McCullagh, the officer responsible for fodder collection in the Dublin area, told a delegation of city councillors that he had checked that very week and found that large quantities of hay had been released by the army for sale. If it could be shown that private suppliers were abusing their position he would cancel their licences and offer the forage to the city and commercial customers at military rates. For their part the city councillors urged the army to extend the catchment area from a ten-mile radius of the city to twenty-five miles to allow military fodder targets to be achieved faster and the balance of the crop to be released onto the market.[15]

Beyond business needs and those of the corporation, the most pressing requirement for fodder came from the city's dairies. There were five hundred of these, with 7,500 head of cattle, represented by the Cow Keepers' and Dairymen's Association. Members ranged in size from relatively large businesses to small dairies such as that of Todd Andrews' parents and even smaller enterprises dependent on one or two animals to keep their owners from penury. Besides fodder, the cowkeepers had enjoyed access to cheap feed in the form of waste from the city's breweries and distilleries. Guinness's brewery found its overseas customers, including the Prussian cavalry, cut off by the outbreak of war. The closing of these markets helped increase the flow of feed to the Dublin market, and, true to its tradition of civic responsibility, the Guinness brewery continued to supply what was prime material at pre-war prices. This helped keep the price of milk at pre-war prices until the summer of 1916.

However, in the long run there was an inexorable decline in the supply of feedstuffs as a result of the production of beer and spirits. The replacement of Asquith by Lloyd George as Prime Minister at the end of 1916 accelerated state intervention in the drinks industry and the economy at large. In December the Dublin distilleries, which had been ordered in August 1916 to cut their already reduced output by a further 30 per cent, were taken over completely by the Department of Munitions. From then on they concentrated on the production of industrial alcohol for the war effort. Beer production had already fallen by 7 per cent in the first two years of the war, but now it tumbled rapidly, from 3.53 million barrels in 1914 to 3.28 million in 1916 and to 1.46 million in 1919, only 59 per cent of production in 1914. Employment in the distilleries and breweries had fallen by 50 per cent by 1917.[16]

From the summer of 1916 onwards the city's cowkeepers had no option but to bid on the open market for fodder, much of it of inferior quality. Higher costs and reduced output caused milk prices to rise from 3d to 4d a quart in October. This was a relatively small increase compared with other staples. Retail prices generally had increased by about 150 per cent by the middle of 1916 and would reach 240 per cent by 1919. However, the increase in milk prices struck a nerve, as the poverty of many Dubliners made them heavily dependent on milk as one of the cheapest and most efficient sources of nourishment. Children were the most dependent of all, and the city's infant mortality rate, already the highest in the United Kingdom when the war began, at 141 per thousand, rose to over 155. As the Minister of Food Control, Lord Rhondda, told a Baby Week conference in Dublin, more British babies died of disease, malnourishment and neglect in 1915 than men on active service in France and Flanders. He believed that infant mortality in a city such as Dublin, where infants accounted for a fifth of all deaths, could be halved by better nutrition and hygiene.[17]

If a major cause of infant mortality was the poor quality of milk, the fines were paltry. The chief medical officer of the city, Dr Charles Cameron, said after a tour of the dairies that 'many were so situated and managed that the chances of milk being uncontaminated are remarkably slight.' It was commonly accepted not only that hygiene in the dairies was poor but that milk sold before 10 a.m. or after 4 p.m. was routinely adulterated, as the food inspectors rarely worked outside office hours.[18]

At its meeting on 9 October the Dublin Trades Council denounced the cowkeepers as members of 'a criminal class' conspiring to rob the public. A Milk Prices Order introduced in November only aggravated shortages, as Dublin dairies followed the example of their Belfast counterparts and began selling milch cows for the export market to Britain. In November the corporation's Public Health Committee debated buying milk in bulk from rural creameries to supply at subsidised prices in the city. But market pressures were such that the corporation was forced to offer 1s 2d a gallon to rural dairies, and even then it was relying on a large measure of good will, because British bulk buyers for the dried-milk industry were already offering up to 1s 8d to meet War Office contracts.[19]

The price of other staples, such as sugar, meat, eggs, potatoes and tea, rose far faster than milk. Tea was one of the worst-affected items, because it had to be imported on ships that ran the gauntlet of mines and German submarines. The price doubled from 3d a pound in 1914 to 6d a pound by 1916 and would rise even faster in 1917 when the German submarine campaign was stepped up.

———

The Irish Sea attracted relatively little submarine activity before the introduction of the convoy system in 1917, because of the richer pickings in the North Sea, the English Channel and the Western Approaches. There had been some serious incidents, most notably in January 1915 when the *Leinster*, one of the City of Dublin Steam Packet Company's mail boats, had a narrow escape east of the Kish Bank on a home run from Holyhead. Its luck would hold out almost to the end of the war; but smaller, slower steamers and fishing boats were not so lucky.

At first German submarine commanders allowed crews to take to the lifeboats before sinking vessels, but attitudes hardened as the war progressed and allied counter-measures made it dangerous for submarines to linger on the surface. The sinking of vessels such as the 3,839-ton *Hartdale* with the loss of two lives in March 1915 and of the 2,114-ton *Aguila* with the loss of three lives in April paled before the almost 1,200 lives lost when the *Lusitania* went down off Galley Head, Co. Cork. Part of the cultural collateral damage for Dublin was the loss of Sir Hugh Lane, a passenger on board. He was not only the director of the National Gallery but had left a bequest of his priceless impressionist paintings to the city. Unfortunately the codicil to his will had never been witnessed, and ownership of the collection would be a matter of controversy for decades.

Meanwhile many of the *Lusitania*'s survivors were brought to Dublin. The *Irish Times*, which had confidently predicted that 'any steamer of moderate speed which gets fair warning can escape' a German submarine, had to revise its opinions after the loss of the *Lusitania*, and it published advice from the Admiralty that British ships should not scruple about sailing under neutral colours to increase their chances of survival.[20]

The British government had moved quickly to pre-empt a collapse of the maritime insurance business by underwriting 80 per cent of potential shipping losses, but the cost of Irish imports was nevertheless bound to rise. By 1917 premiums would increase by almost 50 per cent for relatively new vessels but had almost doubled for the older ships that were the mainstay of the Irish mercantile marine.[21]

If higher tea prices were a hardship, the shortage of coal threatened an already ailing economy. When members of the Irish Association of Gas Managers assembled for their annual general meeting in City Hall they denounced British contractors, merchants and ship-owners for 'availing of their position as monopolists to make huge profits out of the opportunities afforded them by the war.' The behaviour of the ship-owners was singled out as 'very unpatriotic.' They had gone one better than the mine-owners and railways by raising freight prices even faster than the price of coal. While coal was 80 per cent dearer in August 1916 than in August 1914, shipping freight rates were 229 per cent higher. What was particularly galling for the association was that the Price of Coal (Limitation) Act (1915) had not been applied to Ireland, although Irish municipal gas companies were still locked in to price control mechanisms based on pre-war legislation that meant they could not pass on the costs.[22]

When it convened after the rising, Dublin Corporation, hardly a socialist gathering, passed a motion proposed by Alfie Byrne calling on the British government to place all shipping under state control, 'so as to limit the monstrous and utterly indefensible prices charged for coal and food, which is being caused by the extraordinary freights charged by companies who are making vast fortunes out of the War.'[23] The high prices were also fuelled by an increase of 75 per cent in handling charges for stevedoring companies by the Dublin Port and Docks Board and a 10 per cent increase for shipping lines in 1916. At the same time dredging operations were scaled back, and there was a moratorium on purchasing new equipment.

In the new year, dissatisfaction with the performance of the board led city councillors to call for legislation so that the Port and Docks Board could be elected directly by the ratepayers rather than dominated by business interests. However, the *Irish Independent* accused the councillors of 'impertinence' and said they had 'made a muddle of every important undertaking ... attempted during the last twenty-five years.' The lack of a response from the government suggested that it concurred.[24]

When the Ministry of Shipping eventually granted Byrne's wish in late 1917 by taking over control of the industry, it placed the City of Dublin Steam Packet Company under the direction of the London and North-Western Railway. There was outrage at the following meeting of the Port and Docks board. No-one was louder in his denunciations than Alderman Byrne at 'the only Irish company they had' being put under the control of its main British rival. Representatives of the company assured the board that it was all for the best, as the company could no longer afford to pay the insurance premiums needed to cover the loss of vessels, cargoes, passengers or crews. They had no fears about loss of trade, because of the insatiable demand for Irish livestock and other agricultural exports by Britain.[25] Regrettably, their optimism proved ill-founded, and it was the beginning of the end for the world's oldest steamship company.

The primary reason that prices of essential items, such as insurance and fuel, continued to rise was that priority had to be given to war industries and to the armed forces. If coal supplies in 1916 were 'a trickle of the peace time supply and the city faced the perpetual fear of a coal famine,' supplies would fall by a further third in 1917 and another quarter in 1918. The reduction in 1918 was due to the withdrawal of coastal steamers for use by the Admiralty. This affected coal shipments to the south of England as well, but only by 17 per cent, because road and rail traffic in England could make up much of the difference.

The Admiralty's decision reinforced the feeling in Dublin that the city was being discriminated against by the British establishment. A meeting of Dublin Corporation in March 1918 passed a motion protesting against 'the unfair proportion of reduction applied to Ireland as opposed with S. England.' The same motion called for the Public Health Committee to be given powers to investigate the hoarding of coal and food by householders and businesses. Unionist and ratepayer elements on the corporation joined with UIL nationalists, Sinn Féin and Labour in 'demanding that adequate shipping be secured for Dublin to allow the city's trade to continue' and 'proper protection for all Dublin-trading boats.' When P. T. Daly added that they should 'take immediate strong action' if fuel shortages caused the loss of further jobs in the city, Alderman Dinnage, leader of the unionist group, concurred.[26]

These difficulties still lay ahead when the corporation received another unpleasant reminder of the burdens of war at its meeting on 7 August 1916. A letter from Lieutenant-Colonel A. Welby, secretary of the statutory committee for the implementation of the Naval and Military War Pensions Act, demanded to know why the corporation had not established a scheme for making various contingency payments to the dependants of servicemen for loss of income due to enlistment, death or injury. He pointed out that Belfast and Cork had already established schemes and that Dublin County Council was in the process of doing so. Dublin Corporation was given a month to follow suit.

So far the administration of these emergency payments had been done by voluntary bodies, but these could no longer cope with the volume of claims. The government had taken over the responsibility for making all payments and voted £6 million to put the administration of the scheme on a more uniform and structured basis. The need for a more efficient system was vital in ensuring that would-be recruits were not discouraged by worries that dependants might have to wait weeks for separation allowances to be processed. There was also a need to show that war widows and men returning disabled from the war were not suffering undue hardship.

The statutory committee recommended that, in taking over the duties of the voluntary agencies, the corporation should co-opt some members of the latter to the new body. In fact it was quite precise on membership: besides the Lord Mayor and eight members of the corporation it proposed

> two persons (one a lady) nominated by the Soldiers' and Sailors' Families' Association, two persons nominated by the Soldiers' and Sailors' Help Society (one a lady), two persons nominated by Local Representative Relief Committees (one a lady), two persons from the Irish Automobile Club, and four persons from local Labour organisations.[27]

The inclusion of women nominees from so many bodies illustrated their increasing role in the war effort.

———

Nowhere were women more needed for war work than in nursing; but the pay for staff nurses set by the military authorities was only £40 to £45 a year, less than that of an unskilled labourer. Many nurses in Dublin earned even less, and in some country areas pay as low as 11s 6d a week was reported. In contrast, a doctor entering military service received an officer's commission and was paid at least the Royal Army Medical Corps rates and often significantly more, depending on qualifications and experience. Attempts within the profession to set up a nursing register to improve training standards and pay had been disrupted by the war; but such was the demand for nurses that the Queen Alexandra Imperial Military Service and Joint War Committee advertised in Ireland in late 1916 for women aged between twenty-five and thirty-five, single or widowed, with at least three years' training in a large civilian hospital, with the promise of an annual 'clothing and cloak' allowance of £8 to £9 to top up their pay.[28]

The Irish Nurses' Association and Irish Matrons' Association, which tended to share the same leadership, lobbied the Lord Lieutenant and the British government strongly for a system of statutory training and registration. They frequently did so in conjunction with their English counterparts, with whom they enjoyed a love-hate relationship during the war. A relatively large proportion of Irish nurses came from a Protestant middle-class background, which probably helped account for a strong affinity with the war effort. There was also a growing realisation that the high losses of potential marriage partners in the war meant that many nurses would have to be economically self-sufficient in the long run, and their pay and conditions should reflect this.[29]

The Matrons' Association sought to promote these concerns without overtly challenging the British authorities. Its members held much the same views on many issues. For instance, it condemned the shooting of Edith Cavell by the Germans as a spy,[30] and it supported a proposal from Lady Fingall, in her capacity as president of the Conservative and Unionist Women's Franchise Association, to have a woman inspector appointed to monitor separation women and war widows to ensure that they were not cohabiting. These inspections served the dual purpose of reassuring men at the front that their wives were being morally policed and saving the exchequer money by not supporting 'fallen' women.

The Irish Matrons' Association also affiliated to the National Union of Women Workers, the main campaigning body in Britain for working women in a wide variety of occupations during the war. This helped to significantly widen the association's views on women's issues. This wider view of the world fuelled the association's growing resentment at attempts by their British counterparts to dictate policy, including proposals that Irish nurses should go to London to sit qualifying examinations. There was widespread anger when a plan was unveiled for establishing a British College of Nursing in which Ireland would have only six of the thirty-six places on the board. Irish matrons would have none of it. 'Patriotic Irishwoman' wrote in the May 1916 issue of the *British Journal of Nursing*: 'Nurses are mostly strong loyalists, although I know patriots who are not, and it is because it is so difficult for the English to understand the Irish, and to realise their real feelings and convictions, that there has always been trouble in governing them.'

By the time of the association's next annual conference in February 1917 it was ready to condemn attempts at subjecting the governance of Irish nurses to any British institution. Instead it claimed the same professional independence for nurses that the medical profession enjoyed, and it strongly resisted proposals that the

Voluntary Aid Detachment nurses who had played such a vital role in military hospitals should be allowed to qualify on the grounds of wartime experience. 'Three years in the wards of a recognised training school or schools is essential to entitle the VAD to the certificate of a trained nurse,' the matrons ruled. When the war ended, the Matrons' Association secured its objectives with the Nurses Registration (Ireland) Act (1919).[31]

———

Members of the Dublin Metropolitan Police were another group that fared poorly in the fast-changing political environment. After the rising they were issued with arms, only to have them withdrawn the next day. The DMP attracted considerable obloquy, from loyalist and republican alike: many of the former saw them as epitomising the ineffectiveness of the Castle in dealing with sedition, while the latter had not forgotten their role in the lock-out three years before.

Now the DMP had its own industrial troubles. Following the rising, members contrasted the relatively generous compensation paid to members of the military who died or were incapacitated fighting against the rebels with their own frugal payments. This provided a catalyst for a campaign to achieve a long-denied pay increase. Members held a series of meetings in the Irish National Foresters' Hall at 41 Rutland Square. The venue was significant, in that it was a regular meeting place for radical nationalists, including members of the Irish Volunteers and Fianna Éireann.

In an effort to defuse the situation the Commissioner granted them the use of the band room in Kevin Street station. The men availed of the offer, but many also continued to attend meetings outside the stations, using the simple expedient of joining the Ancient Order of Hibernians so as to meet in its hall at 31 Rutland Square. The secretary of the AOH, John Dillon Nugent, raised their case in the House of Commons, along with Alfie Byrne. Representatives of the DMP rank and file and station sergeants also sought help from the Lord Mayor.

They had genuine enough grievances. At the outbreak of war DMP members had received a pay increase of 1s a week—their first since 1884. They received another 3s 6d weekly 'war bonus' on 1 July 1916. They now demanded another 12s a week—a 50 per cent increase in basic pay—with full retrospection from 1 September 1914. Like that of white-collar corporation employees, their demand was driven as much by comparative deprivation as by wartime inflation. DMP men were angered by the spectacle of manual workers in unions passing them out in the pay stakes.

Although Dublin Corporation paid a large contribution towards the cost of the DMP, it had no say in how the force was managed or deployed. The demands of the policemen gave nationalists an opportunity to raise this long-standing grievance and to emphasise how little autonomy the Irish local authorities had when it came to such areas as policing compared with Britain.

Given the disturbed state of Ireland, the government had little choice but to give ground. It provided a pay increase of 2s a week to men with less than three years' service and 3s a week for longer-serving members. However, it gave the same increases to the RIC, and ordered DMP men who had joined the AOH to leave it. Nugent and other champions of Catholic nationalism were outraged, as it was well known that many Protestant members of the force were Freemasons, and the masons were credited with the much higher promotion rate of Protestants.

The government did not seriously dispute the claim, and, rather than argue the point with the Irish Party in the House of Commons, the new Chief Secretary for Ireland, Sir Henry Duke, decided to rule that membership of the Freemasons would be forbidden for future recruits to both the DMP and the RIC. The decision was understandable, given that most Protestant policemen who were Freemasons had been in the organisation for many years, while the influx of six hundred Catholic DMP men—about half the force—into the AOH had occurred over the previous few months and that the AOH had strong links to the Irish Party.

However, this did nothing to assuage the wrath of either side. There was 'a great deal of surprise and indignation amongst the Brethren' over the withdrawal of their right to recruit from within the ranks of the RIC and DMP. Lord Donoughmore, grand master of the Freemasons in Ireland, wrote to Duke protesting at the decision and pointing out that several members of the Cabinet were Freemasons, including Sir Auckland Geddes, who was a member of a Dublin lodge.[32]

Even charitable efforts to help the families of RIC and DMP men killed or injured in the rising indicated the deepening divisions in Dublin. Although William Martin Murphy sent a message of support to the launch of a committee to set up a compensation fund, stating 'it would be a public scandal if the government did not fully compensate the widows and dependants,' it consisted almost exclusively of members of the unionist community in the city, including several prominent Freemasons, thus further fuelling rumours about the influence of the lodges in the police and elsewhere. The president of the committee was the Earl of Meath, the vice-president was Sir John Arnott, the chairman was Sir Maurice Dockrell, and the treasurer was R. W. Booth, a director of the Bank of Ireland. It also included such luminaries as Lord Powerscourt, Sir William Goulding and the Earl of Donoughmore. Donations were largely from the aristocracy, the business community and employees in the enterprises they controlled.[33]

The AOH and nationalists generally felt it was another example of the government and the Castle aligning themselves with the hereditary enemy. This view was reinforced when an example was made of the perceived ringleaders of the DMP rank and file. Constable William Hetherton, who had thirteen years' service, was dismissed, while four other constables were fined or stopped a week's pay and transferred to outlying stations. All four were subsequently dismissed for gross insubordination when they organised a mock funeral, complete with hearse, and marched behind it to Dalkey via the city centre, Blackrock and Kingstown as they accompanied the first of their number to be transferred to his new posting.[34]

———

By then industrial unrest, spurred by the high prices, had become widespread in the city. Coalmen, Glasnevin cemetery workers, gas workers, dockers and others struck for higher wages; but by far the most serious disputes that autumn involved the bakeries and the railways.

The battle in the bakeries was as much about union recognition and a campaign to end night work as about pay. A baker asked in the *Irish Independent*:

What does 'recognition' mean? It simply means the elimination of non-union labour and that the master bakers [employers] of Dublin are required to sit down and arrange working agreements with representatives of their employees—a condition which obtains in every other trade in the United Kingdom. [There is] nothing revolutionary about these demands. Anyone who knows the lot of the operative baker will sympathise with our efforts.

The writer added that the average baker

commences the week's work, in most cases on Sunday morning when he should be attending to his religious duties, and having left everything ready for the night's work, he adjourns at 10 or 11 o'clock to return again at 7 or 8 p.m., working at high crisis until 6 a.m. When other workers are going to their places of employment, after a refreshing night's sleep, they meet the baker wending his weary way home to snatch a few hours rest.

A baker's working life meant he was 'completely cut off from all the activities of society.'

Because of the central role bread played in the city's diet, any strike would cause as great a crisis as the earlier disputes involving coalmen and gravediggers. Once the strike began the Board of Trade quickly intervened and secured agreement within the week. The employers agreed to recognise the Irish Bakers' National Amalgamated Union and to fill positions through the union's hall in Abbey Street. The possibility of eliminating night work would be examined, but not until three months after the declaration of peace.[35]

Even more serious was the railway dispute. The 'war allowance' conceded to Irish railway workers in early 1915 failed to defuse discontent, as it amounted to only half the increase conceded in England at the time. The disparity in pay continued to grow and was aggravated by the fact that English workers employed by British companies, such as the London and North-Western Railway in its Dublin port facility, were earning 10s a week more than Irish dockers for identical work. John Redmond urged the British government to provide funds for removing the anomaly, as most of the Irish railway companies could not afford to pay the increases needed to bridge the gap. The president of the Board of Trade, Lord Runciman, responded sharply that 'as the Irish railways are run for the benefit of the shareholders, the shareholders ought to pay. Any profit made by English railways at present goes to the State.'

In November Irish railway workers gave notice of a strike, although they lacked the backing of their British union, which was bound by the wartime legislation banning strikes. An offer of 2s a week from Sir William Goulding, on behalf of all the railway companies, was rejected: the men were looking for an increase of 6s a week in basic pay or a war bonus of 10s a week. The prospect of a national railway strike in the week before Christmas caused alarm throughout the country. Alfie Byrne joined Redmond in a last-minute appeal for government intervention.

Their wish was granted. The government announced on the eve of the strike that it was putting the Irish railways under the control of the military authorities. The men would receive the increases granted in England, while the companies were to be paid a dividend based on 1913 receipts for the duration of military control. It was probably the most popular decision the British government made in Ireland during the Great War, welcomed unanimously by the railway companies, the unions, the wider business community, consumers and the travelling public.[36]

Chapter 8 ∿

'WOULD ANYONE SERIOUSLY SUGGEST FOR A MOMENT THAT WILLIE COSGRAVE WAS A CRIMINAL?'

B y late 1916 Dublin Corporation had reverted to type, operating in an atmosphere in which members conducted business as they had always done, collegiality giving way to sudden storms over appointments to committees or the filling of vacant posts. The battles over who should be given a job as rate-collector or technical school instructor could often assume Homeric proportions. However, some new trends were proving irreversible, such as the dwindling support for the war and increasing antagonism towards the British authorities.

The fall-out from the death of Francis Sheehy Skeffington and other civilians, delays in the payment of compensation to owners of property destroyed in the rising and the treatment of rebel prisoners—there were city councillors in both categories—fuelled the realignment of loyalties. By contrast, there was little engagement with events on the western front, let alone in the Balkans and Middle East, except for those citizens with relations in the armed forces. As the great majority of the recruits now came from the poorest and least influential elements of the population, their opinions went largely unheeded.

Even the start of the Somme offensive on 1 July 1916 attracted relatively little attention. Never again would Dublin suffer the sort of communal shock inflicted by the news of the Dardanelles casualties a year earlier. Undeterred by recent events at home, the *Irish Times* hailed the gains claimed by the British high command in the opening days of the offensive as 'a new and glorious chapter to Irish history,' giving prominent coverage to the achievements of the 36th (Ulster) Division. 'Her young soldiers have now earned their place beside the veteran Dublins and Munsters and Inniskillings [Royal Inniskilling Fusiliers] who went through the hottest furnace of war at Helles,' the *Times* enthused. While it conceded that the 'blood of Irishmen shed by Irishmen is hardly dry on the streets of Dublin ... out there in the forefront of Ireland's and the Empire's battle the men of all our parties, all our creeds, all our social classes, are fighting side by side.' It predicted that 'no political hates or passions can survive that brotherhood of action.'

However, the activities of the 16th (Irish) Division, which also participated in the offensive, received little publicity, which further alienated nationalist opinion and diluted nationalist identification with the events in France. The offensive coincided with the publication of the report of the Royal Commission on the Rebellion in Ireland. This was highly critical of the Irish administration and in particular of the former Chief Secretary, Augustine Birrell. It also gave rise to renewed calls for a public inquiry into the murder of Francis Sheehy Skeffington and other civilians during the rising.

Most damaging of all were John Redmond's concessions to Lloyd George on partition, which were to be debated in the House of Commons that week. While the *Irish Times* celebrated the 'brotherhood of action' on the Somme, the *Irish Independent* denounced Redmond and the United Irish League for 'surrendering' the fortress of home rule, contrasting their lack of parliamentary effectiveness with Carson's resolve.

Meanwhile Dublin began to receive a new influx of wounded. These men were largely convalescent cases, shipped from hospitals in France to make way for fresh battlefield casualties. They would bring no new stories from the Somme front that might have provided some sense of immediacy and national involvement with the newspaper headlines. For most politically aware Dubliners still at liberty the continuing health and housing problems in the city, illustrated by the Baby Week conference in the Mansion House, were more pressing than the question of how many yards were won in Flanders. Otherwise any sign of returning normality was welcomed, and the news that most impressed itself at the end of the week in which the Battle of the Somme began was that Clery's department store had reopened in temporary premises at the Metropolitan Hall in Lower Abbey Street.[1]

––––

Military recruitment in Dublin virtually dried up in the aftermath of the rising. Although it revived somewhat in the summer, the total fell to 4,292 for the year, less than half the 9,612 who volunteered in 1915 and significantly less than the 7,283 who joined in the last five months of 1914. The latter figure, of course, was somewhat inflated by the recall of reservists.

Reports of hostility towards the military presence grew in the months after the rising. When the honorary colonel of the Irish Guards, Field-Marshal Kitchener, died en route to Russia, John Dillon noted in a letter to T. P. O'Connor that Dubliners 'cheered for the Kaiser and for "the torpedo that sank Kitchener".'[2] By the autumn, people were appearing regularly in the Dublin police courts for assaults on soldiers, usually the result of casual altercations in the street. When a private from the 5th Lancers was knocked down in a fight with a civilian in Wexford Street in early October, onlookers kicked him on the ground; and a military policeman escorting a drunken soldier had to be rescued from a mob by the DMP.[3]

The subscription lists for food, clothing and other aid sent to the Royal Dublin Fusiliers who were prisoners of war in Germany were almost exclusively filled by leading figures of the unionist establishment in the city. Where there were donations from groups of workers they tended to be employees of such companies as Guinness, John Jameson and Son, the Great Southern and Western Railway and the Royal Bank, whose boards of directors were dominated by unionists.[4]

Members of Dublin Corporation showed more concern for the conditions in which men interned after the rising were being kept at Fron Goch prison camp in Wales than for members of the 'Dublins' in German prison camps. Alfie Byrne, who was proving a reliable weathervane of popular sentiment, was far more vocal in calling on an American delegation visiting prisoner-of-war camps for German soldiers in Britain to add Irish rebel prisoners to their itinerary than in expressing concern about the conditions in which Irish prisoners of war were being kept in Germany. However, Byrne, who believed all politics were local, also called for separation women in Dublin to be paid the same cost-of-living allowance as their London sisters. This was passed without a vote, no doubt because the cost would be borne by the British exchequer.

It was only in 1917 that the corporation decided to set up a committee to assist invalided veterans and dependants found to be 'badly in need of assistance' in the city. The committee's main activity appeared to be lobbying the Local Government Board for funds rather than raising money itself.[5]

Unionist councillors were outraged by Byrne's concern for rebel prisoners in Britain; but there was a growing sense of impotence in their ranks. 'Volunteer', an anonymous letter-writer to the Irish Times, articulated the loyalist response to the shifting political environment. After criticising Redmond for expressing himself satisfied with the rate of recruitment to the British army, he added: 'Not only are the loyal Irish ashamed of Irish politicians but hundreds of thousands of Britishers and Colonials are beginning to look on Ireland and the Irish with contempt and disgust.' Young English men recruited to Irish regiments were arriving on Irish soil only to encounter hostility from civilians happy to have the 'bloody and brutal Saxon' fight Ireland's battles abroad.

By contrast, Father Michael Curran, private secretary to Archbishop Walsh, told a sodality meeting in October 1916 that 'those elected to represent them in

Parliament have sold them.' While he did not yet disown his own belief in constitutional politics, he had no faith in the way it had been conducted in recent years. 'The great question at the present moment is not Home Rule, but the right to preserve our young men in this country, which has been so depopulated [by the war].' It is unlikely that Curran would have made such a public statement without the sanction, if not the prompting, of Dr Walsh.

Perhaps even more telling was a letter in the *Irish Independent* from Sergeant R. Walsh of the Royal Irish Rifles, home on leave, who expressed his disgust after attending a rally in Waterford where he saw 'strapping fellows of respectable appearance pummelling and beating young girls, even if the girls were in the wrong,' for heckling Redmond as he sought to simultaneously condemn the British government's reaction to the rising and urge continuing support for the war. Sergeant Walsh added that there was plenty of fighting in Flanders for those who wanted it.[6]

The daily 'roll of honour' in the newspapers and the steady stream of casualties arriving on the hospital ships provided cogent reasons why many hesitated to volunteer, whatever their political convictions. By the end of 1916 the volume of casualties disembarking in Dublin led to sheltered gangways being built so that the wounded, and especially those who had to be brought off on stretchers, could be carried directly from the hospital ships to the ambulances without being exposed to winter weather.[7]

By early 1917 another problem threatening to overwhelm the medical services was the spread of consumption (TB) in the trenches. It was a health problem with which Dublin was very familiar. Although the rate of infection had fallen gradually over the previous decade, because of initiatives by Sir Charles Cameron and Lady Aberdeen's Women's National Health Association, it still accounted for 1,300 deaths a year in the city. Now the Soldiers' and Sailors' Help Society appealed for assistance with men being discharged with TB, much of it the result of gas poisoning. Of 1,100 disabled soldiers and sailors on the society's books in Dublin in February 1917, fewer than half had been found employment, and 114 of the 600 unable to find work had TB. The honorary secretary of the society, Miss P. A. White, told the *Irish Times*: 'That there should be a want of means to carry on this work effectively and render less intolerable the shortened lives of those who have fought for us cannot, I am sure, be the wish of their fellow countrymen.' One suspects that the appeal struck a chill chord among potential recruits.[8]

Her experience is borne out by research into First World War dead at Glasnevin Cemetery by Shane Mac Thomáis. This shows that more than half of those whose records he examined died of respiratory diseases, mainly TB and influenza, compared with fewer than one-twentieth as a result of battlefield wounds. Of course these were men who made it home to die. Like the growing number of maimed veterans who survived, they offered a warning of their possible fate to would-be recruits.[9]

Growing suspicion of the loyalty of Irish units by the military establishment must have had an even more insidious effect on recruitment. The poet Francis Ledwidge, who enlisted in 1914, told his brother that he didn't want to fight the Germans any more, even if they came into his back yard. There were increasing reports of weapons and other equipment going missing. According to F. E. Whitton, historian of the Leinster Regiment, on 4 November 1917 the Irish Volunteers brought a barge up the Grand Canal to the rear of Wellington Barracks (later Griffith Barracks, now Griffith College) on the South Circular Road, and 'every rifle' was handed through the railings and loaded onto the vessel. While this is certainly an exaggeration, the consequences were that 'the command decided they couldn't trust the Irish regiments. They brought over an English regiment to replace each Irish unit and we were put back on the boats that they came over on.'[10]

Another reason why recruitment failed to revive after 1916 was the increasing range of employment opportunities in England. Conscription had stripped vital war industries of manpower, and the shortage was so great that in September the Army Council issued a circular that migrant workers employed in those industries would be exempt from conscription. As an added safeguard, any Irish worker who obtained a job through the labour exchange system would receive a card that would be accepted as evidence by the police and military authorities that they normally resided in Ireland. The only condition was that any man losing his job must return home. Even if other work was available he would have to reapply through his labour exchange in Ireland to retain protection from conscription.

Table 7
Recruitment to British armed forces and war industries after Irish labourers given protection from conscription

	Dublin recruits to armed forces	Belfast recruits to armed forces	Dublin labourers recruited to protected jobs in British war industries	Belfast labourers recruited to protected jobs in British war industries
1917	3,089	4,452	5,023	3,173
1918 (Jan.–Nov.)	3,990	6,549	3,370	2,502

Even so, rumours abounded that 'hundreds of men' were being arrested. At Alfie Byrne's insistence, the corporation made 'an emphatic protest' to the British government at these alleged breaches of the guarantee that excluded Irish workers from the Military Service Act.[11] Some migrant workers returned anyway because of the public hostility they encountered after the rising, especially Dubliners in Liverpool and seasonal workers in Scotland.[12]

Neil O'Flanagan suggests, from an examination of labour exchange records, that between forty and fifty thousand workers, the great majority of them men, migrated to Britain for work. In December 1916, by which time the scheme providing protection from conscription was in full swing, Dublin labour exchanges were providing 30 per cent of total Irish manpower to the British war economy. In 1917 the city provided 5,023 out of 19,551 Irish workers, or 26 per cent; in 1918 it provided 3,370 out of 14,656, or 23 per cent. By contrast, there were 3,089 enlistments in 1917 and 3,990 in 1918. The increase in recruitment in 1918 is probably attributable in part to declining opportunities for war work but also to the potential new employment opportunities available to men enlisting in specialist units, such as signals, transport and the Royal Flying Corps (in 1918 reconstituted as the Royal Air Force). Here they could learn a useful trade without being shot at. There was a saying in the Dublin building trades that it was easier for a brickie's labourer to become Lord Mayor than to become a bricklayer. This nepotistic culture made access to the trades a closely guarded privilege. The British army provided an escape route from permanent membership of the ranks of the unskilled.

Another reason for the declining numbers seeking war work in Britain was that by 1918 Dublin had finally secured some war industries of its own.

It had been a long struggle. Unlike Belfast, there was little in the way of industry suitable for conversion to war work in 1914. As late as 1917 pressure was being exerted by labour exchanges on unemployed workers to accept jobs in Britain. In December 1916 the Dublin Trades Council complained that unemployed craft workers were being denied benefit unless they were willing to work in war industries as labourers.[13]

The obvious question was why Dublin did not get its 'fair share' of war industries. A number of enthusiasts, including the economist E. J. Riordan, involved themselves in the All-Ireland Munitions Committee but found it as difficult to arouse Irish manufacturers to exploit opportunities as it was for the War Office to offer them. When a conference was organised for saddlery and harness firms in Dublin in September 1914 only seven out of a possible twenty companies attended. All seven landed lucrative contracts.

Another problem was that Irish samples and supplies had to be sent to Britain, adding to transport and marketing costs. The Dublin Chamber of Commerce raised the matter with the War Office in March 1915, but progress was slow, and the chamber itself did not establish an Armaments Committee to lobby for war contracts until June 1915.[14] A samples depot was not established until December 1916, operating from the Irish War Office in Dawson Street; a receiving depot for Irish war supplies did not materialise in Dublin until the war was nearly over, in October 1918.

The Minister of Munitions, David Lloyd George, was far more dynamic in providing war work for Dublin—in the shape of a munitions factory—than Irish businesses were in seeking it out, making a commitment to build a munitions factory even before he met a deputation from the Dublin Armaments Committee headed by Patrick Leonard, president of the chamber of commerce, in March 1916.[15] Nor did he allow the rising to disrupt his production schedule. By June 1916 the large-scale production of 9.2-inch shells and fuses had begun at the National Shell Factory in Parkgate Street. In August the committee was informed that full production would be achieved by October. In September the Ministry of Munitions established a branch office in Dublin to co-ordinate Irish production, and the plant was meeting its initial targets shortly afterwards. The Dublin Munitions Committee now concluded that its services were no longer required, and remaining funds were used to meet the expenses of the members.

It appears that poor local management ability was a more significant problem for the minister than the rebels. Two English inspectors reported that Irish factories were poorly run and, unlike their British counterparts, could not be adapted to post-war production. As Neil O'Flanagan has pointed out, 'the replacement of the management ... by directors sent over from England added salt to the wounds.'

Nevertheless the factories provided a much-needed boost to the local economy. By March 1919 the National Shell Factory in Dublin had manufactured half a million shells, worth £569,000, and fuses worth another £98,000. It accounted for 80 per cent of all munitions produced in Irish shell factories and employed the largest proportion of their 2,148 workers, the great majority of them women.[16]

The other bright spot on the horizon was the Dublin Dockyard Company, run by two Scottish shipbuilders, Walter Scott and John Smellie.[17] The Dublin Trades Council and the newly constituted Dublin Port and Docks Board supported the establishment of the business in 1901, both bodies being keen to promote desperately needed local employment. A wise decision to agree Glasgow rates with the unions provided a ready-made formula for pay adjustments that secured industrial peace for many years.

At first the yard provided a ship repair and overhaul service for the seven thousand vessels using the port each year. Later it began to build small to medium-sized steamers, including the fishery protection vessel *Helga*, converted for anti-submarine warfare after the war began but best remembered as the gunboat sent up the Liffey to shell Liberty Hall during the Easter Rising.[18] With the outbreak of war the yard's owners displayed characteristic commercial acumen by securing one of the first war contracts, on 23 September 1914. It was for the repair of Royal Navy ships and any other vessels designated by the Admiralty. Trawler patrol escorts, minesweepers, destroyers, submarines and troop transports were among the vessels serviced, and the yard expanded into supplying and fitting gun platforms, guns, wireless cabins, submarine direction-finders, minelaying appliances, depth-charge throwers, paravanes (for deflecting mines from the hulls of vessels) and battle practice targets.

Shipping losses proved good news for the yard. The Dublin Port and Docks Board provided extra workshop space and water frontage for the creation of two new building berths. This allowed the Dublin Dockyard Company to supply high-demand vessels of 3,000 to 5,000 tons to the Ministry of Shipping. The move was not without its opponents. Representatives of the shipping industry on the board strongly opposed handing over the facilities, leading to accusations from public representatives across the political spectrum that vested interests wanted to keep out competition.

The trades council threw its weight behind the proposal 'to grant these facilities to an industry of so great an importance to Dublin and Ireland.' The position of the shipping companies and brokers was ultimately untenable in a situation where the shortage of shipping was choking the commercial life of the city, as well as preventing the creation of badly needed jobs.[19] Once the opposition was overcome, the yard's expansion in 1917 was so successful that the company had one of its vessels, the c5 collier, adopted by the Admiralty as a standard model for other yards.[20] The firm also diversified into munitions through its subsidiary, Dublin Dockyard War Munitions Company, which produced 50,000 shells for the British army's eighteen-pounder guns.

The company gave the same care and attention to recruitment, working conditions and staff relations as it did to everything else. Within a month of the start of the war it introduced a levy on employees for the Prince of Wales National Relief Fund. This fund was established to channel all charitable donations for relieving distress into one central agency. According to Smellie, employees agreed unanimously to contribute to the fund. The amounts varied from 6d to 1s a week, depending on earnings. In some instances, where men were heavily dependent on piece work, the contribution amounted to 2½ per cent of earnings. The readiness of employees to contribute was probably due in part to supervision by a committee on which all the shipyard trades were represented. Even members of the IRB, Irish Volunteers and Citizen Army, who worked in the yard in significant numbers (and used the facilities to secretly manufacture munitions), would not have wanted to appear mean. There were also significant numbers of skilled workers from Belfast and British yards. Nor did political allegiances overrule financial sense: three times as much was subscribed by employees to war bond schemes as for relief.[21]

The Dublin Dockyard Company's decision to branch out into munitions preceded the establishment of the National Shell Factory; but there was plenty of work to go round. Smellie wrote later in his history of the yard: 'It was determined to make the factory a model one ... and with this in view visits were made to several private plants in England ... and the best features of each incorporated in the designs.' The factory was built of wood, 'with a saw-tooth roof admitting abundance of light.' The machines were laid out in rows, with wide corridors to allow easy and rapid movement of the raw materials as they were transformed from steel bars into shells.

However, 'the getting of suitable girl labour appeared in the early stages to be a difficulty of some moment, as the contract with the Ministry of Munitions permitted only 5 per cent of the total staff to be men or boys, and included in this ... were shift foremen, tool setters, tool makers and any other male labour.' Although Dublin lacked the large reservoirs of female factory labour available in British cities, the misgivings proved groundless.

> The 200 girls employed soon became highly efficient, and were quick in adapting themselves to machine work, and to all the engineering operations of shell turning, including working to gauge limits of but one or two thousandths of an inch. It was perfectly amazing to note with what deftness of hand and eye a cut was made so accurate in judgement as to satisfy forthwith the limit gauges without resort to the usual trial and error process of cut upon cut.

The first batch of 'a dozen chosen young ladies' was sent to the Vickers plant at Barrow-in-Furness for six weeks' instruction, then returned to train the rest of the workers. Soon productivity was so high that the output was three thousand shells per week rather than the two thousand guaranteed by the machine manufacturers. To achieve this target the women worked alternate twelve-hour shifts on piece-work rates that maximised output, and they were not likely to strike.[22]

Despite the efforts of men like Smellie, the Dublin munitions factories failed to keep pace with best practice as advised by the Health Committee of the Ministry of Munitions. Experience showed that twelve-hour shifts lowered productivity and caused increased sickness and absenteeism, as well as putting 'severe mental strain' on managerial staff. Workers on long shifts also experienced an 'increased temptation to indulge in the consumption of alcohol.'

Of course the Irish industry was much smaller than its British counterpart, and the women lived locally, unlike Britain, where they often spent up to five hours commuting. Nor do the Dublin factories appear to have experienced the same wide social mix as the British work force, which listed in its ranks 'dress makers, laundry workers, textile workers, domestic servants, clerical workers, shop assistants, university and art students—women and girls in fact of every social grade,' although one group that was given preferential treatment in Dublin when it came to recruitment was soldiers' dependants, especially wives and widows.[23]

Far from flocking to the National Shell Factories to seek gainful employment, many middle-class Dublin women devoted themselves to charitable war work organised by the Irish Munitions Workers' Canteen Committee; apparently the social stigma of factory work outweighed the lucrative earnings. The Canteen Committee provided subsidised meals in the Dublin Dockyard and National Shell factories. In the canteens every worker received a free cup of tea and bun at the start of each shift. Items such as tea, coffee, cocoa, sandwiches and sausage rolls cost 1d, while a freshly cooked salmon served on a plate with fresh vegetables cost 5d. The social work model in the factories was based on the British system. This relied on Voluntary Aid Detachment networks and 'knitters', who operated under Mrs Hignett, the head knitter for Dublin, who had been trained personally in England by Lady Lawrence, founder of the movement. The planning was meticulous. Based on a realisation that providing subsidised meals helped raise morale as well as reducing the absenteeism caused by malnourishment and associated health problems, it provided useful war work for VAD volunteers who lacked the skills needed for other roles.

The committees of 'knitters' did everything possible to make the munitions workers' dinner hour 'jolly', the Women's Work columnist of the *Irish Times* reported. Before they had finished their meal the workers would be

waiting to hear the news read to them. They always clamoured for this and then listened to the gramophone or sang and danced before filing back to their war work. At tea time they were back for half an hour and it seemed no time again, so crowded with work were the hours for the canteen workers before the hot supper was ready for the new hundreds on the night shift, every one of whom knew the mighty difference between all night work on a parcel of food eaten 'where they could' and this new regime in which delicious meals served by devoted women in attractive canteens serve to break up the hours of hard munitions work ... The steaming food, the flowers, the dance, the gramophone, and the rest when necessary, all combined to vastly increase the output of shells and cartridges. If any ladies seek employment at war work of a wholesome and ennobling character they cannot do better than enrol in Mrs. Hignett's army of workers.[24]

However, Lady Lawrence's 'knitters' would give way to a more professional approach as full-time welfare superintendents and paid catering staff took over the task of feeding the workers. This new system had been piloted in British munitions factories and was found to be superior to the voluntary networks, although they continued to exist.

The superintendent appointed in Parkgate Street was Margaret Culhane, a sister of Hanna Sheehy Skeffington. When objections were raised in the House of Commons to her appointment, the Parliamentary Secretary to Lloyd George,

Worthington Evans, told members that the appointment of professional social workers and managers such as Mrs Culhane was done through the proper procedures and had led to significant improvements on the voluntary system it had replaced.[25]

By early 1917 four-fifths of the munitions workers in the Dublin Dockyard were female; but this revolution in employment appears to have passed the city fathers by.[26] They remained preoccupied with the rapidly changing political situation rather than the feminisation of industry. Concern over the fate of fellow-members and employees of the corporation imprisoned as a result of the rising or who had lost their job as a result of the carnage provided a humanitarian issue on which councillors could unite without having to take positions on the war. In October it was agreed to compensate workers who had lost their employment because of the rising, although the hope was also expressed that the sums to meet this generous policy could be secured from the British exchequer.

The corporation responded sympathetically to a request from the Irish National Aid Association that city employees interned for their part in the rising should retain their positions. No doubt it helped that one of the honorary secretaries of the association, Fred Allan, was also secretary to the corporation as well as a former secretary of the Supreme Council of the IRB. Alfie Byrne went a step further and proposed that the corporation call upon 'the Irish nation ... [to] unite in demanding the release of our fellow countrymen and women interned in English prisons without trial' and for 'an amnesty for those who have been sentenced to terms of imprisonment,' pending which they should be given the status of political prisoners. The motion was seconded by Michael Brohoon, a Labour councillor. Not only did the corporation overwhelmingly support it but councillors agreed to having a representative from each ward actively campaign to establish an all-Ireland convention with various national and labour bodies to establish a Political Prisoners' Amnesty Association.

The same meeting adopted another motion from Byrne condemning conscription, seconded by the recently released Alderman Tom Kelly of Sinn Féin.[27]

The threats posed by the war to public morality were never far from the thoughts of the councillors, or indeed of many respectable Dubliners brought up in an environment of Victorian rectitude. When representatives of the Vigilance Association attended a corporation meeting in October 1916 their views were given careful consideration. A Catholic body, its deputation was headed by Canon Dunne, president of Holy Cross College and a close friend of Archbishop Walsh. Representatives of the Irish National Foresters, AOH and many Catholic sodalities in the city accompanied the canon to express concern at the lack of adequate supervision in cinemas. Their view was shared by the Juvenile Advisory Committee of the Board of Trade Labour Exchange in Lord Edward Street. It wrote separately to the corporation, alerting councillors to the dangers facing idle adolescents who ventured into 'certain censored films' in any of the city's twenty-six picture houses.

The Cinematograph Act (1909) provided for the appointment of censors and inspectors, but the corporation had never appointed any. The earliest it could now do so would be 1917, because, as the law agent, Ignatius Rice, pointed out, it would be illegal in 1916, as no funds had been voted for the purpose. The speed of the councillors' response suggests that the lobbying power of Canon Dunne and his constituency was considerable. While powerless to finance the appointment of inspectors until 1917, the corporation readily agreed to reject an application for picture houses to be opened at 8 p.m. on Sundays rather than 8:30 p.m. It was feared that the earlier opening time could distract the faithful from evening devotions.

In October it also appointed two honorary censors, Eugene McGough JP, a gentleman 'of independent means and education,' and A. J. Murray, headmaster of the Central Model School. Both men would still be acting in an unpaid capacity in 1920, when they requested £78 each to cover expenses for the previous three years.[28] Two honorary lady inspectors, Mrs E. M. Smith and Mrs A. O'Brien, were recruited in early 1917, when a paid corporation employee, Walter Butler, took overall charge. The 'honorary' was a courtesy title, as both women were full-time sanitary inspectors and monitored cinemas as an additional duty. Nor did it mean a pay increase, although their salaries were between £20 and £25 a year less than those of their male counterparts.[29]

The first complaint Walter Butler had to deal with was in early 1917 when a Mr M. J. Barry complained about an 'impure, filthy poster' exhibited by the Carlton Cinema in Upper Sackville Street for a film entitled *The Circus of Death*. 'For sheer audacious and suggestive indecency,' Barry said, it 'had never been surpassed in his experience.' Butler disagreed and found nothing indecent in the poster. Regrettably, no copies appear to have survived.

The emphasis in early inspections was more on safety regulations in cinemas and theatres than on the performances, in ensuring that panic bolts were installed on exit doors and that cinemas adhered to licensed opening hours, especially on Sundays. However, the Dublin Vigilance Committee was soon active again, supplemented by the activities of a Morality Sub-committee of a self-appointed Dublin Watch Committee. This group lodged a complaint about a play entitled *Five Nights*, written by 'Victoria Cross' and performed at the Gaiety Theatre in July

1918. Dublin audiences were spared the film version, which had been banned in some British cities. Charles Eason first raised the matter after refusing to print or distribute advertising material. The controversy was sufficient to persuade the Under-Secretary, James McMahon, to ask the Commissioner of the DMP to investigate, and the manager of the Gaiety was warned that 'if anything grossly immoral were to be shewn in the play' he could lose his licence.

But no action was taken. According to the theatre critic of the *Irish Independent*, the leading man in the play was an artist who 'talks tosh, paints pictures and messes about with his models.' He 'strains after witticisms about models being scarce owing to girls with looks and no brains being employed on Government service.' The female lead is his cousin, who composes 'weird music. Being endowed with the "artistic soul," they feel they are above and beyond all other mere people and must act differently.'[30]

One probable source of irritation was the popularity of the play with British officers. Soldiers generally were great patrons of the theatres and music halls. This could pose problems, as the DMP was responsible for 'policing immorality' in these establishments as far as civilians were concerned but the War Office dealt with military personnel. Much of the material Dubliners found morally objectionable not alone had the blessing of the War Office but was sometimes commissioned by it to boost the morale of the soldiers.

Censorship in the cinemas was less of a problem. This was the beginning of cinema's great era of expansion. When the censorship regime came in there were twenty-two cinemas in the city, including the 'picture houses' that were now being built, as well as theatres that occasionally showed films, such as the Gaiety Theatre and Theatre Royal. Films featured daily as part of the Theatre Royal's variety programme.[31]

One of the few cinemas to fail was the Volta in Mary Street, once managed by James Joyce, in a converted builders' supplies and ironmongery premises. It could not compete with purpose-built new entrants to the market or, apparently, observe safety regulations and control its patrons. On 18 July 1918 there was a complaint that when patrons rushed to the exits after a fire scare they found them padlocked. In his defence the managing director claimed that on the night in question

> about 100 persons had rushed in without paying and one of these shouted "fire" … The operator immediately stopped showing the film and switched on the lights. No one was injured.

Surprisingly, no fine was imposed, although cinemas were regularly fined from £1 to £20 over inadequate access to exits.[32]

1918 was the first full year in which cinemas were monitored. Butler and Smith made 393 inspections of premises, and they or the voluntary censors viewed 707 films. Of these, 600 were approved without changes, 55 were banned 'on account of their immoral tone or suggestions of evil,' and 52 were passed after excisions were made 'to render them free from objection.'

———

What effect the production of lewd cinema posters or films had on republican prisoners being released from British prisons does not appear to have been recorded in any memoirs of the period. It was just before Christmas 1916, the eve of the censorship era, when the British government released a large number of internees, including the Labour councillor P. T. Daly.

Two Sinn Féin councillors, Seán T. O'Kelly (or Seán T. Ó Ceallaigh, as he now became) and W. T. Cosgrave, were less fortunate, as was Daly's Labour colleague William Partridge. Ó Ceallaigh took the trouble to write from Reading Prison, explaining that it was not for lack of interest that he was absent from meetings. Ó Ceallaigh, Cosgrave and Partridge, unlike Daly, had been tried and sentenced for their part in the rising and not merely interned.

Lieutenant Cosgrave, the man who had identified the Nurses' Home as the key to the defence of the South Dublin Union, had been sentenced to death, only to have his court-martial recommend a reprieve because he seemed 'a decent man' who had been 'rushed into this.' In January 1917 a corporation motion calling for his release asked rhetorically, 'Would anyone seriously suggest for a moment that Willie Cosgrave was a criminal?'[33] Councillors expressed no opinion of the character of Captain William Patrick Partridge of the Irish Citizen Army, who had been condemned to fifteen years' penal servitude, commuted to ten years.

Undeterred by government policy, or the law, Dublin Corporation members unanimously co-opted the three imprisoned councillors in January 1917, thus making good the vacancies created by their enforced absence. This action was in marked contrast to the way in which the vacancy created by the death of the unionist councillor John Thornton had been dealt with the previous June, when the seat had been hijacked by a nationalist nominee.

The act was purely symbolic in Partridge's case. He contracted Bright's disease (nephritis) and was released from prison on 20 April 1917. Too ill to resume political or trade union work, he returned to his native Ballaghaderreen, Co. Mayo, where he died of a heart attack in July.[34]

———

While councillors thumbed their noses at the laws governing their own proceedings, held open jobs for rebel prisoners (as they did for employees serving with the Crown forces) and routinely condemned British oppression, the state they saw as the embodiment of foreign tyranny was finding it very hard to sack its own employees suspected of rebel activities. Dealing with subversion, even in a time of war and rebellion, was constrained by the snares of legality, not to mention uncertain guidance from above as well as resistance from employees and nationalist and labour organisations from below. A good example was provided by the case of Patrick Belton, an employee of the Land Commission, who went on to enjoy a colourful career in Sinn Féin, Fianna Fáil, the Centre Party and finally Fine Gael.

After the rising the government established a committee under Lord Justice Sankey to investigate the cases of some 1,800 detainees and other suspects. These included 90 civil servants, half of them employees of the Post Office. It was a cursory trawl, and subsequently Sir William Byrne, an English Catholic recently appointed Assistant Under-Secretary, and another career civil servant, Sir Guy Fleetwood Wilson, conducted a discreet investigation into those 'civil servants who have been suspended from their duties owing to their suspected complicity with the recent Rebellion.' Because of the increasing public hostility to British rule and its agents, the two men adopted a low profile, taking private rooms in Hume Street to conduct interviews rather than using Dublin Castle. They also indicated to departmental heads that they intended recommending whenever possible the reinstatement of civil servants who had been arrested or suspended. They later declared themselves appalled at the advanced views expressed unapologetically by many of those interviewed. One man, who openly admitted participating in the rising, demanded that he be reinstated because circumstances had not allowed him to shoot any British soldiers.

Of the 42 people examined, 23 were dismissed, 1 pensioned off and 18 reinstated. The most senior civil servant dismissed was J. J. McElligott, a first-class clerk who had fought in the GPO and later had a distinguished career in the Free State civil service.[35] In contrast, Belton was only an assistant clerk and does not appear to have participated in the rising, possibly because he feared that it might lead to dismissal and he had a young family to feed. But he was a member of the IRB and has been credited with helping to bring Michael Collins into the organisation when they were both young emigrants in London.[36] His suspected association with the rebels was first brought to the attention of his employer by the RIC. The local sergeant in Finglas reported seeing Belton 'marching' towards his home, Ashgrove House, in the company of four armed Volunteers on 25 April 1916. The Volunteers were encamped in a field nearby. Ordered to investigate further, the sergeant wrote back that a member of the local branch of the National Volunteers told him that Belton spoke 'in a very derisive manner' about their own lack of activity and said, 'Now we are going to get some of our own back.'

While Belton was seen visiting the rebel encampment there was no evidence that he himself carried arms or wore a uniform. The sergeant admitted that the evidence was 'meagre' and that Belton had not previously come to the attention of the police. 'But from what I hear recently I believe he is a dangerous man and one who would cause dissension so long as he could keep out of the conflict himself,' the sergeant commented in a note to his superior at district headquarters in Howth.

On receiving the police reports, by way of Dublin Castle, Belton's superiors in the Land Commission ordered him to account for himself during Easter Week. He duly did so in a written statement. He told the commission he spent the Saturday afternoon working in the garden. On Sunday he walked into town 'for papers' after 8:30 mass in Finglas. On Easter Monday he

> took a message from my wife to Miss Quin's Hospital, 27 Mountjoy Square. Cycled round by Pillar and found that rioting had broken out. Then I went home and walked into town in evening for news, food, tobacco &c. Sojourned in my own house.

On the Tuesday he 'came into town for news, went home and worked in the garden.' On Wednesday,

> friends en route to Cork from London called and remained for a couple of days. They were anxious about their brother in 10th Dublin's whom they believed was in a Barracks convenient to the Park. I went in direction of Park to make inquiries of military, but there was heavy firing in that direction and I came home and sojourned in my own house.

On Thursday, Belton 'heard there was fighting beyond Finglas & cycled out to inquire so that in case of danger I would remove my family to friends in Clonee.' On Friday he 'cycled out on same errand and heard there was firing at Ashbourne.' He returned home and 'sojourned' there once more.

On Saturday, the last day of the fighting in Dublin, he said he went into the city and arranged for a messenger boy to deliver flour to his home from the North City Mills. On Sunday he was once more drawn towards Ashbourne. 'Cycled out to ascertain if the fighting was coming near Finglas and was held on road by Volunteer Sentry and Police Officers who informed me all was over.' Sunday was spent, as it must have been for countless civilians, seeking food, tobacco and other essentials in the city.

Belton's account, given on 5 May, was probably not very different from those that could have been given by most contemporaries. But it could equally cover a multitude of subversive activities; and, unlike McElligott, Belton had no intention of making his dismissal easy for his employers.

Now that he had come to the attention of the authorities, Belton was kept under observation, and in July the RIC in Limerick and in Finglas, and the head of British military intelligence, Major Ivor Price, were reporting that Belton was collecting substantial sums for prisoners on behalf of the National Aid Association. All of this was regarded as 'unseemly' on the part of a government employee, and the Chief Secretary's Office demanded that action be taken.

The Land Commission said it had no information on the aims of the National Aid Association; the police admitted that those collecting the money were not in Sinn Féin; and, crucially, there was nothing in any of the police reports to suggest 'that Mr. Belton is guilty of complicity in the late rebellion.' In fact the commission wrote to the National Aid Association and received a reply that it had no information on Belton, and had not received the funds referred to. This was being somewhat economical with the truth, as Belton was a member of the association's executive committee and had certainly been fund-raising for it.[37]

The commission also consulted the Lords Justices but was informed that 'their Excellencies do not propose to give any directions in the matter, which is one resting directly with the responsible Heads of the Department.' The commission conceded in a letter to the Chief Secretary in September that while Belton 'no doubt ... would have sympathy for the dependants of those who were killed on the rebel side' he was being recommended by the investigating commission for reinstatement. 'I think the matter may be allowed to drop,' the head of the commission added.

It was far from the end of the matter. By April 1917 Belton was reported to be addressing Sinn Féin meetings in his native Co. Longford during the by-election that saw a rebel prisoner, Joe McGuinness, elected to the House of Commons. Belton was reported to have boasted that he had taken part in the rising. Confronted with the allegation, he admitted speaking at the meeting but claimed he spoke only on the division of a neighbour's farm in which he had an interest.

It took until September for him to receive a formal warning to be more circumspect in his public activities. The saga would continue. For the moment, security agents of the state, such as Major Price, could only fulminate that 'it is not healthy for Govt. officials to identify themselves with such things.'[38]

———

Drift seemed the order of the day. A good example was the electricity supply situation in the city. In August 1915 the corporation established a sub-committee to see if savings could be made, given the high price of coal and difficulties in obtaining supplies from Britain. A consultant engineer, Patrick Walter D'Alton, a retired British army lieutenant-colonel, was commissioned to undertake the task. He completed his report by the following February and put down much of the delay to difficulties in obtaining wattmeter certificates from the Electricity Supply Department. When he did receive them he found a deviation of 511,000 units between the records of the Pigeon House power station and the official returns to the corporation. He described some of the measuring equipment readings as 'worthless and misleading.' He also warned that the anticipated winter load for

1916/17 would require 'all your generating sets to be placed in a condition of perfect order during the spring and early summer of 1916,' and required the acquisition of a new turbo alternator if resources permitted. Among the changes he advocated were

(1) a reduction in administrative overheads: the present system was 'unduly complicated as a result of ... dual control by an Engineer who is not a manager and a Secretary who is part manager'; he suggested devolving more managerial functions on the engineer;

(2) reducing the load factor on the overworked and partly outdated equipment;

(3) reducing charges to private customers;

(4) reducing the number of manual and clerical workers but not the professional engineering staff;

(5) transferring members of the outdoor staff, such as canvassers for new business and meter-readers, to the Secretarial Department;

(6) ending the monopoly of the Scottish coal supplier and ensuring greater consistency in the quality of fuel (the calorific value of the coal varied from 10,500 to 12,5000 BTU per ton, which was bad for the boilers as well as poor value for money);

(7) investing more capital in generation plant and expanding the generation and distribution system in the coming year;

(8) cleaning, overhauling, repairing and recalibrating equipment more regularly;

(9) using 'obsolete' Stewart engines only in emergencies, as they made 'extravagant use of fuel.'

Even the 'excellent' Oerlikon turbines 'need to be kept under close observation,' D'Alton warned.

The problem with his report, like that of the Local Government Board on the housing crisis in 1914, was that it was so universal in its condemnation of the system that it united the entire municipal establishment against him. When Dublin's electrical engineer, Mark Ruddle, was asked to respond, he rejected practically all D'Alton's criticisms out of hand. They took no account of the 'special difficulties' under which Dublin laboured, such as distance from coal supplies and a smaller population than comparators cited, such as the London power stations. While Ruddle attributed the high cost of private consumption to the cost of fuel compared with Britain, his own figures showed that householders were subsidising business on a large scale. In the year ending March 1915 private consumers used 53 per cent of all power but contributed 78 per cent of income (£72,300).

Ruddle firmly rejected claims of overstaffing. The wage figure of £12,000 cited by D'Alton included £5,212 spent on capital works and £1,174 for work carried out by the staff of the Electricity Supply Committee on behalf of other sections of the corporation. Ruddle could also point to high interest rates as a justification for not being able to invest in new equipment. In a general defence of the existing regime he gave a potted history of the city's electricity grid, pointing out that its capacity had increased from the equivalent of 1,000 lamps in 1891 to 600,000. Capital invested had risen from an initial £37,000 to £857,000, and income from £5,600 to over £100,000. The cost of generation and distribution had fallen from 2.43d per unit in 1904 to 1.27d in 1915 and, despite the increases in coal bills caused by the war, had been contained at 1.4d in 1916. These improvements were reflected in the financial performance of the committee. A deficit of £12,500 in 1914 had been converted into a surplus of £11,670 in 1915, and the electricity enterprise was still in surplus by £8,840 in 1916.

Ruddle had been with the enterprise from the start and had been appointed city electrical engineer in 1904. He was there long enough to accumulate many allies, including Fred Allan, secretary of the corporation, and Laurence Kettle, city treasurer, who was responsible for the administration of the electricity scheme that D'Alton found so little favour with.

Although the corporation had itself commissioned D'Alton to investigate the electricity generation and distribution system, members could not agree on how to proceed. Suggestions that D'Alton might take over were quickly dismissed. On several occasions a motion was proposed 'to achieve the results which Mr D'Alton has outlined in his report' by giving Ruddle 'entire charge' of the commercial side of the business as well as the engineering section for a trial period of two years. The former Lord Mayor Lorcan Sherlock objected, on the grounds that there was little point in asking Ruddle to implement D'Alton's proposals when he had characterised them in his own report as 'ignorant views, unfounded opinions, stupid suggestions and impossible of realisation.' A compromise proposal that Ruddle be appointed general manager, that Laurence Kettle replace him as chief electrical engineer and that Fred Allan be appointed commercial manager made even less sense. In the end little was done until Kettle succeeded Ruddle in April 1919, when the latter retired because of ill-health.[39]

The controversy certainly took its toll on Ruddle. At a meeting of the Electricity Supply Committee in September 1917 he was accused of manipulating overtime and other payments to favour fellow-members of his 'lodge'. Ruddle felt compelled to state publicly that he was 'not a member of any lodge, whether Masonic, Orange, Hibernian, or Sinn Fein.' The allegations probably said more about municipal politics than about Ruddle's affiliation, which appears to have been Redmondite, like most senior officials. He added to his statement the intriguing postscript that he had 'never been threatened by any members of his staff, either in or out of his office.'[40]

One of his last public acts was to contribute a guinea (£1 1s) to the subscription list for building a memorial to Tom Kettle and his father, Andrew, a veteran Land

Leaguer, who had died within a few weeks of each other in 1916. The Laurence Kettle who replaced Ruddle was another son of Andrew Kettle. Ruddle did not enjoy his retirement for long, dying four months later.

Chapter 9 ∽

'THE BABY WAS THEN NINE OR TEN DAYS OLD, AND THE GIRL SAID THAT SHE WOULD DROWN IT'

The first formal sign that the traditional dominance of the United Irish League in Dublin civic politics was coming to an end was the election of the maverick nationalist councillor Laurence O'Neill, unopposed, as Lord Mayor on 24 January 1917. The establishment nationalist figure, Sir Patrick Shortall, freshly knighted for his services to the war effort, withdrew his nomination. O'Neill had been among those arrested briefly as a suspected rebel after the rising. In his election speech he compared his fate a few months previously as a prisoner 'marched between a company of soldiers with fixed bayonets' with his elevation to first citizen of Dublin. It was the template for many more illustrious political careers to come.

While O'Neill attributed his past relative obscurity to the fact that he 'took a little interest in the uplifting of the poor class of worker in the city,' he was in fact an auctioneer, property-owner and even slum landlord in a small way. His proposer, Alderman Patrick Corrigan, was an undertaker and a slum landlord in a large way; his seconder, Councillor McAvin, was a bakery-owner. Meanwhile O'Neill's predecessor, Sir James Gallagher, the saviour of Grafton Street, was lucky to scrape the traditional vote of thanks by 24 votes to 19 after being denounced as the 'embodiment of British rule in Ireland' by Alderman Tom Kelly.[1]

The shifting sentiment had less impact when it came to hard shillings-and-pence issues, as the bitter battle over the widening of North Earl Street showed. The damage caused during the rising provided an opportunity to widen the thoroughfare, but this was fiercely resisted by owners who would lose frontage as a result. Sir Joseph Downes, 'Lord Barmbrack', was the largest landlord affected, and he used his position as a councillor to fight the British government for every square inch as fiercely as any Prussian. He argued, with some legitimacy, that the best shopping streets in Dublin were narrow ones, such as Henry Street, Grafton Street and, of course, North Earl Street. He had some initial success lobbying his fellow-members, and threatened to sue for £50,000 compensation if the authorities tried to widen the street by more than three feet, even though he was being offered compensatory space at the rear. Eventually a compulsory purchase order was used and the street was widened by 14 feet, rather than the 30 feet envisaged in the original proposal. Sir Joseph Downes and his neighbour, the vintner Philip Meagher, received £33,150 between them, or half the £66,000 paid out in the first tranche of payments to landlords.[2]

It is no wonder that small traders, such as Repetto Byrne, could complain at a meeting of the Property Owners' Association in August that 'the big dogs have all been very well paid but nobody seems to care about the poorer owners.' Their anger was all the more understandable given that in many cases they had lost not only their business but their home.

One 'big dog,' T. Stafford O'Farrell, went so far as to propose that ratepayers would be better served if the government bypassed small leaseholders and bought the damaged sites outright from the owners at pre-rebellion values. Many of these small leaseholders were under-insured, or not insured at all, as well as homeless, making them totally dependent on compensation from the government and the corporation. Some were paying interest on loans to tide them over, which they wanted factored in to the compensation. However, the British government was reluctant to consider any claims for losses other than those directly linked to military activity. Even looting and fire damage were omitted from the terms of reference.

Issues such as bank interest charges and notional lost business were a slippery slope, as claims from the railway companies showed. The Midland Great Western Railway had suffered damage amounting to less than £700 but claimed £20,000 in lost income. The Dublin and South-Eastern Railway was by far the hardest hit, as the rebels had occupied all three of its termini: Wexford, Harcourt Street and Westland Row. It suffered damage amounting to £2,000 as a consequence, particularly through the occupation and desultory fighting around Westland Row, which was out of action from 24 April until 3 May. The company also claimed £14,000 in lost income. The Great Southern and Western Railway suffered relatively little damage directly attributable to the rising but claimed £21,000 in lost income.[3]

It was not until December 1917 that the claims were settled. The MGWR received £10,525, the GSWR £8,543 and the DSER £11,937.[4] By then the British government had taken over control of Ireland's railway network. Ironically, this move, which was to pre-empt the threatened strike in December 1916, had been welcomed by the Irish stock market, which feared that the companies would be sunk by inadequate compensation for the losses incurred during the rising.[5]

The churches, which were among the largest landowners in the city, came out of the rising almost unscathed. The only religious building destroyed was the Presbyterian church in Lower Abbey Street. The General Assembly received £1,150 in compensation and a rebuilding grant of £8,700, plus £2,000 for other property damaged in the city.[6]

One enterprise that did exceptionally well out of the compensation scheme was the *Freeman's Journal*, mouthpiece of the Irish Party. It claimed £74,000, although it was insured for only £32,000. In contrast to its treatment of other claimants, the Defence of the Realm Property Losses Committee made an award of £60,000. The rival *Irish Independent* complained that much of the stock on which the *Freeman's Journal* received compensation, including Linotype machines, vans and horses, was obsolete or had not been lost at all. In fact the paper's premises were badly damaged, and all the Linotype machines destroyed. Whether it was obsolete or not, such equipment was extremely expensive to replace. The paper's ledgers were also destroyed. By June 1917 a modest £800 in funds before the rising had been transformed into a £20,000 overdraft.

Despite the generosity of the exchequer, the *Freeman's Journal* would never again pose a serious threat to the Murphy empire. It passed under new ownership in 1919 and adopted a militant nationalist stance more in keeping with public opinion. Eventually the title was acquired by the Independent group, and it ceased publication in 1924.[7]

――――

The families of civilians killed in the fighting did not fare nearly so well as big business. There were only 450 claims, as opposed to more than 820 from property-owners. There were a little more than sixty awards, and the Dublin Victims Committee was initially restricted to considering cases where the main breadwinner in a household, usually the father, had been killed or seriously injured.

The rates of payment were based on the Workmen's Compensation Act (1906), which covered death and injury at work. Like the act, the scheme applied to those earning no more than £250 a year. There were a handful of cases where claims were based on earnings over this amount, but almost all failed. The largest claim was for £5,216 13s 4d, made by Mrs John Murphy of Delgany, who claimed that her husband earned £360 a year. Unfortunately, all his financial records perished with him in the fire that consumed his offices in the city centre. The committee rejected his widow's claim in the absence of proof of earnings.[8]

The committee did try to apply some flexibility and compassion, but it was confounded by the Irish Treasury and its Remembrancer, Maurice Headlam. He in turn was backed by the new Assistant Under-Secretary, John Taylor.[9] Both men acted as if public funds were their own, except when pressing their own claims. Taylor, in particular, felt that his services were grossly undervalued.[10]

The secretary of the committee, Hugh Love, did succeed in persuading the Treasury to widen its terms of reference so that some payment might be made to parents for the loss of a child, or to a husband for the loss of a wife.

> The loss of a wife represents a considerable pecuniary loss, in view of the fact that the wife acted as an unpaid housekeeper; and where there are young children this loss is increased seeing that some other guardian for them must be provided.

Love's argument prevailed more in principle than in practice. For instance, in four cases where the committee awarded £25 to parents for the death of children aged between three and fourteen the Treasury reduced the amount involved to £10. In four cases where awards of £50 were made to husbands who had lost a wife who was not a breadwinner the Treasury similarly reduced the awards to £10 each. However, it made no reductions in five other cases where parents were awarded £50 each for the loss of children 'who were earning.'

In truth, the sheer variety and complexity of cases would have tried the most compassionate of committees. A case in point is that of Kate Golding, a widow in Longford Street, who claimed first for herself and three children. When visited by the DMP she produced two children and said the third was at the shops. When questioned about the fact that the children appeared to be too old to be hers, she said they were from her late husband's first marriage. Detective-Officer Thomas Mannion concluded that Mrs Golding was unreliable, and 'fond of drink.' Having established that there were no children from the dead man's first marriage, and that the youngest child, Kate Golding Junior, was not the natural daughter of Mrs Golding or her late husband, the detective reported:

> She admitted that ... it was an adopted child. She then said, 'I was living at 132 Townsend Street in April 1913, and saw the child with a girl, whom I do not know and never saw since. The baby was then nine or ten days old, and the girl said that she would drown it. She slept on my landing outside my door for two nights with the baby. I took the baby from her and brought it to City Quay Roman Catholic Church and had it baptised by Fr Gaynor there. He charged me one shilling and said that I would have a great reward for keeping it. The child was christened Kate Golding, my own name. I kept it since. That happened on April 4th, 1914.'

However, the detective could find no reference to a Kate Golding in the baptismal record, and when he enquired of Father Gaynor the priest had no recollection of the incident. The detective concluded that the woman was claiming for more children in the hope of a bigger award, unaware that the amount would be based on her husband's earnings rather than on the number of dependants he left.

In fact the situation was even more complex, and it was not until Detective-Officer Mannion reported again on 13 June 1917 that the real mother of Kate Golding Junior was revealed. She was a Kate Clinton, whose husband had been imprisoned for neglect. Mrs Clinton took up with Patrick O'Neill, a waiter in the Friendly Brothers' Club, St Stephen's Green, who was the father of the child. He was now serving in France. On 26 October 1917 the Treasury concluded:

> If she [Mrs Golding] had declared truthfully that there were no children by either marriage she would have been entitled to the full amount of the award instead of having to take only a share if there were children. Her false declaration has consequently reacted on herself by the diminution, as proposed of her share of the award from £234 to £94 and in our opinion this is a sufficient punishment for her conduct in the matter. As regards the child of whom a soldier serving in France is the reputed father and a Mrs. Clinton the mother, it was adopted as stated when ten days old by Mrs. Golding with the knowledge and consent of the deceased and continues to live with her. The Chief Secretary who has the papers before him agreed to the proposal that the balance of the award should be lodged in Court for the benefit of the child.[11]

Another hard case was that of Margaret Naylor of 101 Great Brunswick Street, who was killed almost at the same time as her husband, John, a member of the Royal Dublin Fusiliers, who died in the Battle of Loos between 27 and 29 April. They left three children. If either parent had survived they would have received an allowance for the loss of the other. In the event, Mrs Naylor's sister was awarded 19s a week for the children and a lump sum of £10 'in full discharge' of compensation. A funeral plot at Blackhorse Lane (now Blackhorse Avenue) military cemetery was also provided for the dead woman.

Nor could other families who provided volunteers for the British war effort expect better treatment. A Mrs Dorgan was denied assistance after her husband was killed because she had four sons, of whom two were unmarried. All four were in the British army. It was not until May 1917 that the Treasury finally agreed to sanction the award of the £150 she was entitled to on the grounds of her husband's earnings, after the committee wrote to 'respectfully suggest that the fact that the deceased had four sons at the front would be reason for generous treatment by Their Lordships.'

Even the most tragic circumstances failed to elicit generosity. The Dublin Victims Committee awarded £25 to Christina Caffrey of 27B Corporation Place (commonly called Corporation Buildings) for the loss of her two-year-old son, only to be overruled by the Treasury. Love asked the Treasury to reconsider, given the very sad nature of the case ... the child having been shot in its mother's arms while the mother was endeavouring to recall one of her other children, which had wandered into the street, on the second day of the Rebellion.

The Treasury finally allowed £5 in compensation, plus the funeral expenses, provided the latter did not exceed another £5. But the second £5 was never released, as Detective-Sergeant John Byrne of Store Street station reported that the family had not incurred any funeral expenses.

In the absence of more adequate social services, the DMP provided the eyes and ears of the Treasury, investigating the details of each case. Most investigations were completed in 1917, but some lasted into 1918. The detective responsible often advised on the ability of individual claimants to handle awards. Sergeant Cummins reported that Bridget O'Grady of 29 Thomas Court was totally incapacitated by a bullet wound to the thigh and faced the workhouse without assistance. She received an award of £150; but he cautioned against a lump sum. She was 'a very respectable woman but she is unable to leave her room in the tenement where she resides, which is not in a very respectable locality and ... the amount awarded to her could not, with safety, be given to her.' He added that the local clergy were of the same opinion. Two local priests at Meath Street church were willing to act as trustees.

Local Catholic clergy were the main source of trustees when the recipient of an award was considered unfit to handle their own finances or when it was feared they might fall prey to unscrupulous relatives or neighbours. But on occasion local public representatives, including the ubiquitous Alfie Byrne, also served.

Many cases required repeated medical examination, and, given the choice between sanctioning a lump sum and extending 'hurt pay' at either the full rate or the 'materially impaired' rate, the Treasury would usually opt for the extension.

Much responsibility fell on Sir Thomas Myles, the government's medical referee. Like Love, he was frequently frustrated at the imperviousness of the Treasury to the situation of the victims. One such case was that of 24-year-old Ann Lovett of 20 Delahunt Buildings, off Lower Mount Street, who had been shot in the stomach. She not alone survived but became pregnant, though injuries left her suffering from numbness in her right leg and unfit to resume work. After she had been kept on weekly payments of between 4s 6d and 3s 4d for more than a year Myles urged the committee to give especially sympathetic consideration to the young woman.

She has a very grave wound; she is weak and anaemic and looks as if she was insufficiently fed; she is about to become a mother and this together with her injuries, in my opinion, quite incapacitates her from heavy and laborious work. I gathered from her conversation that she has had a great deal of domestic trouble lately, her mother died of puerperal fever in June 1916 and she ... has been trying to look after her father's six children; to add to her trouble her father has been out of work for some time past. She is already the mother of one child and has a husband to look after. You can readily understand that the wretched girl has hardly been given the most favourable circumstances for such convalescence.

The committee was not unsympathetic, but the Treasury's response was characteristically minimalist: it approved the extension of the 3s 4d 'materially impaired' payment for another three months.

Even for those who did receive awards the amounts were often too little to preserve victims from the spectre of poverty. Bertha Mackenzie and her two children, aged thirteen and eleven, enjoyed a life of comfort and security until her husband, Robert, was shot dead in his grocery shop at 3 Cavendish Row during the rising. An award of £50 a year or a lump sum of £300 was recommended by the Victims Committee. However, the Treasury expressed concern that she had inadequate records to support her claim, and those she had made no provision for depreciation or bad debts. C. Friery of the English and Scottish Law Life Assurance Association protested over the inadequacy of the award and reminded the committee that he had produced a certificate from Cooper and Kenny, chartered accountants, showing that Robert Mackenzie had made a net profit of £77 7s 1d in the three months before his death. He had also examined Mrs Mackenzie before the committee about the business and satisfied it that she

> took very little part therein. Since deceased's death the widow has been compelled to give up a private house in which she and the children resided during deceased's life time and live in rooms. She is also endeavouring to carry on the business as this is her only livelihood, but I regret to say that the trade is in decline and the profits fast diminishing.

He enclosed accounts from Cooper and Kenny showing a profit of only £86 16s 6d for the six months to 31 March 1917.

> It will be apparent to you therefore that there has been a considerable falling off in trade and if the present decline continues it seems only a matter of a few months when this poor woman will be out of trade altogether. My Client's health has been impaired, and she has been advised that unless an improvement in her health sets in at once she must give up business entirely.

The Treasury relented somewhat and allowed the £300 award; but the widow was to receive only £120, with the balance of £180 to be held by the Recorder's Court for the children. A yearly allowance was out of the question. Even questions in the House of Commons had no effect. The Chief Secretary, Henry Duke, sympathised with Mrs Mackenzie but told MPs that no more money was payable.[12]

A similar case was that of Mrs Harris Abrahams, who claimed £2,500 against her lost husband's earnings of £290 a year. She received £100; another £200 was lodged with the Recorder's Court for five of the couple's eight children. Her eldest, Isaac, had his own tailoring business in Lower Ormond Quay, where her two oldest daughters worked for 18s and 15s a week, respectively. All three were excluded from any compensation.

William Holmes, who owned a tea room in Railway Street and suffered 'drop foot' as a result of a bullet traversing his leg, had a claim for £500 reduced to £150 by the committee and then to £17 5s by the Irish Treasury, even though Detective-Officer John Byrne confirmed that the business was making only £1 a week and Holmes's opportunities for other work had ended because of his injury. He had a couple of slum properties nearby, but these had been closed as unfit for human habitation some time before. The comment that his brother 'occasionally assists the family with small amounts' may have sealed his fate.

Sometimes a man was better off having a good employer than being in business for himself. Patrick Behan of Irishtown claimed £100 against lost earnings of £1 a week. He received an award of only £6 10s for a bullet wound to his left arm and abdomen but in fact was better off than normally because he received 'hurt pay' of 10s a week, half pay of another 10s from his employer, and national health insurance benefit of a further 10s while incapacitated.

On the other hand, an employer's kindness could rebound, as it did on Catherine Hegarty. She was a domestic servant and had been shot during the Northumberland Road fight. Her employer, Frances Neweth, allowed her to return to work in 1917, and when the committee discovered this it immediately stopped her 'hurt pay' and held an investigation into an overpayment of £3 10s 4d. Mrs Neweth protested that Miss Hegarty could carry out only limited duties, assisted by her other servant and herself. 'In my opinion,' she wrote to the committee, 'she is not yet capable, in the open market, of earning the same rate of wages she received before her injury.' This view was confirmed by Sir Thomas Myles, who confirmed that 'Miss Hegarty cannot do any hard work of any kind and ... it is possible the condition may continue for a very long period.' The allowance was not renewed, but it is not clear whether the overpayment was ever reclaimed.

One of the few successful appeals against awards was made by Alderman David Quaid, acting as solicitor for one of his constituents, two-year-old Mary Ann Reilly from Greek Street. She had been shot in the right leg; the wound became gangrenous, and the leg had to be amputated above the knee. It was 'a very serious and permanent mutilation,' Quaid wrote to the committee. The award of £100 offered was 'entirely inadequate for the loss of a leg, practically limiting the earning power of this girl during her life and even preventing her from having marriage chances.' He proposed the Workmen's Compensation Act rate as more appropriate, and he accepted an improved offer of £150 on her behalf. This was the highest payment for an infant and, as in other cases, the award included legal costs.

Amounts paid ranged from £300 to £5. All but five of the claimants had an address in fairly close vicinity to the fighting. Two of the exceptions were a woman who lived in Harold's Cross and a widow in Kingstown. The woman in Harold's Cross had lost a son; the Kingstown widow, who had two children, was partially dependent on her dead brother.

There were three claims from dependants of men living in Cos. Sligo, Limerick and Roscommon. The Sligo case involved a teacher passing through Dublin on his way to a conference in Cork who, according to his brother, was 'shot like a dog' in the street and then robbed of all his possessions. The other men were on bank holiday outings.

Of the remaining sixty successful claimants, thirty-six lived in the north inner city and twenty-three in the south inner city. One woman was committed to the Richmond Lunatic Asylum, which means she had probably lived in the catchment area of the North Dublin Union. Twenty-six of the north city claimants lived between the Five Lamps (Amiens Street) and Capel Street and seventeen in tenements in streets close to Sackville Street, such as Corporation Street, Gardiner Street and Rutland Street. In contrast, only five came from the North King Street area, where the allegations of soldiers shooting civilians had been most prevalent.

The addresses on the south side of the Liffey were more dispersed, again reflecting the spread of the fighting. There was one successful claim from Ringsend, three from the Lower Mount Street area and a scattering from the vicinity of Jacob's factory. The use of the Workmen's Compensation Act inevitably meant that payments were based on lost earnings, with scant regard for the size or circumstances of families. Elizabeth Watson of 55 Middle Abbey Street had no dependants but received £273, while Anne O'Grady of 28 East Arran Street, who had six children, received £265.

There were ninety-nine children altogether among the families covered by awards, including the child of the woman committed to the Richmond Asylum. Eleven claimants were awarded the maximum amount of £300, twenty-eight received between £200 and £293 and the remainder received between £199 and £5.[13]

———

Dependants of participants in the rising fared much better. The Veteran Fenian Tom Clarke had given his wife £3,000 to relieve distress among Volunteers and their dependants. By May there were two bodies collecting funds for the prisoners and their families, the one established by Kathleen Clarke and another one closer to the Irish Party. In August they amalgamated to form the Irish National Aid Association and Volunteer Dependants' Fund, which embraced the Irish Relief Committee in America. More donations flowed in from sympathisers in Britain and Australia. As a result, the fund was able not alone to make small weekly payments to the dependants of prisoners but to invest £20,000 in Dublin Corporation loans in September 1916 and to allocate £1,500 to each widow. This could be taken as a lump sum or in a weekly stipend based on the interest. Unlike payments by the government, no account was taken of the income of the lost breadwinner, but neither was any account taken of the number of dependants: all families were treated equally. In some instances the families were substantially better off than ever before, such as James Connolly's widow, Lillie, and their six surviving children. Instead of having to subsist on her husband's pay of £2 a week as a union official, supplemented by the earnings of her two working daughters, Nora and Ina, Lillie Connolly took the lump sum of £1,500, as well as additional donations worth £325.

Near the other end of the income scale was Éamonn Ceannt, who had earned £220 a year as a senior clerk in the corporation. His widow, Áine, took the £1,500 lump sum together with additional donations worth £300 and used it to set up a market garden for the upkeep of herself and her ten-year-old son.[14] The second in command of the Citizen Army, Michael Mallin, left a wife and five children; his widow, Úna, received £1 7s a week, later increased to £2 10s, plus £100 from American funds. She opted to have her £1,500 invested for her children's education.

The Irish National Aid Association and Volunteer Dependants' Fund decided to set up an education subcommittee to look after the education of all the orphans from Easter Week. The subcommittee, fourteen strong, included no less than four Catholic priests, including Father Aloysius, who heard the last confession of Connolly and other executed leaders. Most of the thirty-nine boys were sent to St Enda's, the school founded by Pearse, and the twenty-eight girls to various boarding schools. Lillie Connolly dissented, asking for the money to be paid to her directly for the education of her son, Roddy.

The commitment to equality of treatment of the widows and orphans of 1916 was commendable, but it was also an inadvertent early indicator that those loyal to the Republic and the values of Irish Ireland could expect preferential treatment under the new political dispensation. The independent Irish state would treat some of its children more equally than others.[15]

––––

Casualties of the rising were not restricted to those who lost their lives, property or homes as a result of the fighting. The largest group of non-combatants adversely affected were ordinary workers, such as employees of the Great Southern and Western Railway. The company had traditionally adopted a very hostile attitude towards trade unions and anything that smacked of radical politics. It had seen off protracted strikes in 1902 and 1911, so successfully that the railways operated normally during the 1913 Lock-out.[16] Nevertheless, as one of the largest employers in Ireland, with nine thousand workers, it contained a microcosm of the national work force.

Fatal casualties in 1916 included the Limerick district auditor, William Moore, shot on an Easter bank holiday day trip to Dublin, and a junior clerk, Seán Heuston, who was executed by order of a court-martial for his role in defending the Mendicity Institute a couple of hundred yards away. Employees who scabbed in the 1911 strike and joined the Royal Dublin Fusiliers in 1914 were among those killed or wounded in the fighting around the Mendicity Institute and the South Dublin Union.[17]

The living proved more of a problem than the dead. Any GSWR employees arrested during the rising were subjected to intense scrutiny and not readmitted to employment on release unless they could prove themselves free from any taint of suspicion. On 6 October 1916 the company received a petition from thirty employees seeking reinstatement after being released without charge. Their plea was supported by Richard Bowden, administrator of the presbytery in Marlborough Street, who wrote to the company urging their reinstatement 'having regard to the difficulty of obtaining employment in the city at the present time.' He testified that 'I know some of these employees personally as being very decent, hard working, sober and good living men.' In April 1922 the Provisional Government of the new Irish Free State was still seeking reinstatement for seventeen of them.[18]

Edward Whelan, a senior clerk in the GSWR Solicitor's Office, with twenty-two years' service, had great difficulty being reinstated. He explained his absence from work between the Tuesday and Thursday of Easter Week by saying he was trapped by the fighting in his elderly father's home in Dorset Street. When military control of the area allowed him to return to work he did so immediately, only to be arrested at Kingsbridge station for being in possession of a circular for the Sinn Féin Loan Fund. He was released from Kilmainham Jail after a few days, and the military authorities confirmed that there was 'nothing known against him.' He still had to sign a declaration stating that he had no involvement in the rising or association with the Irish Volunteers, Irish Citizen Army or Sinn Féin before being allowed to return to work.

Sixteen-year-old Thomas Kavanagh was less fortunate. In 1920 his father, Patrick, who had fifty years' service with the GSWR, was still seeking his reinstatement. In a letter to the chief engineer, E. A. Watson, he wrote:

I beg to address you on behalf of the boy. My son entered the Works in May 1914, being attached to the Fitting and Machine Shop. He was then 14 years of age and then in April 1916, when the Rebellion occurred, he was unfortunately and unconsciously lured into it as a result of which he had to forfeit his job at your works. He was at the time arrested by the Military but owing to his age was released.

Now you will understand what foolish things youths of his age will do, especially when they are led by older and irresponsible persons and only years show them the follies of youth. The boy is now 19 years old with about 40 years more sense than he had when he was 14. Under the circumstances and seeing the boy's foolishness was forgiven by the Military Authorities, I honestly appeal to you to place the matter before the boards and ask the directors to consider the case and give the boy a chance to start afresh.

But even the fact that the boy had lost his mother a year after he was born and was now living with his sister beside the Inchicore works failed to move the directors. Those who were deemed absent from work through no fault of their own, such as signalling staff and the women who cleaned the head office, were refused payment for lost time during the rebellion.

In contrast, the Midland Great Western Railway provided half-pay for all its employees, and the Dublin and South-Eastern Railway provided full pay and even some bonuses, ranging from 10s to £2 5s, to employees who 'went about their work in a whole hearted and loyal way.' P. Franklin, a chargehand smith, and J. Barnwell, a chargehand wagonmaker, received 10s each as a reward for retrieving stolen property from 'a number of boys' on the line near Lansdowne Road station and securing the stores although 'Sinn Feiners' were occupying the premises at the time. Ganger Kearney received an award after being twice arrested by rebels in Enniscorthy. He managed to make his way back to Dublin with 'very useful information ... on the state of the lines.' The same man was struck with a rifle by a rebel in Harcourt Street station for obstructing their activities.

While seventeen employees qualified for a reward, ninety-six absented themselves for anything from one to four days, of whom only five were considered to have acceptable excuses. It is not clear what happened to the remainder.

Passengers of the Dublin and South-Eastern Railway also fared poorly. Requests for refunds on tickets were rejected, on the grounds that the military authorities had ordered the cessation of traffic and, in some cases, had removed track. This did not prevent the company seeking compensation for lost receipts.[19]

————

It was against this background of the little war in Dublin compounding the hardship caused by the Great War in Europe that two parliamentary by-elections took place early in 1917. One was in North Roscommon, caused by the death of the sitting home-rule MP, the former Fenian J. J. O'Kelly. The other was for the vacancy in the University of Dublin caused by the elevation of the junior member, Sir James Campbell, to the bench as Lord Chief Justice of Ireland. Like the mayoralty, both reflected the realignments taking place in Irish politics.

The University of Dublin contest was between the eminent surgeon Sir Robert Woods and Arthur Warren Samuels KC, a distinguished barrister who had previously run unsuccessfully against Campbell. The senior member for the university was another lawyer, Sir Edward Carson, and the challenge from Woods had as much to do with opposition to the near-monopoly the legal profession held on the seats as with the intricacies of southern unionist politics. Since the Act of Union only two MPs for the university had not been lawyers.[20]

The refusal of Woods to espouse any party allegiance alarmed many of the electorate. After he won the seat on a show of hands on 3 February and was carried in triumph by undergraduates up and down Grafton Street, Samuels demanded a full vote by all eligible graduates. He denounced the 'bathos' of an election between a doctor and a lawyer being made the primary issue when the electorate was 'overwhelmingly' composed of southern unionists. It was with some relief that the *Irish Times* subsequently reported the barrister's comfortable election by 1,481 votes to 679 and that Samuels would take his place in Parliament alongside 'our greatest Irishman, Sir Edward Carson.'[21] Samuels would go on to serve as Irish Attorney-General until the general election in 1918.

The North Roscommon election understandably elicited a lot more interest in the city than the contest in the university. The first major political test of public opinion since the rising was the nomination of George Noble Plunkett,[22] father of the 1916 leader Joseph Plunkett, by a radical nationalist coalition conveniently dubbed 'Sinn Féin'. The fact that Plunkett had always been a Whig in politics served to reassure conservative nationalists, while the income he derived from his slum properties in Dublin mattered not a jot.

Dublin's premier Catholic capitalist, William Martin Murphy, had lost all sympathy for what he regarded as Redmond's capitulationist policy on home rule and partition. From now on the *Irish Independent* and its sister publications had free rein to hound the Irish Party establishment in the same way that it had once hounded Larkin and Connolly. When the Roscommon result came in, the *Independent* crowed that the Irish Party machine was 'routed hopelessly.' Plunkett secured 3,022 votes to 1,708 for the UIL candidate, T. J. Devine, and 687 for Jasper Tully, a former Irish Party MP who ran as an independent nationalist.

A certain piquancy was added to the contest by the candidature of Count Plunkett, just home from his post-rebellion banishment, hot on the heels of his expulsion by the Royal Dublin Society, and with the memory of the execution of one of his sons and the imprisonment of two others for association with the rebellion still fresh in the public mind.[23]

The *Irish Catholic*, like the *Independent* a mouthpiece for Murphy, said the result 'sounded the death knell' for UIL constituency machines, although it was sceptical about Plunkett's 'erratic politics.' In a reference to his previous career as director of the National Museum it said 'his capacity for practical usefulness was greater in the Museum than it will ever be in Parliament.' The *Irish Times* dismissed Plunkett as

> a person of no importance, but the Sinn Feiners found in his family's association with the late rebellion an occasion to advertise their disloyalty, and the constitutional Nationalists voted for him—would have voted for anybody—in order to advertise their discontent with the official party.

The *Times* succinctly identified the Irish Party's twin mistakes as acquiescing in the partition of Ireland and agreeing to become 'a hewer of wood and drawer of water to the people who gloried and still glory in the rebellion.' The two sins were equally unforgivable to southern unionists, for whom partition was as abhorrent as it was for nationalists.

Dublin Corporation was in full session when the Roscommon result was announced. Members greeted it with 'wild excitement and much cheering and waving of hats by councillors and the crowd in the gallery.' Alderman J. J. Kelly pinned a celebratory note on the curtains over the Lord Mayor's chair, and Alderman Corrigan, another former stalwart of the United Irish League, proposed the adjournment of the council. The incoming Lord Mayor, Alderman O'Neill, seconded the motion. It was defeated by 39 votes to 24, but only by unionists voting *en bloc* with the main UIL faction.[24]

The reaction of the corporation members was mirrored on the streets. When Plunkett's train stopped at Mullingar on its way to Dublin local councillors and other notables presented him with an address that declared: 'By opposing your candidature in this election your opponents have sounded the doom of their political influence in Ireland.' Their 'puerile policy of inaction, jobbery and sycophancy' had been 'wiped out in a storm of popular indignation.'

In Dublin large crowds awaited the train, which did not complete its triumphal progress into Broadstone station until 10 p.m. Like Sir Robert Woods a few days earlier, Plunkett was carried shoulder-high to a waiting motor car and escorted by crowds through the main thoroughfares to his residence in Fitzwilliam Square. His escort sang nationalist anthems, such as 'The West's Awake', 'God Save Ireland' and 'The Soldier's Song'.

The next day the *Irish Times* correspondent, who had been traversing the snows of North Roscommon on the campaign trail, gave a new view on Plunkett's victory. He attributed it to the activities of 'the Rev. Michael O'Flanagan, the Roman Catholic curate of Crossna ... For twelve days and nights he was up and down the constituency, going like a whirlwind.' The burden of Father O'Flanagan's election speeches was that

> conscription would have been applied to Ireland last year were it not for the rebellion ... As Father O'Flanagan put it in all his speeches, it was better and

easier for the young men to carry their fathers on their backs to the polls to vote for Plunkett than to serve as conscripts in the trenches of Flanders. This appeal went straight home to the parental instincts of the voters with sons of military age.[25]

In Dublin the war itself found myriad ways of exacerbating divisions between local unionists and the new breed of nationalist. Four days after the Roscommon by-election a war loan was launched at a public meeting in the city. The new president of the Dublin Chamber of Commerce, R. W. Booth, urged the banks and life assurance companies to encourage clients to purchase the new bonds, and Sir Maurice Dockrell told the audience that 'if the Empire went down, Ireland would go down with it.'[26]

The Central Advisory Committee of the Royal Dublin Fusiliers' Association passed a resolution the same day thanking the Dublin Women's Unionist Club

for so kindly during the past year granting the use of their office and the services of their secretary ... and bearing the administrative expenses of the branch, thus enabling the grants ... to be spent on ... food and tobacco for the men.

There was no longer even a semblance of nationalist involvement in the Central Advisory Committee: the membership, from Lady Arnott down, was staunchly unionist.[27]

———

Black bread or 'war bread' was introduced at the beginning of the year,[28] and potatoes were becoming a luxury by the time of the by-elections. Although the government had introduced some food controls in late 1916, including fixed prices, there was virtually no enforcement of the regulations. Neither the Department of Agriculture and Technical Instruction, Dublin Corporation nor the DMP accepted responsibility.

The official price of potatoes was set at £9 a ton, but the retail price in the shops was between £1s 8d and £1s 10d a pound, equivalent to between £13 16s 8d and £14 a ton. Even retailers buying in bulk had to pay farmers at least £10 a ton, plus freight and delivery. A ban on potato exports introduced in early 1917 failed to bring prices down. Potato factors in Dublin accused farmers of holding back up to half the crop, and growers could quite legally sell their produce in areas outside Dublin that were not covered by the prices orders, or export them. The vice-president of the Department of Agriculture and Technical Instruction, T. W. Russell, told the *Irish Independent* that if 'British merchants and Ulster exporters had their way ... there would not be a potato left in the country.'[29]

Worse was to follow. The budget for school meals in Dublin ran out at the end of February, and the new rate would not be struck until the end of March. The 1d rate provided £4,150 a year for school dinners in Dublin, but the cost of providing meals for five days a week throughout the year had risen to £12,000, starkly illustrating the shortfall in nutrition for thousands of children in the poorer districts. Unfortunately the corporation could not afford such largesse, nor could private charity. In Britain a grant in aid from the exchequer could make up the difference for local authorities, but the Local Government Board in Ireland lacked such resources. For the same reason appeals to set up communal kitchens similar to those operating in deprived areas of London fell at first on deaf ears. This sort of discrimination was one of the few things that united loyalist and nationalist in Dublin, particularly women activists in the community.[30]

Later in March a probation officer, Miss Gargan, told the *Irish Independent* that starvation was widespread among the poorer classes because of food prices. School meals had temporarily stopped, and even 'Army separation allowances, with the utmost economy, are barely sufficient to provide a family with food—and nothing can be allowed for clothing.' She criticised mothers 'who squandered the allowance on drink,' and she advocated drastic steps 'to stop the rush of women from the post offices to the public houses. I have no hesitation in saying that such women are starving their children.'

Of the 1,500 families on the books of the Women's National Health Association she estimated that 500 of the main breadwinners earned between 15s and 25s a week and most of the rest were dependent on casual work, or were not fit for work. She gave an example from the previous week of a family of eight where the father gave 22s of his weekly pay of 24s to the mother. She spent 16s on twenty-eight loaves of bread, a half pound of tea, a pound of sugar and a pound of margarine. The rent was 3s, and the remaining 2s 4d went on fuel, light and milk. 'Absolutely no provision could be made for meat or cheese and the wage earner had to work hard on his share of the poor quality of food.'

A WNHA doctor said that almost all the fifty-nine children treated in February suffered from malnutrition, and even families with a regular wage coming in were living on dry bread and tea, 'often very black tea.' A clinic had been opened recently to ensure that mothers ate adequately, because 'it was found utterly hopeless to do anything for the children while the mothers were starving.' By making the women eat on the premises it was possible to make sure they would not take the food home to give their children: but only about twenty meals a day could be provided.

The migration of men to jobs in England was aggravating the situation. The WNHA found that the average remittance was only 10s a week and many men left in Dublin were too ill or unfit for work. Miss Gargan said that rebuilding the city centre should be a priority to get the able-bodied back to work, and light employment schemes suitable for 'weak workers' should be developed.[31]

So serious was the potato shortage that in early April the military authorities took the unusual step of opening some of their own stores and setting up a market at Amiens Street station, where retailers were offered produce at the current official price of £11 a ton. Small shopkeepers and community groups were allowed to pool their resources to purchase produce if they could not afford to pay for large orders individually.[32] The measure had at least the temporary effect of forcing large farmers to release stock ahead of the more plentiful supplies that would be available in the summer.

Queen Mary at Maynooth during the royal visit of 1907. The President of St Patrick's College, Daniel Mannix, is on her right and a predecessor, Dr William Walsh, Archbishop of Dublin, is on her left. Mannix was viewed with hostility by nationalists of all hues and was denied an Irish see. He was appointed Archbishop of Melbourne in 1913. After the Easter Rising he became one of the leading champions in Australia of Irish independence. Dr Walsh was the leading political strategist of the Catholic Church in Ireland for thirty-five years. Increasingly disillusioned with the Irish Party, he steered the Catholic hierarchy towards Sinn Féin in 1917 and 1918. (© *National Library of Ireland*)

The funeral cortège of the three fatal victims of the King's Own Scottish Borderers passes the scene of their deaths on Bachelor's Walk, 29 July 1914. Another eighty-five civilians had been wounded in the confrontation three days earlier, which ensured that there was no enthusiasm in the city for Britain's declaration of war on Germany. (© *Getty Images*)

The body of Jeremiah O'Donovan Rossa leaves City Hall for Glasnevin on 1 August 1915. It was the first major demonstration of strength by advanced nationalists and came on the eve of disastrous landings by Irish regiments at Gallipoli. (© *National Library of Ireland*)

Officers of the 6th Battalion, Royal Munster Fusiliers, a volunteer battalion. The commanding officer, Lt-Col. V. T. Worship, secured commissions for Joseph Bagnell Lee and Alfred Tennyson Lee, sons of the prominent Dublin businessman Edward Lee. Joe Lee (standing at back in front of right-hand door panel) was killed at Gallipoli and Alfred (fifth man standing, from right) seriously wounded. (*Courtesy of the Lee family*)

After Gallipoli: Lee family photograph. *Left to right*: Alfred Tennyson Lee, recuperating from wounds at Gallipoli; Annie Lee (née Shackleton), mother, wearing black; Robert Ernest Lee, Royal Army Medical Corps, on leave from the Western Front; Edward Lee (father), and Edward Shackleton Lee, who remained at home to help his father with the family business. A firm supporter of Britain's war effort, Edward Lee served on the recruitment committee for the 10th Battalion of the Royal Dublin Fusiliers. Captain Robert Ernest Lee was drowned on the *Leinster* on 10 October 1918 after giving his place on a lifeboat to a woman in the water. He was on his way back to the Western Front. 'It was a terrible twist of fate that he served four years in France and Flanders saving lives, only to be drowned in the Irish Sea one month and one day before the armistice,' says the family historian, Mike Lee. 'This, to me, was the killer blow to the Lee family, and I think the grief ultimately killed my great-grandfather, Edward.' The family home, Bellevue, in Cross Avenue, Booterstown, subsequently became the residence of Éamon de Valera. (*Courtesy of the Lee family*)

The rebels' failure to disrupt the Great Southern and Western Railway allowed three thousand soldiers from Irish regiments to be rushed from the Curragh to Dublin within hours of the Rising beginning. But the occupation of Westland Row (now Pearse) station meant that British troops arriving in Kingstown (Dún Laoghaire) marched into the city via Mount Street while the Royal Mail piled up in Kingstown. (© *Illustrated London News Ltd/Mary Evans*)

Dublin in flames: Sackville (O'Connell) Street at the height of the fighting. (© *Imperial War Museum*)

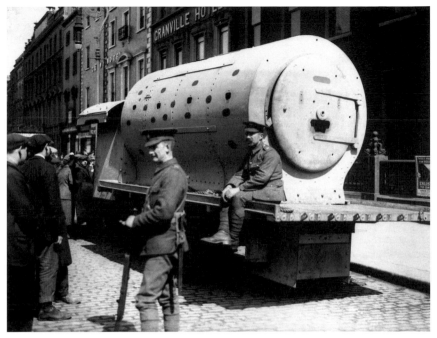

An improvised armoured car manufactured by Irish workers at Inchicore Railway Works to help in the suppression of the Rising. (© *PA/PA Archive/Press Association Images*)

A major casualty of the Rising: the *Freeman's Journal* premises after the artillery bombardment. Generous government compensation was politically damaging and only delayed the demise of this mouthpiece of the Irish Party. (© *National Library of Ireland*)

The British Prime Minister, H. H. Asquith, visited prisoners at Richmond Barracks hours after the execution of Seán Mac Diarmada and James Connolly at Kilmainham. He was more impressed by the political analysis of Father Aloysius, the Franciscan who gave the last rites to Connolly, than by that of his own military governor, General Maxwell. He ordered an immediate end to the executions. (© *Bettmann/Corbis*)

An early straw in the wind: Dubliners hunt for souvenirs among the rubble. (© *PA/PA Archive/ Press Association Images*)

On 14 May 1916 the resumption of tram services and the reopening of theatres and music halls heralded a return to normality, but the military curfew remained. (© National Library of Ireland)

The Rising saw a rapid resolution of the Dublin building dispute as men returned to work on improved rates of pay. The terms were mediated by Captain Fairburn Downie of the Ministry of Munitions, anxious to bring the new shell factory at Parkgate into production. (© *Bettmann/ Corbis*)

William T. Cosgrave— the moderate face of revolution in Dublin. Even the officers of his field court-martial recommended clemency because of his evident decency and respectability. (© *National Library of Ireland*)

The war rolls on: a soldier guards British army recruiting posters on the wall of the battered Four Courts in the wake of the Rising. (© *TopFoto*)

Sir John Pentland Mahaffy, Provost of Trinity College, Dublin, said of the Rising: 'We did not seek this quarrel with our fellow citizens, the thing was thrust upon us suddenly in the twinkling of an eye.' (© *National Library of Ireland*)

JOHN REDMOND and the EXECUTIONS. 🖎

On the evening of the 3rd May, 1916, after the British Premier had announced—amid the cheers of the English Whigs and Tories and the Redmondites—that **Pearse, MacDonagh** and **Clarke** had been shot that morning, and while **Joseph Plunkett, Edward Daly, Cornelius Colbert** and **Michael O'Hanrahan** were lying in the condemned cell, John Redmond rose in the British House of Commons and said :—

> "This outbreak happily seems to be over. It has been dealt with with firmness which was not only right, but it was the duty of the Government to so deal with it . . . I do beg the Government not to show <u>undue harshness</u> or severity to the <u>great masses</u> of those who are implicated, <u>on whose shoulders lies a guilt far different from</u> that which lies upon the INSTIGATORS and PROMOTERS of this outbreak."

Redmond thus signified his approval of the Execution of the Leaders.

Redmond uttered this speech at 4 p.m. in the British House of Commons on May 3rd. Eleven hours later, Plunkett, Daly, O'Hanrahan and Colbert were shot by the British Government's orders.

Who will vote for the nominee of Redmond, the approver and inciter of the execution of Joseph Plunkett?

Printed by O'Loughlin, Murphy & Boland, Ltd., Dublin, and published by J. B. Goff, Solicitor, Boyle, Election Agent for Count Plunkett.

John Redmond and the executions: the Irish Party MPs did not cheer, but Redmond's speeches in the British House of Commons showed he was hopelessly out of touch with events in Dublin. (© *Dublin City Library and Archive*)

Crowds gather to meet released prisoners at Westland Row. 'What a contrast with the humiliating day of our departure,' Sergeant Frank Robbins of the Irish Citizen Army declared on his arrival home. (© *National Library of Ireland*)

Protest meetings took place around the country to demand the release of political prisoners. At this one in Beresford Place, Dublin, on 10 June 1917, Inspector John Wills of the DMP became the first post-Rising fatality of the struggle for independence among the Crown forces when he was felled by a hurley during the arrest of Count Plunkett and Cathal Brugha. (© *National Library of Ireland*)

Thomas Ashe in military custody after the battle of Ashbourne. His calm, commanding presence amidst his captors is at odds with his situation. As he awaited execution he told friends he did not fear death. Conditions in Mountjoy Prison a year later would prove much less humane—and ultimately fatal. (*Courtesy of the Ashe family*)

'The man in the trenches wants shells—Irish shells,' says the slogan on the wall at the National Shell Factory in Dublin. Work in the munitions factories at Parkgate and in the Dublin Dockyard Company saw working-class women earning more than many male counterparts. While the war was a liberating experience for women of all social classes, only those from a working-class background were subjected to regular social censure, usually for spending leisure time in pubs or 'the low saloon' of O'Connell Street. (© *Imperial War Museum*)

Hostility towards 'separation women' and women 'friends' of soldiers led to clashes on Dublin's streets during the celebration of the Allied victory in November 1918. The separation payments caused a major redistribution of wealth to poor tenement communities in the city. The extension of payments to the unmarried mothers of soldiers' children from 1916 further fuelled the flames of resentment. (© *RTÉ Stills Library*)

Youngsters celebrating the end of the war with the Stars and Stripes, the acceptable face of Allied victory. America was the receptacle of hope for international recognition at the Peace Conference. (© *Bettmann/Corbis*)

Crowds gather outside the Mansion House to witness the assembly of the first Dáil on 21 January 1919. Like the radical social and economic principles embodied in the 1916 Proclamation, the Democratic Programme adopted inside could not have been conceived or composed anywhere in Ireland except Dublin. (© *Underwood & Underwood/Corbis*)

Annie Lee with W. T. Cosgrave at a war commemoration in the 1920s. After Fianna Fáil came to power, government ministers ceased attending, but tens of thousands still turned up at Remembrance Day ceremonies until the outbreak of the Second World War. While numbers fell off in subsequent years, there were public commemorations until the end of the 1960s, when they were discontinued because of the renewed Northern troubles. (*Courtesy of the Lee family*)

Letter from Lieutenant Colonel Verschoyle Worship to Edward Lee, dated 19 August 1915. 'What can I say. I have no words that can express my sympathy with you and Mrs Lee and all your family—In the course of my 25 years service I have met many men but I have never met 2 more honourable brave and conscientious than your two sons . . . Forgive me if this scrawl is crude and ill expressed. There is a heavy bombardment going on and I am crouched under a rock.' (*Courtesy of the Lee family*)

Chapter 10 ~

'THE MOST DESTRUCTIVE
BIRD THAT COULD
POSSIBLY BE'

I t was hardly surprising, given the widespread food shortages, that the allotment movement came into its own in Dublin during 1917. It was already a massive success in British cities and in Belfast.

The Vacant Land Cultivation Society had been established in Dublin in 1909 by Sarah Harrison, an artist by profession, a sister of Charles Stewart Parnell's secretary, Henry Harrison, and the first woman to be elected to Dublin Corporation, as an independent (Parnellite) nationalist. The society made little progress until 1915, when food shortages and price increases were posing problems for the city's lower middle class as well as for the poor. In response to the crisis the corporation gave Harrison ten acres at Fairbrother's Fields, between Donore Avenue and Cork Street, which had been earmarked for housing before the war. It acquired other fields and derelict sites in or near the city for allotments.[1] By the end of the year the society had 31 acres under cultivation and by the end of 1917 more than 60 acres.

The Rathmines Technical College and the School of Gardening for Women in Upper Kimmage provided expert advice to smallholders, and the first exhibition of produce at the Leo Hall, Inchicore, in September 1916 was graced by 'massive cabbages' from allotments on the Pigeon House Road, 'burly potatoes' from Broadstone and 'huge onions' from Inchicore. Neither politics nor religion intruded on the society's activities. Harrison served as secretary; other members included the distinguished Trinity College botanist Sir Frederick Moore, the Presbyterian minister for the north inner city, Rev. Dr Denham Osborne, and the Rev J. McDonnell sj, who served as president.[2]

The benefits of the scheme were evident from the experience of allotment-holders elsewhere. In Belfast eight hundred plots had been established by the end of 1915, with produce worth about £10,000 being grown to feed local people, and the lower prices of staple vegetables in Belfast were attributed in part to the 'home-grown' competition faced by farmers. Dublin's smallholders soon proved they could be every bit as productive as their northern counterparts, although removing rubbish, levelling the ground and clearing it of weeds and slugs were problems at first. A more persistent threat was sparrows, which Sir Frederick Moore described as 'the most destructive bird that could possibly be.'

An eighth of an acre was found to be the optimum size for a plot cultivated by a man in his spare time. Women and children joined in, especially when it came to clearing sites of cinders, refuse and old brickwork. Sites varied in price from 6s to 16s 8d, with a proportion set aside for casual labourers and the unemployed to work free of charge.

Sites were taken by a wide spectrum of people, including labourers in full-time employment, skilled workers, teachers, clerks, policemen and a large contingent of Guinness employees. The allotment-holders formed their own committees to allocate sites, organise work, collect rents and purchase seed. Subletting was prohibited; and anyone who failed to work their plot might forfeit it. They erected fences, sometimes with barbed wire, to prevent thefts, such as a dawn raid on a hundred freshly dibbled cabbages from a railway worker's plot in the port in early 1917.

The allotments provided not alone badly needed food supplies and an education in horticulture but a useful exercise in democracy that broadened people's sense of solidarity, their social skills and their horizons. This led eventually to the formation of the Irish Plotholders' Union, which claimed to represent twenty-four associations in Dublin and Kingstown. In an echo of Land League days, their demands included fair rents and fixity of tenure.[3]

As in Belfast, a typical plot could produce well over £10 worth of food a year. The *Irish Times* gave the example of a man with a family of eight who kept £2 10s worth of crops to help feed them and sold the balance for £9 11s 6d. Rent and other expenses amounted to £2 5s.[4]

By October 1916 the Vacant Land Cultivation Society's plots had generated £2,500 worth of produce, and the demand for plots far exceeded supply. Harrison reported 'a pathetic eagerness on the part of men, and women too, to secure plots, and a long list of applicants remains yet unsatisfied.' By then pressure was mounting on the corporation to become more actively involved, and hungry eyes turned on the 1,760 acres of the Phoenix Park, which many citizens wanted turned into one vast allotment. The Chief Secretary, Henry Duke, had no objection in principle, but the Board of Works had other ideas: it took over a section of the park for tillage to meet its own requirements, and pickets placed on the board's operations failed to sway the government. Instead the corporation agreed to acquire sites to supplement those of the society.[5]

The big problem for the corporation and the society alike was that no compulsory powers were granted to local authorities (unlike their counterparts in England, Scotland and Wales) to acquire land either directly or for voluntary bodies. As early as February 1916 a meeting was held in the Mansion House to demand the extension of the Small Holdings and Allotments Act (1908) to Ireland. There was no doubting the wide support for such a measure. Father J. McDonnell presided, and on the platform was the Rev. Denham Osborne, Sir Frederick Moore and most of the city's MPs. Letters of apology were read from the Lord Mayors of Belfast and Limerick and several leading home-rulers, including John Redmond.

The main motion was proposed by Moore and seconded by Tom McPartlin on behalf of the Labour Party and Dublin Trades Council. There was 'some unrest' when J. J. Clancy, the Irish Party MP for North County Dublin, said that the extension of British legislation 'was not only in the interests of workers, but for the general community and even for the British Empire,' and this turned into outright booing when John Dillon Nugent, secretary of the AOH and MP for Dublin City, rose to make an innocuous speech in support of the campaign. By contrast, the Chief Secretary was cheered when it was announced that he supported the extension of the 1908 act to Ireland.[6]

There was no doubting the demand for land. In March 1917 the corporation received 1,200 applications for 269 plots.[7] As a result additional land was acquired at the Model Farm in Glasnevin, at Clontarf and at Islandbridge, so that by the summer the Vacant Land Cultivation Society was able to accommodate 460 plot-holders and the corporation could accommodate another 2,000. While corporation allotment-holders were at first supposed to grow only potatoes and oats, the latter quickly gave way to cabbages, beetroot, turnips, leeks, parsnips, onions, runner beans, carrots, lettuce and celery. Celery was particularly profitable, as it was in demand as an alleged cure for persons of a nervous disposition.

The movement spread to the southern townships of Rathmines, Pembroke, Blackrock and Kingstown. The main restriction on expansion was the ever-rising rent that landowners demanded in the absence of compulsory purchase legislation. What land was available at reasonable prices was on the north side of the city: 96 of the 113 acres available in early 1917 were there. However, such was the demand that Dubliners did not mind trekking across the city to work their allotments.

In an effort to redress the balance, 37 acres were made available at Islandbridge, but only 10 acres were workable, because of the proximity of the barracks with its adjoining gas house and bomb house for training recruits in trench warfare. The site itself was riddled with trenches, and there were hundreds of army horses 'all over the place,' which constantly sampled the produce.[8]

It was not until the end of 1917 that the government finally introduced the Local Government (Allotments and Land Cultivation) (Ireland) Act, authorising local authorities to acquire land in conjunction with the Department of Agriculture and Technical Instruction. In 1918 Dublin Corporation was able to acquire another 100 acres for cultivation, some of it to compensate for the loss of allotments at Fairbrother's Fields, where the housing scheme had belatedly begun. By the end of the war the value of produce grown in the city was estimated at between £150,000 and £160,000.

Once the war was over farmers and landlords generally protested at the continued existence of the allotments. As one substantial landowner in Clontarf, Thomas Picton Bradshaw, put it, the Irish Plotholders' Union was trying to make 'a temporary war emergency scheme' a permanent feature of Dublin life, 'to enable professional men, trade union members and others to oust market gardeners, dairymen, cattle salesmen, schools and sports committees from property on which they had expended money and in which they had an interest.' However, the Plotholders' Union was strong enough to see off the challenge until 1926, by which time agricultural prices had fallen by 42 per cent from their wartime maximum.[9]

———

Fuel was the other major shortage confronting Dubliners, and unfortunately it could be neither mined nor grown in Ireland. Wages were rising, particularly in unionised trades, such as the crafts and in Dublin Corporation, but prices were rising faster. In January the Mansion House Coal Fund and the Lord Mayor's Coal Fund were amalgamated to generate greater efficiency and more effective fund-raising. The proposer was the Rev J. Denham Osborne, the Presbyterian minister actively involved in the allotments movement. He lived and worked in the north inner city and was a regular contributor to the proceedings of the Statistical and Social Inquiry Society of Ireland. He told the society that his pastoral work meant he had recently 'come into contact with cases where people were living in respectable dwellings who were [hit] harder than even some of the very poor' by inflation. He estimated that there were four thousand families in the area of the North Dublin Union unable to afford adequate food or fuel.

The fuel shortage also had other implications. The theft of coal was becoming a persistent problem, especially in the North Wall and East Wall areas, where boys climbed on moving railway wagons to throw it down to accomplices.[10] The Coal Fund was as much for social control as for charity, and it had support across the political and religious spectrum. It provided good-quality coal at 1s 6d a bag, while the market price was 3s 6d. It sought primarily to assist the working poor, families of workmen earning less than 25s a week.

After a sample survey undertaken later in 1917 the chief sanitary officer for the city, Charles Travers, estimated that there were eight thousand families in the city with an income of less than 25s. While this was half the figure for 1913, the year of the lock-out, he said the rising cost of living made 'the economic condition of the working class in Dublin disquietingly unsatisfactory.' He found that the pawning of possessions was on the increase, and that the greatest effect of food poverty was on children. Families lodging in the tenements took it in turns to heat their rooms, cooking food jointly. He found that the traditional cheerfulness of the mothers had given way to concern about procuring adequate food for their families, displacing concern over the sanitary state of their environment.

As we have seen, the consumption of coal fell by 30 per cent in 1917 and a further 25 per cent in 1918. Such large institutions as hospitals, asylums and schools had little choice but to reduce heating levels, public lighting hours were cut drastically and banks agreed to close at 2:30 p.m. each day to reduce energy consumption. However, insurance companies insisted on remaining open until 4:30 p.m. and most retailers until much later. The chairman of the Electricity Supply Committee, Lorcan Sherlock, told the Rotary Club that efforts to conserve energy and to share the burden equitably were received with 'indifference from the general public, sneers from the *Irish Times*, and hardly a word of public support from any section of the press in the city.'[11]

The mood of the chairman of the other major generator of electricity in the city, Dublin United Tramways Company, was very different when he addressed the annual general meeting on 6 February 1917 in the company's head office in Upper Sackville Street. Despite being at the vortex of the rising, Murphy's company had made an even more remarkable recovery than the rebels. Although the company's power station in Ringsend had been occupied by rebel forces it had not been damaged, only two trams had been burnt and, miraculously, the artillery bombardment had not damaged the tramlines, which could have been catastrophic, as it was almost impossible to obtain replacement track during the war. In contrast, the corporation's electricity infrastructure had suffered more than £8,000 worth of damage, plunging its operations into the red for the foreseeable future.

While the fighting had cost the DUTC almost £17,000 (made up of £13,898 in damage and £3,000 in lost business during April and May), traffic had increased. At £335,335, receipts were £1,850 higher in 1916 than in 1915, and further growth was expected despite rising fuel costs. The company had paid 24s 5d a ton for coal in 1916, compared with £18s 5d a ton in 1915, an increase of almost a third. Before the war it had cost the company only 9s 8d a ton. Murphy attributed the company's success to the continuous rise in demand for services, the replacement of some old trams with new cars and the conversion of other vehicles to new and more economical motors. The staff had also played an important role, he said.

Honourable mention is due to our Traffic Manager, Mr. D. Brophy. He remained in charge until the fire reached the opposite side of the lane,[12] when in the early hours of Friday morning, the 28th of April, he succeeded in making his way to the Pro-Cathedral, where many people had taken refuge. While there he found the officer in charge of the military operations preparing to bombard the building in the belief that there were rebels sniping from the windows, but Mr. Brophy was able to satisfy him that the report ... was entirely devoid of truth. To this incident we owe it that we have a convenient place to meet in today, even though it is rather cramped as our old meeting room at the Imperial Hotel no longer exists.

A dividend of 5 per cent was paid to the shareholders for the second half of 1916, up from 4½ per cent for the first half. The rising had actually hurt the DUTC less than the 1913 Lock-out. Murphy could not resist contrasting the company's performance as a private transport monopoly with the tribulations of the corporation's Electricity Supply Committee. Unlike the corporation, the DUTC had absorbed costs rather than passing them on as increases to the customer.[13] Naturally Murphy omitted to mention that the cross-subsidisation of business by Dublin's domestic users benefited the DUTC as a consumer of municipal electricity.

————

P. T. Daly, who had been released from internment just before Christmas 1916, was less resigned about the inability of the corporation to tackle the city's problems than fellow-councillors such as Lorcan Sherlock. He quickly reinvigorated the Food Committee and spurred on the pursuit of dairymen who were adulterating milk. The more rigorous enforcement of regulations had its desired effect. Only one trader had ever been sent to prison under the Food, Drugs and Margarine Acts, and that had been in 1906. By the end of 1917 there were 200 inspections under the acts, compared with 163 in 1916, and £467 5s 6d had been collected in fines, compared with £244 15s 8d in the previous year. One trader had been sentenced to a month's imprisonment and two more had been sentenced to two months each.

Characteristically, Daly insisted on a pay increase for the two inspectors, pointing out that they were paid far less than their counterparts in Britain and £30 to £70 a year less than inspectors of the same grades in Belfast. He did not question the probity of the inspectors, he told the corporation, but decent wages would remove the temptation to take bribes.[14]

He was pushing an open door. Sir James Cameron had just provided councillors with a summary of a report by the Carnegie Trust on mothers and children that was scathing about Ireland. 'I am afraid there is a woeful lack of cleanliness, as well as inattention to such details as straining and cooling,' he said. 'In a large number of cases the milk delivered is so foul and acrid that it cannot stand without curdling,' while Dublin milk showed very few samples uncontaminated by the coliforms found in manure. He believed that a lot of this contaminated milk came from the country, where the delay in getting it to the market allowed bacteria to proliferate, especially in warm weather.

Monitoring milk produced in the city was a major operation. There were 205 dairy yards, accommodating five thousand cows, and 459 shops sold milk. Samples could be taken only from a handful of these places on any given day. In rural areas the situation was even worse, with dispensary physicians and relieving officers doubling as medical officers of health and sanitary officers. Infection by dairymen who were typhoid carriers and by cattle that carried tuberculosis was a further concern.[15]

Milk samples were routinely adulterated with water and the fat content abstracted. A fairly typical case was that of Christopher Dempsey, who ran a milk parlour in Summerhill and had a farm at Betaghstown, Clane, Co. Kildare. He was fined £5 for each of two samples taken from his premises in which the milk was between 70 and 77 per cent water and between 27 and 33 per cent of the fat had been abstracted. While these levels were higher than average, samples with anything up to 25 per cent water and 16 per cent fat deficiency were common, and cases with up to 86 per cent of fat abstracted were uncovered.[16]

Poor people were particularly dependent on milk, but the problems of the dairy industry affected every family with babies and young children, and it was no wonder that public anger rose rapidly when the cowmen again threatened price increases. In October 1917 a mass meeting was held in Smithfield after the Dairymen's Association increased the price from 4d to 6d a quart and warned of another increase to 8d before the winter was out. This compared with a price of 3d a quart twelve months earlier.[17]

The normally moderate Councillor Coghlan Briscoe, executive officer of the Town Tenants' League, denounced 'the octopus grip of the profiteer on the food of the people.' He knew of milk suppliers 'outside the profiteering ring' who were willing to sell milk at 4d a quart, and do so profitably. P. T. Daly commended the police magistrates for taking a tougher line on sentencing adulterators. There was unanimous support for a motion proposed by Percy Robinson of the National Union of Clerks that 'under no circumstances would the workers and the poor of Dublin tolerate the raising of the price of milk.'[18]

Even the *Irish Times* declared in exasperation that there were

people in the trade who would not hesitate to bring about a national famine by giving up their business and selling their cattle for export to England. The vice of the Dublin dairymen is not only that they have no sense of public decency but also [that they] produce milk ... under a most pernicious and costly system.[19]

On the same day as the *Irish Times* editorial the cowkeepers proved that they deserved their reputation by carrying out their threat of raising the price to 8d a quart. The vice-president of the Department of Agriculture and Technical Instruction, T. W. Russell, promptly used his powers to fix the price at 4d or 5d a quart, depending on quality. To make sure the producers complied he prohibited the export of milk. It would be October 1918 before the price was allowed to rise again and then by only 1d.[20]

———

Of course Russell received little credit for his action. The cowkeepers complained, with some justification, that the cost of feed was unacceptably high, because the British army's demand for fodder had pushed up animal feed prices generally. Their last stand came in a protest at a corporation meeting on 10 December when their spokesman, Councillor Michael Maher, told the meeting that his members would defy the Food Controller and sell their cattle on the city's streets if need be, because cattle dealers were exporting cows anyway as 'strippers' only to rehabilitate them as 'milchers' once they reached Holyhead.

There were also claims that 'cows were being milked just before reaching the boats for the purpose of deceiving the portal inspectors,' and they should be detained for twelve hours before sailing to ensure they were not lactating. The department rejected the idea out of hand as impractical and admitted that licences were being issued for about a quarter of Irish milch cows to meet demand in Britain and to contain milk prices generally in the United Kingdom.

It was further grist to the advanced nationalist mill. A few councillors even expressed continued sympathy for the cowmen, but the majority remained sceptical. W. T. Cosgrave, once more the leader of the Sinn Féin group after his release from prison, denounced the British government as the main culprit for depriving cowkeepers of cheap feed by virtually shutting down the city's breweries and distilleries. He demanded that some of the tax on excess profits from Dublin's war industries, such as the National Shell Factory, be used to subsidise milk and other essential foodstuffs.[21]

By the time Cosgrave made his intervention in the dairy controversy he was Sinn Féin's first urban MP, but he was elected for Kilkenny City, not Dublin. He was the fourth Sinn Féin MP in 1917 to defeat a UIL candidate in a by-election.

Redmond and the Irish Party had withdrawn from Parliament on 7 March in an effort to retrieve their political fortunes after Lloyd George confirmed unequivocally that the Government of Ireland Act would exclude Ulster. Redmond accused Lloyd George 'of treason to the interests of Ireland and the Empire.' Before leading his party out of the House of Commons he warned, more presciently than he probably realised, that

> the Prime Minister is playing into the hands of those in Ireland who are seeking to destroy the Constitutional movement. If that occurs the Premier will have to govern Ireland by the naked sword.

The *Irish Independent* commented that the leadership of the Irish Party was now paying the price for fawning 'like nerveless creatures' on successive English governments rather than acting like men and securing home rule in 1912. The *Irish Times* took the opposite tack and bewailed the fact that Redmond had been 'overborne' by John Dillon and other opponents of the war. It believed that had others emulated Redmond's enthusiasm the unity of nationalist and unionist would have been secured, although on what basis and to what purpose was unclear. The paper was on sounder ground when it predicted that partition would only deepen existing divisions.[22]

———

The next day, on the other side of Europe, the Russian Revolution began when Cossacks refused to disperse mass demonstrations in Petrograd, called on International Women's Day to demand bread. Its reverberations would soon be felt in Ireland through the renewed pressure for conscription as the Russian military effort flagged. The revolution was hailed in Irish labour circles and especially in the Irish Transport and General Workers' Union, where tensions between some of the members and James Connolly over the use of Liberty Hall by the Citizen Army before the Easter Rising were long forgotten.

The triumph of the Bolshevik rising in November would strike a particular resonance with some of Connolly's former comrades. As William O'Brien told the Irish Labour Party and Trades Union Congress in 1918, when Connolly

> laid down his life for the Irish working class he laid it down for the working class in all countries, for he believed that an example of action ought to be given to the workers to spur them to resistance to the powers of imperialism and capitalism which have plunged Europe into the war of empire and conquest ... We know the influence it exercised among those great men and women who have given us the great Russian Revolution.[23]

Meanwhile the ITGWU was in the middle of a Lazarus-like resurrection. It had struggled as an organisation in the aftermath of the lock-out. Larkin had departed to the United States on a fund-raising trip that was also meant to provide him with an opportunity to recuperate from the strain of struggle and defeat, while his successor, Connolly, became increasingly preoccupied with the Citizen Army and plans for the rising. Membership fell from 30,000 at its peak in 1913 to 15,000 in 1914, 10,000 in 1915 and probably less than 5,000 on the eve of the rising.[24] To add to its woes, Liberty Hall had been bombarded, its records seized and many leading members shot or imprisoned. The union had to accept an offer of temporary accommodation at the Trades Council Hall in Capel Street. Miraculously, membership reached 14,000 by the end of the year and 25,000 by the end of 1917. Thomas Foran, the president, doubled as general secretary on his release from prison, and he was joined by his fellow-internee William O'Brien, an organiser of genius. Although O'Brien would not be formally appointed general treasurer of the ITGWU until February 1919, he devoted most of his time after his release from internment to the union.

Two other key figures in the revival of the union were Joseph McGrath, who took over management of the ITGWU's National Health Insurance Approved Society, and J. J. (Séamus) Hughes, who served as financial and corresponding secretary. Liberty Hall was renovated through a building fund to which members contributed the first week's pay of any increase achieved by the union. 'In this way [the] Liberty Hall frontage has actually been rebuilt by the employers of Dublin!' the union boasted.

Another critical factor in the union's success was its close association with Connolly and Easter Week. It was becoming patriotic as well as economically beneficial to join the union. Many small 'land and labour' unions in rural Ireland joined the ITGWU *en masse*, and in Dublin new groups of workers, such as cinema projectionists, did so. Of course the authorities and employers were far from happy at the unexpected resurgence of the union. After the rising John Dillon Nugent, the Dublin MP who was also secretary of the Ancient Order of Hibernians, had approached Dublin Castle with a view to 'buying' the union. It is probable that he meant making a bid for the insurance section, as he was head of the Hibernian Insurance Fund, the largest Irish insurance company.

Fortunately for the union, the recruitment of McGrath ensured the continuing financial viability of the union. McGrath had worked for the accountancy firm Craig Gardner before taking part in the rising, was a close associate of Michael Collins and a senior figure in the IRB. Séamus Hughes, also a participant in the rising, was a prominent figure on the cultural scene. A former seminarian and a contributor to the *Irish Worker* in its heyday under Larkin, he saw no problem in people believing in 'economic socialism without attaching themselves to atheistic doctrines.'[25]

———

It was against this surge in the new patriotism that the legacy of the Irish Party had to contend. As it had never opposed political violence on principle and had frequently invoked the memory of the 'hillside men', the party could only criticise the British government for betraying constitutional nationalism and the rebels for subverting it. The futility of its position was demonstrated by a return to Parliament, having made its protest over partition. The alternative was to adopt the abstentionist position of Sinn Féin that it had consistently attacked.

Any hopes that the post-rising mood in Dublin was a passing fancy were dispelled on Easter Monday, 9 April 1917, regarded as the first anniversary of the rising. A proclamation was issued by Lieutenant-General Sir Bryan Mahon, who had commanded the 10th (Irish) Division at Gallipoli and was now general officer commanding the forces in Ireland, banning public meetings and assemblies in Dublin during Easter Week, except for the annual Lord Mayor's procession to the Pro-Cathedral on Easter Sunday. The procession passed off peacefully, but on Easter Monday a large Tricolour was flying at half mast from a temporary flagstaff on the parapet of the GPO. The parapet is 90 feet above ground level, so that the flag was visible over a wide area and drew crowds into Sackville Street. 'Thousands of holiday makers ... raised their hats in passing it, and waved handkerchiefs.' When the flagstaff toppled over at about 10 a.m. a young man promptly walked along the parapet to fix it back in position. 'That was the signal for an outburst of cheering and various other demonstrations of approval on a wide scale,' the *Irish Times* reported.

One such demonstration was by a group of young men who occupied Nelson's Pillar and flew another 'Sinn Fein flag' from the top for about a quarter of an hour. They were allowed to leave the Pillar unmolested, but a policeman then climbed onto the parapet of the GPO to remove the flagstaff. It was secured so firmly that it took an hour to cut it down. As soon as it hit the ground three boys tore the flag off the staff and ran down Prince's Street into the ruins with their prize. Again there were loud cheers, and a large section of the crowd made its way down Lower Abbey Street to Liberty Hall, where there were further cheers and flag-waving.

Many in the crowds that gathered at Liberty Hall and continued to occupy Sackville Street wore black armbands surmounted by ribbons with 'Sinn Fein colours.' Flags appeared on other buildings, and during the afternoon gangs of youths used the debris on derelict sites to stone the police. The fighting grew particularly fierce outside the Abbey Theatre, where a DMP superintendent and inspector were among the casualties. Eventually the police retreated to Sackville Street, while an unarmed military detachment passing along Eden Quay had to flee across Butt Bridge.

Some rioters turned their attention to the Methodist church in Lower Abbey Street, while others made for the richer pickings in the shops erected in temporary buildings nearby. The worst of the rioting was at the junction of Talbot Street and North Earl Street, and several trams were damaged as well as shops. Peace was eventually restored when a sharp hailstorm just after dark scattered the crowds.

Only two arrests were made on a day when a mixture of rebel sympathisers and what the *Times* termed 'young toughs' effectually took over the north city. Republicans had retrieved their honour by defying the authorities; but the only people able to re-enact fully their role in the rising were the looters from the slums.[26]

Meanwhile, in the stately atmosphere of City Hall across the river, the Irish Drapers' Assistants' Association, Ireland's largest, oldest and richest white-collar union, was holding its annual general meeting. At the top of the agenda was the lack of compensation from the government for members who had been laid off as a result of the destruction of department stores during the rising. Although the Drapers were the wealthiest union in Dublin, their resources had been severely tried. During the winter £3,000 had been paid out to offset hardship and another £3,000 by the insurance section. Despite the disturbed state of the country and the lack of sympathy from government and employers alike, the association's president, W. J. McNabb, appealed to members not to allow politics to affect their work.

Membership had reached a record figure, largely because of expansion in Belfast and the North; it had also held up in Dublin, although £500 had had to be paid out in unemployment benefit. Despite McNabb's plea, politics did intrude with a debate on a motion dealing with conscription. Southern delegates insisted that the issue was an 'economic matter,' while northern members insisted it was 'political.' There does not appear to have been a vote. Delegates adjourned to dinner at the Dolphin Hotel, where the general secretary, Michael O'Lehane, a long-standing member of Sinn Féin, assured them that with the growth of education labour could, without bloodshed, achieve all its objectives.[27]

———

The militant mood on Dublin's streets was about to be further inflamed by news that another six hundred jobs were to go in the city's breweries and distilleries. Distress was now so widespread and so obviously feeding into civic disorder that the Local Government Board finally sanctioned £1,250 for setting up communal kitchens in the poorer areas of the city.

Any kudos from the measure was cancelled out by the angry public reaction to a letter from Lieutenant-General Mahon, published in the *Irish Times*, urging the men who lost their jobs 'owing to the limitations placed on brewing and distilling industries and allied concerns' to join the British army. He described the attractions of increased separation and dependants' allowances and stated that skilled workers would be welcome in technical services such as the Royal Flying Corps and Royal Engineers.

The *Times* welcomed the general's 'attractive' offer to recruits and contrasted their prospects with those of men who went to England under the National Service scheme to work 'among strangers in a strange land.' Army recruits, even if they ended up in a strange land, would be among their own 'gallant Irish regiments.' The general boasted, quite truthfully, that 'there are more Dublin men in the trenches today than in all the Dublin breweries and distilleries.'[28] It was not an argument to boost recruitment: most Dubliners now preferred to see fewer fellow-citizens in the trenches.

———

If the events of Easter Monday 1917 demonstrated the mood on the streets, the first serious attempt to channel that anger organisationally came with a conference convened by Count Plunkett in the Mansion House on 19 April. Well over a thousand representatives of various organisations attended. They included delegates from local authorities, boards of Poor Law guardians and other bodies that were traditionally dominated by Irish Party stalwarts, as well as thirty divisions of the Ancient Order of Hibernians. They were leavened by representatives of radical nationalist bodies, such as Sinn Féin, the Irish National League, Cumann na mBan, and nineteen trades councils. The prevalence of Tricolours, including one carried by a fourteen-year-old boy who had allegedly been interned, indicated the prevailing mood.

There was a minute's silence for those who had died in the rising and a call for those still in custody to be treated as prisoners of war. But the most significant action was the adoption of a declaration asserting 'Ireland's right to freedom from all foreign control.' The conference further demanded representation at the post-war Peace Conference convening in Paris so that it could release 'the small nations from the control of the Greater powers.' The delegates affirmed their commitment 'to use every means in their power to obtain complete liberty.' The Dublin Trades Council delegation, led by Thomas Farren and William O'Brien, 'wished God-speed to the great work begun that day for Ireland.' O'Brien declared that 'Irish labour was absolutely united against partition—even those [workers] opposed to Irish self-government in the North.'

Plunkett stressed that the National Alliance he was launching was not another party 'to machine public opinion' but was for building an organisation in every parish 'prepared to deal with any emergency such as the introduction of a fraudulent Home Rule business.' However, Arthur Griffith made it clear that Sinn Féin would continue to pursue its own policies, and it was agreed that all interested bodies, including the Irish Volunteers, then reorganising, should hold talks on creating a new movement to 'smash' the Irish Party.[29] Calls from the floor for food exports to be banned and for conscription to be resisted reflected the more immediate concerns of delegates.

The editorial in the next day's *Irish Independent* summed up the conundrum now facing many moderate nationalists. The paper admitted that Plunkett's programme appeared increasingly attractive, although his gathering 'would have been inconceivable three or four years previously' and was possible now only because of the

> repeated muddling, chronic weakness and inactivity of the Nationalist leaders and Party ... On the other hand we are not believers in the methods or policy of the Party whose battle cry is an Irish Republic.

It questioned how much support the abstention policy advocated by Plunkett and Griffith really had.

———

It would receive the answer three weeks later in the South Longford by-election. The Sinn Féin candidate on this occasion was not a Papal count and grieving father of an executed leader of the rising but a draper's assistant in Dublin convicted of armed rebellion. What was worse, Joe McGuinness was a native of Co. Roscommon and had no links to the constituency in which he was standing. In fact he did not even want to stand, and most of his imprisoned comrades did not want to nominate him, including Éamon de Valera, who felt that participation in a parliamentary election was tantamount to recognising British rule in Ireland.

His only fellow-prisoners who felt strongly that he should run were Thomas Ashe, the teacher from Lusk who had won the battle of Ashbourne, and Harry Boland, a Dublin tailor. Both were senior members of the IRB—Ashe was to be elected president on his release from prison—and they worked closely with another rising IRB man on the outside, Michael Collins, to promote McGuinness's candidature. When the candidate still refused to run they nominated him anyway under the famous slogan 'Put him in to get him out.'

It was a dirty campaign, even by Irish standards. No fewer than twenty Irish Party MPs campaigned for their candidate, Patrick McKenna, while Dublin radicals, such as Michael Collins, Arthur Griffith, William O'Brien and the ITGWU's new financial officer, Joseph McGrath, invaded the constituency. The large convoys of Sinn Féin motor cars bedecked with Tricolours touring the county were denounced as evidence of 'German gold', while the Irish Party members were accused of cheering the executions of the 1916 leaders in the House of Commons.

Past internecine strife within the Irish Party came back to haunt it when one of McKenna's supporters, J. P. Farrell, editor of the *Longford Leader*, was reminded that he had described the candidate 'as a dyspeptic visaged humbug ... from the Irish Pig Buyers' Association.' There was also a destructive dimension to the Irish Party's campaign. On the weekend before polling the mothers of two of the executed 1916 leaders, Mary Josephine Plunkett and Margaret Pearse, together with the widow of a third, Kathleen Clarke, were stoned in Longford by a number of 'drunken and abandoned females ... from suitable cover behind the Bludgeon men' of the Irish Party. The *Irish Independent* intimated that the women had been plied with free drink before the incident. On his return to Dublin, John Dillon Nugent was alleged by the same newspaper to have sacked a number of employees for travelling to Co. Longford in their own time to canvass for McGuinness.[30] This brought the Irish Party more bad publicity; but far worse was to come.

On the eve of the election more than twenty senior churchmen, including three Protestant bishops, signed a manifesto opposing partition; one of them, Archbishop Walsh of Dublin, issued a letter denouncing the Irish Party for political cowardice.[31] Dr Walsh's letter was in effect an endorsement of McGuinness, who won the hard-fought contest by 1,493 votes to 1,461.

If the Irish Party could be defeated in its heartland it could be defeated anywhere in Ireland. The Walsh letter symbolised the alienation of many traditional supporters of home rule from the Irish Party and their despair at its inability to prosecute the nationalist cause effectively. But the archbishop had gone even further: he had made support for McGuinness and the other Easter rebels politically respectable.

———

Now that a rebel prisoner was a member of Parliament, the emphasis of advanced nationalists shifted quickly to securing the release of the 120 remaining prisoners in Britain, all of whom had been sentenced to varying terms. On the evening of Sunday 10 June a demonstration was held in Beresford Place in support of the prisoners in Lewes Jail in the Isle of Wight who had begun a hunger strike for prisoner-of-war status. It had been banned by Lieutenant-General Mahon, but that did not prevent three thousand people turning out to greet the hackney car carrying the speakers, Count Plunkett and Cathal Brugha.

As it drew up in front of Liberty Hall at 7:30 p.m. Inspector John Mills of the DMP arrested the two men. A large force of police was needed to clear a route to Store Street station nearby, and stones were thrown freely. As they neared the station Mills was felled by a blow to the head from a hurley. His assailant was pursued by two constables down Abbey Street, but one was obstructed by the crowd and the other was himself attacked when he attempted an arrest. Inspector Mills was taken to Jervis Street Hospital, where he died shortly afterwards, leaving a widow and three children aged between thirteen and nineteen. A carriage-driver at an undertaker's was subsequently arrested, but it proved impossible to find any witnesses to give evidence. The DMP would find this to be a recurring pattern over the next few years. Four policemen were injured that night in riots along South

Great George's Street and Aungier Street as word spread of the arrests of Plunkett and Brugha. Again looters were busy.

A fund was set up to assist the inspector's family, but, as with the Royal Dublin Fusiliers' Association, its membership was dominated by the old ascendancy and southern unionists, with the Earl of Meath as president, Sir John Arnott and Sir Maurice Dockrell as vice-presidents, and the baker John Mooney as deputy chairman. Apart from Alderman Laurence O'Neill, the Lord Mayor, there were no prominent nationalists on the committee.[32]

——

Five days after the death of Inspector Mills, Lloyd George announced the release of the prisoners. It was timed to coincide with the launch of the Irish Convention, which would be a forum of 'Irishmen of all parties for the purpose of producing a scheme of Irish self-government.' The hope that the prisoners' release would create an atmosphere of good will in which the spirit of compromise could flourish proved ill-founded. The Irish Party claimed credit, with some justification, for the government's change of heart, but the opening of the convention received none from the ecstatic crowds who greeted the prisoners.

The government, while wishing to appear conciliatory, made the releases as low-key as possible, with no prior announcement to the prisoners or their families. Nevertheless by 4:30 a.m. on Monday 18 June a crowd of three thousand with a convoy of wagonettes was waiting at the North Wall to greet their heroes. Word that they were being transported via Holyhead to Kingstown did not filter through until the prisoners were reported disembarking shortly after 8 a.m. While the crowd was marching quickly across the city the released men found themselves having to share the railway carriages from Kingstown with soldiers on leave from France; but the only unpleasantness, as reported by the *Irish Times*, was when some civilian passengers demanded that they be moved to another part of the train.

As they left Westland Row the prisoners were seized by the crowd and led up Great Brunswick Street before the organisers of the welcome could rescue them and install them in the wagonettes for their triumphal return to the scene of their defeat at the GPO. There was some confusion over the identity of some released prisoners, who stood out only by the uniformity of their cropped heads and unshaved stubble. They were loudly cheered as they were led past the ruins of the GPO and on to Fleming's Hotel in Gardiner Place for a celebratory luncheon. Later they called on the Lord Mayor at the Mansion House before heading home.

Frank Robbins of the Citizen Army probably spoke for most of the prisoners when he described his homecoming as one of the greatest surprises of my life. What a contrast with the humiliating day of our departure. The reception given to us by the Dublin people was beyond description. A very large force of D.M.P. was around Westland Row but they were simply overwhelmed by the throng of people that greeted us on our appearance at the exits. From there up to Tara Street not one of us had a moment without some man's or woman's arms around us, kissing us, slapping us on the back, and practically carrying us through the streets. It was our moment of real triumph which well repaid us for our day of surrender and the subsequent insults.[33]

The *Weekly Irish Times* reported it as 'noteworthy that there was no enthusiasm and no cheering along the footpaths, or the tram cars,' as the procession of prisoners and their supporters made their way through the city. But these would have been early-morning commuters on their way to shops and offices and largely unaware of the nature or significance of the event they were witnessing.

As the paper reported later, a festive mood gradually took hold of the city as word of the releases spread. Crowds of young men and women colonised the city centre with 'Sinn Fein' flags. Not one but two Tricolours were flown by 'an athletic young man' from the top of the GPO, and wooden hoardings around shelled sites were torn down for a bonfire at 10:30 p.m. More railings were used by youths for mock military drill.

Even the *Times* had to concede that whenever a released Sinn Féiner, or anyone remotely suspected of being one, was observed they were warmly congratulated. When, however, a detachment of soldiers went through the city on its way to France 'not a cheer was given.'

Similar scenes occurred over the next few days as other prisoners returned home, most notably Constance Markievicz, who was released on the day following the main batch of prisoners. She was met by a fellow-veteran of the rising, Dr Kathleen Lynn, in her car. Lynn had been chief medical officer of the Citizen Army and, as a captain, actually outranked Lieutenant Markievicz. She drove her through cheering crowds from Westland Row to Liberty Hall, where Markievicz addressed the crowd in her usual fiery style. The *Irish Independent* reported that she looked 'very well and was most cheerful.' While she declined to talk about the political situation until she had acquainted herself with the facts, she was scathing of the British prison system, which she denounced as dirty in both the material and the moral sense. She called for prisoners to be allowed to join trade unions as the best means of cleaning it up. She was attired in a blue silk dress and wore a large water-lily. Her sister, Eva Gore-Booth, explained that Constance had chosen the flower because it combined the Sinn Féin colours of green, white and orange. By Friday the Dublin cinemas were showing newsreels of her return.[34]

———

Almost as a protest at the way the country was drifting, on the Saturday after the release of the prisoners the *Weekly Irish Times* published a large block of sixteen photographs of Irish soldiers who had been killed recently at the front alongside its report of the rebel prisoners' return to the city. Pride of place went to Major Willie Redmond, brother of the Irish Party leader, who had died in the attack on Messines Ridge on 7 June. It was a combined operation by the 36th (Ulster) Division and the 16th (Irish) Division, in which Redmond served, and it typified the type of sacrifice he believed could form the basis for Irish unity in the future, although there were few enough Irish replacements to fill the gaps in the ranks of either division by this stage in the war.

Redmond's passing was widely mourned, but its main significance was that it left a vacancy in the House of Commons. When the released prisoners gathered in Fleming's Hotel on their return to Ireland they decided to nominate Éamon de Valera, the senior surviving commandant from 1916.

Willie Redmond's popularity, his personal integrity and the manner of his death should have been strong cards for the Irish Party to play, even with de Valera nominated to run against its candidate, Patrick Lynch. A ditty to the tune of 'The Wearing of the Green' summed up the Irish Party's hopes.

> Oh, Paddy dear, you need not fear
> The Spaniard going round,
> For we are Irish, and our hearts
> To Redmond still are bound.

The 'Spaniard' won East Clare by 5,020 votes to 2,025.

———

There was another by-election on the same day in South County Dublin. It attracted far less attention but was no less an indication of the political gale now blowing. It had been caused by the death of Alderman William F. Cotton, chairman of the Alliance and Dublin Consumers' Gas Company, who had narrowly won the seat from the unionists in the second election of 1910. He was described by the *Irish Times* as 'one of the most widely known and most popular members of the business community in Dublin,' though 'his political opinions were … of the most fluid and contradictory character.' In putting him forward in such a solidly middle-class constituency, where many Catholic voters had supported unionist candidates in the past, 'it was hoped that a good many Unionists, being satisfied of Mr. Cotton's harmlessness as a politician would give him their vote for personal reasons.'[35]

As Cotton had been defeated by the unionist candidate, Captain Bryan Cooper, by a mere 65 votes in the first election of 1910 and had in turn defeated Cooper by only 133 votes in December 1910, the unionist bloc remained a force to be reckoned with. At first it appeared that there could be a crowded field in 1917, with a unionist, independent unionist and at least two nationalist candidates running. The UIL candidate was Michael L. Hearn, a solicitor and chairman of the board of directors of the *Freeman's Journal*. Sinn Féin was not expected to put forward a candidate in such a conservative constituency; but on 30 June Dr James S. Ashe, a unionist, wrote to John Redmond as a precautionary measure, proposing that all the declared candidates withdraw in favour of Sir Horace Plunkett. Plunkett had represented the constituency previously as a unionist. A man of progressive views who had been nominated by the British government to chair the forthcoming Irish Convention, he could be seen as a champion of moderation and reconciliation.

The initiative might have appealed to Redmond had it not been scuttled immediately by one of the unionist candidates, Sir Frederick Falkiner. He said that rather than allow the constituency to be handed over to Plunkett 'as a gift' he would prefer to see a nationalist elected 'on the ground that an avowed opponent whose views are unmistakable is to be preferred to an administrator whose views on important questions seem colourless.' This effectually sealed the outcome of the election in favour of the main nationalist candidate.

Still fearful of the danger of Sinn Féin romping home between the warring home rule and unionist blocs, all the other candidates agreed to withdraw in favour of Hearn. As James Creed Meredith told a meeting in support of Sir John O'Connell before Hearn was endorsed as the agreed candidate, they could not blind themselves to the fact that 'the machinery of the Nationalist organisation in almost every respect has broken down.'

As it happened, Sinn Féin decided not to contest South County Dublin but to concentrate its efforts on getting de Valera elected. Unfortunately for unionists and home-rulers, there was not another constituency in Ireland where such an unlikely pact was possible.[36]

___

The Irish Convention, designed to allow the leaders of unionism and constitutional nationalism to reach a settlement that would deny advanced nationalists their victory, opened on 25 July. Far from smoothing the way, the release of the prisoners had served to alarm unionists, north and south. The Ulstermen insisted on continuing acceptance of partition by Redmond as a precondition for talks, while the choice of Trinity College as a venue further alienated nationalist opinion.

The mood of the crowd outside was unenthusiastic. An attempt by supporters to raise a cheer for Redmond as the first session ended backfired, serving only to attract a group of hostile youths who followed him all the way back to the

Gresham Hotel.[37] The following month brought further humiliation for Redmond and his party when the recently released councillor for the Liberties, William T. Cosgrave, was elected comfortably in Kilkenny to take Sinn Féin's first urban seat. The victory was celebrated in Dublin with a rally outside the Sinn Féin meeting rooms in Westmorland Street.

One particularly damaging tactic of Sinn Féin in Kilkenny had been to emphasise the opposition of the Irish Party to the increase in the old-age pension introduced by the British government in June to help offset wartime inflation. Redmond had told the House of Commons that the increase of 2s 6d a week was an 'extravagance which would not have been indulged in by an Irish Parliament comprised of Irishmen responsible to the country and knowing the country.'[38] He may well have been right, and defending the ratepayer was good politics for the party in normal times. It was one of history's little ironies that when normality did return in the 1920s it was an Irish government headed by W. T. Cosgrave that cut the old-age pension for precisely the same reasons Redmond had outlined in the House of Commons in June 1917.

————

Meanwhile the death of Cotton had left a vacancy for alderman on Dublin Corporation. The agreement between Labour, Sinn Féin and nationalist councillors on filling these posts by co-option frayed at this point. There were two nationalist candidates for Cotton's seat in the South Dock ward. The official candidate was a sitting councillor, Thomas Murty O'Beirne, a temperance hotelier and tenement-owner. However, some Labour councillors opted to support a challenge by Sinn Féin for the seat on behalf of Charles Murphy, a local man nominated by Alderman Tom Kelly and seconded by the independent nationalist Lorcan O'Toole. O'Beirne, who had the support of the UIL and AOH machines, won comfortably by 44 votes to 14.[39]

Labour's support for Murphy backfired the following month when the vacancy for a councillor in New Kilmainham arose. This had been caused by the death of William Partridge in July from Bright's disease, contracted in prison. Peter S. Doyle was a mechanical engineer at the Inchicore railway works, where Partridge himself had once worked, and, like Partridge, he had been 'out' in 1916. He received a plethora of endorsements, including the Inchicore United Workmen's Club, the local branch of the Town Tenants' Association and the Number 1 Branch of John Saturninus Kelly's 'scab' Railway Workers' Trade Union, as well as numerous 'local merchants and traders.' By contrast, the official Labour nominee, Thomas Lawlor of the Tailors' Society, only had the endorsement of Dublin United Trades Council. It had expected this to be sufficient, as it was effectually the nominating body for Labour candidates in the city; but when it came to a vote

Doyle won by 32 votes to 16. Some Sinn Féin councillors voted with the dominant nationalist faction, as did the renegade Labour councillor John Saturninus Kelly.[40]

It then became necessary to fill O'Beirne's vacancy as a councillor, and the same battle was played out in the council chamber. The Sinn Féin candidate, Joseph Curran, had a petition signed by two thousand local residents in his favour, but he was rejected in favour of J. J. O'Looney, who had endorsements from the Irish National Foresters' Benefit Society and the City of Dublin Stonecutters' Trade Union. The latter endorsement was a reminder that some of the craft unions still had strong links to the old nationalist machine.[41]

In exasperation, Alderman Tom Kelly of Sinn Féin said that the sooner direct elections to council seats were restored the better.[42] Meanwhile Alderman Laurence O'Neill, the man who had been marched through Dublin after the rising 'between fixed bayonets,' would continue to preside with his increasing political dexterity and would remain in the mayoral chair for the next seven years.

| 'I DIE IN A GOOD CAUSE'

When the men released from Lewes Prison met at Fleming's Hotel in Gardiner Place, a large number wanted to nominate the schoolmaster from Lusk, Thomas Ashe, to contest the East Clare by-election. Ashe, however, who had acted as de Valera's second in command in Lewes, declined in order to avoid disunion in the ranks, and he went on to campaign vigorously for de Valera.

Although de Valera was the senior surviving officer from the rising, Ashe was equally well known. Besides leading the only militarily successful rebel force in 1916, he was highly regarded by advanced nationalists for his involvement in the Gaelic League, GAA and other cultural organisations. Handsome, with a commanding presence,[1] he had a reputation as the best speaker and public advocate of the advanced nationalist cause. When Cosgrave—not the most charismatic of candidates, although a very businesslike one—arrived in Kilkenny to contest the seat in August 1917 he sent to Dublin the laconic message: 'I want Ashe.'

Unlike many prisoners, Ashe found that his job as school principal had been kept open for him by the parish priest, Father Byrne, despite their past differences. But he never resumed the post, visiting the area only to speak at an aeraíocht in Donabate and to meet members of the Irish Volunteers and the IRB, of which he was now president. With other former prisoners based in Dublin, including Michael Collins, he rewrote the organisation's constitution.

Ashe was very like Collins in his drive and his ability to carry out multiple tasks simultaneously, but he never came across as a braggart or bully. Like Collins, he spent most of his eight weeks of freedom setting the country alight with seditious speeches and rebuilding rebel structures; and, like Collins, he found time to socialise. One of his favourite haunts was number 1 Brendan Road in Donnybrook. This was the home of a fellow-Kerryman, Batt O'Connor, a stonemason and building contractor from Castleisland who had begun installing secret compartments in selected houses he was working on, which proved invaluable in the War of Independence. O'Connor's daughter Eibhlín recalled:

We as children remember him as a very gentle man during his stay with us and his delightful way with children, talking to us about his interests in country life, the Cause of Ireland and books. He had sung for my mother and father his poem 'Let me carry your Cross for Ireland Lord' … and one night they gathered us children around him and asked him to sing it for us. My father asked us to pay great attention. We were very impressed too and I remember it so well that summer evening with Tom sitting with his back to the dining room window with the sun pouring in on him as he sung his poem. He had set it to his own music.[2]

He knew he faced the strong possibility of re-arrest, and had no permanent base, other than the family farm at Kinard, near Dingle. When one of many female admirers asked him to write a list of prisons where he had stayed since 1916 he finished with the words 'To be continued.'

He was eventually arrested by detectives from G Division of the DMP while waiting for a tram at Nelson's Pillar on Saturday 18 August 1917. He was first held at the Curragh Camp, where the military regime was relatively relaxed, but this changed when he was transferred to Mountjoy Prison in Dublin on 29 August. A medical examination found him to be in good health, and he appears to have taken the change philosophically. His only complaint was the lack of air in his cell—a problem he remedied by smashing some of the glass panels in the window.

He was charged with making a seditious speech at Ballinalee, Co. Longford, on 25 July. He could as easily have been charged with half a dozen other speeches. He was tried on 3 September and the sentence was handed down on the 11th: two years' hard labour, remitted to twelve months from the date of the trial—a sentence out of all proportion to the alleged comments Ashe made. The RIC witnesses could produce no notes of what he had actually said at the meeting.

Ashe was on a collision course with the authorities from the first day of his sentence, as he refused to sew mailbags and insisted on talking to his fellow-prisoners in the exercise yard, something forbidden to men serving a criminal sentence. As a punishment his mattress was removed from his cell and he was denied any secular reading matter.

The new coercion policy would rebound not alone on the British government but also on the Irish Party as public interest in the battle grew. Part of the evidence against Ashe had been an alleged attack in his Ballinalee speech on T. P. O'Connor, a senior nationalist MP, who had gone on a fund-raising tour of America only to return, according to Ashe, 'with his tail between his legs.'

In his widely published defence speech Ashe described the statements by RIC witnesses as 'the most choice item of the evidence.'

> I have made many statements in public but had not been arrested until I criticised Mr. O'Connor. I would not mind going to prison for a decent charge, but it would be unfair to be sent to prison in order that Mr. T. P. O'Connor might collect forty thousand dollars in America.

Nor were Ashe's supporters outside slow to mention the fact that the chairman of the Prison Board overseeing the coercion strategy, Max Green, was a son-in-law of John Redmond.[3]

The confrontation escalated rapidly as other rebel prisoners joined the protest and adopted similar tactics to those used in Lewes Prison to secure concessions. In retaliation the cells were raided and stripped of bedding and the men had their personal belongings removed. Boots were taken to prevent the prisoners kicking cells doors or otherwise damaging prison property. The prisoners then brought forward a threatened hunger strike from 1 October to 20 September.

From the beginning the Prison Board made it clear that it would take a hard line and would resort to forced feeding to break the strike, a controversial practice that had led to deaths in Britain in the past. The prison authorities also tried to suppress news of the strike, but Ashe managed to send word to the Lord Mayor, Laurence O'Neill, who visited him and other prisoners in Mountjoy. Prisoners who had been in Lewes with Ashe considered the regime there to be humane compared with that adopted by the Prison Board in Mountjoy.

During the forced-feeding sessions each man was strapped by his arms and legs in a high chair. A tube was forced down the gullet through either the mouth or the nose so that food could be pumped directly into the stomach. As there were only four pumps in the prison, it was not possible to feed all forty prisoners each day. Nor was the equipment sterilised. Dr William Lowe, who administered the forced feeding, had no previous experience in the procedure.[4]

On Sunday 23 September there was a mass protest in Smithfield, followed by a march to the prison. It was to be the first of many such protests over the coming years. Ashe was visited again by the Lord Mayor and Sir John Irvine, chairman of the Visiting Justices Committee. The bedding and clothing had been restored to the cell, but Ashe remained adamant that the men would continue their protest until they achieved prisoner-of-war status. 'Even though I do die, I die in a good cause,' he told his distinguished visitors. A deeply religious man, Ashe appeared to have a premonition of his death.

On Tuesday 25 September, Ashe was forcibly fed by Dr Lowe shortly after 11 a.m. Lowe claimed later that Ashe did not resist having the tube inserted down his throat, but other prisoners recalled Lowe as a particularly rough practitioner, and the subsequent examination of Ashe's body uncovered extensive bruising and scratch marks around his mouth, chin and throat. Whatever happened, it resulted in fatal damage to his lungs. He was taken to the prison hospital ward after the forced feeding session and transferred to the Mater Hospital at about 5 p.m. In a scene reminiscent of the executions a year earlier, two Capuchin friars, Father Albert and Father Augustine, called to give him the last rites. He told the priests: 'I was splendid this morning until forcibly fed.' As they were leaving he added: 'We made a great fight.' Father Augustine gave the traditional blessing in Irish: 'God is good, and he has a good mother.' Ashe replied in Irish, 'Yes, indeed, father.' Those were his last recorded words. Water slowly filled his damaged lungs, and he died of oedema at about 10:30 p.m. while Dr Kathleen Lynn was taking his pulse.

A large crowd had already gathered outside the hospital. Among the mourners was his old friend and fellow-piper Seán O'Casey. The next few days saw an outpouring of grief such as Ireland had not witnessed for many years. It was as if the feelings of fear, confused anger and uncertainty that had haunted Dublin and the country at large since the events of Easter Week and the subsequent executions had been resolved in an overwhelming outburst of sorrow for the loss of the dead man.

O'Casey wrote a lament for Ashe, but Ashe had written his own epitaph.

Let me carry your Cross for Ireland, Lord!
The hour of her trial draws near,
And the pangs and the pains of the sacrifice
May be borne by comrades dear.
But Lord take me from the offering throng,
There are many far less prepared
Though anxious and all as they are to die
That Ireland may be spared.[5]

The song would be published in every nationalist newspaper and news-sheet in the country.

Long before then both the British administration and the Irish Party had to undergo their own political purgatory. As Ashe's biographer Seán Ó Lúing put it, 'Thomas Ashe's death changed the mood and mind of Ireland almost overnight.' Until then the Irish Party leadership had clung to some hope that Sinn Féin's political progress could be halted. The next morning the party's mouthpiece, the *Freeman's Journal*, voiced their despair.

There must be a hidden malignant and malevolent influence somewhere in the government of Ireland, whether in the War Cabinet or the Castle, determined that Ireland shall not have peace in freedom and that there shall be no reconciliation between the British and Irish peoples.

The *Irish Independent* put the dilemma faced by the Irish Party with brutal bluntness. The death of Ashe had driven the country 'to the verge of desperation' and had

> embittered thousands of Irish nationalists who had no real sympathy with the policy of Sinn Fein. The Irish Party ... is now fighting for its life and ... hates the Sinn Feiners more than it does the Unionists, and longs for their complete extermination. Yet it is holding out the left hand as if to succour them, whilst with the right it would deal them the death blow should the chance be theirs.

Much of the provincial press was already turning against the old guard. The *Waterford News*, in Redmond's own stronghold, denounced the 'cataracts of crocodile tears' for Ashe, while the *Kilkenny People*, which had witnessed Cosgrave's victory, drew attention to the role of Max Green in the whole affair.

The only newspaper in the south to play down Ashe's death was the *Irish Times*, which gave more prominence to the annual meeting of the Ferns Diocesan Synod of the Church of Ireland. Predictably, the synod in its debate ruled out any notion of a 'Republic' for Ireland, but the president, Dr Gregg, pointed out with more prescience than he probably realised that an Order in Council of 1801, made after the Act of Union was passed, provided for 'dominion' government under the crown. 'The dissolution of the Legislative Union did not mean either quitting the Empire or losing their King,' he told his fellow southern unionists.[6] He had unknowingly described the constitutional arrangement that would be made at the end the War of Independence in 1921.

Meanwhile in Dublin the British military guard on the Mater Hospital withdrew and Ashe's old comrades took charge. A guard of honour composed of men from Fingal stood over the body, which was cleaned by nurses and dressed in Volunteer uniform. Sister Juliana recalled: 'He was such a handsome young man, with lovely hair. He looked beautiful.'[7] The body was then taken to the Pro-Cathedral for requiem mass.

An application was made to the Estates Committee of Dublin Corporation by the Wolfe Tone Memorial Committee (an IRB front chaired by Seán McGarry) for Ashe to lie in state in City Hall. This elegant Georgian building by Thomas Cooley represented the last great display of civic pride by Dublin's mercantile elite, serving as the Royal Exchange before becoming the meeting place and head offices of the corporation. It was also within shouting distance of Dublin Castle and had been under permanent military guard since being recaptured from the rebels during the rising the previous year.

When the Estates Committee granted permission for Ashe's body to be brought there under a Volunteer escort, the Under-Secretary for Ireland, Sir William Byrne, wrote immediately to the Lord Mayor warning of the likely consequences. He suggested, not unreasonably, that Ashe could as easily lie in state at the Pro-Cathedral. But O'Neill was not to be moved and was strongly supported by two of the most conservative nationalist members of the Estates Committee, the undertaker and slum landlord Patrick Corrigan, who had disposed of Alderman Kelly's explosives store after the rising, and the builder who had locked his men out in 1913 and had been knighted for his wartime services, Sir Patrick Shortall. All three met Byrne and senior officials in the Castle, even as Volunteers were assembling across the Liffey to bring Ashe's remains to City Hall.

O'Neill proposed that the administration could easily avert a crisis by withdrawing the military guard temporarily from City Hall. According to the Lord Mayor, Byrne remained implacable and informed the deputation that he had a regiment of soldiers 'armed to the teeth' in the Castle Yard. Fortunately, Lieutenant-General Mahon was also present, and he took it on himself to withdraw the guard.[8]

Even as the troops withdrew, the giant funeral procession wound its way through the crowded streets. Tens of thousands would come to pay their respects to the martyr between then and the funeral on Sunday 30 September.

Incredibly, the administration continued its forced feeding of the remaining prisoners in Mountjoy for several days, further fuelling public anger, before conceding the hunger-strikers' demands.

The danger of a confrontation arose again when the Chief Secretary heard that there was a Volunteer guard of honour in City Hall. He banned the possession or carrying of arms in the building. Fortunately, Duke was not in Ireland, and Mahon simply ignored the Chief Secretary's instruction.[9] Troops were virtually confined to barracks until after Ashe was buried.

The funeral was generally admitted to be 'larger and even more impressive than the funeral of Parnell.' References to the death of Parnell were to be common in the coming days and weeks, as if nothing of comparable significance to the nation's psyche had occurred between those two events. Because of the wartime ban on excursion trains, some Volunteer detachments took extraordinary measures to reach Dublin. Two hundred men from Ashe's native Kerry travelled for days to reach Dublin in time for the funeral, and another contingent was said to have marched all the way from Athlone. In all, nine thousand Volunteers took part, along with the Irish Citizen Army and virtually every Catholic fraternity and every trade and business association in Dublin. The largest contingent was made up of 18,000 trade unionists, of whom 8,000 were members of the ITGWU, marching behind their general president, Tom Foran. The Catholic Archbishop of Dublin, Dr Walsh, attended, despite his increasingly poor health. 'I feel it a duty,' he wrote to the Lord Mayor, 'to take part in the public protest that will find expression in the funeral.' The *Irish Independent* commented next day:

This was the real significance of yesterday's unprecedented demonstration. The people from the Archbishop down to the humblest citizen, while paying tribute to the memory of the dead also desire to register a protest against a regime and a practice which they regard as needlessly vindictive and harsh.

At the graveside Michael Collins gave perhaps the shortest funeral oration ever made in Ireland. Stepping forward after the firing party had fired three volleys and a Fianna bugler had sounded the Last Post, Collins said a few words in Irish that were never recorded and then in English: 'Nothing additional remains to be said. That volley which we have just heard is the only speech which it is proper to make above the grave of a dead Fenian.'[10]

With that, the official ceremony ended; but thousands flocked to the grave over the next few weeks, not alone to pay their respects but some also to secure souvenirs. Margaret Connery of the Irish Women's Franchise League protested that the grave 'had the appearance of being trampled by a herd of cattle' and 'Irish "Huns" were busy cutting up wreaths, cards and even a temporary cross erected by Corporation employees.'[11]

———

Meanwhile meetings of local councils and boards of guardians throughout Ireland passed votes of sympathy on Ashe's death. The quarterly meeting of Dublin Corporation took place on the day after the funeral, and all regular business was put aside to consider a motion from the Lord Mayor. Inevitably, O'Neill referred to his own meetings with Ashe and the dead man's famous words, 'If I do die, I die in a good cause'; but, conscious of the explosive atmosphere in the city, he made no reference to the meeting with Sir William Byrne and Lieutenant-General Mahon.

An independent nationalist, O'Neill was ideally placed to be Chief Magistrate of Dublin at a time when the UIL still dominated the corporation but had lost its popular mandate. He did not allow any discussion of the dead man's politics 'or whether Thomas Ashe was right in his methods,' but he was scathing in his criticism of the government. So were other speakers, including the former Lord Mayor and UIL stalwart Lorcan Sherlock, who drew loud applause when he declared the government of the country to be turning patriots into criminals. No government had done more to generate 'the strongest and bitterest feeling of national resentment and national hatred against oppression and hypocrisy ... since the days of Mr. Parnell.' The council voted unanimously for the motion of sympathy by a standing ovation.

Unionist councillors appear to have absented themselves from the vote, and there were misgivings over a similar motion in the old unionist heartland of Blackrock. Unionist councillors agreed to support it only if it was restricted to offering sympathy to the dead man's family and deploring the circumstances in which his death occurred. While voting for the motion, Lady Dockrell commented wryly that five women suffragists had died of forced feeding in British prisons and not a word had been said about it in Ireland.

Nor did Ashe's death attract much notice in Britain. Londoners and residents of east-coast towns in particular were far too preoccupied with the long moonlit nights that facilitated Zeppelin raids from across the North Sea.

There was one last ordeal for the Irish Party and the British administration concerning the death of Thomas Ashe and, appropriately, it was provided by Tim Healy, who represented the Ashe family at the inquest. Healy condemned the authorities in searing tones for using confrontational tactics that breached their own penal regulations in order to punish the prisoners. He too referred to Max Green and the Prison Board, claiming that if it had not been for the intervention of the Lord Mayor of Dublin and the outrage of its citizens they could well be investigating forty deaths in Mountjoy Prison rather than one.

Even at this late stage the government's legal team had no instructions to offer any words of regret to the Ashe family, or a credible explanation to the public of how the death had occurred.

———

Immediately Thomas Ashe Cumainn of Sinn Féin sprouted up throughout Ireland. One of the first was in the Rotunda ward in Dublin's north inner city. It was ironic, given Ashe's radical social views, that he would now be transformed into a quasi-religious figure, like Pearse. On the other hand, his piety reconciled many naturally conservative Catholics to the cause of advanced nationalism and drew significant numbers of clergy into the ranks of Sinn Féin. At Mount Bolus, Co. Offaly, the Rev. J. Kane said he did not blame older men for clinging to the Irish Party, but 'when they knew Sinn Féin they would come in.' He attacked the Irish Party for its powerlessness to address basic grievances, such as the crippling of the cattle trade to meet the demands of Britain's war economy.

In Belfast, Laurence Ginnell, a nationalist MP who had deserted the Irish Party for Sinn Féin, assured a meeting held to found a new Thomas Ashe Cumann that the organisation was not advocating 'red ruin and revolution' but had policies 'similar to those of the Dublin Chamber of Commerce in promoting Irish industry.' Several local priests attended the meeting; and when the Gaelic League decided to launch a fund for a memorial hall to commemorate Ashe there was a massive response from the clergy, both as individuals and in forwarding collections from special masses held for the repose of the dead man's soul. Subscription lists for the Ashe fund frequently carried expressions of gratitude from Gaelic League and Sinn Féin branches to parish priests for allowing them to hold church gate collections. Within a few weeks the league had enough money to acquire 14 Rutland Square for the promotion of Irish, Irish music and the reconfigured ideals of the late Thomas Ashe.[12]

———

There could have been no better backdrop to the Sinn Féin convention that gathered in Dublin on 25 and 26 October than the Ashe funeral. Even more delegates attended than were at Count Plunkett's conference in April: 1,700, compared with 1,200.[13] But the most significant difference was that they all represented Sinn Féin branches—1,009, to be precise, from virtually every parish outside Ulster and quite a number within the province. The disparate organisations of the spring had been subsumed into one political party committed to 'securing the international recognition of Ireland as an independent Irish Republic.'[14]

It had been a hard-fought struggle between the moderate incumbent faction of Sinn Féin, represented by such figures as Arthur Griffith and Darrell Figgis, and the militant newcomers led by de Valera. Agreement was secured only in the final phase of negotiations the previous night.[15] The new constitution committed Sinn Féin to the 'use of any and every means available to render impotent the power of England to hold Ireland in subjection by military force, or otherwise.'[16]

A pen portrait of his local cumann in Rathfarnham by a very youthful Todd Andrews provides an insight into the type of 'Sinn Féin Clubs' springing up.

The membership included some very old men, usually tradesmen and labourers, as well as women of various ages and conditions of life. There were girls who served in shops or worked in laundries and some secretaries. Other of the women members were housewives with very strong feelings on the subject of women's rights. Although they never had any clear notion of what these rights should be they had a feeling that something was wrong with the status of women in the community. This was a sufficient grievance on which to hang many a debate.

As for the male membership, they

were astonishingly conservative … It might be expected that men who were prepared to support a rebellion against the political status quo would have shown some liberality of view but … social questions such as housing, land division, public health, education were seldom discussed.

Instead subjects for debate revolved around 'England's difficulty, Ireland's opportunity.'[17]

Much to his disgust, Andrews was relegated to stewarding the crowds outside the convention, but he would not have been surprised at the debate, which resembled a meeting of his own cumann writ large. Reflecting the innate conservatism of many members, some delegates, including a number of priests, expressed more concern about how a republic should be achieved than about the substance of the proposed new state. They wanted the constitution amended to ensure that Sinn Féin would adopt only 'legitimate' methods in pursuit of its goals. One of the movers of this amendment, Father O'Meehan, let the cat out of the bag when he said he would have used the word 'constitutional' in his amendment but it had acquired a 'bad flavour.' On the other hand, Father Gayner from Ennis, in de Valera's new constituency, urged the delegates to set up a provisional government and declare themselves a constituent assembly.[18]

In keeping with Andrews's analysis of his local cumann, the only delegates to cause disharmony at the convention were women. They were Constance Markievicz, Helena Molony and Kathleen Clarke, all of whom attacked Eoin MacNeill for his role in attempting to abort the rising. Less controversial was their demand that Sinn Féin make votes for women part of its policy in the coming general election. All three were members of Cumann na dTeachtairí, which had been established by leading female activists within Sinn Féin to secure greater equality and representation for women within the organisation. MacNeill was staunchly defended by de Valera, but the conference did agree to support votes for women. A proposal from Markievicz urging craft workers to leave British unions and form Irish ones, a project she would help bring to fruition three years later, was also adopted.[19]

Members of the Irish Volunteers, such as Todd Andrews, were important facilitators of Sinn Féin's growth but did not take it very seriously. They certainly did not accept the primacy of politics in achieving a republic: they saw politics and politicians as totally discredited. Less than a month later, in Croke Park, they held a convention at which de Valera was elected president of the Volunteers. He now led both the political and the paramilitary wings of the movement. The only man who might have challenged him, the late commandant of the Fingal Battalion, victor of Ashbourne and former president of the IRB, Thomas Ashe, was now a national icon.

————

High political drama soon gave way to the perennial concerns of Dubliners over the basics of life. If little could be done to control food prices, there was some short-lived optimism that the price of coal might be reduced and renewed efforts to tackle slum clearance. Largely because of pressure from the trades council, the corporation undertook to examine alternatives to the near-monopoly enjoyed by the Scottish coal suppliers McKelvie and Company, whose fuel was regarded as too expensive and of poor quality. The first attempt was made by a deputation to Scotland consisting of P. T. Daly, James J. Kelly, a nationalist councillor and manufacturer, Mark Ruddle, the city's electrical engineer, and the old IRB hand Fred Allan, secretary to the corporation.

However, they discovered that cutting the city adrift from McKelvie and Company might leave them in a worse and colder place. Belfast and several British cities had found to their cost that it was much easier to ditch a supplier than to find another on better terms. While the corporation stayed with the Scottish supplier, it was protected by the Price of Coal (Limitation) Act (1915), which would set the price from time to time until six months after the war ended.

However, the committee did come back with two proposals. One was to adapt the furnaces used by the power station to take more varied types and sizes of coal; the other was to consider the purchase of its own steamer. A suitable vessel would cost £20,000, while shipping charges on the 35,000 tons of coal required by the city already amounted to £21,000 a year. Daly argued that the investment would more than pay for itself and would provide security of supply. But it was a step too far for his fellow-councillors, some of whom feared that one German torpedo could scuttle the whole project.[20] Their fears were not unfounded: Tedcastle's, a large commercial coal importer, lost the *Adela* off Holyhead on 27 December 1917.[21]

Councillor W. T. Cosgrave tried a different tack: he explored the possibility of exploiting Irish coal. There were two possible sources, Arigna (Co. Roscommon) and Castlecomer (Co. Kilkenny). The latter was preferable because of the better-quality coal, but distance from the market, an inadequate railway network that would require laying extra track and a bridge across the Barrow to make it accessible, as well as the high cost of motor fuel for lorries to supplement railway deliveries, made the option as unrealistic as Daly's scheme.[22]

———

By contrast, a corporation report on the city's pressing need for housing contained the seeds for future development and provided up-to-date information on how the war was affecting families in the tenements of the north inner city. It followed, and to some extent grew out of, a more ambitious scheme promoted by Archbishop Walsh and the MP for the St Stephen's Green division, P. J. Brady, to raise funds in the United States for slum clearance. Despite support from the chamber of commerce, the idea of applying to the American investment market for funds frightened most members of the corporation, who felt that ultimate responsibility for the problem lay with Dublin Castle and with London.

The new report produced by the Housing Committee under the former internee Tom Kelly proposed slum clearance on a more modest scale, renovating the better class of tenements rather than demolishing them. It provided a graphic history of the rapid decline of fine residential housing into slums since 1850. For instance, Buckingham Street, where one house had been let out in tenements that year, had four more houses converted to tenements by 1875 and fifteen by 1900; the number had risen to seventeen by the time the report was compiled. Another thoroughfare, Dominick Street, had one tenement in 1850, but 75 of the 145 houses had been let out in tenements by 1917. The number of houses let out in tenements in Gardiner Street (Upper, Middle and Lower) was also seventy-five. In Dorset Street ninety houses (including the birthplace of the dramatist Richard Brinsley Sheridan) had been let as tenements. Another thoroughfare, Gloucester Street, had eighty-one tenements by 1917.

The report identified areas where new housing could be built. These included the grounds of the Richmond Asylum at Grangegorman to the north-west of the city centre, open spaces in Glasnevin, Drumcondra, Clonturk and Cabra to the north, and Killester, Marino and Clontarf to the north-east.

In selecting tenements for renovation the Housing Committee proposed using the existing criteria and selecting first-class housing, which was structurally sound. It proposed that 2,192 of the 3,791 families living in the district's 627 first-class houses could remain once the properties had been improved; the rest would be provided with new homes in areas identified for rebuilding. It would cost £3,074 per acre to acquire the slums, because of the generous compensation terms for landlords, who were entitled to ten years' rent when a house was purchased compulsorily. The compensation system actually encouraged them to neglect their properties, as it added to the pressure on the corporation to demolish tenements unfit for human habitation or in a dangerous condition.

During eviction proceedings in November 1917 in the Crabbe Lane and Boyne Street area, between Great Brunswick Street (Pearse Street) and Denzille Street (Fenian Street), the solicitor for the Dublin Tenants' Association, James Brady, argued that the landlords of derelict slum properties should have their properties confiscated rather than bought. He added that 'the military should have blown them down instead of perfectly good buildings in the city centre.'[23]

The cost of acquiring the slum dwellings in the eighty acres encompassed by the survey under the existing compensation scheme was £254,920. Turning to the cost of rehousing the displaced slum-dwellers, the report estimated that

the average cost of a self-contained dwelling of sufficient size to prevent overcrowding, and which admits of the separation of the sexes, and which would provide living accommodation with a scullery and w.c. [toilets] for the sole use of each family, is £380 based on the most recent competitive prices.

However, the cost of land clearance, sewerage, road construction and other charges would bring the total cost to £553 per dwelling, and it would cost £1.1 million to provide the two thousand houses needed for the first phase of the plan. It would cost more than £5 million to house the eight thousand families living in the area, compared with £3 million before the war to house all the city's slum-dwellers.

A considerable amount of thought went into the sites to be chosen for the new developments. It was considered important to ensure that people were housed as near as possible to their place of employment. 'The more remote sites [should be] reserved for the better paid class of artisan who could afford the expenses of transit.' The DUTC would be required to extend its tram services to the new areas and to introduce cheaper fares for the corporation tenants 'during the time when they are going to and from their work.'

The project was no more than a pipe dream without adequate government funding. The only part of the scheme remotely feasible from within the corporation's own resources was the renovation of the tenements, which could be carried out for an estimated £150 each, or less than a third of the amount required to build and service a new house.

In a further setback, Alderman Kelly's colleague W. T. Cosgrave, the new Sinn Féin MP for Kilkenny City, published a minority report that dissented strongly from the proposal to renovate existing dwellings. He questioned the accuracy of the estimate of £150 per flat and pointed out that many of the houses classified as first class and second class in 1914 had deteriorated considerably since. He estimated the life of the renovated buildings at no more than twenty years and predicted that the social problems associated with tenement living would continue to fester. His objections to perpetuating tenement life in renovated buildings included the continuing absence of privacy, the lack of open-air amenities for children living in the upper storeys, the difficulty of keeping common areas clean and secure and the question of problem tenants imposing on their neighbours. Other problems included the noise and disruption caused by tenants who worked irregular hours, and the generally cramped conditions.[24]

———

The survey accompanying the report provides an insight into tenement life in the inner city towards the end of the First World War. The great majority of tenants lived in one room. A total of 5,506 lettings were for one room, compared with 2,087 for two rooms and 909 for three or more rooms. 1,068 of the one-room tenements had one occupant, and 1,572 of them had two. A further 1,141 had three occupants, and the remainder were occupied by between four and nine people each. Only 136 of the two-room tenements had one occupant and 34 of the tenements of three rooms or more.

The 5,506 one-room tenements accommodated 15,930 people, an average of slightly less than three people each. Rents were between 6d and 5s 6d a week. There were 8,361 people living in the two-room tenements, an average of a little over four people each. Rents ranged from 1s to 10s a week. There were 4,348 people living in the flats with three or more rooms, an average of slightly less than five people each. Rents for these larger tenements ranged from 5s to 15s a week.

The lowest rents were usually paid by tenants in the worst-kept rooms or who undertook various duties for the landlord, such as letting out other rooms, cleaning the common areas or carrying out repairs. The higher rents for the larger lettings often included a shop or business premises.

No fewer than 1,599 lettings, accommodating 8,503 families, were in premises classified as unfit for human habitation.

The relatively low rents reflect the low income of most tenement-dwellers. The average wage of 324 'heads of families' in 'first-class' tenements was only 10s a week, although the rents ranged from 1s to 4s 8d. This means that other family members must have contributed to the weekly budget, a pattern replicated in all categories of dwelling, as can be seen from the figures below.

A further 466 heads of families earned between 10s 6d and 19s 6d, with 324 earning 20s a week. This was the basic pay for many manual workers in the city. For most of these families the weekly rent on a two or three-room tenement would have absorbed most of the main breadwinner's income.

A further 398 heads of families earned between 20s 6d and 24s 6d a week, and 250 earned 25s. Another 236 earned between 25s 6d and 29s 6d, and 139 earned 30s. The remainder of the first-class tenements were occupied by 207 families, whose principal breadwinners earned between 30s 6d and 39s a week.

As might be expected, no fewer than 595 families occupying second and third-class tenements were headed by breadwinners earning no more than 10s a week. These tenants paid rents as low as 6d for one room. A further 459 heads of families earned between 10s 6d and 14s 6d, while 192 earned 15s a week. They paid rents ranging from 1s to 6s 6d.

516 heads of families earned between 15s 6d and 19s 6d, with 549 earning 20s a week. Another 754 earned between 20s 6d and 24s 6d, with 408 earning 25s a week. They paid rents ranging from 1s 6d to 6s for a single room and up to 13s 6d for three or more rooms.

587 heads of families earned between 25s 6d and 29s 6d, with 256 earning 30s a week. The rents they paid ranged from as little as 1s 6d for a single room to 12s 6d for three or more rooms. A total of 326 heads of families living in second and third-class accommodation earned between 30s 6d and 37s 6d, although there were only sixteen earning more than 36s a week.

There was no strong correlation between income and the amount of rent paid. In many instances rents were high compared with the earnings of the head of the family, which suggests not alone that spouses, children or lodgers must have contributed but also the existence of a significant black economy.

———

The range of occupations in the tenements is immensely varied. The lists include an actor, a fisherman, a photographer, a signwriter, a cinema operator, a pig jobber, a tree-feller, a jockey, two policemen, two donkeymen and two sculptors.[25] But by far the largest group was that of the 3,476 labourers. Their earnings ranged from 7s to 60s a week, suggesting that this occupational heading covered anyone from part-time night watchmen capable only of light work to dockers and employees in relatively secure unionised employments, such as Dublin Corporation and the Port and Docks Board.

The next-largest occupational group comprised charwomen, of whom there were 603. Their income ranged from 2s 8d to 36s a week. The upper figure is surprisingly high and suggests that many charwomen were far better off than domestic servants, who could expect to be paid only between £10 and £20 a year, depending on their duties and the prosperity of their employer. However, servants living in also received free board and lodging, worth between 5s and £1 a week. The same applied to female drapers' assistants who lived on the employer's premises and could expect to earn between £10 and £25 a year, while female factory workers could expect to earn as little as 4s a week. Even Jacob's biscuit factory, the premier employer of women factory workers before the munitions industry arrived, paid only between 6s and 10s a week, with forewomen earning 16s 10d.[26]

Among the best-paid, predominantly female occupations in the tenements was that of dealer. Despite their 'Molly Malone' image, these women earned between 10s and 60s a week. There would also have been some men among the 179 dealers listed for the north inner city.

Other large occupational groups included 262 carters earning between 10s and 40s a week, 180 clerks earning between 10s 6d and 60s and 159 carpenters earning between 15s and 50s. There were 79 factory hands listed (a term that suggests they were all men), earning between 7s 6d and 30s a week. By contrast, 184 munitions workers (the vast majority women) were earning between 10s and 60s a week. However, the average earnings for female munitions workers was only 33s a week: far more than many male manual workers but well below what male munitions workers earned.[27]

Craft workers were well represented in the north city tenements, as table 8 shows. The wide discrepancy in pay among some trades, such as printers, is probably explained by the fact that it includes apprentices and, in the case of the printing trade, those employed in small jobbing houses as well as bigger employers, such as the newspapers. In other trades, such as building, the divergence in rates probably reflects differences in seasonal work and permanent versus temporary employees. The rates suggest that wage inflation had yet to take a grip on the Dublin trades.

Table 8
Numbers and earnings of craft workers in north inner-city tenements

	Number	*Weekly earnings*
Bakers	57	18s to 40s
Blacksmiths	29	15s to 43s
Boilermakers	12	20s to 43s
Bookbinders	23	15s to 42s
Bootmakers	89	15s to 50s
Bricklayers	47	13s to 45s
Butchers	28	17s 6d to 45s
Cabinetmakers	46	25s to 40s
Carpenters	159	15s to 50s
Carters	262	10s to 40s
Charwomen	603	2s 8d to 36s
Clerks	180	10s 6d to 60s
Compositors	39	24s to 49s
Coopers	28	20s to 50s
Dealers	179	10s to 60s
Electricians	20	20s to 45s
Engineers	13	36s to 50s
Factory hands	79	7s 6d to 30s
Fitters	61	15s to 60s
Labourers	3,476	7s to 60s
Munitions workers	184	10s to 60s
Painters	155	15s to 47s 6d
Plasterers	31	23s to 45s
Plumbers	51	20s to 50s
Printers	84	13s to 50s
Shopkeepers	303	14s to 30s
Soldiers' dependants	1,705	6s to 60s
War widows	34	12s 6d to 35s
Pensioners (state)	460	7s 6d
Pensioners (private)	296	5s to 60s

The other large occupational group was that of the the 303 shopkeepers, although there were only 21 shop assistants, suggesting that the shops were mainly family-run businesses operating on the ground floor of tenements. The income of these shopkeepers ranged from a surprisingly modest 14s to 30s a week, while no income at all was listed for 51. In contrast, shop assistants earned between 6s and 40s a week, which means that most if not all worked in the large department stores in the main commercial streets nearby.

Another 92 people are listed as house-owners or landlords, with no income given. This suggests that they did not let out rooms. They may also have included individuals such as William Holmes, the tea-room owner wounded in the rising whose properties had been closed down as unfit for human habitation. There were three lodging-house keepers, with incomes of between 35s and 40s a week.

———

Three other large groups played an important social and economic role in the tenements, although they were not engaged in any occupation. The first, and the largest after labourers, was that of soldiers' dependants. Some 1,705 adult dependants are listed, with incomes ranging from 6s to 60s. This suggests that the category covered everyone from a mother or other relative partly dependent on a young private to the wives of senior NCOs, warrant officers and possibly even some officers, as some senior NCOs were promoted to fill gaps created by the high casualty rate among junior officers. There were also 34 war widows, receiving incomes between 12s 6d and 35s a week. Women in both categories with large families could also help account for the higher incomes.

These War Office payments were very significant and no doubt played a role in ensuring that there was a steady trickle of recruits from working-class districts. The changing pattern of recruitment in 1917 and 1918, with the majority of recruits able to apply to technical branches and learn valuable trades, also increased the attractions of what had once been solely the resort of the unemployed or the adventurous.

The other large groups in the tenements were pensioners and widows. There were 460 old-age pensioners living in the north inner city, all of them on the standard pension of 7s 6d a week. Practically all would probably have been consigned to the workhouse before the introduction of Lloyd George's scheme, which allowed them to remain in the community and to contribute to the local economy. Another 296 pensioners, presumably with occupational pensions predating the state scheme, were receiving between 5s and 60s a week.

There were 222 women listed in the tenements as widows with an income derived from family earnings that ranged from 5s to 40s a week.

Surprisingly, given the image that has come down to us of tenement life, there were only 24 people listed as receiving outdoor relief. While many tenement-dwellers were poor, the vast majority were economically very active.

Finally, there were small numbers of professionals and middle-class tenants living in the area, including a dentist, a chemist, three civil servants and fifteen nurses. There was one piano-tuner and six musicians, but only one of the latter was a street musician.

Table 9
Occupancy of first-class tenements

Number of families consisting of—	One room	Two rooms	Three or more rooms
one person	529	41	8
two persons	764	147	32
three persons	568	168	26
four persons	423	173	45
five persons	252	117	33
six persons	119	84	26
seven persons	54	62	22
eight persons	22	29	10
nine persons	7	6	7
ten persons	2	3	6
eleven persons	1	3	1
twelve persons	—	1	—
thirteen persons	—	—	—

Table 10
Earnings of heads of families in first-class tenements

	One room	Two rooms	Three or more rooms
10s per week or less	324	34	1
10–15s per week	266	49	5
15–20s per week	524	119	17
20–25s per week	648	198	17
25–30s per week	375	147	36
30–35s per week	142	90	16
35–40s per week	118	72	22
40–45s per week	14	11	3
45–50s per week	11	10	—
50s per week or more	3	2	—
Unascertained	316	102	99

Table 11
Second-class and third-class tenements

Number of families consisting of—	One room	Two rooms	Three or more rooms
one person	1,086	136	34
two persons	1,572	393	113
three persons	1,142	390	145
four persons	868	410	141
five persons	510	323	142
six persons	218	218	152
seven persons	85	105	89
eight persons	31	68	33
nine persons	12	23	30
ten persons	—	14	24
eleven persons	—	5	4
twelve persons	—	1	—
thirteen persons	—	1	2

Table 12
Earnings of heads of families in second-class and third-class tenements

	Total number of families	Families in one room	Families in two rooms	Families in three rooms
10s per week or less	653	595	51	7
10–15s per week	756	631	111	14
15–20s per week	1,471	1,065	320	86
20–25s per week	1,781	1,222	382	177
25–30s per week	1,436	848	515	73
30–35s per week	549	257	196	96
35–40s per week	556	237	185	134
40–45s per week	74	42	26	16
45–50s per week	44	7	10	27
50s per week or more	22	7	10	5
Unascertained	1,161	606	281	274

The rising cost of living contributed to a resurgence of trade union militancy in 1917, though it was more marked in the provinces than in Dublin. Often the threat of strikes in the city could secure significant pay increases, as P. T. Daly demonstrated yet again in Dublin Corporation. In March 1917 the corporation had agreed to extend the war bonus of 3s a week from men earning up to £100 a year to those earning up to £200, which meant it would cover craftsmen and semi-skilled workers as well as labourers. In August he proposed that the bonus be paid to all male employees earning up to £250 a year, and that it be increased to 5s a week, backdated to 1 October 1916. When the only female member of the Corporation, the nationalist Martha Williams, asked why it was not being extended to female employees, Daly readily accepted an amendment to that effect.

There were strong objections from the usual champions of the ratepayers, including all the unionist councillors. Alderman David Quaid of Drumcondra said the cost could not be met in a city devastated by war and suffering from a serious loss of rates revenue because of the destruction visited on its commercial centre. Councillor Sir Andrew Beattie, who also represented the predominantly middle-class Drumcondra ward, said he sympathised with the low-paid corporation employees but sympathised even more with the unemployed and small shopkeepers.

Councillor W. T. Cosgrave proposed that the matter be referred to the Estates and Finance Committee for consideration, but Daly refused to withdraw the motion. Cosgrave then agreed to support Daly's motion, though he would have preferred it to go through his own committee so that Sinn Féin could claim the credit for any subsequent pay increase. Daly must have had his votes counted, for the motion was passed, by 34 to 18. Besides securing all the Labour and Sinn Féin votes, it obtained the support of the Lord Mayor, of Martha Williams, and of a large segment of nationalist councillors who realised that to refuse the pay increase was to invite serious industrial unrest.

However, councillors reacted very differently to a motion put forward by John Saturninus Kelly at the end of the year, presumably in the hope of invoking the Christmas spirit, when he proposed that the war bonus be extended to corporation employees serving in the forces. There was certainly a logic to Kelly's argument that the men fighting the war should benefit from the war bonus; but he could find no seconder. Even unionist councillors opted to put the ratepayers' interests first, while it was now impossible for nationalist councillors to support such a deeply unpopular move.[28] There was no longer any credit to be obtained from supporting a highly unpopular war.

––––––

If the casualties from the bloody battles on the western front in 1917 did not have the same emotional impact in Dublin as those of earlier years, one reason was that the falling off in recruitment meant that the ranks of Irish regiments were increasingly filled by British conscripts. As early as the summer of 1916 the *Irish Times* had condemned the antagonism with which bemused young recruits from England were met *en route* to regimental depots; and by 1917 a majority of men in the 10th and 16th divisions were not Irish. After a stint in the Balkans following Gallipoli, the 10th Division had been transferred to Egypt, where casualties were lower and replacements came largely from the Indian army.

The last bloodletting for the 16th Division would be in the Third Battle of Ypres in 1917 and the resistance to the German spring offensive of 1918. After that it was effectually stood down as an operational force.

There was one loss at Ypres that did register in the wider public consciousness, and that was the death of Father Willie Doyle sj. He had served as chaplain with the Royal Dublin Fusiliers at the front from November 1915 and had taken risks few other chaplains matched in tending the wounded and dying. He had been mentioned in despatches on numerous occasions and was awarded the Military Cross. On 17 August 1917 he had insisted on going forward to give the last sacraments, and four men had been killed by shell fire as he attended to them. Then a nearby shell-burst killed him too. He was deeply mourned as well in the 36th (Ulster) Division 'for his saintliness.' The *Evening News* (Glasgow) quoted one Ulsterman as saying:

> Father Doyle was a good deal among us. We couldn't possibly agree with his religious opinions, but we simply worshipped him for other things. He didn't know the meaning of fear, and he didn't know what bigotry was. He was as ready to risk his life to take a drop of water to a wounded Ulsterman as to assist men of his own faith and regiment.[29]

It was one of the last flares of generosity born of the 'common sacrifice' of Irish soldiers at the front that John Redmond had set so much store by in 1914. The only newspaper that still paid homage to the idea was the *Weekly Irish Times*. In September 1915 it began publishing a block of photographs of 'Irish Heroes Killed and Wounded' on its front page every week. It also included members of the armed forces who received awards for bravery, such as the Military Cross and Military Medal, and men attached to the Royal Flying Corps who died as a result of accidents.

The list was far from exhaustive and reflected the newspaper's constituency, with greater prominence being given to officers and to members of unionist families. By far the greatest number of those featured were from Ulster, but Dublin provided the next-largest contingent. In the first half of 1917 men from Dublin, or with Dublin connections in the case of Commonwealth units, amounted to 138 out of 484 featured. A significant minority of those mentioned were private soldiers from a working-class Catholic background in the city.

By contrast, the *Irish Independent* restricted itself to lists of dead, missing and wounded, with only the occasional mention of particularly prominent individuals, such as Major Willie Redmond or Captain James O'Shaughnessy Beveridge of the Royal Army Medical Corps, who was a son of the late J. B. Beveridge, former Town Clerk of Dublin.[30]

Chapter 12 ∿

'A COERCIONIST, CONSCRIPTIONIST LORD LIEUTENANT'

s the last year of the war dawned in Ireland, the dominant thought in the minds of most Dubliners was food. Exports from Ireland to Britain were virtually uncontrolled, but Dublin was subjected to the same controls on imports as any British city. These shortages helped ensure that prices rose much faster than wages.

Communal kitchens were now a reality in the city. Some were in traditional venues from the lock-out, such as the ITGWU head offices in Liberty Hall and the Little Flower in Meath Street, but others were new, such as the canteen run by a British charity, the White Ribbon Society, in Charlemont Street. A typical White Ribbon menu consisted of stew twice a week and corned beef with turnip or cabbage on other days. During the previous year its twenty women volunteers and a paid cook provided twelve thousand dinners.[1]

If submarine warfare in the Irish Sea was not as intensive as elsewhere, it was still sufficient to disrupt services. Between May and December 1917 nine vessels had been sunk in the central corridor between Dublin and Holyhead, compared with seventeen in the North Channel between Belfast and the Clyde and more than fifty off the south coast of Ireland. Many of the losses, such as Tedcastle's coal ship *Adela* off Holyhead on 27 December 1917, with the loss of twenty-five lives, were at first kept from the public by the military censors. Then, on 31 March, the submarine war was brought home with the sinking of two fishing smacks off Howth, the *Geraldine* and the *St Michan*, with the loss of five lives.

The incident led to fierce controversy in Dublin, with rumours abounding that it was the work of a British submarine. Eventually the Rev. James Williams, a Presbyterian minister in Howth trying to raise funds for the victims' families, including the eight men and three boys who survived the attack, wrote to the newspapers to point out, not unreasonably, that the Royal Navy would hardly attack fishing vessels when one of its strategic priorities was the protection of food supplies. He sought to stem the rumours because they were affecting subscriptions to the relief fund. He probably did not help his cause by adding that one of the survivors had been 'a strong Sinn Feiner, pro-German, and anti-English' but was now 'a Britisher, longing to take service in the Navy that he may have an opportunity of avenging the injury and outrage caused by this German submarine.'

As this letter demonstrates, fund-raising activities had become highly politicised. A general Submarine Victims Fund set up in Dublin the previous year had raised little more than £700 by the end of 1917, reflecting the relatively low impact of the U-boat campaign on the life of the city in lives lost. As with so many funds directly related to the war effort, subscriptions tended to come primarily from the Protestant community. The largest donation was from the Dublin Dockyard Company, which gave £100. Unionist councillors and Protestant clergymen were also prominent among the donors.[2]

A separate Howth Submarine Victims Fund was set up in April 1918, and the list of subscribers was headed by the Catholic Archbishop of Dublin, with a donation of £100. While Commander J. C. Gaisford St Lawrence, Lord of Howth, also gave £100 and Alexander Findlater and Company another £25, the great majority of other donations, large and small, came from members of the Catholic community and nationalist politicians, including the local MP, J. J. Clancy.[3]

All told, the number of Dubliners losing their lives so far in the war at sea had been a small fraction of those on the five hundred British merchant vessels sunk during the previous eight months; but that did not make Dublin immune from the relentless squeeze on supplies that the submarine war was causing. As well as food it included essential materials for industry and trade, newspapers, and even construction materials needed for the rebuilding of Sackville Street.[4]

The prospect of more merchant shipping being diverted from civilian use in 1918 to meet the needs of the American Expeditionary Force in France led the British Food Controller, Lord Rhondda, to try to manage the expectations of civilians by predicting that 'food is going to be scarce throughout the world in 1918 and 1919, and probably long afterwards.' Although his comments were directed as much at the British as the Irish public, they reinforced the view in Dublin that, in the words of the *Irish Independent*, British 'Food Controllers' and 'Economy Controllers' were 'no exception to the rule of discrimination against Ireland ... and ... are indifferent to the fate of this country.'[5] The famine analogy was never far away. Constance Markievicz, commenting on the disappearance of animals from piggeries in the city, said that if things got any worse Sinn Féin would have to 'consider how they could get and hold food for the poorer people. Ireland was not going to allow England to starve her this time.'[6]

The ITUC representatives on the Irish Food Control Committee resigned on 7 January 1918 in protest at what they regarded as official interference in their activities. One of them was Thomas Farren, the Stonecutters' leader, veteran of the 1913 lock-out and Labour candidate in the College Green by-election of 1915, who represented Dublin on the committee. The last straw had been a decision by the vice-president of the Department of Agriculture and Technical Instruction, T. W. Russell, to amend the price of milk in Dublin and of bread in Derry before the committee had completed its own investigations. The Executive Council of the ITUC promptly endorsed the decision of its representatives to resign, and the president of the congress, William O'Brien, personally congratulated Farren.

The fact that Russell had cut milk prices and imposed tighter controls on exports appears to have weighed not at all with the union representatives.[7] It was another example of the growing resentment against any manifestation of British control, even when the effects were beneficial. As Farren put it, Russell's decision had exposed the 'fatuity' of Irish efforts to tackle problems that were a direct result of Britain's fateful decision to go to war.

The British authorities were well aware of the problem. T. P. Gill, secretary of the Department of Agriculture and Technical Instruction, told a meeting of allotment-holders in Blackrock Town Hall that it would be counter-productive to impose controls on food, because most imports were 'the cheap necessaries of the poor, while the exports from Ireland were mainly the dearer luxuries of the well to do.' He assured his audience that 'the farmer is not a profiteer and could not be expected to do his business at a loss.' However, there was a widespread belief that someone was profiteering; and on the same night that Gill was making his speech the Irish Clerical Workers' Union was proposing that a Vigilance Committee be set up in Dublin by workers to carry out house-to-house searches and expose 'the hoarders of food.'[8]

There was a steady trickle of prosecutions of profiteering shopkeepers through the magistrates' courts. Persistent offenders who overcharged on staples such as bread, butter, jam, margarine and bacon would receive fines of up to £10 for 'slight errors of judgement,' as defendants usually described their behaviour. This in turn provoked criticism of the magistrates by the Dublin Retail Purveyors', Family Grocers' and Off-Licence Holders' Association over what it claimed were entrapment tactics by inspectors. The fact that the association called in long-standing political debts by forcing some UIL councillors to support its claims cannot have helped the Irish Party's election prospects in the city. The association's special pleading received short shrift from the Irish Times, which commented that infringements of food orders were far more harshly punished in Britain. Dublin's magistrates were 'scrupulously fair,' and 'if £10 fines do not suffice to cure these "slight errors of judgement" … committed at the expense of the poor of Dublin, the penalties will be increased.'[9] Official statistics supported the popular view. For instance, live pig exports in the year ending 24 April 1918 came to 2,297, compared with only 686 over the previous twelve months.

Eventually it was not Sinn Féin or the labour movement that took action along the lines threatened by Constance Markievicz but the Irish Volunteers. At the end of April 1918 a series of consignments of pigs were intercepted at the corporation pens in Portland Place *en route* for export from the North Wall nearby. When one young Volunteer, Charlie Dalton, reported for duty he found

> twenty or thirty Volunteers at work. The yard was strewn with carcasses of pigs, which had been slaughtered by one of the Volunteers who was a butcher by trade ... I was given a yard brush and was told to sweep up the blood which was being hosed into the channel. I felt very superior engaged in this work of national importance.

According to Dalton (whose older brother was serving with the British army in France), the main reaction of the watching crowd was to bemoan the loss of all the blood, 'which would make such grand black puddings.' At last the carcases were loaded on lorries and taken to local curing factories. Afterwards the Volunteers were plied with tea and slices of bread. Dalton commented:

> I drank the tea with great satisfaction, recalling the time when I had seen the very same refreshments handed to the British Tommies ... during the Rising. The tide had turned. We were now the heroes of the people.[10]

What might be termed the active citizenship of the Volunteers would reach a peak in the 1918 general election, when they provided the electoral muscle for Sinn Féin. Often IRB personnel acted as the conduit between political and paramilitary organisations. The link was personified in this instance by Diarmuid Lynch, the Sinn Féin Food Controller. When he was deported for his role in the pig-slaughtering campaign his prison van was accompanied to the docks by a posse of prominent Sinn Féiners, headed by de Valera.[11]

It certainly made the traditional lobbying tactics of the Irish Party look anaemic. A few weeks earlier T. P. O'Connor and the veteran Dublin MP William Field led a deputation to meet the Parliamentary Secretary of the Admiralty, Dr MacNamara, to seek more support for shipbuilding and stronger measures against the submarine menace. When McNamara pointed to the very light losses on the Irish Sea from submarines, and said that Irish yards were already receiving substantial Admiralty business, he was inadvertently highlighting the continued indifference of the military machine to Irish concerns and the impotence of the Irish Party in changing that mindset. The exercise also smacked of support for the war effort.[12]

On 9 February 1918 there were 'animated scenes' at the Mansion House when socialists gathered 'to congratulate the Russian people on the triumph they have won for democratic principles.' The Round Room was unable to accommodate the crowds of people wanting to celebrate the Bolshevik revolution, which had taken place two months previously. The Supper Room was also filled to overflowing, and the crowd spilled out onto the street. A large Red Flag was brandished at the main meeting to accompany a lusty rendition of 'The Red Flag'. The president of the ITUC, William O'Brien, acclaimed the revolution for attaining 'the most complete political and economic freedom that the world has yet seen.' Cathal O'Shannon of the ITGWU proposed the motion 'that the people of Dublin are at one with the Bolsheviks and ... the Russian interpretation of the democratic principle is the only one that will be acceptable to the people of Ireland.' Thomas Johnson, former president of the ITUC and future leader of the Labour Party in the early years of the Irish Free State, asked the crowd whether they were ready 'to follow the action of the Russian revolutionaries and do the whole job at once.' There were some shouts of 'No' as well as 'Yes.' Undeterred, Constance Markievicz offered congratulations to the representative of the new Soviet government, Conrad Peterson of the Lettish Rifles, on behalf of the Irish Citizen Army. Other speakers included Maud Gonne, Margaret Connery and the most prominent defector to Sinn Féin from the Irish Party, Laurence Ginnell MP.

Only Dr Kathleen Lynn, who had served in the Citizen Army garrison in City Hall during the rising, struck a more cautious note. She told this band of enthusiasts that

> some people were shy of acclaiming Russia for fear of the cry of anti-clericalism. That cry had been raised against men and movements which the British government had reason to fear, because it knew that cry was the most potent to cast a slur on any cause in this country and make the ordinary unthinking person afraid of it.'[13]

Like Constance Markievicz and other Citizen Army members, Lynn had gravitated towards the post-rising reincarnation of Sinn Féin. The independently minded daughter of a Church of Ireland Canon, Lynn could not be accused of undue religious deference, but unlike Markievicz, she was acutely perceptive of the public mood among the middle classes, a mood reflected in the enormous response to the Thomas Ashe fund. Six of the ten largest subscribers to the latest subscription list were Catholic clergymen, and there was an ample sprinkling of reverend mothers. Conservative Catholic Ireland was drawing the Irish revolution to its bosom with a power that a handful of socialist enthusiasts in the Mansion House would be unable to counter.[14]

Ironically, the victory of the Irish Party candidate, Patrick Donnelly, in the Armagh by-election the previous Saturday was a demonstration of how bankrupt constitutional nationalism had become. Unionists in the constituency voted tactically for Donnelly so as to deny the seat to Sinn Féin. This did not prevent the *London Express* from asking naïvely, 'Orangemen and Hibernians have clasped hands in South Armagh: cannot they clasp hands in Dublin?'[15]

Meanwhile the Russian Revolution was to have more immediate consequences than expected for Irish socialists and nationalists of all complexions. The decision of the Bolsheviks to sue for peace released German divisions for redeployment in the west and a last bid to defeat the allies before the American army made a decisive intervention. That offensive would begin on 20 March, and each German advance brought nearer the threat of conscription in Ireland. Fortunately, the labour movement's remarkable recovery after the rising left it better placed to meet the challenge than any other organised force. It had arisen phoenix-like from the burnt-out shell of Liberty Hall.[16] As in the period leading up to the lock-out, it was the ITGWU that spearheaded the revival, especially outside Dublin. Séamus Hughes, who had fought in the rising, believed that 'Easter Week saved the union. It … linked up the labour movement with the age long aspirations of the Irish people for emancipation from political and social thraldom.' A former seminarian, Hughes combined a socialist vision with a strong Catholic faith.

Many unions in the city suffered significant disruption as a result of the fighting and subsequent repression, but none more so than the ITGWU. It even had to use the good offices of Thomas Johnson, president of the ITUC in 1916, to recover its records from the British military authorities.[17] Yet the union would achieve spectacular growth over the next few years, reaching a peak of 120,000 by the end of 1920, with most of its members outside Dublin in such industries as agriculture, where workers were benefiting from the increase in tillage vital to the war effort. In Dublin the Irish Women Workers' Union and the British National Federation of Women Workers were the main beneficiaries of growth in employment and the new wartime arbitration structures in such areas as clothing, hosiery and, most importantly, munitions.

Usually the mere threat of a strike was enough to secure intervention by the arbitration bodies and a settlement resulting in pay awards on a par with, or at least related to, the traditionally higher British rates. But there were penalties for workers as well as for employers for defying the state. When sixteen apprentices went on strike at the Dublin Dockyard Company in late 1917 they were fined between £10 and £5 each, although the deductions were deferred until the new year to help them get over Christmas—and demonstrate their compliance with procedures.

It is an indication of the vulnerability of war industries to industrial action that this strike cost the yard £10,000 in lost business. The company also agreed to concede the apprentices an extra 7½ per cent for war work in the yard, even though this forced it to breach the Admiralty list of pay rates. The Munitions Tribunal stated that the fines might be remitted if the apprentices behaved and did not allow themselves 'to be led astray' in future. By whom they might be 'led astray' is not stated.[18]

———

There was much more industrial unrest generally in 1917 because inflationary pressures had become intense. The price of basic items was up by 57 percentage points on the base year of 1900—by far the largest general increase in prices of any of the war years.[19] It was against this background that the Dublin Trades Council held a special conference of affiliated unions on 30 October 1917, the largest such gathering seen until then in the city, attended by representatives from other centres, including Belfast.

More than a thousand bakers were once more threatening strike in the city, as were two thousand members of the ITGWU with the Alliance and Dublin Consumers' Gas Company. Printers and shipyard workers were already on strike, and the newly formed Irish Clerical Workers' Union had served a pay claim on the city's employers. Fears of the loss of jobs and of price increases were aggravated by news that the British government was introducing further punitive taxes on distilleries. A further five hundred jobs would be abolished, and the loss of grain and wash as cheap animal feed for the city's dairies would renew pressure on milk prices. The debate came down to a choice between a general strike in the city and more effective price controls combined with a conciliation board for dealing with pay claims.[20]

None of these things happened. In large part the failure to agree a strategy stemmed from deep divisions within the movement in Dublin. The trades council had already paid a price for this conflict when Thomas Lawlor failed to secure the vacant Labour seat on the corporation caused by the death of William Partridge. While complacency appears to have played a part in the debacle, William O'Brien was laying most of the blame on P. T. Daly, the leader of the Labour group, who was his main rival within the ITUC, ITGWU and Dublin Trades Council.

If Daly had been Jim Larkin's protégé, O'Brien had been James Connolly's. O'Brien's long period of incarceration with republican prisoners in England had seen him develop close personal ties with the leaders of advanced nationalism, including Éamon de Valera, Michael Collins and Cathal Brugha. O'Brien had been involved in the Longford and Clare by-elections and had helped to secure for Michael Collins the job of secretary of the National Aid and Volunteer Dependants' Fund, his first step on the road to power. O'Brien saw his liaison with Sinn Féin and Irish Volunteer leaders as very much in line with Connolly's political legacy, of which he regarded himself the custodian. Daly too had been interned but for a much shorter period, and he remained a determined advocate of Larkin's project for a politically independent Labour Party.

When the All-Ireland Convention had been called by Count Plunkett in early 1917 Daly had opposed it. He told the trades council that 'we have started an independent movement and I will always use my influence to maintain that independence and to be under no circumstances subservient to any other party in the state.' But a close ally of O'Brien, Tom Foran, president of the ITGWU, was probably more representative of mainstream opinion when he said that 'if a man could not be a good trade unionist and a good nationalist it was better to have no trade unionism at all.'

O'Brien's ultimate triumph in the battle with Daly was based in part on the strong alliances he was building between the Dublin labour movement and Sinn Féin, which reflected the rapidly changing balance of power in the city. Up to 1916 Labour had been the main opposition to the UIL. Daly warned the trades council in the autumn of 1917 that Sinn Féin was growing rapidly in the city and was in the process of nominating candidates for constituencies that Labour regarded as its legitimate prizes. But few were listening as the new year dawned. The pressure of events was too great; and the mass mobilisation of workers against conscription, particularly in Dublin, was to be Labour's finest hour.

———

Fear of conscription was never far below the surface of Irish life. In 1917 only 3,089 Dubliners joined the British army, and not many more, 5,023, would travel to Britain for work, despite strong incentives and assisted passage from the Prince of Wales Fund. Reports still proliferated of Irishmen being forcibly conscripted in British cities despite exemption orders. In 1918, when the conscription scare was at its height, only 3,370 Dubliners would travel to Britain for work, while the number joining the armed forces would rise slightly to 3,990, although mainly in non-combatant and technical branches.[21]

There was undoubtedly a lot of truth in the claim by the *Irish Times* that 'Ireland has deserted her regiments at the front. She still praises them in her newspapers and talks about "Irish valour" ... but it is mere talk.' The paper predicted that if the war lasted another year, 'and the Irish regiments receive no help from Ireland, they will have disappeared altogether from the British Army or will be Irish in nothing save their name.' Two days later the MP for the Harbour division, Alfie Byrne, put down a motion for the city council warning the government that any attempt to introduce conscription 'would be resisted violently in every town and village ... and [would lead to] the establishment of a battle front in Ireland that would not be to the advantage of the Allies.' Kingstown Urban District Council, which unionists had controlled up to the 1914 municipal elections, voted to oppose conscription, with only four councillors voting against the motion. Even the unionist spokesman in South County Dublin, Sir Thomas Robinson, admitted that 'this was perhaps the worst time to conscript Ireland.'

The battle against conscription was the most complete victory ever won by nationalist Ireland, and it was won without a drop of blood being spilt. Indeed its triumph lay precisely in its saving thousands of young Irishmen from the pointless bloodletting on the western front. It was also the first time that the new alliance between Sinn Féin and what might be termed the O'Brienite wing of the Labour movement swung into action to secure a common objective.

An early hurdle easily cleared was securing the support of the Executive Council of the British TUC for the Irish stance on conscription. At its own conference in January the TUC had called on the British government to give a commitment that conscription would end immediately hostilities ceased.[22] In fact one of the reasons the War Cabinet wanted to at least be seen to be considering the extension of conscription to Ireland was to make measures such as sending eighteen-year-olds to fight in France more palatable to the British public.[23]

Dublin was the focal point for the anti-conscription campaign. Alfie Byrne and the former Lord Mayor Lorcan Sherlock worked with the incumbent, Laurence O'Neill, to form a national committee. O'Brien drafted a motion for the Dublin Trades Council meeting on 8 April that the Executive Council of the Irish Trades Union Congress and Labour Party should send delegates to any anti-conscription conference, provided that Sinn Féin and the Irish Volunteers decided to attend. As O'Brien was president of the ITUC, there was little doubt about what the response of the congress would be.[24]

Proceedings in Dublin Corporation were somewhat more fractious. The language of Alfie Byrne's motion, calling for a conference to organise resistance to conscription in 'every town and village in the country,' alarmed some councillors. However, most were reassured by Sherlock's addendum that the Lord Mayor should invite the Irish Volunteer and Sinn Féin leaders Éamon de Valera and Arthur Griffith to the conference 'to arrange a united Irish opposition to conscription,' along with the new leader of the Irish Party, John Dillon, his Belfast lieutenant, Joe Devlin, and representatives of the ITUC.[25]

The only member of the corporation to speak against the motion was the independent alderman David Quaid, whose Drumcondra ward contained many Protestant ratepayers. He said that a campaign of resistance to conscription would only earn Ireland 'the contempt of all the nations of the world.' When he asked members how they could vote against conscription when they had just passed a vote of sympathy for the families of the Howth fishermen killed by a German submarine he was met with the jibe, 'Who told you they were Germans?' When the motion was put to a vote there were only three votes against: Quaid and the two unionists present, Alderman William T. Dinnage from neighbouring Glasnevin and Councillor William M. Coulter from Clontarf West. The other thirty-nine councillors present voted for the motion.[26]

Once the decision was made, a flurry of meetings followed, and the Mansion House Conference was held on 18 April, two days after the enactment of the new Military Service Act, which extended conscription to every Irish male between the ages of eighteen and fifty. In the House of Commons debate preceding the vote Lloyd George taunted the Irish Party with reminders of its pledges of support for the war, including those of their recently deceased leader, John Redmond. He reminded Dillon that he had said he would support conscription if necessary. Dillon responded feebly that he had done so because he had believed 'it was [for] a war for small nationalities,' but 'we found out that was not true.' After the legislation was passed, the Irish Party would withdraw yet again from the House of Commons, and in a weaker position than ever.

————

The Mansion House Conference has been described as the convening of a 'National Cabinet'. It was in fact a remarkable gathering of the old guard of constitutionalism about to depart, although not without a fight, and the new guard representing a younger generation of radical nationalists and separatists. Perhaps the biggest divide was the cultural one, with the new guard championing a more assertive and 'purer' sense of nationality that was all the harder for the old guard to counter for being intangible.

There was certainly a lot more public interest than there had been in the anaemic Irish Convention set up by the British government the previous July. It had achieved nothing and had met for the last time on 5 April 1918, largely unremarked as public attention turned to the threat of conscription.[27] The contrast in public interest with the opening of the Anti-Conscription convention at the Mansion House two weeks later could not have been greater. Crowds gathered long before the opening time of 10 a.m., even though the proceedings were to be in private. According to the *Irish Independent*, there were 'young and old, rich and poor, with ... a considerable sprinkling of the Unionist element.' While the demeanour of the crowd was orderly, 'the intensity of feeling caused by Mr. Lloyd George's proposals' was shown by the 'perfect roar' that greeted the arrival of de Valera and Griffith.[28]

The meeting adjourned at 1 p.m. to allow a deputation to confer with the Catholic hierarchy at Maynooth. The bishops had already decided to oppose conscription, though they were somewhat divided, between Cardinal Logue and other advocates of purely passive resistance on one side and those prepared to go further, such as Archbishop Walsh of Dublin, on the other. Characteristically, Walsh had been conspiring feverishly behind the scenes to ensure the maximum unity between the emerging generation of radical nationalist leaders and the hierarchy.

De Valera had given an early display of his famous obstinacy that morning by insisting that the Mansion House Conference endorse his version of the anti-conscription policy before going out to Maynooth. Years later he would tell William O'Brien that he had already cleared the wording confidentially with Archbishop Walsh and that his refusal to accept amendments was for fear that any change might unravel the agreed strategy. Walsh had also arranged for the Lord Mayor to phone him from the Mansion House when the delegation would be ready to travel to Maynooth to seek the hierarchy's blessing. Even the speaking order of the delegation was decided in advance, with de Valera giving the opening position on behalf of the Irish Volunteers, that they would not limit themselves to passive resistance, and William O'Brien speaking last, pledging the support of workers to the cause.

The bishops gave the campaign their blessing. Their statement against conscription contained the key phrase engineered by Walsh that it was being imposed in 'an oppressive and inhuman law, which the Irish people have a right to resist by all means that are consonant with the law of God.' They also decreed that a Mass of intercession would be offered up in every church the following Sunday, at which details would be announced of rallies where people could sign the pledge against conscription. Indeed many Mass-goers found that they were able to sign the pledge at tables outside the church gate on the next Sunday.

As O'Brien said afterwards, 'we were getting all we asked for and more.'[29] It was a far cry from his speech in the Mansion House a month earlier, acclaiming the Russian revolution for attaining 'the most complete political and economic freedom that the world has yet seen,' but it was also of much more practical value; and O'Brien, unlike his mentor James Connolly, usually came down on the pragmatic side of any political question.

The delegation then hurried back to the Mansion House, where the crowds were still thronging 'every foot of the thoroughfare' and singing rebel songs to while away the time. The delegates were delayed by the breakdown of the car in which O'Brien and John Dillon were travelling, so that proceedings did not end until 9:45 p.m. While there were cheers for all the departing leaders, de Valera was carried shoulder high down Dawson Street, and it was only with some difficulty that he freed himself to catch the Dalkey tram home to Booterstown.[30]

––––

It was one thing for the Mansion House Conference and the Catholic hierarchy to make ambitious declarations asserting the rights of the Irish people, but only the trade union movement could give them effect. William O'Brien came into his own when the conference reconvened next day and endorsed a proposal for a national strike on 23 April. A special All-Ireland Trades Conference was held in the Mansion House on Saturday 20 April to plan the action. Uniquely, it took place with the support of the nationalist press. Even William Martin Murphy's *Independent* group of newspapers threw its weight behind the strike and warned workers of the dangers of not showing solidarity with each other!

It was left to the Church of Ireland Archbishop of Dublin, Dr J. H. Bernard, and a Labour Party member of the British government, George Barnes, to champion conscription. In a sermon preached in St Michan's church on Sunday 21 April, Dr Bernard not only advised people to respect the new conscription laws but urged young men not to wait to be conscripted.

Offer your services as voluntary recruits without delay. Do not hesitate because others hold back. Your duty remains the same, whether others are cowards, or shirkers, or traitors, or not.

An interview given by Barnes to the Press Association the same weekend, urging Irish workers to support the war effort, was a deliberate attempt to appeal to them over the heads of the local trade union leadership. Although Barnes was serving as Minister for Pensions in the Lloyd George government, he had been one of the strongest supporters of the men locked out in 1913, speaking at public meetings in Dublin, including the funeral of one of the men killed. He had been shocked by the 'traces of battered humanity' he had seen as the funeral procession passed through the city and had attempted to move an amendment to the King's Speech in early 1914 to address the workers' grievances. But he completely misjudged the mood of the city in 1918.

He tried to reassure workers that home rule was coming and that it would be 'a tragic thing if that settlement were lost again through hasty and needless conflict.' As far as Irish workers were concerned, 'there is no need for them to fight conscription. Home Rule is right ahead.' The 'settlement of the Irish question has become a necessity of the war, and ... organised labour in this country [Britain] is pledged to see this thing through.' The only danger was that Ireland was 'full of combustible material,' and 'a spark from either side may kindle ... disaster.' He considered the 'disaster of separation' to be even worse than 'the disaster of revolution.'[31]

The strike itself was effective everywhere outside Belfast and its environs. Far from Barnes influencing Irish workers, even those in British unions, such as the National Union of Railwaymen and his own Amalgamated Society of Engineers, played a crucial role in ensuring its effectiveness. More than 100,000 workers were reported to have signed the anti-conscription pledge at trade union offices and at meetings around the country.

In a demonstration of the strong bonds now developing between the Catholic Church, the new national movement and Dublin workers, thousands of strikers attended Mass in Dublin's working-class parishes. Churches in Gardiner Street, Dominick Street and North William Street, as well as the Pro-Cathedral in Marlborough Street, were reported to be particularly well attended. Elsewhere 'there were many little discomforts connected with the day, which the public bore with cheerfulness,' the *Irish Independent* said. 'There was, for instance, no bread delivery, grocery or victualling establishments [butchers] and restaurants were closed.' The absence of trams 'cut thousands off from the seaside' and prevented day trippers from enjoying the fine weather. During the day the Parnell Monument was bedecked with a Tricolour and a 'No conscription' sign.

The only places of any consequence where business was conducted in the city that day were Dublin Castle and the Stock Exchange. Even licensed premises were closed, together with theatres, cinemas and music halls.

Some of the main hotels in the city tried to defy the strike, but by early afternoon 'practically all of the male staff,' including waiters, had left work, and guests had to collect their own meals from the kitchens. The *Irish Independent* awarded the accolade for the greatest self-sacrifice to the hackney car owners, 'in view of the rich harvest presented by Punchestown Races.'[32] O'Brien and his comrades had reason to be proud and no reason to expect that Labour had reached its apogee in leading the national struggle.

On the night of the Mansion House Conference, after de Valera had headed home on the Dalkey tram, several hundred young men of military age finished off the proceedings by marching in formation to the Shelbourne Hotel in St Stephen's Green, where Field-Marshal French was staying. They stood chanting 'No conscription!' for about ten minutes, then dispersed peacefully. French, who had commanded the British Expeditionary Force in France during the opening phases of the war, had arrived on a fact-finding mission. A fortnight later he would be appointed Lord Lieutenant of Ireland to replace Lord Wimborne.

Wimborne had survived the fall-out from the Easter Rising because he had urged a pre-emptive arrest of the rebel leaders, a proposal rejected by the then Chief Secretary, Augustine Birrell, as too provocative. Now he was dismissed for being too weak, refusing to support the introduction of conscription.

Henry Duke, who was thought to have 'gone native,' was replaced as Chief Secretary by another lawyer, Edward Shortt, to implement the new strategy. French represented the symbol rather than the substance of the new policy. He was regarded as old and tired after being relieved of his command in France in 1915. The real architect of the new policy was the former Unionist leader and member for South County Dublin, Walter Long, who was now Secretary for the Colonies in the War Cabinet.

That policy was put into operation immediately. On the night of 17 and 18 May more than seventy Sinn Féin leaders, including de Valera, Griffith, Markievicz and Cosgrave, were arrested on suspicion of being involved in a plot with Germany. Many senior figures in the organisation had been warned in advance of the arrests but had decided that this latest move would backfire on the authorities and consolidate popular support before the forthcoming parliamentary by-election in Co. Cavan, where Arthur Griffith was the Sinn Féin candidate. They were certainly correct in that assessment. Some fifteen thousand people attended a rally in Cootehill the following Sunday to denounce the arrests; and Griffith defeated the nationalist candidate comfortably by a margin of 1,200 votes.

The tip-offs about the arrests came from within the Dublin Metropolitan Police, where demoralisation was turning to disaffection. The treatment of the ringleaders of the police strike in 1916, the increasing support for radical nationalism and the continuing grip of Protestants on most promotions were sources of grievance, and many members of the DMP, like the RIC, had signed the anti-conscription pledge.

At least three members of G Division had gone a step further and, independently of each other, had approached the Irish Volunteers to offer information. Ironically, one of them, Ned Broy, a police typist in his mid-twenties, was given the task of typing the list of senior rebel suspects for the swoop. He passed a copy of the list to a cousin who worked as a clerk for the GSWR in Kingsbridge, who passed it to Harry O'Hanrahan (a brother of Michael O'Hanrahan, one of the executed 1916 men). Another G Division detective, Joe Kavanagh, who had been in touch with Michael Collins for some months, passed word to him through an established contact, Thomas Gay, an IRB member who worked in Capel Street Library.

It was probably no accident that these detectives, and others who switched their allegiance within the DMP, tended to be in the lower ranks. It was an indication of the sea change in the feelings among many public servants about what the future might hold.

It was ironic that the decision to carry out the arrests led to the most militant and committed separatists taking control of the radical nationalist movement—most notably Collins, who heeded his own advice and avoided the police raids that night. He would go on to reorganise the intelligence department of the Irish Volunteers' GHQ in Dublin, replacing the miscast Dublin solicitor Éamonn Duggan as Director of Intelligence. Duggan was more useful to the movement representing members in the courts.[33]

———

The thinking behind the sweep by Dublin Castle was based on a belief that 'the brain power of these organisations which are the chief disturbing element in Ireland is mostly centred in the City of Dublin.' The same 'Report as to the State of Ireland' prepared later in the year for the Cabinet by Lord French stated that the clamp-down was vindicated by a reduction in the number of indictable offences, from 269 in May to 174 in June. The report conceded that there had been less progress in the provinces than in Dublin, and it lamented that 'moral courage is not one of the great attributes of the Irish people.'[34]

The report also contained details of the surveillance of extremists by the DMP in May and June 1918 to support French's analysis. There were certainly plenty of Dublin activists who travelled to Co. Cavan to campaign for Griffith in the first two weeks of May. They included Dr R. Boyd Barrett, Kathleen Clarke, George Gavan Duffy, Eoin MacNeill, Darrell Figgis, Joe McGuinness and Éamon de Valera, as well as Griffith himself. While the Inspector-General of the RIC, Sir Joseph Byrne, reported that the subsequent arrests made speakers more cautious at meetings, cries of 'Up the Kaiser' and 'Up Germany' were frequent, and defections from Sinn Féin were unlikely while 'the dread of conscription' bound young men of military age and their families to Sinn Féin and the Irish Volunteers.

Nor was surveillance restricted to members of the separatist movement. The RIC monthly report for June stated that Labour was

> organising all over the country under the Irish Transport and General Workers Union, and is likely to become a powerful and troublesome force. The Union professes to be non-political but its recognised journal *Irish Opinion* or *The Voice of Labour* is edited by an advanced Sinn Feiner and the tone of the paper is Sinn Fein. The principal organisers of the Union are Sinn Feiners and so also are the members.[35]

It is not surprising, therefore, that the RIC took a close interest in the movements of William O'Brien. Although he was still technically a member of the National Union of Tailors and Garment Workers and would not be appointed treasurer, or *de facto* general secretary, of the ITGWU until February 1919, it was clear that he was already carrying out extensive organising work for the union. The police report for June 1918 showed O'Brien travelling to Carlow, Longford, Limerick and Navan to establish branches of the ITGWU or to deal with industrial disputes.

Meanwhile there was close surveillance of separatist and Labour activities in Dublin itself by the DMP. These included sports fixtures at Croke Park and an aeraíocht held there on 12 May to commemorate members of Fianna Éireann who fell in Easter Week, as well as social events such as the May Day concert at Liberty Hall. The latter attracted about six hundred people, mainly ITGWU members, including 'known suspects.' A much larger and, as far as the police were concerned, more respectable crowd attended a Whist Drive and Labour Concert organised by the trades council in the Mansion House on the following Friday night.

The sheer size of the crowds at hurling and other sports fixtures, usually 3,000 to 8,000, must have made surveillance difficult, and police note-takers infiltrating meetings and concerts were no longer readily tolerated, so that the intelligence notes yielded little more than lists of names. Nevertheless the police authorities sought to explain the apparent futility of persistence by explaining to their superiors that 'these entertainments, which generally border on sedition, afford opportunity to the disaffected of meeting together in furtherance of their organisation.'

And occasionally this work did yield results, such as a number of arrests for illegal drilling in open ground at Dean's Grange and at the Conservative Workingmen's Club in York Street in June, as well as the seizure of forty thousand rounds of rifle ammunition concealed in sacks of oats in the city and of explosives on a ship from Ardrossan in Scotland.[36] But despite the claims of Lord French, the arrests did not stop protests and public meetings in the city. On 19 May, the day after the mass arrests of Sinn Féin leaders, five hundred people attended an anti-conscription rally in the school yard attached to Meath Street church in the Liberties, where members of the local clergy spoke in place of the advertised speakers. The meeting agreed to organise house-to-house collections for the anti-conscription fund, which the police believed now totalled £250,000.

Public defiance also took more blatant forms. On 2 June thousands of people attended the funeral of John Cullen, a 1916 veteran who had never recovered his health after being released from prison. Cullen's remains, his coffin draped in a Tricolour, were brought from his home in Prussia Street on a tour of the north city before reaching Glasnevin cemetery. Fifty Volunteer companies marched behind the hearse as well as four hundred members of Fianna Éireann and three hundred members of Cumann na mBan, along with a large crowd of ordinary citizens. A revolver volley was fired over the grave and the Last Post sounded. The DMP managed to prevent a group of Fianna members forming up afterwards, but the Cumann na mBan contingent proved too much for them and were allowed to march off in formation. On 23 June shots were fired and the Last Post sounded at the funeral of another Volunteer, John Byrne from City Quay. The crowd was much smaller, but again the funeral procession was made a demonstration of strength.

By now the police were admitting that the 'German plot' arrests had

stirred up a bitter feeling against England which shows no sign of abatement. The young men are unwilling to take part in the War on any terms and therefore the Police see no prospect of a general and satisfactory response to the Lord Lieutenant's appeal for 50,000 voluntary recruits, unless it is supported by the Bishops and the Nationalist Party.

Nevertheless, the rate of recruitment more than doubled in the four weeks ending 15 June 1918, to 538, compared with 1,079 in the four months ending 15 May.[37]

———

Southern unionists had a more realistic assessment of the state of the country than Dublin Castle. Hopes that some accommodation might be reached under the home-rule dispensation had died with the convention in April and the irresistible rise of Sinn Féin. This was reflected in the election of hard-liners to the Unionist Council in the first week of June 1918. The *Irish Times* commented:

Three months ago a large number of moderate Nationalists were anxious for a reasonable settlement; that party no longer asserts itself in public affairs. The basis of the Irish Convention was national recognition of the supreme authority of the Imperial Parliament. Within the last few weeks the most powerful force in Ireland—the Roman Catholic Hierarchy—has defied that authority on an essential point of principle, and has rallied the whole of Nationalist Ireland to its support. These hammer blows, following one another in rapid succession, have killed every hope that moderate Irishmen founded on the work of the Irish Convention.

The *Times* blamed the new leader of constitutional nationalism, John Dillon, for the dilemma of southern unionists. It said the Mansion House conference convened by the Lord Mayor had helped Dillon in his 'undertaker's task of driving the last nail in the coffin of Home Rule by rejecting the Empire's final appeal to Ireland for voluntary service in the war.'[38] While the editorial seriously misrepresented Dillon's role in the process, and there was a large element of 'it's everybody else's fault' in the diagnosis, it did reflect the growing belief among southern liberal unionists that the time for compromise was over.

On Sunday 9 June there was a small demonstration of the widening gulf between the majority of the Protestant unionist community and their co-religionists who had embraced the nationalist position. A group of Protestant anti-conscription women arrived early at Christ Church Cathedral to hold a private prayer session. They had written to the Dean notifying him of their intention. Although they had received no reply, they were surprised to find the doors closed. The group, which included such well-known figures as Alice Stopford Green, Sarah Harrison, Susan Mitchell, Nelly O'Brien and Alice Milligan, knelt down in the pouring rain to hold their prayer meeting. As they were about to leave, an unidentified church official came out, took a copy of the anti-conscription pledge from one of the women and tore it to pieces, saying he 'would not allow any rubbish of that kind in the church.'[39]

The prayer meeting and the rain were both a foretaste of 'Woman's Day', when thousands of women took to the streets of Dublin and braved gales of up to 55 miles per hour and torrential rain to demonstrate their opposition to conscription. Up to fifteen thousand signatures were collected for the anti-conscription pledge in the vestibule of City Hall, a short distance from Christ Church. Many women's groups marched to City Hall and other venues to take the pledge. The largest was the contingent of 2,400 from the Irish Women Workers' Union, who marched from Denmark House in Great Denmark Street,[40] with Louie Bennett at their head.

Louie Bennett was a member of that remarkable generation of women activists to emerge from Dublin's Protestant middle classes to campaign for social justice. The daughter of an auctioneer in Killiney, who was himself shunned by his family for being 'in trade,' Louie showed her independence from an early age when she formed an 'Irish League' at the boarding school she was sent to in London. Her time there either led to, or reinforced, feelings of 'intense hatred of the English people,' but her primary interest was female suffrage and women's rights. In her late forties by 1918, she was highly regarded for her work in such bodies as the Irish Women's Suffrage Federation and her editorship of the *Irish Citizen*. By then she had become a convinced pacifist, although one ready to engage in strenuous and sustained passive resistance when necessary in pursuit of her objectives. After the rising the IWWU was in crisis, as its leading figures, Helena Molony and Winifred Carney, both members of the Irish Citizen Army, were in prison for their activities. Bennett agreed reluctantly to take up the baton but soon realised that trade union organisation provided an ideal vehicle for mobilising women, especially working women, to demand their rights. Her first recruit was her lifelong friend Helen Chenevix, a neighbour in Killiney who was the daughter of a Church of Ireland bishop and, like Bennett, a combination of militant suffragist and advocate of passive resistance.[41]

Other large contingents included 1,400 members of the Irish Tailoresses' Society and 700 members of Cumann na mBan, which did not prevent the latter claiming ownership of the event.[42] Similar demonstrations were organised at Rathmines Town Hall and the Bottle Makers' Hall in Ringsend.

While Christ Church may have disowned some of its flock, Archbishop William Walsh encouraged expressions of unity of purpose between the anti-conscription movement and the Catholic Church. There were two processions to the Carmelite church in Whitefriars' Street by two thousand women and girls, on each occasion combining a demonstration against conscription with attendance at the Exposition of the Blessed Sacrament. Another two thousand women and girls attended the Passionist church at Mount Argus in Harold's Cross, where special devotions took place, including recitations of the Rosary and the Consecration of the Sacred Heart, to accompany the taking of the anti-conscription pledge. A group of two hundred IWWU members attended Mount Argus bearing banners, while the priest at the Church of the Three Patrons in Rathgar allowed 'an energetic committee of ladies' to collect 1,100 signatures.

In the working-class area around Sheriff Street hundreds of local women signed the anti-conscription pledge after Mass in St Laurence O'Toole's Christian Brothers' School and then marched in a body to City Hall. Similar demonstrations took place late into the evening at Fairview, Inchicore, Goldenbridge and St James's churches, where thousands of women braved the rain and wind. Altogether an estimated forty thousand signatures were collected in Dublin, dwarfing the numbers elsewhere.[43] It was yet another example of how the anti-conscription campaign was reasserting the traditional bonds of nationality and religion in new ways.

———

Equally remarkable in its own way was the extraordinary general meeting of the Dublin Chamber of Commerce five days later. When the traditional address of welcome to the new Lord Lieutenant, Field-Marshal French, was proposed by the president, E. H. Andrews, there were 'wild scenes of disorder and confusion.' Gone was the unity of 1913, when Catholic and Protestant employers stood shoulder to shoulder against the threat of Larkinism. On that occasion William Martin Murphy had been the first Catholic to hold the presidency of the chamber, and Andrews had been his lieutenant, organising the Loyal Tramway Fund so that grateful citizens could pay a handsome bonus to strike-breakers.

On this occasion Murphy was absent, but members of one group who had remained largely silent during the lock-out, the city's Irish Party MPs, now found their voice. William Field, Alfie Byrne and Patrick J. Brady were vocal in their opposition to the proposal, as were a number of councillors. E. J. Carton, an egg and poultry merchant, said the address was inopportune, given the state of the country. It might have been traditional to offer such addresses in the past, but he reminded the president that the rules had been amended as far back as 1915 to ban such initiatives as being outside the chamber's remit. The address was unnecessarily contentious. Belfast Chamber of Commerce had offered no address to the Lord Lieutenant, nor had the Irish Agricultural Organisation Society, and was anyone suggesting that its founder, Sir Horace Plunkett, was disloyal?

However, the former unionist councillor Sir Maurice Dockrell, who ran the city's largest builders' providers and was junior grand deacon of the Grand Lodge of Free and Accepted Masons of Ireland, insisted that merchants in the city would be labouring under a disadvantage if they could not protect their property against sedition by upholding the lawfully constituted authority of the state. Alderman Quaid, who had opposed the holding of the Mansion House Conference against conscription in April, supported Dockrell; and at that point 'pandemonium' broke out.

James Brady, a solicitor who had been one of Murphy's few critics during the lock-out, mounted the platform and attempted to speak, only to be drowned out by cries of 'Vote' from the dominant unionist faction. A heated exchange followed between Andrews and Byrne, who denounced 'the old Tory regime' and threatened to hold a public meeting on the steps outside. The language grew stronger, with shouts of 'Low bounder' being thrown and members having to be separated.

> Alderman Byrne, amid a deafening uproar, sprang on a chair and, gesticulating wildly, cried out, 'I claim you must listen to minorities.' The uproar increased rather than subsided and Alderman Byrne threw the chair on the floor. A member approached him in a very threatening manner and a collision appeared imminent, all of the members having risen and joined in the general yelling. The President here put the question and declared it carried.

But the opposition refused to accept defeat and accused the president and his sixteen fellow-members of the executive of speaking for no-one but themselves. Byrne, once more in full flight, shouted:

The address was prepared by seventeen gentlemen, every one of whom is seeking a title. They do not care how they represent the views of the traders so long as they get their titles from a coercionist, conscriptionist Lord Lieutenant.[44]

He hoped that French would be informed of the true state of affairs. There was little doubt that he would, given the coverage the meeting received in the newspapers.

In fact French had already retreated significantly over conscription. On 1 June he had issued a proclamation seeking no more than 50,000 volunteers by October, 'to replenish the Irish Divisions in the field, and after that date to raise 2,000 to 3,000 recruits per month in order to maintain those divisions.' The proclamation stated that there was 'no intention to disturb farming interests or food production ... hamper or curtail the essential industry of the country': instead 'the Government look almost entirely to the large number of young men in the towns, far greater than is required to carry on ordinary retail trade, to furnish the necessary contingent.'

In an effort to attract these men, many of whom had come from rural Ireland to work as clerks, barmen or drapers' assistants, the proclamation contained vague assurances that steps would be taken, 'as far as possible,' to provide land for volunteers when the war was over. It was a far cry from the 200,000 men that conscription would have yielded; and the appeal fell largely on deaf ears.

Dublin supplied a mere 3,990 recruits between January and the end of November 1918. Even Belfast managed only 6,549. Nor, to the disgust of the *Irish Times*, were there any proposals to drive the large number of young men of military age out from 'under the gigantic umbrella of the Irish Civil Service' in Dublin to the front. It described Lord French's 'astonishing moderation' as a 'final test of Ireland's loyalty to the Allied cause and, therefore, of her fitness to self government.'[45]

One of those sheltering under the civil service umbrella was Patrick Belton, assistant clerk at the Land Commission. He had escaped dismissal with a warning not to engage in political activities after the investigation of his actions during the Easter Rising and his foray into the South Longford by-election during 1917.[46] He was in trouble again by June 1918. However, the most striking aspect of Belton's treatment was how bungling, how fair and how bureaucratic the instruments of repression were in dealing with an inveterate rebel.

When local RIC men reported on Belton's activities in Co. Longford they were required to travel to Dublin and pick him out among the commission's staff to make sure it was not a case of mistaken identity. Belton was unable to deny that he spoke from a Sinn Féin election platform alongside Michael Collins, but his denial of the statements recorded by the RIC note-takers was accepted. The case ended up on the desk of the Under-Secretary, Sir William Byrne. He concluded that Belton was 'a slippery and rather defiant person,' whose loyalty was 'doubtful' but who had a knack for 'explaining away' his actions. The fact that Belton's case came to the most senior civil servant in the Irish establishment, and that Belton was merely instructed 'to be more circumspect in his conduct,' showed how ill prepared bureaucratically or psychologically the British state was for confronting serious disaffection in Ireland.

Meanwhile Belton, convinced that he had enemies within the Land Commission who would keep the authorities posted on his activities, requested a transfer to the Department of Agriculture, on the grounds of his farming background. T. P. Gill refused to take him. Police reports from Finglas that Belton had 'poisoned the minds of the youth and made them all Sinn Feiners' could not have helped his career prospects, and the note that 'he himself keeps far from all danger of detection' no doubt confirmed the judgements already made by his superiors.

In June 1917 Belton moved from Finglas to Belfield Park in Drumcondra to become a tenant farmer in his spare time. Presumably Collins, the Irish Volunteers or some other agency helped finance the move. It was to become part of a recurring pattern in Belton's career, in which politics and business developed a symbiotic relationship. The police reported in May 1918 that 'large bodies of Sinn Feiners assembled on his lands … and carried out drilling in secluded parts of his fields, where they could not be observed.' Besides the drilling there was a steady stream of visitors, and after a particularly large group descended on the farm, the police carried out a raid on 30 July. A number of the visitors managed to escape, but Belton and another man calling himself John Murphy were still on the premises, as were two revolvers and more than fifty rounds of ammunition. Belton's papers were found to include subscription forms for the Irish National Aid Volunteer Dependants' Fund, various Sinn Féin pamphlets and rebel songs, and documents showing that Belton was a member of the executive of the Dependants' Fund and the Patriot Graves Committee. There was a pass admitting the bearer to the graveside of Thomas Ashe on the day of the martyr's funeral and correspondence from Patrick Sheehan, secretary of Sinn Féin.

On 31 August, Belton was sentenced to six months' imprisonment with hard labour. He had already written to his employers while in custody in Mountjoy Prison explaining that his annual leave had expired but that his host had prevailed on him to stay a little longer 'and revel in the romantic scenery.' The Land

Commission suspended Belton without pay but stopped short of dismissing him, as he had appealed the conviction for unlawful possession of firearms and ammunition on the grounds that he needed them to protect his poultry from thieves. It took until 14 September 1918 for his appeal to be rejected, and it was 7 January 1919 before he was finally dismissed from the Land Commission.[47] By then things had gone from bad to much worse in Dublin as far as his superiors were concerned.

———

While the activities of men such as Belton attracted police interest and newspaper reports, it was the burden of war on the quality of life in the city that caused alienation among ordinary Dubliners. On the same day as Lord French's proclamation rowing back on the threat of conscription the corporation received a letter from Fred Allan, in his capacity as secretary of its Electricity Supply Committee, on a matter of more immediate and greater consequence. It was a warning that continuing restrictions on coal imports meant that the city would receive no more than three-quarters of the 1917 figure. Imports that year had been between 7,000 and 8,000 tons short, and the demand for electricity had been met by eating into the fuel stockpiled from previous years.

Unfortunately H. G. Burgess, wartime Director-General of Transport, Shipping Controller and Coal Controller, had rejected pleas to facilitate the shipping of extra coal needed to make up the shortfall. No more than 18,000 tons was approved, or 45 per cent of what was required. There was also the added problem of cost. Coal was now 33s 7d a ton, compared with 9s 6d before the war. Fred Allan and P. T. Daly, chairman of the Coal Committee, decided to go over Burgess's head, but their trip to England proved unfruitful and was probably not helped by the fact that as former veteran Fenians (and in Allan's case a reactivated Fenian) their movements were kept under police surveillance.[48] They may well have reminisced on the mail boat about their exploits together in the early 1900s.[49]

On their return Burgess rejected Allan's figures and, while admitting that there would have to be a significant cut in supplies for domestic users, assured him that it was intended to ensure adequate supplies to maintain essential utilities, such as the sewage and water works.

Further pressure was put on electricity generation by military requirements. The Admiralty had commandeered supplies from the corporation for the Dublin Dockyard Company, and when the corporation sought to secure replacement supplies from the DUTC power station the army claimed precedence so that it could use its power to process fodder for the cavalry at its depot at the East Wall. In desperation, the corporation decided to apply for a loan of £175,000 to buy new plant and equipment to boost electricity production from its dwindling fuel stocks.

This in turn provoked protests from the Citizens' Association and the City House Owners' Property Association, fearful of further increases in the rates.

Subsequently the corporation's plans to augment its electricity-generating capacity were bogged down in a Local Government Board inquiry that summer. The Town Clerk, Sir Henry Campbell, an old Parnellite MP not normally given to intemperate language, told the hearing that it was 'a scandal' for Dublin Corporation to be treated in this fashion. 'I warn the Government that it is this sort of pin-pricking that will irritate the people, and make it impossible for the proper Government of this country to go on.'[50]

'THE TORPEDO EXPLODED IN THE MIDDLE OF THE POST OFFICE, DESTROYING THE STAIRS, THE ONLY MEANS OF ESCAPE'

On 12 July 1918 the commander in chief of the forces in Ireland, Lieutenant-General Frederick Shaw, proclaimed Sinn Féin, the Irish Volunteers, Cumann na mBan and the Gaelic League as 'dangerous organisations.'[1] No meetings could be held except with police permission, and public addresses in Irish were banned. A number of race meetings and football matches also fell victim to the ban. As the proclamation was only announced on the Twelfth, Orange marches that day were not affected, neither were loyalist demonstrations that were planned for the coming weekend.

While the move caused widespread anger outside Ulster, the Dublin ratepayer had other matters to consider. On 3 July the boards of the city's two workhouses were notified that they were to be amalgamated. The issue, which had been debated for years, made sense in that it would lead to a better use of resources and provision of services, as well as (it was hoped) reducing the financial burden on the city. But the final decision was the result of military diktat. The British army requisitioned the North Dublin Union complex as winter quarters for troops, and the guardians were given until 1 September to transfer inmates across the river. Any surplus could be sent to the workhouses at Pelletstown, near Dunshaughlin, and Cabra.

Outrage among the guardians was only partially mitigated by the expectation of economies that might accrue for ratepayers from this forced rationalisation. When those paladins of the ratepayers, the Dublin Citizens' Association, met for their annual general meeting the following week they speculated in celebratory mood that with good management the savings could be between £20,000 and

£30,000 a year. There was also heated speculation by members, councillors and guardians alike (often the same people) about how much the military might pay in compensation for the use of the North Dublin workhouse, which was valued at £87,688.[2]

All were to be disappointed. The Local Government Board notified the two Poor Law unions, now to be amalgamated as one Dublin Union, that the army authorities did not pay compensation for the use of workhouses. Nor were ratepayers happy that the North Dublin Board of Guardians agreed to top up pensions for redundant employees by crediting them with, in some cases, as much as twenty-five years' extra service.

———

On the positive side, the forced amalgamation did not pose the serious accommodation problem it might have done a few years earlier. The advent of Lloyd George's old-age pension and the establishment of outdoor relief had seen the number of inmates fall drastically. The workhouse was no longer the inevitable destination of working-class people who had outlived their capacity to support themselves: if they survived long enough to claim the pension—to the age of seventy—they could live out their days in the community.

Although the elderly still made up 30 per cent of the population of Dublin's workhouses in January 1915, the figure had fallen to 20 per cent by January 1919. The number of other poor people seeking admission also fell. The total population of Dublin's two workhouses was only 4,800 in 1916 and 3,500 in 1919. By then there was more than enough room for all those seeking shelter in the South Dublin complex, which had housed 5,000 people at the beginning of the century.

On the other hand, the number claiming outdoor relief rose from 1,980 in 1916 to 3,009 in 1919; and this upward trend would continue when the post-war recession struck. While the cost of the old-age pension fell on the British exchequer, as did the newfangled unemployment and health insurance schemes, the cost of relieving the poor, either inside or outside the workhouse, continued to fall on the ratepayer.

Wartime inflation aggravated the upward spiral in the poor rate. The increase in rates was particularly sharp for ratepayers on the south side with the amalgamation of the two Poor Law unions, because of the disproportionate number of poor north-siders claiming either outdoor relief or indoor sanctuary. The North Dublin poor rate had been 3s 6¼d in the pound (17½ per cent) in 1914 and the South Dublin rate 1s 10½d (9½ per cent). By 1918 the North Dublin rate was 4s 9½d (24 per cent) and the South Dublin rate 4s 0½d (20 per cent). On amalgamation the joint rate was set at 4s 6d (22½ per cent). It would continue to rise over the next four years that led to the establishment of the Irish Free State.[3]

An amalgamation driven by military imperatives did not augur well for inmates either. While some unmarried mothers with young children were banished to Pelletstown and rural isolation, others found themselves sharing living quarters with the elderly, the mentally handicapped, and beggars.[4]

——

Not that life was easy in the outside world. In August 1918 Dublin experienced a wave of strikes generated by rising prices. The biggest group to come out were the city's ten thousand building workers; but yard men in the shipping companies, bakers, butchers, printers, hotel and restaurant workers, coalmen in Kingstown and agricultural labourers in the county also pursued pay increases.

Building workers sought an increase of 3½d an hour and had been offered ¾d before striking on 19 August. The original claim on the Dublin Building Trades Employers' Association had gone in during July and was based on a 12½ per cent increase in war industries conceded by the government's Committee on Production.[5] Building employers resisted, on the grounds that they had already paid an increase of 16s 8d a week in April and that conceding union demands would cost another £4 a week. Besides, they were outside the Committee on Production's arbitration system. The strike dragged on for almost a month, during which time work stopped on all public works, including the restoration of the bombed-out area around the GPO. The sheer number of unemployed building workers also hit shopkeepers and other businesses hard. An agreement was eventually arranged through the Lord Mayor, Laurence O'Neill, which conceded 1½d an hour to the men, or a minimum of 6s 3d a week. This was a doubling of the original employers' offer but less than half the amount sought.[6]

The hotel and restaurant strike was also settled through negotiation under the aegis of the Lord Mayor. Some waiters had been earning as little as 6s a week, while some received only tips. They were seeking a standard wage of 25s a week for male waiters and 15s for female waiters in hotels, with 17s 6d for men in restaurants and 12s 6d for women. Chefs were looking for an extra £1 a week. Other male manual workers sought an extra 15s a week, and female non-waiting workers were looking for an extra 7s 6d. All the major hotels and restaurants were closed, except Bewley's, which agreed to pay an increase as an advance on whatever was finally agreed.[7]

Negotiations for the Hotel Workers' Union were undertaken by the president of the ITGWU, Tom Foran. He managed to secure most of the strikers' objectives by the following Saturday, showing how strong the demand for hotel space was in Dublin during the latter stages of the war. Many of the travellers discommoded by the dispute were Americans *en route* to Britain and France.

Similar success was achieved in the agricultural labourers' dispute in Co. Dublin. With the harvest coming in, the ITGWU had picked its time well. The settlement demonstrated the growing power of the union, and the rates finally struck with the Agricultural Wages Board were higher than those achieved in England, Scotland or Wales. The rate for summer work was increased by 3s 6d a week and for winter work by 4s 6d, bringing the top rate to 28s 6d for both summer and winter work. The age at which full wages were paid was reduced from twenty-one to twenty. The maximum rent for a labourer's cottage was set at 1s 6d a week.[8]

By contrast, industries covered by state arbitration bodies, or having relativities with war industries, remained relatively trouble-free in late 1918. A new pay claim by general labourers and craft workers in Dublin Corporation was practically inevitable after the concessions to the building workers in the summer strike, especially as the Lord Mayor had brokered the agreement. But there was no industrial action. Nor was there any action on the part of such unions as the United Building Labourers or the United Brassfounders', Turners', Finishers' and Gasfitters' Society, which had put in claims to the corporation the previous May. They were not adjudicated upon until mid-October, and backdating varied considerably, but the general result allowed for increases ranging from 1s 9d a week for boys to 12s 6d for some craft workers. In contrast to the uncontrolled sector, the existence of arbitration structures meant that these increases were determined without the loss of an hour's pay or production. This did not prevent the Citizens' Association and their champions in the corporation fighting a vigorous rearguard action to block the increases, but the decisions of the Committee on Production and the Wages Regulation Orders took precedence over Dublin's ratepayers' concerns.[9]

By 1918 a new phenomenon was clearly emerging in pay resolution for Dublin workers, whereby unions representing workers in uncontrolled industries based claims on the outcome of the arbitration awards for workers in the controlled sector; this in turn led workers in controlled industries to put in new claims based on restoring their eroded differentials with the uncontrolled sector. It was the invention of a 'pay round' system that would re-emerge during the Second World War, but on this occasion it was less structured and was swept away by the employers' counter-offensive of 1921.

It should be stressed that the controlled and uncontrolled sectors were not the same as the present-day public and private-sector systems of collective bargaining. The controlled sector did include many public employments but it also included any area of economic activity considered essential to the war effort.

Nor did it mean that all was plain sailing where the military exercised control. In a tightening labour market there was a bad employment scare in the autumn of 1918 solely attributable to the military. The owners of Boland's Mills announced on 4 September that they would have to close, as no compensation had been paid by the military authorities since they appropriated the plant in May 1917 to meet the needs of the army. As a result almost four hundred bakers, labourers, van men and yard men faced the dole. Once again the British state's dispute resolution machinery swung into action and a mutually acceptable agreement was reached by 9 September under the auspices of the Flour Mills Control Committee in London.[10]

———

The growing air of militancy in Dublin displayed itself in other ways. The British government thought it had achieved a coup for its recruitment campaign when the home-rule MP Arthur Lynch, former commander of one of the Irish Brigades that fought for the Boers, agreed to join the army, with the rank of colonel. But when he made his debut as a recruiting officer at one of Dublin's traditional recruitment hustings, the Fountain in James's Street, he was met with 'a veritable tornado of cheering and booing.' Every time he tried to speak sections of the crowd would sing 'The Soldier's Song' or cry 'Up de Valera,' or 'What about MacBride? Why weren't you with him?' Lynch's 'brigade' in fact had been little more than a company, and its record had been much poorer than that of the illustrious unit led by the 1916 martyr—a fact not lost on the crowd. Eventually Lynch had to be escorted from the meeting by a detachment of twenty DMP men. He met a similar response at another meeting in the more salubrious setting of Kildare Place in Rathmines. There he told the hostile crowd that he had 'endured great trials and faced great dangers in the cause of home rule.'

Heckler: 'Why not stop in Ireland and share our dangers?'[11]
    'Colonel Lynch—Stop in Ireland and share your cowardice. [Hisses] Hide your cowardice behind the high-sounding name of patriotism.'[12]

———

Industrial unrest subsided in the autumn, and the police reported to Lord French that the attention of the Executive Council of the ITUC was turning towards election strategy as an end to the war appeared to be in sight. Sinn Féin was doing likewise, and police reports informed the Lord Lieutenant that 'great efforts' were being made by some trade union leaders 'to bring about a compromise so as to enable Sinn Fein to obtain the full support of the working classes.'[13]

In August, when the ITUC&LP had still been riding high on the back of its success in the anti-conscription campaign, and widespread industrial militancy was achieving improvements in pay and conditions, it announced that it would be contesting the post-war general election. However, it soon became clear that there was considerable disagreement on electoral strategy within its ranks.

Because of the large membership among Protestant workers in Ulster who were loyalists, the ITUC&LP could not take a clear position on what, if any, constitutional link there should be with Britain. Many Dublin trade unionists, including P. T. Daly, secretary of the ITUC&LP and leader of the Labour group in the corporation, saw the defeat of the Irish Party as the priority, because of its corruption and its close ties with the employers. By contrast, relations with Sinn Féin remained cordial. That organisation appreciated the need to keep a good working relationship with Labour, especially in Dublin, if it was to defeat the constitutional nationalists.

A year earlier Daly had warned the Dublin Trades Council that Sinn Féin was setting its sights on 'legitimate' Labour seats. William O'Brien, as president, had cut Daly out of the ITUC&LP delegation to the anti-conscription conference in the Mansion House, ostensibly because of the need for wider geographical representation by including delegates from Cork and Belfast; but Daly's hostile attitude at the time towards Sinn Féin may also have been a factor in O'Brien's thinking.[14]

But in late 1918 the men's roles were reversed. In September O'Brien led a delegation that met Sinn Féin and asked the latter to give Labour a clear run in Dublin. Then, at the October meeting of the Dublin Trades Council meeting, it was Daly's turn to argue that a clear field should be given to Sinn Féin to beat the Irish Party across the country.

Daly's proposal was defeated, by 27 votes to 9. He was then nominated, along with O'Brien and three other candidates, including the absent Jim Larkin, to fight one of the Dublin constituencies. Daly declined the nomination and was replaced by Louie Bennett, who was now the leading woman trade unionist in the city, having taken over direction of the IWWU. In the event the decision proved immaterial, as the Sinn Féin campaign had gathered so much momentum that it proved impossible for Labour to find credible candidates willing to run elsewhere in the country.

Nor was the problem restricted to the provinces. By October, Dublin Trades Council was being informed by the National Union of Railwaymen that its members would be supporting Sinn Féin; and Tom McPartlin, one of the leading figures in the 1913 Lock-out, who had been nominated to contest a Dublin seat only a few weeks earlier, was told by his own members in the Tailors' Society that they would not vote for him if he ran against Sinn Féin.

Prominent members of the Irish Citizen Army, such as Constance Markievicz and Kathleen Lynn, had already joined Sinn Féin, as had several rank-and-file Citizen Army members. The experience of the rising had forged new bonds. Neither Markievicz nor Lynn was entirely satisfied with Sinn Féin's social programme, especially as it related to women, but they saw the national movement as capable of being remoulded and realised in their different ways that the national question had claimed centre stage. Both were, above all, 'doers'. Markievicz would soon run as a Sinn Féin candidate in the general election, while Lynn would gain prominence as joint director of the Sinn Féin Public Health Department with Dr Richard Hayes, a dispensary doctor from Lusk who had been a close comrade of Thomas Ashe.[15] The Public Health Committee was one of a number of committees set up by Sinn Féin to explore initiatives for transforming Irish life once it assumed state power.

It was yet another indication of the new political reality that, while Sinn Féin was transforming itself from a niche political party into a movement for national liberation, Labour was transforming itself from a movement for social and economic liberation into a niche political party. Ironically, Labour's success in bridging the sectarian divide in the economic field crippled it in a situation where the survival of the link with Britain was the defining issue of the day. As the historians of Dublin Trades Council put it, 'in essence Labour was the trade unions in politics ... With Nationalists, Republicans and Unionists in the trade unions the leadership was bound to compromise.'

If the increasingly bitter and open rivalry between O'Brien and Daly damaged Labour's strategic ability to deal with the Sinn Féin challenge, the political ground had shifted since 1916 in ways that Labour was no better equipped to tackle than its old protagonists in the UIL and AOH. The moratorium on municipal elections since 1915 had also deprived the party of its usual platform on the hustings to make its distinctive voice heard. By 1918 Labour in Dublin no longer represented the aspirations of the majority of the city's workers.[16]

Another force in more permanent decline was Dublin unionism, although it had one final surprise for Sinn Féin in the coming general election. Meanwhile, on Saturday 5 October 1918, the unionist establishment in the capital held a Mammoth Auction in aid of the Royal Dublin Fusiliers Prisoners of War Fund. It opened at the Mansion House and continued until the following Tuesday. Some five thousand items were sold to help the men held in captivity.

It was fitting that the last great public outing of this former political elite should be dedicated to demonstrating its continuing support for the war effort and a celebration of the coming allied victory by remembering the remnants of the 'Dublins' in German prison camps. The patron was Lord French, the president was Lady Arnott, and the other officers and organisers included Viscount Powerscourt, Sir Edward Shortt (Chief Secretary), Andrew Jameson (of the distilling dynasty), Robert Moore (Rotary Club), Sir James Campbell (Lord Chancellor and Lord Chief Justice of Ireland), Sir Maurice Dockrell, and Henry Hanna KC. The latter two individuals were to run as unionist candidates in the general election, while the Lord Chancellor, James Campbell, was a former Unionist MP for the University of Dublin.

The prices of the items sold were an indicator of the continuing relative wealth and social exclusiveness of the milieu. A satinwood writing table donated by Andrew Jameson sold for £17, a Sheraton escritoire donated by Millar and Beatty also sold for £17, while a spray brooch donated by Rose Vernon sold for £26 and a gold, sapphire and enamel necklace donated by Mrs Ernest Guinness of the brewing dynasty was sold for £27. The event culminated on Tuesday with the auction of a 'hold fast' letter from the Prime Minister, David Lloyd George, to Lord Powerscourt and a stone of sugar. Both items were sold and resold until they reached a combined value of £116 15s.

Political niceties were also observed. The auction had been planned for Merrion Square, then the property of Lord Fitzwilliam, but strong winds blew down the tents on the Friday night. The Lord Mayor, Laurence O'Neill, readily agreed to put the Mansion House at the disposal of the committee. Apart from this ecumenical gesture there appears to have been no involvement by any leading representative of the nationalist tradition. The DMP, Dublin Schools Cadet Corps and Rotary Club were mobilised to transfer the items for auction from Merrion Square to the Mansion House.[17]

———

Two days after the auction ended, on 10 October 1918, the *Leinster* was sunk by a German submarine, with the loss of 587 of the 780 passengers on board. It was almost as great a loss of life as that during the rising; but after the initial shock public memory subsided almost as rapidly as the *Leinster* itself. It was one of the ironies of the naval war that submarine activity in the Irish Sea intensified only after convoys were introduced for transatlantic shipping in late 1917. The vessels were now easier targets after they shed their escorts at Queenstown (Cóbh) and dispersed for Dublin and Liverpool.

Naval vessels and newfangled airships provided escorts if important individuals were on board a ferry, or very large troop contingents, as happened on 24 July 1918, when the US Secretary of the Navy, Franklin D. Roosevelt, travelled from Dublin to Holyhead on the *Leinster*. Roosevelt was one of many senior American political, military and naval personnel to use the mail boat. While far from luxurious by modern standards, it was the preferred mode of travel for senior British officers, politicians and even enlisted men anxious to avoid the cramped conditions on troop transports.

In recognition of the threat posed to the mail boats they were provided with 12-pounder guns that could engage a submarine on something like equal terms if subjected to surface attack. While this provided no protection against underwater attacks, it shortened German submarine cruises by forcing them to use up their limited supplies of torpedoes.

In many ways the *Leinster* was living on borrowed time. As the longest-serving mail boat on the Dublin–Holyhead route it had experienced the first of several narrow escapes in January 1915.[18] The last near miss had been on 27 December 1917, when U-100 could fire off only one torpedo, because its tubes were blocked with debris. It was after the tubes were cleared that it claimed the coal ship *Adela*. The *Leinster*'s sister ships, *Ulster*, *Munster* and *Connacht*, all of which were used extensively as troop ships in 1917, had their own narrow escapes; and the *Connacht*'s luck had run out on 3 March 1917, when it was sunk while 'trooping' in the English Channel.[19]

It was UB-123, one of the most up-to-date submarines and one of the last to come from the German yards, that claimed the *Leinster*. It was actually the larger vessel of the two, at 3,000 tons to the 2,641 tons of its victim. It could range as far as the east coast of America; but the convoy system had made for dangerous prey in the Atlantic.

The 10th of October was overcast with a heavy sea running when the *Leinster* passed the South Burford buoy at 9:37 a.m. At 9:45 a passenger spotted the first torpedo crossing the *Leinster*'s bows. Captain William Birch, a very experienced sailor and commodore of the City of Dublin line, ordered a sharp turn south, away from the attacking submarine. If successful, the manoeuvre would have brought the ship on a return course for the safety of Kingstown. But the *Leinster* was struck by a second torpedo on the port bow before it could complete the manoeuvre. It exploded in the ship's post office, killing all but one of the twenty-two sorters.

The sole survivor was J. J. Higgins, who was momentarily stunned. He recalled later:

> The torpedo exploded in the middle of the Post Office, destroying the floor and the stairs, the only means of escape. All the men working in the fore part of the office were either killed instantly by the explosion or engulfed by the falling structure and drowned by the tons of water pouring in through the hole in the side of the ship.

Higgins swam towards a large hole above, where the top of the stairs had been, and hung on to some loose wiring until the water rose to a point where he could clamber out. Realising that there would not be enough places in the lifeboats for 'the mass of people' on deck, and expecting help to arrive before the ship sank, he returned to the uppermost section of the post office to retrieve a lifebelt. When he returned on deck he saw that

> one of the forward lifeboats was being lowered and [I] concluded that this was an opportunity not to be overlooked ... We were only a few yards away when the second torpedo struck the Leinster and she was practically broken in two pieces, the whole centre being blown sky high.
>
> The lifeboat, being so near the sinking ship, it was in danger of being drawn into the vortex; and it was only the good seamanship of the crew that saved the boat. After being adrift for some hours we were rescued by a British destroyer.[20]

The debris from the second explosion posed a further threat to survivors. John Hood, a commercial traveller, said it came

tumbling down all around us. We feared our boat would be swamped but
fortunately got away, rowing through a great deal of wreckage, mingled with
which there were many bodies.

While almost all those still on board when the second torpedo struck died, there
were some extraordinary escapes. Mrs Leo Plunkett of Lansdowne Road (whose
husband was a lieutenant in the Royal Dublin Fusiliers in France) survived, while
her sister-in-law, Sheila Plunkett, drowned. Both women were standing on the
deck when the explosion flung them into the sea. Mrs Plunkett told reporters:
'Miss Plunkett's lifebelt was so insecurely fixed that it fell off at the moment she
was washed overboard, and to add to her helpless plight she was unable to swim.'

Hannah Doe of Camden Buildings was on the promenade deck when she was
'pitched into the sea.' Her leg was injured by wreckage, and although she made it
to a life raft she was twice washed off. She received no help from anyone on the raft
until an officer in the water shouted to the men on board to help her. She reported
seeing numerous bodies floating around her.

Pressure on space aboard lifeboats and life rafts was intense. Some of them had
been destroyed or thrown too far away by the explosions to be of any use. Some
women survivors had 'anything but praise for the conduct of some of the male sex,'
the *Irish Independent* reported. An exception was Captain Robert Lee of the Royal
Army Medical Corps, who had been returning from leave to join his unit in France.
He gave up his place on a life raft to a woman and subsequently perished.[21]

Ironically, the sinking of the *Leinster* occurred on the same day that the new
Chancellor of Germany, Prince Max of Baden, made his inaugural address to the
Reichstag and used it to appeal for peace on the basis of President Woodrow
Wilson's 'Fourteen Points'. German armies were in retreat on the western front, and
it was only a matter of time before the allied armies reached Germany itself.

Most public events in Dublin, including the Phoenix Park Races, were cancelled
for the weekend following the sinking. Survivors flooded into Dublin's hospitals,
and worried relations flocked to the mortuary at St Michael's Hospital in Kingstown
to identify the dead. Among them was the Dublin retailer Edward Lee in search of
his doctor son.

The *Irish Times* expressed the hope that after such an outrage 'Germany has no
longer any dupes in Ireland. Many Irishmen are fools, but we do not think that
many of them are callous renegades from all instincts of patriotism.' It was
'incredible' that any Irishman 'should wish or dare to claim political alliances with
the murderers of Irish women and children.'[22]

However, the advanced nationalist press would have none of it. One pamphlet
entitled *Who Sunk the Leinster?* claimed that the two explosions could be explained
by the vessel hitting a mine of the 'duplex kind' used by the Royal Navy. Even
publications that accepted that it was the Germans, such as the new bulletin of the
Irish Volunteers, *An tÓglach*, put the primary blame on the British government for

using mail ships to carry troops. Reports of people being abandoned were deftly rationalised by nationalist propagandists, who explained that the culprits were British soldiers. The author of *Who Sunk the Leinster?* claimed that nine hundred British soldiers had been on board and they had driven back women and children from the lifeboats at gunpoint, shouting, 'To 'ell with the bloody Hirish.'[23]

The Royal Navy never responded to the claims about the 'duplex mine', nor explained why the *Leinster*'s sister ship *Ulster*, which was on its way from Holyhead to Kingstown and in sight when the attack occurred, did not come to assist.[24] One reason was undoubtedly the need to maintain operational security; but some of the explanations, such as the direction to merchant vessels not to go to the assistance of other ships under attack in case they too became targets, would have won no kudos. At the subsequent inquiry, members of the crew of both ships were instructed not to mention the large number of soldiers carried by mail boats. As the assistant purser on the *Ulster*, Bill Sweeney, said in an interview sixty-one years later, that 'was giving information to the enemy.'

What is without question is that if the German submarine commander, Robert Ramm, had not fired the third torpedo the number of deaths on the *Leinster* would have been much lower. However, despite the efforts of Admiralty censors, German intelligence would have known from even a cursory examination of Irish newspapers that the mail boats were regularly used as troop carriers. The *Irish Times* had published enthusiastic reports about 'daily drafts of newly enlisted men' being seen off by 'sweethearts, wives and mothers.' The paper even warned Belfast that it 'had better look to its laurels if Dublin intends, as seems likely, to keep the steady forwarding of daily drafts of newly joined men across the Channel.'[25]

Unfortunately, the sinking of the *Leinster* marked a critical stage in the decline and fall of the City of Dublin Steam Packet Company, reputedly the oldest steamship company in the world, having begun its cross-channel service in 1816. The London and North-Western Railway had been competing with it for the mail contract since the late 1840s, when the Admiralty had ceased providing the service. With berths in Dublin port, the LNWR could provide a direct capital-to-capital service, but the City of Dublin usually won the contract, through superior lobbying prowess. However, its hostility to unions, which led to the bitter dispute of 1915–16 with the ITGWU and the consequent serious disruption to services, had severely tried the patience of Dublin Castle.[26] It also meant that it enjoyed precious little sympathy from nationalist politicians.

This did not prevent howls of outrage when the government reorganised cross-channel traffic because of the exigencies of war and shipping shortages in 1917 and the City of Dublin line was placed under the control of its rival. The LNWR employed the City of Dublin vessels for the least remunerative and most dangerous work, including troop transport. As the LNWR now had the government contracts, the City of Dublin line had to seek remuneration from its rival.[27] Disputes over amounts due ended up in the courts and, combined with the loss of half its mail-boat fleet, saw the rapid demise of the City of Dublin line in the 1920s, when it was finally absorbed into the British and Irish Steam Packet Company. It was one of many situations in which advanced nationalists received no favours from their 'gallant allies' in Europe.

———

Perversely, despite the food shortages, the war had a relatively benign effect on some of Dublin's poorest and most vulnerable children. Annual reports by the National Society for the Prevention of Cruelty to Children reported that the number of complaints and the number of children neglected or ill treated dropped to lower levels than ever recorded before. It was a trend in Britain as well.

There had been a sharp drop in complaints and confirmed cases of cruelty during the 1913 Lock-out. In 1914 the NSPCC reported that, although money had been scarce in the previous months because of the strikes and disturbances, 'the children, owing to various agencies, received a sufficiency of food more regularly than usual.' In other words, the strikers' children were better fed on British trade union food shipments than when their fathers and mothers were working.

As can be seen from table 13, the number of complaints rose again after the lock-out and continued rising in the early months of the war. This may well have been due to the social disruption caused by the war itself. Among complaints up to 31 March 1916 were 'many cases of soldiers' wives and children with whom we have been asked to keep in touch during the war.'

Table 13
Complaints of cruelty to children, 1912–25

1 April to 31 March	Complaints	Children
1912–13	1,538	4,411
1913–14	1,441	3,993
1914–15	1,503	4,273
1915–16	1,352	3,981
1916–17	1,238	3,669
1917–18	1,083	3,023
1918–19	740	1,913
1919–20	867	2,162
1920–21	841	1,987
1921–2	860	2,043
1922–3	801	1,866
1923–4	829	1,966
1924–5	856	2,015

While the 1914 report used the word 'complaints', it also suggested that some contacts were primarily expressions of concern about how young mothers were coping on their own, especially in the first year of the war, when delays were reported in the payment of separation allowances. Quite a number of complaints appear to have come from fathers serving in the forces. The report stated:

> It is of common occurrence for soldiers on furlough [leave] or serving abroad, either to come direct to the office in Molesworth Street, or write asking us to see to their children's welfare during their absence, and it gives us much pleasure ... that from time to time we have been able to send these men reassuring and satisfactory reports as to the ways things are going on with their respective families.

No doubt in some instances suspicious husbands were also using the NSPCC to check on their wives as well as their children.

The importance of NSPCC work for the morale of the armed forces was publicly acknowledged by the military establishment. Recognising the enormous strains the war imposed on the society, the Army Council praised its 'depleted and overworked staff' for their commitment

> to continue in the interest of soldiers' families ... The timely intervention of your society has been instrumental in saving many families from dire distress and has at the same time relieved many fighting men of anxiety for the welfare of their children.

Although there is plenty of anecdotal evidence of the profligacy of 'separation women' in Dublin, the NSPCC reports provide little evidence of it. However, the figures in table 14 do show that significantly more women than men were offenders during the war years, a reversal of the usual pattern; but this could be expected in wartime.

Between August 1914 and March 1917 the NSPCC carried out 14,746 inquiries concerning soldiers' families, covering 33,234 children. Warnings and various interventions, mainly in the form of supervised visits, were usually successful, but in 116 cases the society had to take over the administration of separation allowances for the children, who were either found foster homes or put in institutions.

Table 14
Inquiries concerning soldiers' families, 1914–21[28]

	Men	Women	Total
1914–15	931	833	1,764
1915–16	695	847	1,542
1916–17	590	774	1,364
1917–18	509	679	1,188
1918–19	401	435	836
1919–20	582	437	1,019
1920–21	588	402	990

What is more striking is the rapid fall in the number of cruelty cases during the war years and the upward trend afterwards. The post-war reversal of the trend was entirely attributed to men, suggesting that offenders were returning soldiers, many of whom probably had physical or mental health problems. The number of women offenders continued to fall, suggesting that the educational and preventive work of the NSPCC was having significant long-term benefits.

The society itself was unequivocal about the reasons for the decline in the number of cases of ill treatment, neglect and abuse of children during the war years. In a report for the year April 1917 to March 1918 it attributed the decrease to

uniformly more employment and better wages. The bulk of the cases under investigation this year relate chiefly to the families of soldiers and sailors on active service. Most of these families are better off financially than they have ever been, and consequently the homes are better provided with food and clothing than during normal conditions in times of peace when there were no funds or separation allowances available.

The society also felt that

restrictions on the sale of alcohol and its prohibitive cost—apart from the question of adulteration of spirits—has materially assisted the cause of sobriety. Experience tends to show that the women generally are more abstemious than the men, and lapses appear to be most frequent in homecomings of husbands on leave.

The relations that developed between the NSPCC inspector (the 'cruelty man') and the families he visited could become quite close. The same annual report cites the case of a soldier killed at the front who appointed an NSPCC inspector executor of his will and guardian of his children. The inspector had been instrumental in having the dead man's wife committed to prison for six months for neglect. 'The woman has happily made good,' the report said.

The affinity of the society with the armed forces may well have been at least partly due to the dominance of women from upper and middle-class unionist families on its ruling bodies and local committees. The Marquis and Marchioness of Aberdeen continued to serve as principal patrons throughout the war years, despite their departure from the Viceregal Lodge in 1915; but the other long-serving patrons were from leading unionist aristocratic dynasties, such as the Dowager Duchess of Abercorn, the Marchioness of Londonderry, Viscountess Powerscourt, Viscountess Midleton and Viscountess Wolseley.

With the end of the war the NSPCC reported that the corruption of morals was on the rise, and it found itself having to act as intermediary in disbursing weekly and monthly payments to separation women whose husbands were now living apart from them and to take control of pensions in the case of some widows with child dependants.[29]

It is not widely known that only 100,000 veterans of the Great War returned to civilian life in Ireland between the armistice in 1918 and the early summer of 1920— fewer than half of those who enlisted.[30] Some 30,000 had died, but others decided, for whatever reasons, not to return to Ireland or, if they did come home, to leave again.

For their families, the reasons for the absence of those men was less important than the absence itself. It is no wonder that many women felt themselves abandoned, including the unmarried mothers to whom the government decided to award separation allowances from 1916 onwards, especially as those payments would cease with demobilisation. Even a war widow with a pension was far from secure, for the War Office took a dim view of what it regarded as illicit liaisons, and any woman who fell under suspicion of 'immoral behaviour' could find her pension confiscated. Such rigour not only reflected the official mores of the time but saved the British exchequer considerable sums of money.

––––––

During the war Dublin Corporation took some modest measures to protect child welfare under the Employment of Children Acts. These might more accurately have been named the Self-Employment of Children Acts, for they related primarily to illicit street trading and to begging. There was a crackdown on both in 1914, and the by-laws were thoroughly overhauled in 1915. From 1 August 1915 only children aged fourteen and over could legally trade on the streets; and to do so they had to have a licence in the form of a badge, worn where it could be easily seen. They could lose the licence if they were reported to be trading during school hours, and they were barred from trading in streets where prostitutes or thieves were known to reside. Nor could they obstruct the footpath or annoy members of the public. Girls were not allowed to sell newspapers, one of the staples of their male counterparts.

The hours of trading were set as strictly as those for public houses. The summer licensing season ran from 1 April to 30 September, and the winter season from 1 October until 31 March. In the summer, girls could trade outside school hours only until 8 p.m. or until 7 p.m. in winter; boys were allowed to trade until 9 p.m. in summer or 8 p.m. in winter. The aim was to protect youngsters as much from exploitative parents as from members of the public or from employers.

A report published by the *Irish Times* in the debate before the introduction of the by-laws described the problems and also the outlook of those trying to grapple with the crisis of child poverty in a city where many citizens saw nothing wrong with barefoot or half-naked children of all ages wandering the streets and where the physical and sexual abuse of poor waifs was hardly thought worthy of public debate. Any blame attaching to such problems was generally thought to rest with the parents, insofar as it was considered at all by the comfortable classes.

The anonymous correspondent, who obviously had close contacts with such bodies as the NSPCC and the Dublin Advisory Committee for Juvenile Employment, pointed out to readers that the employment of children was 'precarious' and that experience confirmed a tendency by employers 'to keep wages down to the lowest possible subsistence level.'

The deleterious influences of the slums, combined with wretched housing accommodation, prevent the proper and effective training of children, and seriously lessen the feeling of parental responsibility ... And the living conditions under which the boys and girls grow up leave an indelible influence on the life and character of the future men and women. To this upbringing may be ascribed those characteristics peculiar to the working classes of Dublin, which are evidenced in their free-and-easy habits.

There were

boys and girls of school going age who, with a persistence worthy of a better cause, solicit alms from all and sundry; there are girls from fourteen to twenty, who cling to the streets with the tenacity of the Arab to the desert; and strong healthy young men, with raucous voices, who flaunt their wares in the faces of passers by; but have not done and probably never will do a regular week's work in their lives. Then, in the back mean streets and slum areas are to be seen all the appanages of poverty, drunkenness and wretchedness envisaged in slatternly women, indescribably dirty rooms, ill nourished and anaemic children.

Given the attitude displayed by this well-informed and clearly influential commentator, it is hardly surprising that the onus of ensuring that children complied with the legislation was placed completely on parents. As there were no fixed rates of pay or conditions of employment for these youngsters, it would of course have been difficult to penalise employers.

Perhaps it was just as well, because, as table 15 shows, there was poor enforcement of most of the laws for protecting adult workers. A much more rigorous approach was adopted towards children and their parents. In 90 per cent of cases it was the mother who attended court and paid the fine for the errant child offender.

Table 15
Prosecutions under employment laws, 1914–19

	Intimidation by workers on strike picket	Offences against special trades acts	Offences against the Shops Acts[31]	Offences against the Factory Acts	Offences against the Employment of Children Acts
1914	16	8	45	18	250
1915	0	2	56	1	318
1916	1	0	0	0	417
1917	1	0	47	10	415
1918	2	0	23	45	282
1919	4	4	5	0	157

The end of the war brought cuts in the few social supports that had been introduced for the civilian population. This began before the end of 1918 as part of the exchequer's new policy of retrenchment to restore the health of the public finances. Among the first casualties were communal kitchens, including those for 'necessitous school children.' Ironically, the funding was being cut just as demand was increasing because of 'the increasing difficulty of procuring nourishing meals in the homes of the poor,' as Father George Turley of the Lourdes House communal kitchen in Upper Rutland Street reported.

Since April 1918 this kitchen had been feeding nine hundred children daily, at a cost of about 2d a day. Even when in funds the project found it hard to feed eight hundred comfortably. This project was one of many, mostly organised by religious, to supplement the work of the corporation's School Meals Committee, which fed almost ten thousand children during term time. 'To cease supplying these warm meals to the poor children during this cold and wet weather would cause much suffering,' Father Turley wrote to the *Irish Independent*. 'The Committee therefore appeals with confidence to the charitable public to assist them in carrying on the work while the Corporation grant is stopped.' He hoped that with Christmas less than a week away 'those in more comfortable circumstances' who were 'filled with thoughts of happiness and good cheer' would respond generously.[32]

Funding for communal kitchens catering for adults was hit even earlier. When the kitchen at Eden Quay closed because of the 'withdrawal of public grants,' the committee thanked the many generous subscribers, 'particularly the Irish Transport and General Workers Union, but for the use of whose premises the step would have to be taken sooner and the Plotholders' Union,' which had supplied provisions.[33]

———

Poverty was not confined to children, or to families. Dublin and the south of Ireland had an exceptionally high level of pauperism in the early twentieth century compared with Belfast or with British cities. After the initial disruption of the war caused a momentary surge in the number of paupers throughout the United Kingdom to 650,737 by August 1915, or 41,261 more than a year earlier, the number fell steadily after the establishment of the Committee on the Prevention and Relief of Distress and of the National Relief Fund to assist local authorities.

In Dublin hardly any progress was made. In January 1915 there were 5,583 people dependent on indoor relief and another 5,125 dependent on outdoor relief—11,062 altogether, or 272 per 10,000 of population, compared with 3,981 in Belfast, or 95 per 10,000. The total figure for the United Kingdom was 347,281, or 191 per 10,000. By December 1918 there were still 10,832 people in Dublin dependent on relief (261 per 10,000), compared with 2,988 in Belfast (69 per 10,000) and a total in the United Kingdom of 232,416 (125 per 10,000). Nor was the Easter Rising a major aggravating factor: the damage and social disruption caused by the fighting added less than 300 to the number seeking relief in Dublin.

In Britain the advent of peace was more calamitous than war. The rate of pauperism rose with unemployment, which was only 0.81 per cent in 1917 but grew to 2.54 per cent in December 1918 and reached 6.71 per cent by January 1919.[34] Just as Dublin benefited relatively little from war industries, so it was not as severely affected by the return to a peace economy. By November 1919 the number of destitute citizens had risen only to 11,006, or 263 per 10,000 of population. Belfast's higher level of integration in the British war machine was demonstrated by an increase in the rate of those dependent on relief to 89 per 10,000, almost as high as at the beginning of the war.

However, in Britain the social and employment initiatives adopted in wartime paid off to some extent. The United Kingdom average rate of pauperism rose only to 130 per 10,000 by November 1919, still much lower than the figure of 191 in early 1915.

Dublin was not unique in its failure to tackle pauperism: the other southern cities, Cork, Waterford and Limerick, performed equally poorly.[35] They too lacked the expertise, financial resources, municipal infrastructure and political leadership at the local level to tackle basic social problems. This was part of the socially bankrupt legacy of the home rule movement. Rural radicals, such as Redmond's chief lieutenant, John Dillon, never came to terms with urban problems.

The extension to Ireland of social reform schemes introduced in British towns and cities was resisted by the Irish Party, in deference to the ratepayer, and as a result Dublin was still dependent on the old Poor Law system. It was only when the British government was willing to provide central funding for relief, health care and old-age pensions that the majority of city authorities were willing to go along with such initiatives. Slum clearance was also predicated on London's largesse, and with the war having first call on limited resources this urgent problem continued to fester.

———

The one bright spot was the old-age pension. The lack of adequate records meant that many Irish people applying for a pension received the benefit of the doubt. In 1912, of the 942,000 pensioners in the United kingdom 205,000 were in Ireland.

However, outdoor relief continued to be a feature of life in the city. The fact that it was open to abuse and was highly politicised only made corporation members all the more determined to defend the system. The councillor who could be an ardent defender of the ratepayer at corporation meetings could be an equally passionate defender of the poor when lobbying for a claimant as a member of the Board of Guardians of the North or South Dublin Union. He saw no more contradiction between these two roles than a barrister did when switching from a defending to a prosecuting brief.

Relieving officers were appointed by the Boards of Guardians, just as the rate collectors were appointed by the councillors, politicising what should have been important offices whose holders had wide-ranging discretionary powers and who should have been independent of interference. The intense level of clientelism that the local government and Poor Law systems bred had totally corrupted the dominant nationalist clique on the corporation over the years, so that it was held in increasing contempt not only by social reformers and the British administration but by the citizens it was supposed to serve.

———

Perhaps the most unfortunate victims of the system were young children and workhouse inmates with intellectual or physical disabilities. The Irish Party had opposed the extension of the relevant British legislation for reforming the health and social services, on the usual grounds that it was unfair to the Irish ratepayer.

In January 1914 the Minister of Local Government, John Burns, finally lost patience and ordered the transfer of all children over three years of age from the Irish workhouse system to foster homes where available, or to more suitable institutional care. The timing was regrettable, as the Home Office, which oversaw an extensive system of child-centred reform in the United Kingdom, lost its remit for the 26 Counties in 1922. Thousands of Irish children would be consigned to the tender mercies of the religious orders and the industrial school system, at minimal cost to the newly established Free State. The victims included children in trouble with the law, who would be dealt with through the Probation of Offenders Act in Britain. The continuation of the discredited capitation system in the Free State provided a powerful financial incentive for a parsimonious state and for religious orders hungry for funds. By 1924 industrial schools would be accommodating more children than their counterparts in England, Scotland, Wales and Northern Ireland combined. Other vulnerable groups would also experience tortuous escape routes from the workhouse system, such as those covered by the Blind Persons Act (1920), one of the last pieces of progressive British legislation to be passed before the Treaty settlement.[36]

———

Dublin did at least have a mental asylum in the Richmond Asylum at Grangegorman, which had increased its capacity in 1912, although it still proved inadequate to meet demand in the war years. While the Richmond admitted 58 patients from the South Dublin Union in 1913, the number of mental patients in the South Dublin Union itself rose from 198 to 202, and there was similar pressure on space in the North Dublin Union. The Richmond was only supposed to take patients who were certified as dangerous, but the North Dublin Union used it as a dumping ground for old, senile and bedridden inmates. The inadequate training of the staff meant that they were often little more than guards and work supervisors. Occasional incidents of brutality were reported, but neither patients nor staff were inclined to inform on the perpetrators. In one of the few incidents that were investigated a patient complained that he had been punched on the jaw by an attendant after he refused to clean spittoons. The attendant denied the allegation and said that the patient had attacked him and was 'a very low class of man, he was a corner boy and often in jail.' In another incident a patient was allegedly beaten for refusing to get out of bed and help move a coffin. No member of the staff was dismissed as a result of these incidents, which, ironically, fuelled the popular image of the asylum as a dangerous place to work because of the violent nature of the patients.

The informal agreement between rebels and military to treat the Grangegorman complex as neutral ground had spared it the destruction visited on the rest of the north inner city. As a result, a few weeks after the rising a section of the institution was converted into a war hospital for soldiers suffering from shell shock and other psychiatric disorders. The military agreed to pay 21s 6d per bed per week, providing a profit of 8s 2d a week on each of the thirty-two beds involved. The money was useful in bridging the growing gap between the capitation grant of 4s per patient per week, which had remained unchanged since before the war, and the rapidly rising cost of food, coal, drugs and clothing for patients.

The Dublin Citizens' Association was constantly questioning the expenditure of ratepayers' money on the Richmond. The failure of wages to keep up with the cost of living greatly exercised the staff, who attended a meeting in the Trades Hall with staff members from other hospitals to form the Irish Asylum Workers' Union. This would lay the basis for a wave of industrial action in psychiatric hospitals once the Great War ended.[37]

Meanwhile the military hospital had played an important role in breaking down popular prejudices against psychiatric illness, with the military patients accepted as 'brave soldiers who have risked their lives and sacrificed their health in their country's service.' The introduction of a more therapeutic regime and the involvement of voluntary bodies, such as the Royal Irish Automobile Club and the Red Cross Society, in the soldiers' recovery were harbingers of a more benign future. Of the 362 soldiers admitted to the facility before it closed in December 1919 more than half were treated successfully for their condition. However, a quarter of the patients were described as 'of low mentality for whom treatment could do little.' It is not clear what their fate was after the hospital closed.

Many members of the hospital's staff were glad to see the back of the soldiers; some had refused to have anything to do with them or with the Red Cross Society. Donations to the latter organisation were now seen very much as a political act. In vain did the *Irish Times* try to upbraid readers by pointing out that in late 1917 Ulster had collected £27,750 for the Red Cross Society, while Munster, Leinster and Connacht between them had managed only £21,340 4s 8d. The paper cited a message from the commander of British forces in France, Sir Douglas Haig, that asked: 'Are you amongst those who are remembering the men who are now GIVING MOST, DARING MOST, ENDURING MOST?' The provocative style of the notice, like that of much of the recruitment literature in Ireland, may well have been counterproductive, in that it crystallised the question of where the reader's commitment lay. Indeed the phrase 'enduring most' would be adopted by one of the nascent Irish Republic's future heroes, Terence MacSwiney, in his *Principles of Freedom* as part of a strategy for resistance to the very forces whose welfare the Red Cross Society held so dear.[38]

On a lighter note, one unsung saga of the war that would be resolved only after its close was the battle of the bands. Public concerts in the city's parks and open spaces had been subsidised by the corporation's Public Health Committee for several years before 1914. Some concert venues, such as Fairview Park, fell victim to allotment fever, but the concerts remained popular. Brass bands were paid 4 guineas (£4 4s) and flute and drum bands 3 guineas (£3 3s) for each performance. However, in 1915 there were complaints 'that some of the bands were not *bona fide* bands, or not proficient, or consisted of an insufficient number of performers.' It was also alleged that one band 'was receiving engagements under two names.' The committee therefore decided to invite the Feis Ceoil Association to hold a qualifying competition, and only those bands that secured a mark of 70 per cent or more would be allowed to perform.

The choice of the Feis Ceoil Association did not please everyone. It was less than twenty years old—much younger than some of the bands it was judging—and critics felt its emphasis on traditional music meant that it lacked empathy with the performers. In May 1919 the Irish National Fife and Drum Band Association lodged a complaint with the corporation that only one of its members—the O'Connell Flute and Drum Band—had qualified. It said the judges had failed to take account of the absence of many of its most experienced musicians, who were serving in the British army. These men would be returning shortly, only to find they would be denied the right to perform before their fellow-citizens.

The Public Health Committee decided to add St Kevin's Band, the City of Dublin Band and the United Builders' Labourers' Band, all of which had close associations with the corporation, to the list. However, this failed to appease everyone, and in June 1919 the secretary of the Irish Municipal Employees' Trade Union Band put the corporation on formal notice that the city would be sued for breach of contract, as well as the costs incurred by participating in the Feis Ceoil competition and the loss of earnings for band members, if it was not allowed to perform. Within a fortnight of receiving the union's letter the corporation set down new criteria, and the approved list of bands was expanded to include the complainants. It was also agreed to increase the payment for concerts to five guineas (£5 5s) for a brass band and four guineas (£4 4s) for flute and drum bands.[39] At least one conflict in the city had ended harmoniously.

———

Less fortunate were many of the inmates of the Royal Dublin Zoological Society's gardens in the Phoenix Park. Established in 1831, Dublin Zoo had been one of the cultural gems of the capital as well as providing a venue for an educational day out for citizens. It was hard hit by the war. As early as September 1914 gate receipts fell by 60 per cent, and Lieutenant-General Shaw appealed to the public for windfall apples, pears and plums that had no market value, as well as cauliflowers that had bolted, old turnips and peas. The zoo even offered to send out carts to collect produce.

Despite the shortages, the inmates faired reasonably well in the early years of the war, and an *Irish Times* editorial praised the zoo for maintaining a collection 'that boasts a gorilla, a chimpanzee, an orang-utan and a gibbon, and these four types of anthropoid have never been all exhibited together previously in any zoological gardens.' There was even a little gloating at the next annual general meeting of the society that Dublin Zoo had not had to resort to shooting some of its larger exhibits, such as elephants and bears, because of food shortages, as had happened in the zoos of the Central Powers. Instead the war brought extra business as contingents of wounded soldiers came to enjoy the amenities.

However, the mood of self-congratulation was somewhat dented by the disruption caused by the Easter Rising. Food shortages required some of the smaller inmates to be fed to the larger ones, which was arguably more barbaric than the measures resorted to in the zoos run by the 'Hun'. Appropriately enough, the lions were among the animals that prospered most in the war years. Not only had the zoo learnt how to breed them successfully in captivity but they required less food than many of the other animals, such as the antelope, bison, chimpanzee or eagle. The sale of lion cubs to other zoos also provided a substantial income—£500 in 1916 alone.

The introduction of a young leopard in January 1917 was less successful. It managed to escape from its cage and killed a duck that was trying to hatch nine eggs. 'He kicked up quite a fuss before he would let the duck be taken from him,' the meeting was told, 'and, being about nine months old, he can make his point of view listened to.' One prize exhibit that did not survive the war was the gorilla called 'Empress'. She died of a gastric disorder in May 1917, and was much mourned by the chimpanzee.

Nevertheless, the zoo quickly recovered its fortunes after the war and was able to resume the traditional summer fete in 1919.[40]

Chapter 14 ∾

'YOU HAVEN'T GOT A REPUBLIC YET, SO GET OUT OF THE WAY!'

On 31 May 1918 reports of 'mysterious maladies' in Spain and Sweden vied for attention with news of the great German offensive in France on the leader page of the *Irish Times*. It was some time before the source of the pandemic was identified as an unusually powerful variant of the H1N1 flu virus that attacked children and healthy young adults. It was first identified in these neutral states because there was no war censorship to suppress the details. After King Alfonso XIII of Spain fell ill with the mystery malady it was dubbed the 'Spanish flu'.

Dublin was singularly ill prepared to meet the challenge. In the first decade of the twentieth century it had the highest rate of urban mortality in Europe, exceeding those of many Asian cities. James Connolly seared the figures into the collective consciousness of the trade union movement when he quoted them at length in *The Re-conquest of Ireland*, his most important work after *Labour in Irish History*. A temporary improvement in 1912 and early 1913 was negated by the suffering inflicted during the lock-out.

Mortality rates provide the simplest criterion of Dubliners' health. During the First World War they showed an initial deterioration followed by a continuous improvement until the influenza pandemic drove the figure up again in late 1918. However, once the pandemic was over the rate resumed its downward trend, suggesting that, in general, the war had been good for the health of Dubliners.

The figures for the first quarter of every year tend to be the worst, as winter takes its toll, especially on the young, the old and the poor. As can be seen from table 16 (p. 277), the mortality rate in the city in the first quarter of 1913 was 23.3 per thousand; this rose to 25.9 in the first quarter of 1914, when the lock-out had been in force for four months.

After recovering somewhat later in 1914 the rate rose again in the first winter of the war. It reached 29.5 per thousand in the first quarter of 1915 for the greater metropolitan area and 31.4 per thousand within the city itself. The main cause appears to have been a rise in the incidence of infectious diseases, particularly for children, with diarrhoea, enteritis and dysentery (DED) and whooping cough featuring prominently. The birth rate also rose temporarily with the onset of the war; but the figure for the first winter of the war is not exceptional in the context of pre-war mortality rates. What is more striking is the general improvement in the mortality rate as the war progressed.

This is not to say that seasonal trends no longer mattered. On the contrary, they continued to assert themselves, but to a less pronounced degree. The Easter Rising also had a small but significant impact on mortality for the second quarter of 1916, which broke with the seasonal trend. However, even within the city boundary the fighting was less lethal than General Winter's yearly visitation. Once the spring of 1917 arrived, the mortality rate showed a steady improvement on previous years until the third quarter of 1918. This suggests that the reforms adopted by the Public Health Committee of the corporation, under the chairmanship of P. T. Daly, and the work of such bodies as the NSPCC, the Women's National Health Association and the voluntary bodies running communal kitchens had a beneficial effect, as well as the financial impact of separation allowances to mothers with young families in the tenements.

It was from mid-1918 until the end of March 1919 that Dublin felt the full brunt of the influenza pandemic. There appears to have been an initial surge in deaths in July 1918, followed by a short remission, before the rate soared to 34.1 per thousand in the metropolitan area and 36.1 in the city for the last quarter of 1918. It rose again in the first quarter of 1919, to 35 per thousand in the metropolitan area and 37.7 in the city. These rates were between 75 and 100 per cent more than for comparable quarters in the previous years.[1]

Figures published in the newspapers suggest that mortality was even higher in some weeks, especially for children, a high proportion of whom had fallen ill in June 1918, leading to the closure of about 120 schools. Sunday schools were cancelled, and 'a notable falling away at ... Church services' was reported. The effectiveness of these measures was probably limited, as factories, shops, cinemas, pubs and theatres remained open.[2] What stayed open and what closed was determined by commercial considerations, not concern for public health.

On 1 July 1918 the Local Government Board placed public notices on the 'Spanish influenza epidemic' in the newspapers. These warned readers that the disease was 'most infectious' and the symptoms 'readily recognisable, consisting of extreme lassitude, aching of the limbs and headaches. There is generally but not always nasal catarrh.' It recommended Formamint tablets (highly dubious throat lozenges made from formaldehyde and lactose), which were used by the Royal Army

Medical Corps, the Red Cross Society and hospitals. They cost 2s 2d a bottle—a not inconsiderable sum for tenement-dwellers with large families.

Military censorship prevented full reportage of the pandemic, and considerable discrepancies in the figures provided by different newspapers added to the confusion. For instance, the *Irish Independent* reported a significantly higher number of deaths in Dublin in the week ending 3 July than the *Irish Times*. It also stated that almost a third of those who died were children, while the *Times* quoted the Registrar-General's returns as containing no child fatalities.[3]

The reports were too vague to be useful for the purposes of public health or education. A typical example from the *Irish Times* in July reads: 'Several fresh cases were reported yesterday, especially among members of the police force and employees of the Dublin United Tramways Company, while the staffs of many commercial firms are being seriously depleted.' Occasionally the indisposition of a prominent individual, such as the Lord Mayor, Laurence O'Neill, was mentioned because it meant that public engagements had to be cancelled.[4] However, all the reports agreed that the infection rate was increasing. Of deaths in the second week of July, 92 were from influenza, compared with 35 the previous week.[5] By late November the death rate from influenza had reached 250 a week, seriously disrupting many businesses and services in the city. The Dublin and South-Eastern Railway, which provided most of the commuter services, complained of significant loss in income because 'fraudulent passengers' were taking advantage of sickness among checkers to avoid paying fares.

Dr Kathleen Lynn, who was working as a GP in Rathmines, advised people to avoid overcrowding and to eat nourishing food. Oatmeal porridge would suffice, with milk and eggs 'for those who could afford it.' More controversially, she called on soldiers returning from Europe to be quarantined 'until they were certified all right before being allowed to mix with the population.' At the very least she believed that uniforms and demob clothes should be thoroughly disinfected.[6] There was a lot of sense in what she advocated, and it was probably inevitable, given her politics, that she would hold the British military authorities primarily responsible for the serious threat now posed to the health of Dublin's civilian population. She would describe the battlefields of Flanders as the 'factory of fever'; and she had already jointly written a circular in February 1918 with her fellow-director of Sinn Féin's Public Health Committee, Dr Richard Hayes, warning of the threat that sexually transmitted disease would pose for the civilian population, especially women, when mass demobilisation began.

The same arguments applied, with even greater force, to highly infectious diseases such as influenza and TB. But both positions were charged politically. While the city's Chief Medical Officer, Sir Charles Cameron, was capable of taking a broad view of the situation, his natural conservatism and desire to avoid unnecessary conflict, which had made him more accommodating than he should have been of vested interests such as slum landlords, now led to procrastination. About the flu virus Lynn wrote in exasperation to Arthur Griffith:

People say it is the work of the Corporation or L.G.B. [Local Government Board]. Well, my experience is that the epidemic will be over before they had done considering the matter.[7]

She was almost right: it was not until 25 February 1919 that the corporation made influenza and pneumonia notifiable diseases. Even then its powers were limited. It could not force social events to be cancelled, or places of public entertainment to close. The British government, which was quick enough to ban public protests or seditious speeches, could have undertaken such measures, but it failed to do so.

When the Registrar-General's annual figures for 1918 were finally published in March 1919 they showed that in the Dublin Registration Area, which included the suburban townships and Co. Dublin, there had been 9,008 births and 9,397 deaths, a net excess of 389 deaths over births. The total mortality rate for 1918 had been 23.6 per thousand, compared with an average of 20.6 for the previous ten years.

In the first quarter of 1919 the influenza pandemic reached a peak at 35 deaths per thousand in the metropolitan area and 37.7 in the city. However, in the second week of February the death rate went as high as 44.8 per thousand in the metropolitan area and 50.2 in the city.[8] This translates into 2,476 births in the Dublin metropolitan area, offset by 3,544 deaths. In the city there were 2,030 births but 2,923 deaths; in other words, in the first three months of the year 1,961 more people died than were born. As in 1916, severe restrictions were placed on the number of mourners permitted to accompany the dead to the cemetery.

The higher mortality rates are entirely accounted for by the flu pandemic. The number of people dying from influenza in 1918 was 1,506, against a yearly average over the previous decade of 95. Deaths from pneumonia, which also affected many flu victims, tell a similar story: there were 1,140 deaths from pneumonia in 1918, compared with an average of 667 a year in the previous decade.

———

Hampered by lack of resources, and of adequate statutory powers, Sir Charles Cameron did what he could to meet the crisis through public education, the closing of schools, the disinfection of buildings, including cinemas and theatres, the nightly cleaning and disinfecting of trams, and the spraying of streets and laneways with disinfectant. At one point so much disinfectant was being used that the Street Cleansing Committee wrote to Cameron complaining at the cost. Extra stocks to the value of £64 14s 9d had been purchased in the last quarter of 1918.[9]

The money was well spent. By contrast to the soaring death rate from influenza and pneumonia, there was a general falling off in cases of other infectious diseases. For instance, there were only 906 deaths from bronchitis in 1918, compared with a yearly average of 1,001 over the previous five years.[10]

Altogether, deaths from the principal infectious diseases in the metropolitan area fell from 1.4 per thousand in the fourth quarter of 1917 to 1.0 per thousand in the fourth quarter of 1918. The comparable returns for the city show that the rate fell from 1.6 per thousand to 1.1 per thousand. In the first quarter of 1918 the rate of deaths from infectious diseases was 1.7 per thousand; this fell to 0.8 in the first quarter of 1919. The comparable figures for the city were 2.0 in 1918 and 1.0 in 1919.

Another anomaly was that the infant mortality rate, horrifying as it was, at 149 per thousand, was actually lower in 1918 than the rate of 152 in 1917 and 153 in 1916. The big killers of babies were diarrhoea, enteritis and dysentery (DED). These diseases accounted for 148 out of 192 deaths from infectious diseases in the third quarter of 1918, but the figure fell to 51 out of 81 deaths from infectious diseases in the last quarter of 1918. In the first quarter of 1919 the number of deaths from DED fell to 40, and the total number of deaths from infectious diseases was only 74. However, once the public disinfecting campaign ended, mortality from these diseases rose again: by the third quarter of 1919 it was back at 194, and DED accounted for 177 of them.

No doubt some of the other measures taken by Cameron to reduce the transmission of influenza, such as closing schools, also helped reduce the level of other infectious diseases.[11] Even more lives could have been saved if places of public entertainment had closed, not to mention the appallingly insanitary tenements themselves.

Meanwhile Cameron had to apply moral suasion in his liaison with the hospitals and medical profession throughout the city to co-ordinate interests with colleagues such as Kathleen Lynn, his complete antithesis. She was a modern, ground-breaking professional and political radical; he was the last standard-bearer of the old corporate unionist identity of Dublin. He personified the old regime, in part because of the sheer number of responsibilities, both public and private, that resided in his person. He was medical superintendent officer of health, executive sanitary officer, secretary to the Public Health Committee and city analyst. In a private capacity he was deputy grand master of the Freemasons, and *de facto* grand master while the head of the organisation, the Earl of Donoughmore, was a serving officer who spent most of the war abroad.

The link with the Freemasons was a familial one. Cameron came from an old Scottish military family. An ancestor was beheaded in London for his part in the '45, and his father had fought under the Duke of Wellington at Talavera in the Peninsular War. However, after studying philosophy and qualifying as a doctor in Germany, the centre of academic excellence in his youth, Cameron returned to Dublin to practise medicine and to write extensively on the arts as well as medical and scientific matters. He undertook much voluntary work and campaigned vigorously for public health reforms before being appointed city analyst in 1862. By 1879 he had assumed responsibility for most aspects of public health policy in Dublin. A grateful city awarded him a salary of £1,000 per annum in 1911, but by the outbreak of war he was in his eighties, and some of his policies had begun to attract criticism and even ridicule, such as his campaign to eradicate houseflies by offering 3d to every child who handed in a bag of dead flies. (It was estimated that it would take six thousand flies to fill one of his bags, and the bounty was never claimed, even when the size of the bags was halved.)

His sons reverted to the family's military tradition,[12] and the death of the youngest, Ewen, a lieutenant in the 'Pals Battalion' of the Royal Dublin Fusiliers, cast a shadow over his declining years. Cameron's diary entries for August 1915 tell their own story.

[Thursday 26 August] Meeting at the Mansion House on food question. Presided at Council of the RDS.

Ewen came today. He appears very upset, apparently by the bad news from Dardanelles—death of Major Tippet and some of his late companions in the Seventh Battalion of the Royal Dublin Fusiliers.

[Friday 27 August] The dreadful news that poor Ewen had shot himself in the train between Greystones and Newcastle came today. He and Maitland went by the 10.30 train. After leaving Greystones Ewen went to the lavatory and shot dear head with revolver. I was telephoned to come home at once. Gladys Collins told me that something very serious had occurred to Ewen. I knew at once what had happened and I said has (Ewen died?) and [she] said Yes. I nearly fainted. Later on Sir Lambert Connolly told me the whole tragedy. This terrible blow will [make] the little of life left to me joyless. I was prostrate for the rest of the day.

Cameron would resign as deputy grand master of the Freemasons in 1919, citing ill health, and in March 1919 surrendered most of his day-to-day duties as chief medical officer of the city to his deputy, Dr M. J. Russell.[13]

If the Freemasons were regarded with suspicion, fear and envy by Catholic nationalists because of their hidden influence in the professions, the government, the police and the armed forces, they certainly paid the price in the Great War, especially in the case of the British army. The losses suffered by Sir Charles Cameron were not uncommon among masons. More than 350 members of the Dublin lodges served in the war, including members of such well-known families as Arnott, Atkinson, Ball, Bewley, D'Alton, Dawson, Dickinson, Dockrell, Fry, Goulding, Hewat, Jellett, Lawrence, Lee, Overend, Shaw, Swifte, Taylor, Watson, Weir and Wynne. There were also Dublin masons in the Curragh and Dublin Garrison lodges. Other members formed lodges in units to which they were assigned, including D Company of the 7th Battalion of the Royal Dublin Fusiliers. Some of these lodges were able not only to hold meetings at the front but to engage in 'Masonic labour' behind the lines. The last wartime commander in chief of the forces in Ireland, Sir Frederick Shaw, was in a Dublin lodge, as was Sir Auckland Geddes, a member of the Cabinet.

Cameron does not appear to have allowed his politics to interfere with his duties. He enjoyed a good working relationship with councillors of all political complexions as well as with professional colleagues. When Kathleen Lynn was arrested in October 1918 because of her membership of the executive committee of Sinn Féin he joined with the Lord Mayor, Laurence O'Neill, in securing her release in recognition of the important work she was doing in combating the influenza pandemic and raising public awareness of health issues.

In many respects Cameron was not far from being indispensable. After his death the corporation ceased publishing quarterly health breviates—a retrograde step with regard to collating information and identifying important social as well as health trends. This had serious implications for policy planning. If he often expressed nostalgia for the long-departed nobility who had populated the city of his youth, he also welcomed the emergence of trade unions to champion workers' rights.[14] In short, he represented much of what was best in Dublin's liberal unionist tradition.

————

The greatest impact of the flu pandemic was among the poor. The fate of the Phelan family in Corporation Buildings was unusual only in that it took them all. On Saturday 22 February 1919, not having seen them for some days, neighbours forced the door of their flat. The mother was dead in the bed. Her husband and their daughter were lying beside her, too weak to move. Mrs Phelan's sister lay on the floor at the foot of the bed, also unable to move. They were brought to the Dublin Union hospital, where all died within a few hours.

————

The influenza pandemic obscured a greater long-term health threat for Dubliners from the prostitution and sexually transmitted diseases that had been bred for generations by the poverty of the slums. In 1914 deaths from the main sexually transmitted diseases, such as syphilis, gonorrhoea and phagedaena, were 1.4 per 10,000, compared with 0.51 in Belfast and 0.76 in London. STD-related deaths, especially those of infants, were often attributed to other causes.[15]

Even before the war began these closely linked problems had assumed social and political dimensions. The British army had been regarded as the main source of the problem for decades, and public figures who agreed on very little else, such as Arthur Griffith and Jim Larkin, routinely denounced soldiers as the despoilers of Irish maidenhood.

Table 16
Mortality rate (per thousand), 1913–20

		First quarter	Second quarter	Third quarter	Fourth quarter
1913	Metropolitan area	22.3	20.4	19.1	19.0
	Municipal area	23.3	21.5	19.8	20.4
1914	Metropolitan area	24.2	21.7	17.4	20.1
	Municipal area	25.9	23.6	18.6	21.2
1915	Metropolitan area	29.5	20.4	16.3	20.9
	Municipal area	31.4	20.8	17.4	25.4
1916	Metropolitan area	21.9	22.5	16.3	20.3
	Municipal area	23.5	23.8	17.6	21.8
1917	Metropolitan area	25.0	20.3	15.2	16.2
	Municipal area	25.9	21.4	16.0	16.9
1918	Metropolitan area	20.6	19.5	20.0 (32.7 in July)	34.1
	Municipal area	21.7	20.4	21.8 (32.7 in July)	36.1
1919	Metropolitan area	35.0 (44.8 in February)	18.6	14.1	16.0
	Municipal area	37.7 (50.2 in February)	19.3	14.6	16.8
1920	Metropolitan area	19.6	n.a.	n.a.	17.6 (39 weeks to 1 January 1921)
	Municipal area	20.6	n.a.	n.a.	18.6 (39 weeks to 1 January 1921)
1921	Metropolitan area	25.5 (January)	n.a.	n.a.	(16.1)
	City area	26.5 (January)	n.a.	n.a.	(16.8)

Note: These figures exclude those who died after being admitted to public institutions in the city and county from other places. Quarterly breviates do not appear in the Corporation Reports after the first quarter of 1920; an annual summary is provided for that year and the first four weeks of 1921.

There had been improvements over the years. There was a marked decline in the number of arrests for prostitution from the 1890s onwards, when the advent of large-scale factory employment for women in enterprises such as Jacob's began providing alternative sources of income. By the early 1900s the number of prostitutes in the city was reckoned to have fallen by three-quarters, though the DMP estimated that there were still 1,677—about 2 per cent of the city's female population.[16]

A 'white slavery' scare in the years immediately before the war brought renewed interest in the problems of prostitution, sexual mores and disease. Groups expressing concern included conservative Catholic nationalists, for whom it was the most sordid manifestation of English materialism and its power to corrupt traditional Irish values, as well as feminists fighting for the dignity of women and for equality. The two strands were brought together in the person of Alice Abadan of the Catholic Women's Suffrage Society, who made well-publicised tours of Ireland in 1912 and 1913. More than a thousand women attended her meeting in Dublin in 1912 to hear her denounce the evils of 'white slavery', and many people supported the demand that the Criminal Law (Amendment) Bill (1912) should include Ireland in its remit. Fears that the country would be excluded from the legislation appear to have been unfounded, but they gave added momentum to the campaign for women's rights in general. As Abadan reminded her audience on her return trip to Dublin in early 1913, 'where there was one slavery, there were many.'

The outbreak of war brought with it more soldiers, Irish and British, and with the deluge of uniforms on the streets came renewed concern for the morals and health of Irish women.

Table 17
Prosecutions of brothel-keepers and prostitutes, 1912–19

	Prosecutions of brothel-keepers	Prosecutions of prostitutes for soliciting or unruly conduct
1912	1	1,067
1913	0	689
1914	3	645
1915	13	740
1916	14	552
1917	11	447
1918	8	260
1919	4	198

The anxiety of feminists and nationalists would be shared by the military authorities, which helps explain the vigour of the DMP's crackdown on brothels.

The absence of any prosecutions in the year preceding the outbreak of the war is easily explained by the lock-out, as is the dramatic falling off in arrests of women for soliciting, because police resources were fully stretched in the second half of the year in dealing with labour unrest. Once the war began, and especially from 1915 onwards, there was a considerable increase in the number of prosecutions of brothel-keepers.

The temporary increase in the number of arrests for soliciting on the streets in 1915 probably reflects the suppression of the brothels. The DMP could also use new powers under the Defence of the Realm Act to arrest women they suspected of having sexually transmitted disease in order to prevent them infecting soldiers.

At the same time voices as varied as the advanced nationalist journal *Hibernian* and the Church of Ireland Archbishop of Dublin, Dr Bernard, expressed concern over the corrupting influence of the military on Irish recruits. The *Hibernian* warned that

> conscription leads to immorality ... It has happened too often that decent young Irishmen removed from the restraint of home life, and placed in the corrupting surroundings of a barracks, have taken to drink and got into the habit of keeping company with the unfortunate women who are found wherever soldiers are stationed.

Dr Bernard bewailed the fact that it was impossible to police the situation, as there were hundreds of single women living in single rooms in Dublin. The view that single women living alone could become prostitutes and 'contaminate the other respectable women living in the house' worried churchmen of all denominations. The Catholic Primate, Cardinal Logue, asked rhetorically, 'Shall we allow the brightest jewel in the crown of Ireland to be wrested from her?' And the revolutionary socialist James Connolly told the authorities: 'If you want to make Dublin clean in its moral standards remove your garrison.'[17] At the other end of the social spectrum Lady Fingall organised a committee to establish a hostel for young domestic servants who were between jobs, where they could live free from the risk of contamination by vice.[18]

Two days after Lady Fingall told a meeting of the Catholic Truth Society in the Mansion House that 'the state of the City of Dublin and its suburbs at night are a disgrace to Christianity and above all a disgrace to Catholic Ireland,' P. T. Daly was relating to fellow-members of the corporation that fathers in his constituency could not let 'the females of their families' go out after nightfall in the area between the Custom House and the end of the North Wall. 'The immorality that is going on is scandalous.' He was 'informed that the men responsible were not Dublin men,' and stated that if the police did not do their duty others would. 'I do not want to see bloodshed, but I may tell you that a vigilance committee is being formed, and it will be stopped once for all.'[19]

The Irish Women's Suffrage and Local Government Association had already launched its own patrols under the leadership of its redoubtable founder and driving force, then eighty-six years old, Anna Haslam. A Quaker by religion and unionist in politics, she had no difficulty taking the initiative in conjunction with the National Union of Women Workers in Britain and the Chief Secretary's Office. The patrols were made up of women, usually working in pairs, who policed what were considered the worst areas, from Sackville Street eastwards along the quays and into P. T. Daly's North Wall area. They were usually accompanied by plain-clothes DMP constables. The association was affiliated to the National Union of Women Workers, whose support for the war effort did not lessen its commitment to advancing women's rights through trade union organising and educational, political and philanthropic activities.

In the same week that the *Weekly Irish Times* published the speeches by Lady Fingall and P. T. Daly a member of the women's patrol said she was 'aghast at the scenes my night walks have shown me.' She normally patrolled from 9:30 until 11:30 p.m., when Sackville Street

> appears to be one great, low saloon, where young girls, soldiers, sailors and civilians loiter about. It goes to one's heart to see how very young most of the girls are; also how drunk many of them are. They accost one another without apparently any shame, and more times than I can count have I turned my flashlight on to dark doorways and corners in laneways and disclosed scenes that are indescribable.

The culprits were 'too cute' for the police to catch them. 'We try to impress these poor girls with the fact that we are their friends and out in their interests, but it is very hard.' Some of them 'are quite gentle,' but

> more often they give us great abuse and they have even raised their hands to us. The drunken ones are particularly hard to deal with.

The men included many foreign sailors but also well-dressed locals. Nor was economic need the only imperative.

> Factory girls that I know do not care to go to their miserable homes till bedtime; so they frequent the streets, where mischief is just waiting for them. The filthy, ill-lighted, uncared for, and unprotected laneways in the city are veritable nurseries of evil.

This type of activity allowed suffrage campaigners and feminists generally to raise the issue of women's rights and the vulnerability of children in such circumstances. The *Irish Worker*, on the other hand, had no time for the 'new form of inquisition' by 'a number of ladies to interfere with the lives of the poor, to boss, to direct, to control and ... keep in subjection ... their poorer sisters.' Over time, however, the women won grudging admiration, even from their critics, for their courage and their determination to prosecute men who used prostitutes, including 'suburban swanks,' thus seeking to redress the traditional attitude that dissolute women were the cause of the problem. If they were not particularly successful this was mainly due to the prevailing attitudes among the DMP and police magistrates.

Although their numbers were tiny, the publicity these patrols generated raised public awareness of the problem, and by January 1916 a Dublin Watch Committee had been set up, with sub-committees to tackle drunkenness, vice, immorality, moneylending, gambling, child abuse and, in early 1917, sexually transmitted disease. Later in 1917 the women's patrols were incorporated in the DMP, with eight paid full-time workers.

As the war dragged on, a consensus would emerge that drew together different strands of opinion that shared concerns about its effects on Irish society and where it was taking the country morally. As a result, none of these groups appears to have allowed the DMP returns for the years after 1915 to revise their opinions, even though the number of arrests for soliciting continued to fall.

The main reason for the declining rate of prostitution in the city was increased prosperity, including the flow of separation allowances into the tenements and the growth of gainful employment for women in munitions, clothing and other war-related industries. This meant that far fewer engaged in more desperate ways of earning a living. Ironically, as the war progressed the concerns and fears of many nationalists would crystallise instead around the issue of separation women.[20]

––––

'From 1914 a new figure to the Irish scene became an odious symbol of British rule in Ireland, and a symbol that overtook the prostitute in the public understanding of immorality.' This is how Maria Luddy characterises the way that separation women were regarded during the war years, and after.[21] No figures exist for the number of women receiving allowances as dependants of men serving in the British forces, but it must have been significant.

Separation women formed the second-largest group in the corporation's survey of the north inner-city tenements, after labourers, when classified by source of income. There were 3,476 heads of households who were labourers and 1,705 who were separation women. Coincidentally, the range of incomes was almost identical, with labourers earning between 7s and 60s a week and separation women between 6s and 60s. The returns do not provide details of the spread of incomes, but for labourers the great majority are likely to have been earning under 30s a week;

and, unlike separation women, the amount a labourer earned bore no relation to the number of mouths he had to feed.

Most craft workers and even shopkeepers in the north city earned no more than 40s or 50s a week, so that resentment against separation women is easy to understand as regards comparative deprivation, especially given the widespread perception that much of the money the women received was spent on drink rather than on children.[22] This view crossed the political spectrum, and the decision by the British government in 1916 to extend the payment of separation allowances to unmarried mothers outraged Irish public opinion. The military authorities were accused of promoting 'illegitimacy' and immorality; but the city's councillors were relieved all the same that these women and their children were not thrown on the mercy of the workhouse system and the charity of the ratepayer.

The DMP reports during the war years do lend support to the popular nationalist perception of these women. Indeed the figures suggest that there was some truth, in Dublin at least, in the old maxim that when it came to drink 'the women were worse than the men.'

Table 18
Drunk and disorderly offences, 1911–19

	Total	Drunk Men	Women	Total	Drunk and disorderly Men	Women
1911	1,913	1,165	748	944	479	465
1912	2,345	1,542	803	1,087	517	570
1913	1,814	1,191	623	861	451	410
1914	1,488	981	507	847	390	457
1915	1,842	887	955	821	277	544
1916	1,550	750	800	561	169	392
1917	1,047	473	574	391	107	284
1918	790	403	387	274	66	208
1919	884	394	490	315	89	226

Even before the war a significant proportion of those arrested for drunkenness were women, and in 1912 they actually outnumbered male offenders for being drunk and disorderly. Arrests generally for this offence fell during the war years, but the proportion of women arrested rose, so that in 1918 and 1919 there were almost three times more female offenders than male offenders. The general falling off in arrests for both sexes after 1915 can be put down to declining consumption because of the increasing price of drink, shortage of supply, especially where spirits were concerned, reduced specific gravity levels, and the restrictive licensing laws. All of this was in tune with the thinking of David Lloyd George, who famously denounced the 'drink traffic' as 'a greater danger even than Germany.'[23]

But perhaps some credit for increased sobriety can also be given to the pioneering work of the NSPCC and other voluntary bodies.

Separation women were not, of course, the only ones in the city with high incomes. These included dealers and, in the latter stages of the war, munitions workers. Many of these women would have frequented pubs just as much as prostitutes—or men, for that matter—because, as the woman vigilante referred to above recognised, Dublin tenement life was so appalling.

Ultimately the behaviour of some separation women towards rebel prisoners would seal their fate in the popular collective national memory. The recollections of the prisoners are almost unanimous in condemning what Dr Brighid Lyons Thornton referred to as 'savage women' from whom they had to be protected by their guards. What many prisoners probably did not know, and popular Dublin opinion quickly forgot, was that the rising coincided with the anniversary of the attack on Saint-Julien, where the 'Old Contemptibles' element of the Royal Dublin Fusiliers, including many working-class reservists, suffered such heavy losses. At least some of the women who abused the rebels would have been mothers, widows, wives, daughters or sisters of the dead and wounded.

People took what they wanted from the drama played out on the city's streets during and after the rising. For increasing numbers of Dubliners, drunken separation women—like the slums, the raging inflation, food and fuel shortages, lewd music-hall shows, censorship and military repression—were a manifestation of the blight that Britain's imperial war machine had visited on the city. Conversely, they believed that Irish freedom would banish immorality along with its most visible and potent source, the British army.

The most extreme expression of this view came from the Irish Society for the Combating of the Spread of Venereal Disease, an *ad hoc* body in which Sinn Féin and Cumann na mBan members were particularly active. They seemed to develop a particular obsession with the threat that syphilis posed to young children. Maud Gonne MacBride, widow of the executed 1916 leader John MacBride, told one meeting that the village of Artane was 'crowded with war babies and some of them were suffering from syphilis.' But, as Ann Matthews points out, the general effect of their campaign was to push 'unmarried mothers and their children beyond the margins of social respectability' rather than to generate informed debate.[24]

In reality, of course, the problems of poverty, prostitution and sexually transmitted disease could not be banished by the demonising of separation women, the British army or Dublin Castle. If Kathleen Lynn and Richard Hayes were correct in demanding that the military authorities take responsibility for treating the fifteen thousand Irish soldiers they estimated would have contracted syphilis before returning home, they were also wishfully misdiagnosing the bigger problem. As events proved, the blight of sexually transmitted disease could not be laid solely at the door of the British army. However, this does not mean that their efforts were wasted. The concerns raised by Dr Lynn in particular helped mobilise other feminists, political activists and champions of public health reform to support the establishment of St Ultan's Hospital in Charlemont Street in early 1919. However, to gather public support its aims had to be broadened beyond that of eradicating the threat posed by syphilis to young mothers and their babies.[25]

Meanwhile the corporation moved to tackle the threat from STDs to adults by using recently activated Local Government Board legislation. In June 1918 a two-ward unit was set up in Dr Steevens' Hospital to supplement existing facilities at Sir Patrick Dun's Hospital and the Westmorland Lock Hospital in Townsend Street (an old facility for treating prostitutes and their children). It was proposed by P. T. Daly, chairman of the Public Health Committee, who had been so exercised by scenes on the North Wall in 1915 and had even advocated vigilantism. The unit opened in January 1919 and in its first three months recorded 452 male attendances and 59 female attendances; by the first quarter of 1920 the figures were 2,298 and 529, respectively, a fivefold increase in male attendances and a tenfold increase in female attendances. The number of cases increased after the establishment of the Irish Free State: there were 10,624 attendances at Dr Steevens' Hospital in 1921/2, and the figure rose to 19,531 by 1924/5, when the British army could no longer be blamed for the problem.

At Sir Patrick Dun's Hospital over the same period the figures were 3,737 and 6,545, respectively, and a similar trend occurred at the Westmorland Lock Hospital. Altogether, attendances at outpatient clinics did not reach their maximum of 40,086 until 1934/5, when the number of inpatient days was 10,487. The number of inpatient days in 1922/3 had been 6,783.[26]

An Interdepartmental Report on Venereal Disease in 1926 found that infection was widespread, not only among prostitutes and members of the new Free State army but the wider population as well. Salvation came in the form of Salvarsan (arsphenamine), an organo-arsenic compound developed in 1910 that treated syphilis without the damaging long-term side effects of the old mercury-based treatments. There was also final acceptance by the new regime that sexually transmitted disease was primarily a health problem and not a malign manifestation of British oppression. Indeed the government even considered adopting the Continental model of registering prostitutes and regulating their trade to contain the threat to public health; but the moral guardians of Irish society, the Catholic hierarchy, vetoed any such revolutionary measure.[27]

The end of the war on 11 November 1918 no doubt provided countless occasions of sin, but it is unlikely that public health concerns were uppermost in anyone's mind. The *Irish Times* reported:

> Dublin gave itself over to rejoicings. The feelings that had been pent up for years were suddenly let loose and the whole city seemed to go mad with joy.

Flags of the Allies 'were profusely displayed from the principal buildings ... the Union Jack being, of course, in largest request.' In the afternoon a dense crowd filled the area from College Green to St Stephen's Green

> and cheered themselves hoarse. The windows of the houses were occupied by people waving flags; the tops of tramcars were packed with cheering passengers; motor cars were laden with jubilant occupiers; the jarveys had more 'fares' than their cars could carry; military wagons bedecked with flags and carrying scores of happy 'WAACS' [members of the Women's Army Auxiliary Corps] pushed their way cautiously through the crowds,

while overhead, 'areoplanes' could be seen 'gracefully gambolling in a cloudless sky, their wings flashing in the sunlight.'

The only reference to local political differences was a mock funeral for the Kaiser organised by students from the Royal College of Surgeons. They wheeled an effigy of Wilhelm II through the streets wrapped in 'a Sinn Fein flag.'[28]

Arthur Lynch, whose recruitment efforts had been booed a few weeks earlier, was cheered by the crowd and a speech demanded in College Green. He declared that 'barbarism is killed, now and for ever,' before being carried shoulder high to Trinity College by British soldiers. However, the college authorities had ordered the gates closed, and Lynch had to make a less dramatic entrance through a side door.[29]

Sinn Féin was caught on the hop by news of the armistice. It had organised a meeting in the Mansion House that night, addressed by Alderman Tom Kelly and Harry Boland, where all the speakers could do was declare that the Allies' victory would not deflect them from the campaign for independence. To raise morale, Boland predicted that the party would win 'between seventy-five and eighty seats' in the general election that must follow the ending of the war.

The celebrations continued on Tuesday with a military display at Wellington Barracks for the children of the Liberties. It was also the day when spontaneous joy at the ending of the war gave way to events driven by conflicting political agendas and aspirations about what the peace should bring.

For most soldiers it was a holiday, and they thronged the streets. The only incidents during the daylight hours were some stone-throwing by youths at a military band on St Patrick's Hill and a few attacks on Union Jacks. The most prominent incident was at the head office of the National University in Merrion Square, where a group of students overpowered the staff and tore down a large Union Jack. A Sinn Féin supporter in Glasnevin hit on the simple expedient of mounting a lighted piece of turf on a pole and setting fire to flags on display.

Serious trouble erupted in the evening. Staff members in the Sinn Féin offices at 6 Harcourt Street received a last-minute warning that a group of Trinity students were planning an attack at 7 p.m. They barely had time to bar the doors before the building was bombarded with stones. The besieged workers retaliated with lumps of coal from the cellar but were finding it hard to hold out until two Irish Volunteer officers, Simon Donnelly and Harry Boland, arrived and dispersed the students by firing over their heads.[30]

The appearance of Donnelly and Boland marked the beginning of a counter-mobilisation by the Volunteers. Joseph McDonagh, a member of the 1st Battalion of the Dublin Brigade, recalled: 'At seven o'clock that Monday evening members of the Dublin Brigade, including my own unit, acting on orders from GHQ proceeded to clear the streets of the British Military and their supporters.' The main confrontation came when a group of soldiers decided to hold an impromptu victory march from St Stephen's Green to Sackville Street at about 7:30 p.m. There were no incidents until they were approaching the GPO, where a large number of Volunteers and Sinn Féin supporters had gathered with flags. The soldiers turned into Middle Abbey Street to avoid a confrontation, only to be set upon by a fresh crowd. They were driven back across the river, and a rush of young men and youths waving Tricolours pushed though a DMP cordon on O'Connell Bridge and reached Grafton Street before being dispersed by a baton charge. During the riot a window in Switzer's drapery shop was smashed and a group of British officers set upon in Wicklow Street.

Fresh trouble erupted north of the river when a group of women marched up Sackville Street carrying a Union Jack. After reaching the Parnell Monument they turned around and marched back to the GPO, taking up a position around Nelson's Pillar. This was too much for the Volunteers and Sinn Féin supporters gathered nearby: they drove off the women, grabbed their Union Jack and burnt it to the accompaniment of rebel songs and shouts of 'Up Dev!' Undeterred, the women returned with a larger Union Jack and an escort of off-duty soldiers and sailors. Battle resumed at the corner of Henry Street, where the Sinn Féin supporters were once more victorious. However, on this occasion the flag was too large to burn easily and had to be torn into fragments first.

Other fights flared in the area between local people and off-duty soldiers. The latter were often accompanied by women 'friends', as the Irish Independent called them, and it was this factor that seemed to spark the most violence. In one instance where a woman collapsed at the O'Connell Monument the hostile crowd let an ambulance through but blocked it again when a soldier tried to accompany her to hospital.

The Independent stressed that most of the soldiers and sailors involved in the disturbances were from 'England, Scotland and Wales,' while the Irish Times played down the scale of the trouble and pointed out that 'soldiers and civilians mingled in harmony' in many parts of the city that night. But Volunteers claimed that they had control of the streets by 11 p.m., having defeated the 'military, Dublin Metropolitan Police and loyalists.'[31]

———

Lloyd George called a general election for 14 December. The British Parliament also enacted the long-promised Parliament (Qualification of Women) Act, enfranchising women over the age of thirty as voters and as candidates. By calling the election quickly and presenting voters with an opportunity to re-elect the war-winning coalition before the disillusionment of peace set in, Lloyd George ensured his own return to power with the loss of a few dissident Liberals. But it was a strategy that did the Irish Party no favours. It did not even attempt to contest twenty-five seats that were claimed by Sinn Féin, mainly in Munster. It would also have to secure a pan-nationalist electoral pact with Sinn Féin to ensure victory in some of its Ulster strongholds.

Another difficulty it had to contend with was the hostility of William Martin Murphy and his newspapers. Like many home-rulers, Murphy had lost relatives in the war and had also been disgusted by Redmond's acceptance of partition. While not openly supporting Sinn Féin, Murphy's papers subjected the Irish Party and Redmond's successor, John Dillon, to relentless criticism. Most editions of the *Irish Independent* in the weeks before the election had front-page displays attacking the record of the Irish Party. On 5 December 1918 the display was printed under the heading 'The Policy of Parnell.' It used the lost leader's famous statement that 'no man has a right to fix the boundary of the march of a nation' and listed opposite this 'What the Party Did.' Among the climb-downs catalogued were:

1905–18	Customs and Excise given up
1905	Devolution accepted
1910	Party declare for a Provincial, NOT a Dominion Parliament
1914–1917	Partition of Ireland agreed to

It also contained damaging quotations from John Dillon and concluded: 'Whoever Represents Parnell Mr. Dillon Definitely DOES NOT!'

On 6 December it listed all twenty-five constituencies where Sinn Féin was standing uncontested:

EXCELSIOR!

474,778 Electors have now declared for an INDEPENDENT IRELAND!

and urged other voters to do likewise. On 7 December the display included a 'Message from the Poles Defence Committee, New York,' declaring:

The sympathy of the world is with Ireland. Will you help Sinn Fein to make Ireland worthy of it by VOTING FOR INDEPENDENCE?'

On 10 December the paper published two quotations from Éamon de Valera in Lincoln Prison, '(As passed by the Censor).' The next day the headline was 'WHY DID THEY DIE?' followed by a list of national martyrs from Brian Bórú to Thomas Ashe and Richard Coleman,[32] who 'died to secure the liberation of the oldest political prisoner in the world—IRELAND!' Finally, on the day before the election, under the heading 'TE DEUM!' it quoted Cardinal William Henry O'Connell of Boston declaring that

IRELAND must be allowed TO TELL the world freely what she wanted, how she wished to be governed, and IRELAND must make the world hear HER.

The *Independent* added that '25,000,000 Irish-Americans back this demand AND 474,788 Irish Electors at home affirm it.'

———

In Dublin every constituency would be contested by the Irish Party. Only three sitting MPs had survived since 1914: William Field in the St Patrick's division, P. J. Brady in the St Stephen's Green division and J. J. Clancy in North County Dublin. The number of constituencies in the city and county had also been increased, from six to ten, reflecting changes in population and, most significantly, the massive increase in the electorate resulting from women having a vote for the first time. Other sitting MPs were Alfie Byrne, who would be defending his seat in the Harbour division, and John Dillon Nugent of the AOH, who would be running in the new St Michan's division.

Suffrage groups were at first hopeful that many women would be nominated. There was certainly no lack of eligible candidates. Cissie Cahalan, one of the few working-class women to play a leading role in the suffrage movement and secretary of the Irish Women's Franchise League, wrote to the newspapers urging Sinn Féin to nominate such figures as 'Mrs. Sheehy Skeffington, Madam Markievicz, Mrs. Tom Clarke ... Mrs. Wyse Power ... Dr. Kathleen Lynn, Madam Gonne McBride, Countess Plunkett, Miss Gavan Duffy and Miss Nora Connolly.' She also suggested Prof. Mary Hayden, Alice Stopford Green, Sarah Harrison, Mary Louisa Gwynn (wife of Stephen Gwynn) and Mary Kettle (widow of Tom Kettle) as candidates for the Irish Party. Only when it came to the Unionists were most of the candidates on her list from outside the capital, but even here she could propose Lady Dockrell, a Unionist member of Blackrock Town Council.[33]

Constance Markievicz would be the sole candidate who had been on Cissie Cahalan's list, although Hanna Sheehy Skeffington was nominated for the Harbour division. Why she did not stand is not clear.[34] It may have been that she felt, like many members of Sinn Féin, that Alfie Byrne's position was unassailable. Whatever the reason, it was the second time in four years that the most working-class constituency in Dublin was denied the opportunity to vote for one of the country's leading republican socialists. Instead a local publican, Phil Shanahan, who had been 'out' in Easter Week, was nominated for Sinn Féin.

The party's campaign got off to a brisk start with a rally in the Liberties presided over by the long-standing local Sinn Féin councillor William T. Cosgrave. As he had been re-elected unopposed for Kilkenny, the party used the tried and tested tactic of nominating a prisoner for the seat. In this case it was the ITGWU finance officer and 1916 veteran Joseph McGrath, who was serving a sentence for sedition in Usk Prison in Monmouthshire. More than two thousand people attended the rally at the Fountain, including five hundred Volunteers in military formation.[35]

It was a symptom of the bankruptcy of the Irish Party in Dublin that its candidate in the Liberties should be John Saturninus Kelly, a renegade Labour councillor widely reviled for his attacks on Larkin during the lock-out, his condemnation of Connolly as a 'pro-German' and his unstinting support for the British war effort. He was general secretary of the Irish Railway Workers' Trade Union, whose members 'scabbed' in numerous disputes, and he was suspected of surviving on secret subsidies from employers.

The early display of support by the Volunteers for Sinn Féin candidates was ominous for the Irish Party. The DMP estimated that there were twenty-three Sinn Féin 'clubs' in Dublin on the eve of the election, with a membership of 4,640. It warned that these activists would be supplemented by the efforts of the Irish Volunteers, which contained 'all the younger members ... and most fanatical Sinn Feiners.'[36] Irish Citizen Army members would also canvass for Sinn Féin, especially for Constance Markievicz in the St Patrick's division.

Markievicz benefited even more from the support of many Dublin women activists, angry as well as disappointed at the party's failure to nominate more women. Some even suspected that Markievicz would be left without support by the organisation's national office. Hanna Sheehy Skeffington described St Patrick's as 'the worst managed constituency in Dublin' and said that women had a duty to go there to campaign for Markievicz.[37]

Her opponent was the old Parnellite and friend of 'craft' labour, William Field. Field's problem was his voting record, which was exemplary for a Redmondite. His only policy initiative was the advocacy of a 'dead meat' plant for Dublin. It evoked an appropriate electoral image for the party.

Councillor Coghlan Briscoe, executive officer of the Town Tenants' League, former sheriff and a pillar of the old political order in the city, ran as an independent against the long-established Sinn Féin councillor Seán T. Ó Ceallaigh in College Green. Rather than make any attempt to defend the Irish Party's record, Briscoe urged electors to vote for him because of his expertise on rent legislation. As with Field, his programme did not inspire voters.

John Dillon Nugent faced another 1916 veteran, Michael Staines, in the St Michan's constituency. Dillon ran the weakest of all campaigns in the city, pleading ill health as the reason for his absence from the hustings. Staines was a senior member of the IRB and the Irish Volunteers and had served as a very effective quartermaster of the Dublin Brigade in the period before the Easter Rising. However, his main claim to fame with the wider public at this point in his career was that he had been one of Connolly's stretcher-bearers at the GPO.[38]

In Clontarf East the Irish Party candidate was Sir Patrick Shortall, whose anti-union record as an employer in 1913 would not be as damaging to his prospects as it would have been in one of the main city divisions, and he could hope for tactical support from the substantial Protestant electorate in the absence of a Unionist candidate. However, he faced a strong Sinn Féin opponent in Richard Mulcahy, Thomas Ashe's lieutenant at Ashbourne.

The Unionists contested five seats. One of the most interesting contests was in Rathmines, where Sir Maurice Dockrell was the candidate. Dockrell was a pillar of the Unionist Party in Dublin. Since the outbreak of the war he had served on the Dublin Recruitment Committee and in 1918 had been appointed to the Recruiting Council of Ireland. He was chairman of the British Red Cross Society and of the St John Ambulance Brigade in Co. Dublin and was Deputy Lieutenant of the city. Although he had been involved in the 1913 Lock-out and had even issued revolvers to strike-breakers in his capacity as a justice of the peace, he had not initiated any lock-out at his own builders' supply business. Rather he had to close when employees engaged in sympathetic strike action. As a consequence he was widely regarded as a 'good employer.'

His own campaign was directed at the new women voters. He presented himself as a champion of women's rights, especially those of soldiers' wives and widows. He accused Sinn Féin, not without justification, of abandoning this group who had suffered so much in the war. Lady Dockrell campaigned actively for her husband, as did Lady Arnott, president of the Dublin Women's Unionist Club. A coup for Dockrell was the endorsement of the veteran suffrage campaigner Anna Haslam, who had pioneered the women's patrols. She and her late husband, Thomas, had been campaigning for women's rights since the 1860s. She told women that their long-term interests were best served by being united with a large urban liberal democracy such as Britain rather than being tolerated in a small peasant society as a subordinate sex.

P. J. Little, the Sinn Féin candidate, laboured under the handicap of not having been 'out' in 1916. He was the editor of New Ireland and had been involved in the

Irish National League, one of the more conservative groups that merged with Sinn Féin in its 1918 reincarnation. He was probably considered suitably conservative to be acceptable to the Rathmines electorate.[39] His nationalist rival was George Moonan, a businessman and founder-member of the Knights of Saint Columbanus. Little was approached by UIL members to discuss an electoral pact against Dockrell. He immediately denounced Moonan, only to have to apologise when Moonan claimed that the proposal had been made without his knowledge. Moonan in turn embarrassed one of his most important supporters, Mary Kettle, by drawing her into another spat with Little about women's rights. Dockrell left them to it.

Henry Hanna KC was the Unionist candidate in the St Stephen's Green ward, where P. J. Brady had narrowly won the seat for the Irish Party in 1910. Hanna had hopes of winning it back. He was a liberal unionist, and he had defended Larkin and other strike leaders in the courts in 1913. He argued that the slum clearance and health reforms Dublin needed could be achieved only through the largesse of the British Treasury, and that meant maintaining the Union.

Alderman Tom Kelly was the Sinn Féin candidate in the constituency. If Kelly had not been 'out' in 1916 he had at least been interned and was also widely respected as a long-standing advocate of slum clearance. The Irish Party incumbent, Brady, could reasonably claim to have done what he could in Parliament to secure funds for slum clearance. He had worked with Archbishop Walsh to mobilise support from the business community for a housing programme to be financed by the American loans market but had failed, like many before him, to achieve anything of substance. He was perceived, rightly or wrongly, as a relatively weak and colourless candidate whose main power base lay in the Society of St Vincent de Paul.

The Pembroke division also had a three-cornered contest. Another 1916 man, Desmond Fitzgerald, was the Sinn Féin candidate, and John Good was the Unionist, with Charles O'Neill standing for the Irish Party. O'Neill was chairman of Pembroke Town Commission and was popular; but he had also been a member of the ill-fated Irish Convention and had to defend himself against allegations of being a 'conscriptionist'. Good was a leading figure in the Dublin Master Builders' Association and had recently secured the contract to build Collinstown aerodrome (precursor of Dublin Airport) for the Royal Air Force. He had been one of the hard-line supporters of William Martin Murphy in the lock-out. His position was simple and uncompromising: he opposed partition and predicted that the 'flow of capital' would cease 'if the Sinn Feiners got into power.' Fitzgerald was an IRB London-Irish blow-in but, as well as having served in the GPO garrison, was the beneficiary of a new phenomenon whereby leading figures in the old home rule establishment endorsed Sinn Féin candidates. In his case the blessing came from Michael Davitt Junior. Few expected Good to win, but nationalists were hopeful that O'Neill could see off the Sinn Féin challenge.

Unionists believed they had a good chance of winning South County Dublin, where the seat had often hung in the balance between nationalist and unionist.

With the nationalist vote split, Sir Thomas Robinson, a hotelier and popular businessman, might have done better if he had not tried to tar the Irish Party candidate, Thomas Clarke, with the Sinn Féin brush. He said the only difference between the Irish Party and Sinn Féin was that Sinn Féin wanted a Republic 'at one swoop' while the Irish Party was willing 'to take two bites of the cherry.' In turn, any hope Clarke had of winning unionist votes evaporated when he asked the electorate of South County Dublin if they wanted to be 'represented by an Orangeman,' while one of Clarke's supporters, J. J. Kennedy, chairman of Kingstown Urban District Council, said that Robinson represented 'Carson, the "King of Ireland" of whom the present Government was afraid.' By contrast, the Sinn Féin candidate, George Gavan Duffy, who had an impeccable nationalist family background, was moderation itself and sidestepped the sectarian row.

In North County Dublin, J. J. Clancy fought a rearguard action against Frank Lawless, who had been with Thomas Ashe at Ashbourne and was yet another Sinn Féin candidate in prison. The outcome was regarded as a foregone conclusion.

Unlike some parts of Ireland, most notably the Dillon heartland of Co. Roscommon and East Mayo, there was relatively little violence between Volunteers and Irish Party 'bludgeon men' in Dublin. But it was by no means absent, particularly in the Harbour division, where Alfie Byrne had a formidable election machine. Thomas Leahy, an Irish Citizen Army veteran of 1916 who worked for Sinn Féin in the area, recalled:

> During one of our meetings down … East Wall, we met with a very hostile crowd who were mostly all Scotch people working in the Dockyard, and the followers of Alfie were also strong there. When I rose to open the meeting and to introduce Seán T. O'Kelly and … Phil Shanahan, we were met with a shower of sods and Union Jack Flags waving all around us. But it did not last long, as the precaution was taken … for this and a company of the Second Battalion Volunteers were near at hand and, with batons, cleared the place of the objectors in quick time. We were allowed to hold our meetings without interruption after that.[40]

The reality was that the remnants of the Irish Party's strong-arm men were no match for the Volunteers. On polling day Sinn Féin 'peace patrols' appeared alongside military pickets, underlining the supremacy of the advanced nationalists over their opponents on the ground. Only in one instance did this innovation threaten to turn ugly and serve as a warning of what the future might hold for their opponents. This was in South County Dublin when Sir Thomas Robinson visited the Shankill polling station with Robert Potterton, an election worker and unionist solicitor in Kingstown. They arrived in their touring car at the top of the lane leading to the polling station to find it blocked by 'a cordon of young men.'

'Who are you?' demanded Potterton.

'Soldiers of the Irish Republic,' was the reply.

'You haven't got a republic yet, so get out of the way,' said Potterton.

The situation was defused by the appearance of an RIC constable. He explained that the 'peace patrol' was assisting him with the direction of traffic, as the lane was too narrow for vehicles to turn in. They had done such a good job that he had left them in charge while he took a break.

———

The remaining Dublin constituency was that of the University of Dublin. Elections for these seats, as for the National University, would take place over a number of days, hence the delay in counting the ballot papers until 28 December. As Carson had opted to run in Belfast, there were two vacancies to be contested in the university. The Irish Attorney-General, A. W. Samuels, was defending his seat, and Sir Robert Woods, professor of laryngology and otology, was renewing his challenge to the lawyers' monopoly of representation for the university. The other candidates were William Morgan Jellett KC, another lawyer, and Captain Stephen Gwynn.

Samuels and Jellett were both unionists labouring under the handicap of having to defend government policy on Ireland, while Woods was a unionist in principle but reserved the right to freedom of action in representing the college's best interests and in seeking a negotiated political settlement for southern unionists with the nationalist majority. Gwynn's politics were a vaguer version of those espoused by Woods. The one firm assurance he gave the electorate was that he would oppose partition, although the implication was that he would prefer home rule or dominion status if necessary in order to do so. His main assets were his youth and his war service. The fact that his proposers were also junior officers in the armed forces showed that he was a rank outsider. By contrast, Samuels was nominated by the Primate of the Church of Ireland and seconded by the vice-provost of the university, while Woods was proposed by the Archbishop of Dublin and Jellett by the Bishop of Cashel.

Samuels and Woods would be returned, showing that an endorsement by the Unionist Party was not sufficient in itself to guarantee election. Eoin MacNeill would secure a National University seat for Sinn Féin.

When the votes in the other Dublin constituencies were counted, Sinn Féin failed to secure only one seat, that in Rathmines.

The margin of Sinn Féin victory was comfortable in most of the constituencies. Michael Staines defeated John Dillon Nugent by 7,553 votes to 3,996 in the St Michan's division. Nugent did surprisingly well, given that he failed to campaign and had a knack of antagonising the electorate when he did. Just as Farren had to appeal to the crowd to allow the victorious Nugent to address them in 1915, so Staines had to repeat the request in 1918 for Nugent in defeat. Staines took the

opportunity of his own acceptance speech to respond to the charge by Nugent's
AOH election workers that he only represented poor people. To loud cheers, he said
he was proud of the charge and proud of the poor people of St Michan's who had
put him at the head of the poll. Many of the voters in the hall that day were probably
men and women who would not have had a vote when Nugent defeated the Labour
candidate, Tom Farren, three years earlier.

Joseph McGrath won the most crushing Sinn Féin victory in Dublin, with 8,256
to 1,389 for John Saturninus Kelly in the St James's division. In College Green,
Seán T. Ó Ceallaigh won by 9,662 votes to 2,853 for the former sheriff,
Coghlan Briscoe.

Sir Patrick Shortall did better than expected in Clontarf, polling a respectable
3,228 to the 5,974 votes for Richard Mulcahy. Shortall clearly benefited from tactical
voting by Protestants in the absence of any unionist candidate in a constituency
that regularly returned an alderman and at least two unionist councillors.

In North County Dublin, Frank Lawless won by 9,138 votes to 4,428 for the Irish
Party veteran J. J. Clancy. It was the same in the other constituencies where a straight
fight took place between Sinn Féin and the Irish Party. In the St Patrick's division
Constance Markievicz secured a comfortable win—despite the fears of
Hanna Sheehy Skeffington—with 7,835 votes to 3,752 for William Field. J. J. Kelly,
the publican who had run as an unsuccessful 'Home Rule Labour' candidate in 1914,
ran again as an independent, securing 372 votes.

In the Harbour division Alfie Byrne put up the most redoubtable fight of any
Irish Party candidate in Dublin. He won 5,368 votes, but it was not enough to see
off the Sinn Féin challenge from his fellow-publican Phil Shanahan, who won with
7,707 votes.

In the three-way contests with unionist candidates, Sinn Féin also outperformed
the Irish Party. In St Stephen's Green, Alderman Tom Kelly topped the poll with
8,461 votes. This was more than double the combined vote of P. J. Brady, with 2,902,
and Henry Hanna, with a disappointing 2,775.

In Pembroke and South County Dublin the results were much closer. In
Pembroke, Desmond Fitzgerald won by only 6,113 votes to 4,137 for John Good and
2,630 for Charles O'Neill. In South County Dublin, George Gavan Duffy won with
5,133 to 4,354 votes for Sir Thomas Robinson and 3,819 for Thomas Clarke. In both
these constituencies the unionist candidates might have won if the nationalist vote
had split more evenly, or if significant numbers of conservative middle-class
Catholics had opted, as they had in the past, for the unionist candidate. But those
days were gone.

In Rathmines, however, Sir Maurice Dockrell secured a convincing victory by
polling more votes than the combined total of his opponents. Little won 5,566 votes,
Moonan 1,780 and Dockrell 7,400. Rathmines was also the only Dublin
constituency where the votes of servicemen played a significant though not a
decisive role. More than 1,500 soldiers and sailors were entitled to vote in

Rathmines. Of the 539 who bothered to do so, 459 voted for Sir Maurice Dockrell, 50 voted for Moonan and 30 for Little. Given the demographics of Rathmines, the high turn-out by servicemen probably reflected the relatively high proportion of middle-class and Protestant recruits from the constituency, although Dockrell's championing of the rights of war widows and their families no doubt secured votes from the families of nationalist servicemen as well.

It would be January 1920 before municipal elections would consolidate the power of Sinn Féin on Dublin Corporation—supplemented by a large Labour contingent. But the 1918 general election had served formal notice on the old home rule regime in City Hall.

Nationally, Sinn Féin had won 73 seats to 6 for the Irish Party, of which 4 were in Ulster constituencies, where pan-nationalist electoral pacts had allowed it a clear run against the unionists. The other big losers were Asquith's anti-coalition Liberals, who won 28 seats. The *Irish Times* quipped that if the dissident Liberals could fly to London in a Handley-Page aeroplane, an Irish jaunting car could accommodate the remnants of the Irish Party.

———

Unfortunately, the spectacular Sinn Féin electoral victory of December 1918 made very little difference to the practical lives and problems of Dubliners. One threat that neither Sinn Féin nor the end of the war could remove was that of power cuts. In fact the situation grew more critical in the city during the winter of 1918/19. Reduced heating in hospitals and the temporary closing of public baths were already in force when the corporation's Electricity Supply Committee produced new proposals on 1 October 1918 for conserving dwindling coal supplies. These included the introduction of lighting restrictions and increased charges to dampen demand. The committee told councillors that consumption would have to be reduced by two-thirds compared with the winter of 1917/18. The only alternative would be to cut power supplies to industry, causing even greater disruption to the economic and social life of the city. The committee proposed, therefore, that offices close by 4:30 p.m. and shops by 5:30 p.m. four days a week. This was rejected in favour of an amendment from an alliance of shopkeepers and ratepayers' champions that shops would remain open until 7 and keep their lights on until 7:30. It was also agreed that the restrictions would last only until 28 February 1919, instead of the end of March, as proposed by the committee.

While industry was spared power cuts, it would have to bear the brunt of the price increases. Lighting rates for consumers would rise by 1d per unit from 1 October, but rates for machines used in workshops and factories would rise by between 2½d and 5¼d per unit. Vital utilities and large-scale employers, such as the corporation's pumping station and the National Shell Factory, would be charged at the lower rate of 2½d per unit.[41]

The restrictions on opening hours were quite acceptable to the banks, which had repeatedly expressed a willingness to close at 2:30 p.m., and to the insurance industry, which had stated that it could close offices by 4:30; but even in their modified form the restrictions provoked a strong reaction from shopkeepers. The Irish Retail Confectioners' Association complained that the proposed Early Closing Order was unacceptable, 'as it affects so many small traders and also causes great inconvenience to the general public who are compelled to be in business all day.'

However, the power to determine lighting orders lay ultimately with the British government. On Armistice Day, 11 November, the Lord Lieutenant made orders for all cities in Ireland. Under these, every retail shop in Dublin, Belfast, Cork, Limerick, Derry and Waterford had to close no later than 5:30 p.m. on weekdays, no later than 7 p.m. on Fridays and no later than 9:30 p.m. on Saturdays. Businesses such as hairdressing, temperance bars and fish-and-chip shops could remain open until 9:30 p.m., provided they closed for an equivalent number of hours during the afternoon to make up the difference. Fines of up to £100 could be imposed under the Defence of the Realm Act for breaches of the regulations.[42]

——

On the coal supply front, an offer of help came from an unexpected quarter when the Director-General of Transport, H. G. Burgess, who also represented the British Coal Controller's Department in Dublin, advised Fred Allan that a shipment of 1,000 tons of high-quality coal could be purchased for 42s per ton—admittedly a high price but no more than the market now commanded. Perhaps mindful of the power of the retail lobby, Burgess said it would be available only if it was kept in reserve for emergencies, when all other stocks were exhausted. P. T. Daly immediately proposed that the offer be accepted, with the proviso that it would be used only in extremity to provide fuel at cost to families with a weekly income below 8s per capita. This was agreed by the corporation.[43] Even the situation of better-off households was now desperate. Since the summer, coal merchants had had their daily ration reduced from 3¾ tons to 1¼.[44]

The battle for supplies continued into December, with Allan complaining that councillors did not appreciate the gravity of the situation. He had never been able to secure supplies for more than four weeks at a time over the previous six months, and as Christmas approached he reported that there was only a fortnight's supply left in the city. Consumption was exceeding supply by 30 per cent.

Nevertheless, the retailers continued their lobbying, with some success. Eventually the Under-Secretary, Sir William Byrne, met a corporation delegation on 16 December and agreed to lift lighting restrictions for shopkeepers from 20 December until the 24th, so that they could avail of the pre-Christmas sales bonanza.[45] As so often in the past, the old UIL machine had proved its ability to focus on the short-term interests of the 'shopocracy' before the common good of Dubliners.

The longer opening hours did at least make the peace seem a little more tangible, and all the newspapers dipped into their reserves of ink and newsprint to carry the largest advertisements for the Christmas and January sales since before the war. It would be March before restrictions on the importation of such luxury items would be relaxed.[46]

——

It was April 1919 before coal supplies improved, partly because of industrial unrest in Britain and the chaotic state of the mining industry there.[47] Nevertheless, the general situation was improving, and a sense of normality began to prevail from 1 March, when businesses were allowed to light their premises until 9:30 p.m. every evening.

The price of essential items such as coal and food would begin to fall only when controls on production and imports were relaxed. Once more the British government was blamed for the slow relaxation of controls, with nationalists of all hues blaming the coal shortages in particular on the British government's reluctance to allow cheap American coal into the market. By March coal merchants were warning that the stock for domestic use had fallen to one week's supply and supplies for industry to four weeks. The Dublin United Tramways Company could maintain its services only with assistance from one of its directors, William Hewat. He was also one of the city's leading coal merchants and helped ensure a continuity of supply.[48]

The retail price of coal in Dublin was now between 56s and 60s a ton, while Londoners paid 30s. The merchants pointed out that allowing in cheaper American coal, even if freight and shipping costs remained the same, could cut prices by 7s a ton. They also protested that shipping rates remained unchanged, despite the disappearance of the German submarine menace.

Even wholesale customers in Dublin were paying more than household consumers in Britain for supplies, because of the high shipping and freight rates. The corporation's Electricity Supply Department was still paying 42s 6d a ton in early 1919. As a result, wartime tariffs on customers had to be extended into the second quarter of 1919. On the positive side, many large drapery shops and other businesses had managed to reduce their bills to pre-war levels through cost-efficiency measures.

Similar discrepancies persisted in prices for other staple items, some of them hard to explain, such as the price of Irish eggs at between 3s 9d and 5s 6d a dozen in Dublin and only 3s in Britain.[49]

———

Meanwhile, Laurence O'Neill was re-elected Lord Mayor for the third time on 25 February 1919. In many respects the election resembled the two previous occasions, not least in that some leading councillors, most notably W. T. Cosgrave, were in prison. O'Neill admitted that practically all his promises to keep down rates, contain costs and build new houses for the working class had not been honoured. He had pushed new housing schemes in Spitalfields, the McCaffrey estate (Mount Brown), St James's Walk and Fairbrother's Fields as far as he could without central government funds, and he sharply criticised the failure of the government to notify Dublin Corporation of the availability of grants in aid for housing, unlike its British counterparts. In his own defence and that of the corporation he reminded his colleagues, not unreasonably, that 'all our critics, whether of the press or public, invariably left out the fact that there had been a war on.'

The only discordant note came with the vote of thanks to the outgoing high sheriff, Sir Andrew Beattie, whom Tom Kelly criticised for entertaining Lord French in the middle of the conscription crisis. Beattie said he 'may not have pleased everyone, any more than myself, but I have the satisfaction of knowing I have conscientiously done my duty.'[50] It was an apologia for all the aldermen and councillors of the old regime as they awaited the events that would inevitably sweep them away.

———

The first step had already been taken a month earlier, on 21 January, when the twenty-four Sinn Féin MPs at liberty met in the Mansion House to constitute themselves as Dáil Éireann and to issue the Declaration of Independence, which gave democratic ratification to the Proclamation of the Irish Republic and its establishment in arms on Easter Monday 1916.

The Dáil, the first legislative assembly to gather in Ireland since the Act of Union, also adopted the Democratic Programme. The idea for such a document, outlining the social and economic aspirations of the infant Republic, had first been mooted by the Dublin Trades Council. The invitation to draft it came from the Sinn Féin leadership, in recognition of the role Labour had played in its own victory, especially in Dublin. The main author was Thomas Johnson, assisted by William O'Brien and

Cathal O'Shannon of the ITGWU. It was amended by Seán T. Ó Ceallaigh to meet objections from Michael Collins and other senior IRB members. They wanted the removal of explicit affirmations of socialist principles, such as the right of the nation 'to resume possession' of the nation's wealth 'whenever the trust is abused or the trustee fails to give faithful service.' Ó Ceallaigh also had to remove a reference that encouraged 'the organisation of people into trade unions and co-operative societies.'[51]

Nevertheless, the document finally adopted reasserted the claim in the Proclamation that national sovereignty 'extends not only to all men and women of the Nation, but to all its material possessions, the Nation's soil and all its resources, all the wealth and all the wealth-producing processes within the Nation.' It further reaffirmed 'that all right to private property must be subordinated to the public right and welfare.'

'In return for willing service,' every citizen had the right to 'an adequate share of the produce of the Nation's labour,' and 'it shall be the first duty of the Government of the Republic to make provision for the physical, mental and spiritual well-being of the children, to secure that no child shall suffer hunger or cold from lack of food, clothing or shelter, but that all shall be provided with the means and facilities requisite for their proper education and training as Citizens of a Free and Gaelic Ireland.'

Thomas Johnson would cry as he sat listening to the declaration being read into the Dáil record by 'the Alderman', Tom Kelly.[52] Whether they would have been tears of joy if he could have seen the future is a moot point; but the fact remains that such a radical document could not have been conjured into existence anywhere in Ireland other than Dublin.

On the same day a group of Irish Volunteers in Co. Tipperary shot and killed two RIC constables who were escorting a consignment of gelignite. The ringleaders would soon be on their way to Dublin to assist Michael Collins, the man who objected to the Democratic Programme's socialist content, in bringing the war to the streets of the capital.

The unfolding situation was neatly summed up in the editorial of the *Irish Times* on 1 January 1919. 'We stand on the threshold of a New Year. It is the year of a new order in international affairs, of a new order in British politics, of a new and strange disorder in Irish life.'

Chapter 15 ∿

A FLICKERING GREEN LIGHT AT THE END OF A LONG TUNNEL

D ublin was a divided city in 1914. It was divided by nationality, religion, class, culture and conflicting loyalties. All those divisions had deepened by 1918 and resulted in significant realignments.

The most obvious change was the increasing isolation and marginalisation of the Protestant and unionist community, which was ironic, given that the British Empire had just emerged triumphant from its greatest test. The total mobilisation of state resources to win the war brought significant benefits in the form of jobs and the redistribution of wealth to 'separation women' and their families in the Dublin tenements; but Lloyd George's Government received little thanks.

The vast majority of Dubliners never saw the war as their quarrel. Indeed the Bachelor's Walk shootings at its outbreak overshadowed more momentous events in Europe. While a relatively small number of middle-class Catholics joined the forces in response to John Redmond's appeal for nationalists to fight for the rights of small nations, enthusiasm soon evaporated because of the crass mishandling of Irish nationalist sensitivities by the War Office and the dawning awareness of the awful price that was being exacted in blood at Gallipoli and on the western front.

Most Dubliners who joined the British army were economic recruits from the city's working-class communities, for whom the decision had no great political or ideological significance; the first batch of reservists called up did not even have a choice in the matter. Later the chance for unskilled young men to learn a trade and break out of the rigid caste system that governed craft apprenticeships in the city provided a strong incentive to join the technical branches.

Meanwhile a gap quickly opened between soldiers at the front and civilians at home. Inevitable in any conflict, it was aggravated by the difficulty soldiers had in obtaining leave and by the unique turn of events in Dublin itself. The rising changed everything. The deaths, the looting, the destruction of property, imprisonment and repression happened on people's doorsteps. Tens of thousands of Irishmen may have perished in Flanders, the Balkans or the Middle East, but that was 'over there.'

All politics are local. The fact that so many soldiers who survived the war either never came home or decided not to resettle in Ireland, often abandoning their families in the process, also lessened awareness of cataclysmic events abroad. This failure to return is worthy of more study than the 'collective amnesia' theory promoted by some commentators.

Far from being forgotten, thousands attended annual Armistice Day commemorations in the Phoenix Park for decades. Free State ministers attended ceremonies in Dublin and London until Fianna Fáil came to power and the political establishment turned its back on Remembrance Day. But forty thousand were still reported attending the 1939 commemoration, twenty years after the war ended. During the Second World War restrictions were imposed on commemorations, as they were in Britain.[1] Subsequently, as the collective memory receded, so did the numbers who attended the ceremonies. Their discontinuation at the end of the 1960s was because of concern about the public reaction to events in Northern Ireland, where a unionist tradition of a harsher kind had outlived its political usefulness. Modern attitudes towards Irish participation in the Great War have been more determined by developments since 1968 than by anything that went before.

Many families in Dublin with a unionist background continued to commemorate their fallen members within their own social circle and religious community. In the wider nationalist population the lack of enthusiasm for commemorations in the immediate aftermath of the war was certainly due to changing political sentiment. The great majority of Catholic Dubliners who served with the British forces were members of the working class, with no particular allegiance to the Crown or the Union. They rarely had a voice outside of organised labour—and organised labour in the city was totally opposed to the war effort.

The apolitical nature of Dublin working-class involvement in the First World War is demonstrated most emphatically by the failure of returning soldiers to provide a reserve army for the right, unlike many ex-servicemen in other combatant countries. Far from displaying any affection for either unionism or home rule, many ex-servicemen joined the IRA in the War of Independence, and more would have done so, particularly in Dublin, but for the misgivings of some Volunteer officers. J. J. O'Connell, assistant chief of staff of the IRA, testified to their contribution, and a high proportion of those who were accepted into the IRA rapidly rose through its ranks. In Northern Ireland there were no such obstacles to loyalist veterans of the First World War joining the RUC and its reserves when that force replaced the RIC.

––––––

The most important social initiative of the war in Dublin was the introduction of separation payments to support the wives and children of serving soldiers. This was widely denounced as a plan for degrading and corrupting Irish womanhood, especially after it was extended in 1916 to the unmarried mothers of servicemen's children. The fact that the organisation working most closely with the families of servicemen, the National Society for the Prevention of Cruelty to Children, was unequivocal in its assessment of the beneficial effects of the scheme was dismissed by advanced nationalists, who saw the society as a cat's-paw of the British establishment.

Similar disapproval extended to manifestations of independence or self-indulgence by young female factory workers, especially those in munitions factories, who were better paid than many male workers. That they would go out and enjoy themselves, helping to turn Sackville Street into an outdoor 'low saloon', outraged their social betters. The filth, the poverty, the prevalence of infectious disease and above all the lack of privacy in the tenements explains not alone the preference of these young women for the 'low saloon' of Dublin's main boulevard but also the popularity of the pubs frequented by their elders. The social benefits of overcrowding in the slums—the camaraderie that brought neighbours together to combat shortages and share hardships—have been much exaggerated. Tenement life also left weaker tenants a prey to theft, threats and abuse by unscrupulous neighbours.

By contrast, young middle-class women who joined the Volunteer Aid Detachments or Cumann na mBan were spared the censorious scrutiny applied to munitions workers and soldiers' wives. They too enjoyed a degree of freedom unattainable before the war, and there is no reason to believe they were any more, or less, virtuous than their working-class contemporaries. Yet the women's patrols established by Anna Haslam were focused firmly on the behaviour of their working-class sisters and the threat this posed to society.

The threat that most preoccupied the middle classes, of all political persuasions, was the high incidence of sexually transmitted disease, a scourge whose prevalence was persistently laid at the door of the British administration. It was only after independence that it became obvious that the causes ran much deeper than the presence of a dissolute military.

The enormous amount of energy expended in denouncing the effects of prostitution has to be contrasted with the glaring failure to tackle the slums that bred this and other social problems. During the Great War nearly a thousand tenements were closed as unsafe, and 3,563 of the 4,150 families living in them were thereby made homeless. Only 327 new houses were built in a city urgently needing to rehouse 50,000 of its poorest people. While much of the blame can be laid at the door of the Local Government Board for failing to show greater alacrity in taking advantage of the funds available to British local authorities, the achievements of Pembroke Urban District Council show what could be achieved where the political will existed.

A similar situation arose with regard to wider social and health reforms. The amalgamation of the two Poor Law unions arose not out of any decision by the city to rationalise and improve services for its most vulnerable inhabitants but from military diktat. More consideration was given to ensuring that workhouse employees' pensions were protected than to how the opportunity might be used to radically improve services to inmates. Improvements in psychiatric services were introduced by the military authorities at Grangegorman for soldiers suffering from shell shock, but many Irish staff members refused to work with them, so that a valuable learning opportunity was lost. The one great advance achieved by the forced amalgamation of the Poor Law unions was that citizens on the more prosperous south side of the city had to contribute a more equitable share to the maintenance of the city's poor. However, the policy priority remained minimising the burden on the ratepayer. The level of pauperism in Dublin remained virtually undiminished during the war years.

———

A major reason for the unpopularity of the war was that it brought plenty of hardship and only a small fraction of the economic benefits enjoyed by Belfast and British cities. Dublin was unfortunate in that its principal industries did not lend themselves easily to war production. However, far more energy was spent in resisting inevitable tax increases on the drinks industry than in exploring opportunities for replacement enterprises. It was fitting that the last great rally of constitutional nationalism in the city in 1915 was to oppose heavier taxes on alcohol. Nothing better demonstrated the political bankruptcy of that movement.

The largest employment initiative was the National Shell Factory, which Lloyd George pushed through, despite the rising, with very little assistance from Dublin's business community. The success of the Dublin Dockyard Company was achieved by two outsiders who saw opportunities that local businessmen had missed and who had to overcome 'dog in the manger' resistance from other port companies. Trade unions, anxious to generate jobs, were the company's strongest supporters.[2]

———

The revival of the labour movement in the city after 1916 was one of the great achievements of Dublin workers. It was all the more remarkable given the punishment inflicted on the movement by the state, with the death or imprisonment of so many leading figures and the near-destruction of Liberty Hall. In many ways the execution of Connolly was a blessing in disguise. While he was a brilliant polemicist and propagandist, his insistence on mastering opponents in debate and his 'prickly integrity' led to a career marked by splits and resignations in any organisation with which he was involved. His dogmatism could also breed intolerance at times, as is illustrated by his attitude to the dependants of reservists forced to rejoin the army on the outbreak of war, as well as towards conscripts and separation women. Nor was this hostility very revolutionary: the Bolsheviks seized power in Russia by courting soldiers and nurturing their grievances, not by denouncing them.

As a martyred leader of the rising Connolly was of infinitely greater value to the movement than he would have been alive. He provided an icon sedulously cultivated by William O'Brien, an organiser of genius. O'Brien, however, was a follower rather than a leader. During his internment after the rising he became close to the rebels and began forging an alliance with advanced nationalists, especially de Valera, which would lay the basis for the continuing closeness of unions to Fianna Fáil in the decades after independence.

In many respects O'Brien's strategy was inevitable in a society that was still overwhelmingly rural. Even in Dublin many trade unionists made it clear during the period before the 1918 general election that they would prefer to vote for Sinn Féin than for Labour candidates. If Labour had run candidates, the results of the split radical vote in the city would have allowed the Irish Party or Unionist candidates to secure seats in Pembroke, South County Dublin and possibly the Harbour division.

The only alternative Labour leaders to O'Brien were Thomas Johnson and P. T. Daly. Johnson was handicapped by the fact that he was English, spent much of the war in Belfast, and was an ineradicable moderate, despite his brief verbal flirtation with Bolshevism. Daly proved no match for O'Brien as a political infighter, and the principal result of their power struggle was the further incapacitation of Labour as an independent actor in national politics after the rising—even in Dublin. In the wider national context, the need to preserve working-class unity across the sectarian divide prevented Labour taking a position on the central constitutional issues of the day. This inevitably led to its relegation from being the movement of social, economic and national liberation envisaged by Connolly to being a niche party. Meanwhile Sinn Féin moved in the opposite direction, from niche party to national liberation movement.

Union growth in Dublin and throughout Ireland in the war years owed an enormous, if unacknowledged, debt to the British government. The state structures established to mediate in industrial disputes and to minimise disruption to war production meant *de facto* trade union recognition. Because Irish industry was largely peripheral to the war effort, the repressive elements of the system used to curb militancy and to try, unsuccessfully, to suppress the emerging shop stewards' movement in Britain had no real role in Dublin. Conversely, it was one reason why a shop stewards' movement independent of official union structures never emerged here.

While wages never caught up with inflation, the arbitration structures did allow for the emergence of a 'pay round' system of sorts. Industries and occupations outside the remit of the Committee on Production used its awards as a basis for their own claims, which, when successful, were used in turn by workers in controlled industries to lodge new claims aimed at restoring their differentials. Unfortunately for the workers, the dismantling of the state industrial relations machinery coincided with the post-war recession, which would see a massive counter-offensive by employers, first in Britain and then in Ireland.

———

The delay in the Irish employers' counter-attack was partly due to the disturbed state of Ireland in 1921 but also to their own disunity, dating from the war years. The Dublin Chamber of Commerce, which had entered the war period greatly strengthened and unified by its victory in the 1913 Lock-out, was now deeply fractured.

Like Labour, employers were divided by the constitutional question. This eventually manifested itself in the extraordinary scenes at the Chamber of Commerce meeting in June 1918 when E. H. Andrews tried to move an address to Lord French. An ill-advised initiative by an executive still dominated by a Protestant aristocracy of capital that felt the need to endorse legitimate authority in disturbed times superseded the sensitivities of nationalist colleagues. It probably did not help that many of the chamber's luminaries, such as Sir William Goulding, Sir Maurice Dockrell and John Good, were also leading figures in the city's Unionist organisations and in the Freemasons.

Ironically, the most vocal opposition came from such figures as Alfie Byrne, campaigning on a 'rights of minorities' principle that they would themselves eschew after independence.

———

The alienation of nationalist businessmen from the war effort took place over a relatively short period and sprang from an early realisation that there was no percentage in it for them. They gave Redmond's gambit the benefit of the doubt, and it might have worked if there had been a quicker and cheaper Allied victory—

or even any indication by unionists and their allies in the British political establishment that something of substance would be conceded to nationalists in return for Redmond's generosity. The Irish Party's pursuit of the Holy Grail of home rule blinded it to the growing power of the city's various pressure groups, including feminists, trade unionists, cultural nationalists, and social reformers. Redmond did not bother making many public appearances in the city; when he did, it was to address recruiting meetings. His principal lieutenant and his successor, John Dillon, made even fewer efforts to communicate with Dubliners, although he lived in the city.

The Irish Volunteers provided an ideal organisation around which advanced nationalists and others disenchanted with the Irish Party could coalesce. The fact that it was not a political party facilitated this role. At the same time its opposition to conscription and its objectives of national unity and the replacement of 'Dublin Castle and British military power' with an unspecified form of independent Irish government provided a *de facto* alternative political programme.

Right from the split with Redmond, a high proportion of Dublin Volunteers cleaved to the Provisional Committee. After Gallipoli, when the full scale of the sacrifices required by Britain in the war were understood, there was no question but that weekend soldiering and route marches through the city's streets and its environs were infinitely preferable to the carnage at the front. The Volunteers also provided political education and a forum for debate in a democratic milieu that was inconceivable in the British army, where manifestations of Irish nationality were suspect and the performance of Irish troops frequently denigrated. It is no wonder, given the scant official recognition for the Irish contribution to the war effort, that Dubliners themselves felt little ownership of 'their' regiments as time passed and the ranks were filled increasingly from outside Ireland.

——

The rising forced Dubliners to choose sides, between continuing identification with the British Empire and those fighting British imperialism at home. The performance of the rebels and the military decision to use artillery made even their inveterate enemies acknowledge their courage. It also exposed the real divisions within Dublin, and Ireland as a whole, when members of the Officers' Training Corps at Trinity College and the Dublin Veterans' Corps assisted British troops in retaking the city centre. Irish soldiers serving in British units fighting the rebels had no choice, but in the Trinity OTC and the Veterans' Corps every man was a volunteer, and many took substantial risks in order to participate in the fighting.

In August 1916 swords were presented to OTC officers and souvenir cups to other participants in the defence of the college. The presentations were made by

Sir Maurice Dockrell on behalf of 'the citizens and property owners of Dublin.' Responding, the Provost, John Pentland Mahaffy, recalled that his great-grandfather had received a similar presentation from the citizens 120 years earlier for his role in combating 'Defenderism'. While Mahaffy took pride in his ancestor's achievements, he did so 'with mixed feelings,' because the Defenders of the 1790s corresponded 'to the Sinn Feiners of the present day.' Describing the conflict bluntly as 'a civil war,' he declared:

> I am very sorry indeed to think that the virtues of my family should have been shown not in combating an external enemy but the dangers of home rebellion ... We did not seek this war; we did not seek this quarrel with our fellow-citizens, the thing was thrust upon us suddenly in the twinkling of an eye.

Yet quarrel there now was.

Even without the executions it was inevitable that the restrictions imposed on the civilian population after the rising had been suppressed would alienate Dubliners further from British rule. Even committed unionists, such as Wilmot Irwin, found military rule irksome.

The appalling parsimony of the British government in providing compensation for civilian casualties was a lost opportunity to retrieve ground. The contrast with amounts paid to businesses and property-owners, especially the extremely generous settlement for the official mouthpiece of the Irish Party, the *Freeman's Journal*, spoke eloquently of where priorities lay. Another opportunity to literally repair the political as well as the physical damage done by the rising was lost by the mismanagement of the reconstruction of the city centre. This was an area where the British government should have exercised more, not less, authority, especially when it became clear that neither the corporation nor the property-owners were going to embrace the challenge. Decoupling the compensation payments from the planning process was a fatal error.

The apotheosis of the rising came with the death of Thomas Ashe eighteen months later. Although largely forgotten today, Ashe came to personify the new nationalism in ways that even conservative elements within Irish society could embrace. (How they would have reacted had he lived is another question.) But of all the post-rising leaders of the advanced nationalist cause he was the only one of a calibre to match de Valera or Collins. In many ways he seemed to combine the best qualities of both, and with a more attractive personality than either.

Another forgotten figure is Archbishop William Walsh. He managed to bring the Catholic hierarchy, Sinn Féin, the Irish Volunteers, the Irish Party and Labour together in a common campaign to oppose conscription. In the process he reinforced the bonds between all elements of the Catholic nationalist population and their church, from the working-class communities of Sheriff Street and the Liberties to the middle-class townships of Rathmines and Rathgar. His diplomatic ability in moulding alliances and his capacity to anticipate problems would be sorely missed during the Treaty crisis and the Civil War.

———

All this was happening against the background of constant shortages in the necessities of life, some of which were attributed directly to the military, such as distortions in the fodder market caused by the requirements of cavalry regiments. This in turn affected milk supplies in Dublin. As we have seen, many of these complaints were ill founded. There was no praise for the military, even for its work in feeding the population after the rising or for releasing some of its own potato stock in 1917 to break the grip of profiteering farmers on the market.

It is true that the authorities were much slower to activate price controls on essential items, such as food, in Dublin than in British cities; when they did eventually act it led to charges of interference and discrimination, even when the results were beneficial. The one occasion when the use of its draconian powers by Dublin Castle might have achieved something worth while was during the flu pandemic of 1918; but it was left to Sir Charles Cameron to take what limited measures he could with the totally inadequate resources of the corporation.

———

On 4 February 1919 Mr Justice Moore was presented with white gloves by the county sheriff to signify that there were no criminal cases serious enough for him to hear. He congratulated the sheriff and the grand jury on this state of affairs.[3]

There was never a high incidence of serious crime in early twentieth-century Dublin. Yet the dramatic decline during the First World War may not necessarily reflect an improvement in the 'law and order' environment—possibly quite the opposite. The 1916 Rising had, in the words of the Commissioner of the DMP, 'rendered ordinary police duty an impossibility,' and members of the force appear to have conducted a strategic withdrawal from the city's streets.

Given the low rate of indictable offences in Dublin, this retreat can more readily be seen by looking at the number of arrests and summonses served. The total number of summonses fell from 21,618 in 1912 to 11,867 in 1919; the fall in the number of arrests is even more dramatic, from 13,338 in 1912 to 4,394 in 1919.

Table 19
Arrests and summonses served, 1912–19

	Arrests	Summonses	Total
1912	13,338	21,618	34,956
1913	11,065	17,269	28,334
1914	10,181	16,620	26,801
1915	9,629	18,051	27,680
1916	8,587	12,850	21,437
1917	6,606	12,903	19,509
1918	5,672	12,359	18,031
1919	4,394	11,867	16,261

The decline in the number of assaults on DMP constables and in common assaults would also support the notion of a retreat from the streets, or at least from active law enforcement. After reaching a peak in 1913 during the lock-out, the number of assaults reported, together with attacks on property, theft and public order offences, fell steadily in subsequent years. The more structured forms of protest engaged in by the Irish Volunteers, at least until the rising, appear to have exacted a less serious toll on the DMP than the amorphous disturbances that surrounded the great industrial dispute.

However, the continuing fall in the number of assaults after the rising mirrors that in the number of arrests made and summonses served. This suggests, therefore, that there was some validity in the belief among senior figures of the British administration that the DMP had become too demoralised by 1919 to enforce the King's writ. The scene was being set for a direct conflict between the Volunteers, the military and the future paramilitary formations of the British state. The fact that the latter bore the misnomer of the RIC fooled no-one. They would go down in history and popular memory as the Black and Tans and the Auxiliaries.

Table 20
Assaults, 1912–19

	Assaults on constables	Common assault	Aggravated assault
1912	250	1,285	77
1913	338	1,311	75
1914	185	1,173	67
1915	126	947	52
1916	139	709	40
1917	92	422	13
1918	63	231	8
1919	51	401	6

One of the few unambiguous success stories of the war years in Dublin was the emergence of the allotments movement. It provided badly needed nourishment for the city, and the Irish Plotholders' Union donated produce to the communal kitchens in Liberty Hall during the severe food shortages at the end of the war. By 1919 the area under cultivation had grown to 440 acres and the number of plotholders to three thousand. Like the Irish Volunteer movement, it was an important educational exercise in civics and local democracy as well as meeting more immediate and mundane objectives. By 1919 Dublin Corporation had two thousand applicants on a waiting list for allotments; but, far from expanding, the movement faced the prospect of shrinking acreage as many of the sites on which crops were grown were awaiting funds for housing development.

Another success story was the mass mobilisation of women for war work. Unlike some British cities, there was a sharp class division of duties in Dublin. Working-class women went, by and large, into the factories, while occupations for middle-class recruits included nursing and organising hospital supply depots, running soldiers' clubs, providing meals for the poor and sustaining such voluntary bodies as the NSPCC. If the leading honorary positions in such bodies continued to go to the aristocracy, there was a growing reserve of women with the leadership, organisational and professional skill to provide real benefits to the wider community—as well as the war effort—such as Alice Brunton Henry, quartermaster of the Irish War Hospital Supply Depot. The great majority of these women came from Protestant and unionist upper and middle-class backgrounds. It was the last great flowering of good works by this community before independence.

There were, of course, prominent converts among this group to radical nationalist politics and social reform movements who were prepared to challenge the status quo, such as Constance Markievicz and Louie Bennett, who involved themselves in the advanced nationalist and labour movements, respectively. Markievicz also converted in a literal sense, becoming a Catholic, one of several prominent Protestant women activists to do so. The desire to more fully legitimise their commitment to the cause of independence with fellow-revolutionaries probably played a role in the process, as well as purely spiritual motivations. This is a phenomenon worthy of more study.

Of course many Catholic middle-class women, such as Hanna Sheehy Skeffington, played a similar role in nationalist ranks to that of their Protestant counterparts. As with labour, the national question proved the rock on which the feminist movement foundered. It is one of the reasons why the advent of votes for women in 1918 failed to propel them into leadership positions in either nationalist or unionist ruling circles in significant numbers—although there were important structural obstacles to the advancement of women in society as well.

Many of the obvious changes wrought in Dublin by the war were superficial. If the commercial centre of the city had been gouged out by British artillery shells, it was soon repaired, while within a stone's throw the city's most glaring social problem, its slums, stood intact.

On the other hand, the gathering of the first Dáil in the Mansion House in January 1919 at least showed the willingness of a new generation of political leaders to assert control of the nation's destiny rather than trust to concessions from London. For the first time since the crushing of the lock-out in 1913, militant hope was a viable political commodity on the streets of Dublin, even if it had assumed a greener hue.

NOTES

Chapter 1: First blood (pp 1–25)

1. Bureau of Military History, Witness Statements, ws 1043, Joseph V. Lawless. He subsequently rose to the rank of lieutenant-colonel in the Free State army. Captain Judge appears to have been a naturally argumentative individual, as he subsequently managed to fall out first with the Redmondite faction in the Volunteers and then with republicans, resigning his commission and his place on the Executive in December 1914.

2. The manner in which the guns were spirited away also told a story. The upwardly mobile Kathleen Boland, widow of a Fenian and mother of the future republican leaders Harry and Gerry Boland, hid some of the Howth Mausers in her garden at 15 Marino Crescent while the confrontation with the Crown forces took place a few yards away. Volunteers retrieved them later. Rifles left in the grounds of the ITGWU premises at nearby Croydon Park that day were moved into the union's head office in Liberty Hall and retained for use by the Citizen Army. Fitzpatrick, *Harry Boland's Irish Revolution*, p. 15; Bureau of Military History, Witness Statements, ws 1043, Joseph V. Lawless.

3. Tynan, *The Years of the Shadow*, p. 140–41.

4. The account of the Howth gun-running and subsequent events is based on contemporaneous reports in the *Irish Times*, *Irish Independent* and *Freeman's Journal*, supplemented by Martin, *The Howth Gun-Running and the Kilcoole Gun-Running*.

5. British unions and socialist organisations sent more than £110,000 to help the strikers. The Dublin relief fund set up by the Lord Mayor raised less than £6,500 to help the families of non-unionised workers. See Yeates, *Lockout*.

6. Yeates, *Lockout*.

7. *Irish Independent*, 14 and 15 July 1914; Keane, *Ishbel*, p. 201–9; O'Brien, *Dear, Dirty Dublin*, p. 69.

8. O'Brien, *Dear, Dirty Dublin*, p. 69.

9. Tynan, *The Years of the Shadow*, p. 139.

10. One commentator in 1912 expressed the fear that 'the Irish parliament will be similar in character to the present Dublin Corporation, which is shunned by all decent men and … is an object of contempt to the citizens.' John Moynihan, quoted by Ferriter in *The Transformation of Ireland*, p. 41–2.

11. Yeates, *Lockout*, p. 109.

12. Tenants received only six months' rent to cover the cost of moving.

13. Dublin Corporation Reports, 1916, vol. 1, p. 341–3.

14. O'Brien, *Dear, Dirty Dublin*, chap. 4 and 5; Report of the Departmental Committee into the Housing Conditions of the Working Classes in the City of Dublin, appendix 15; Yeates, *Lockout*, chap. 9.
15. McManus, *Dublin*, p. 23–4.
16. Father Finlay's 1901 quotation is from Pašeta, *Before the Revolution*. The 1914 quotation is from the *Irish Times*, 7 March 1914.
17 Housing Committee, Dublin Corporation Reports, 1914, vol. 3.
18. For a discussion of the falling numbers of Protestants in Dublin during the eighteenth and nineteenth centuries see Hill, *From Patriots to Unionists*, p. 291–5; O'Brien, *Dear, Dirty Dublin*, p. 39–40; Pašeta, *Before the Revolution*, p. 82.
19. Yeates, *Lockout*, p. 440–46.
20. Most of the details on Dublin's Protestant community are taken from Maguire, 'The Church of Ireland and the problem of the Protestant working class of Dublin, 1870s–1930s,' in Ford, McGuire and Milne, *As by Law Established*, Maguire, 'The organisation and activism of Dublin's Protestant working class, 1883–1935,' *Irish Historical Studies*, May 1994, Maguire, 'A socio-economic analysis of the Dublin working class, 1870–1926,' *Irish Economic and Social History*, 20, 1993, and Maguire, 'The Dublin Working Class, 1870s–1930s: Economy, society, politics,' in Bartlett, *History and Environment*.
21. Andrews, *Dublin Made Me*, p. 9–10.
22. Andrews, *Dublin Made Me*, p. 20.
23. The gunfire did not prevent the mob from wrecking the Conservative Working Men's Club premises.
24. Ó Maitiú, *W. and R. Jacob*, p. 17.
25. Geraghty, *William Patrick Partridge and His Times*, p. 15–16; Yeates, *Lockout*, p. 608, n. 6.
26. Goulding was reputedly the richest businessman in Ireland after Lord Iveagh. Ironically, the Belfast shipping magnate Lord Pirrie, a Liberal, threatened to lock out workers if they opposed home rule.
27. Maguire, 'The Church of Ireland and the problem of the Protestant working class of Dublin, 1870s–1930s,' in Ford, McGuire and Milne, *As by Law Established*; Maguire, 'The organisation and activism of Dublin's Protestant working class, 1883–1935,' *Irish Historical Studies*, May 1994; Maguire, 'A socio-economic analysis of the Dublin working class, 1870–1926,' *Irish Economic and Social History*, 20, 1993; Maguire, 'The Dublin Working Class, 1870s–1930s: Economy, society, politics,' in Bartlett, *History and Environment*. See Greaves, *The Life and Times of James Connolly*, p. 22–6, Morrissey, Introduction to McKenna, *The Social Teachings of James Connolly*, p. 14, Newsinger, *Rebel City*, p. 148, and Murray, *Seán O'Casey*, p. 34–5.
28. He was also chairman of the Johnston, Mooney and O'Brien bakery and therefore a major employer in the city.
29. Herbert may also have felt circumscribed in what he could say because he was related by marriage to the general officer commanding the forces in Ireland, Sir Arthur Paget.

30. McDowell, *Crisis and Decline*, p. 33.
31. Up to eighty members of the corps joined the Dublin 'Pals Battalion' shortly after the war broke out. *Dublin Evening Mail*, 14 September 1914.
32. *Irish Times*, 28 January and 1 and 3 April 1914; Dublin Chamber of Commerce, Annual Report, 1914; Yeates, *Lockout*, p. 445, 537–8.
33. Yeates, *Lockout*, p. 423.
34. Nationalist MP for West Belfast and founder of the Ancient Order of Hibernians. See the confidential report on proselytism in the Walsh Papers, Laity File, Dublin Diocesan Archive, for a flavour of the proselytism wars; also Montefiore, *From a Victorian to a Modern*. For a general overview see Yeates, *Lockout*, especially chap. 20–23; *Irish Times*, 26 November 1913.
35. *Irish Times*, 27 and 28 October 1913.
36. Morrissey, *A Man Called Hughes*, p. 14–15; Maume, *D. P. Moran*, p. 19–20; Bolster, *The Knights of St Columbanus*, chap. 1.
37. Morrissey, *William J. Walsh*, chap. 12.
38. Yeates, *Lockout*, p. 85–93.
39. Yeates, *Lockout*, p. 75.
40. Maume, *The Long Gestation*, p. 125; Yeates, *Lockout*, p. 44–5.
41. It is now the head office of the Irish Congress of Trade Unions.
42. Dublin Chamber of Commerce, Annual Report, 1914; *Irish Times*, 28 January 1914 and 19 February 1914; Yeates, *Lockout*, p. 104.
43. Bew, *Ideology and the Irish Question*, p. 16, 47.
44. Yeates, *Lockout*, p. 102–3.
45. Shane Leslie, 'Archbishop Walsh,' in Cruise O'Brien, *The Shaping of Modern Ireland*.
46. O'Malley, *On Another Man's Wound*, p. 23.

Chapter 2: 'The desolating cloudburst of war' (pp 26–49)

1. *Freeman's Journal*, 4 August 1914, *Irish Times*, 4 August 1914, *Irish Independent*, 5 August 1914, *Dublin Evening Mail*, 5 August 1914, and *Irish Times*, 14 August 1914.
2. *Freeman's Journal*, 1 September 1914.
3. Peter Martin, 'Dulce et decorum: Irish nobles and the Great War,' in Gregory and Pašeta, *Ireland and the Great War*, p. 32–3.
4. *Irish Times*, 5 August 1914.
5. Ironically, the British government lifted the ban on the importation of arms into Ireland on 5 August, largely in response to complaints from Unionists that their isolated brethren in the South were vulnerable to attack by armed nationalists.
6. Irish Railway Record Society Archive, GSWR, General Correspondence on Great War, Part 1, file 2314.
7. *Irish Worker*, 22 August 1914; O'Riordan, 'Connolly reassessed'; O'Brien, *Dear, Dirty Dublin*, p. 252.
8. *Dublin Evening Mail*, 17 August 1914.
9. *Dublin Evening Mail*, 17 August 1914; O'Riordan, 'Connolly reassessed.' In 1920 Dublin councillors voted unanimously to restore the now dead Kuno Meyer to the city's roll of freemen.

10. *Irish Times*, 11 August 1914; *Dublin Evening Mail*, 21 August 1914.

11. *Freeman's Journal*, 21 August 1914.

12. The non-residential unemployment assistance.

13. *Irish Times*, 11 August 1914; Dublin Corporation Minutes, 10 August 1914.

14. O'Flanagan, 'Dublin City in an Age of War and Revolution.' The act provided grants of 10 per cent for approved schemes, plus loans repayable at 4½ per cent.

15. O'Flanagan, 'Dublin City in an Age of War and Revolution.'

16. O'Flanagan, 'Dublin City in an Age of War and Revolution.'

17. O'Brien, *Dear, Dirty Dublin*, p. 69.

18. O'Brien, *Dear, Dirty Dublin*, p. 69; McManus, Dublin, p. 46.

19. *Irish Independent*, 13 August 1914.

20. *Irish Independent*, 21 September 1914. Despite their name, the United Irishwomen had no republican overtones. The organisation was sponsored by the liberal unionist Horace Plunkett and was a forerunner of the Irish Countrywomen's Association. Likewise, the Irish Volunteers Aid Association had been set up in the wake of Redmond's pledge to support the war effort and was dominated by moderate nationalists and members of the gentry, including Anglo-Irish peers such as Viscount Gormanston and the Earl of Fingall.

21. See Eileen Reilly, 'Women and voluntary war work,' in Gregory and Pašeta, *Ireland and the Great War*.

22. Eileen Reilly, 'Women and voluntary war work,' in Gregory and Pašeta, *Ireland and the Great War*; Fingall, *Seventy Years Young*, p. 363–4. O'Farrelly won the post against stiff opposition; among the unsuccessful candidates was Patrick Pearse. McCartney, *UCD*, p. 29.

23. Eileen Reilly, 'Women and voluntary war work,' in Gregory and Pašeta, *Ireland and the Great War*.

24. Many of them were placed in workhouses. They do not appear to have stayed long, because of the poor accommodation, and moved to Britain. O'Brien, *Dear, Dirty Dublin*, p. 252; O'Flanagan, 'Dublin City in an Age of War and Revolution,' p. 96.

25. Eileen Reilly, 'Women and voluntary war work,' in Gregory and Pašeta, *Ireland and the Great War*.

26. Eileen Reilly, 'Women and voluntary war work,' in Gregory and Pašeta, *Ireland and the Great War*.

27. *Irish Independent*, 21 September 1914; Keane, *Ishbel*, p. 219–20.

28. Asquith Papers, Bodleian Library, Oxford, ms. 38, f. 236.

29. An indication of Lady Aberdeen's wide range of friends, and poor political judgement, was that among her confidants was Margaret MacNeill, sister of Eoin MacNeill, first chief of staff of the Irish Volunteers.

30. *Irish Independent*, 21 September 1914; 'Redmond's double-refusal to Lord Kitchener,' in Tierney, *Eoin MacNeill*, p. 151.

31. Though a founder-member of the Volunteers and secretary of the organisation, Kettle was a moderate nationalist. His father, Andrew Kettle, had been a leading member of the Land League and a Parnellite; his brother Tom was a former Irish

Party MP, professor of national economics at University College, Dublin, and a leading commentator on public affairs. Kettle himself served in a number of senior posts with Dublin Corporation, including Treasurer and manager of the municipal power station in Ringsend.

32. Martin, *The Irish Volunteers*, p. 152–5.

33. O'Brien, *Dear, Dirty Dublin*, p. 241.

34. O'Flanagan, 'Dublin City in an Age of War and Revolution,' p. 37.

35. Augusteijn, *From Public Defiance to Guerrilla Warfare*, p. 51. He accepts the low figure of 350 from the statements of some former Dublin Volunteers in the Ernie O'Malley papers, while police intelligence figures are noticeably higher. The police had obvious reasons for exaggerating the nature of the threat; but four thousand men joined the Volunteers at the launch in November 1913, long before the movement had Redmond's blessing. Large numbers were also mobilised for the Howth and Kilcoole gun-running, and the indications are that the militants hung on to the rifles. This suggests that there was a substantial appetite for militant nationalism in Dublin. DMP estimates may include Citizen Army and Fianna Éireann members.

36. Dublin Castle Special Branch File, National Archives, CO 904/193/1.

37. Dublin Castle Special Branch File, National Archives, CO 904/193/1.

38. Ashe Papers, mss 46,788, NLI. Ó Lúing, *I Die in a Good Cause*, p. 32.

39. Ó Lúing, *I Die in a Good Cause*, p. 35.

40. Ó Lúing, *I Die in a Good Cause*, p. 56.

41. O'Farrelly wanted to reduce the Coiste Gnótha to 25, but an amendment proposed by Éamon de Valera to reduce it to 30 was accepted. De Valera was perceived as less radical than Ashe, who unsuccessfully proposed increasing the size of the committee to 35.

42. Ó Lúing, *I Die in a Good Cause*, p. 29.

43. *Irish Freedom*, November 1913. Blythe had moved from his native Magheragall, Co. Antrim, to work as a boy clerk in the Department of Justice and was soon immersed in radical nationalism. He was inducted into the IRB and worked for a season on the Ashe family farm in Co. Kerry to learn Irish.

44. Ó Lúing, *I Die in a Good Cause*.

45. Ó Lúing, *I Die in a Good Cause*, p. 41–2.

46. Ó Lúing, *I Die in a Good Cause*, especially chap. 15.

47. Ashe Papers, mss 46,788. The comments were actually made to a Gaelic League meeting in Cork as Ashe was about to depart for America. Ó Lúing, *I Die in a Good Cause*, p. 63.

48. Ashe Papers, mss 46,788/2, NLI. Ó Lúing, *I Die in a Good Cause*, p. 66; Hugh Oram, "An Irishman's Diary," *Irish Times*, 24 February 2005.

49. Ó Lúing, *I Die in a Good Cause*, p. 66; Cathal O'Shannon, *Evening Press*, 15 September 1961.

50. See, for instance, Bureau of Military History, Witness Statements, WS 284, Michael Staines. The venue was the Broadmeadow Estuary, just north of Malahide.

51. Ó Lúing, *I Die in a Good Cause*, p. 72.

52. 20,000 Dublin servicemen would survive to be demobilised in 1918.
53. O'Brien, *Dear, Dirty Dublin*, p. 245. From 1899 to 1913, 12,561 men joined the regular army in the Dublin recruiting area, compared with 8,067 in Belfast. The total recruitment figure for Ireland was 44,975.
54. Daly, *Dublin*, p. 102–7; O'Brien, *Dear, Dirty Dublin*, p. 199–210.
55. Yeates, *Lockout*, Prologue, xxii. *Irish Times*, 7 March 1914. *Dublin Evening Post*, 14 September 1914. Not only did dockers earn a bonanza in overtime in August 1914, but ITGWU records suggest that many men blacklisted during the lockout were re-employed on a temporary basis. Ms 3097, NLI.
56. Dooley, *Irishmen or English Soldiers?*, Introduction.
57. *Dublin Evening Mail*, 8 August 1914; Strachan, *The First World War*, vol. 1, p. 160.
58. The chief medical officer for Dublin, Sir Charles Cameron, attributed the 'Pals' soubriquet to the Dublin music-hall entertainer Alfred 'the Great' Vance, whose song 'He's a Pal o' Mine' was a great favourite with Dublin audiences. In fact several wartime battalions in Britain had already been given this nickname. Cameron, whose father and sons served as officers in the British army, believed Vance's 'song clung to public memory' and was adopted by 'the heroic 7th Battalion of the Royal Dublin Fusiliers ... How little Dublin thought when it chanted and whistled that song which Vance sung many years ago, at the Rotunda, that the name of "The Pals" was destined to thus live in the fighting record of our island story.' Cameron Papers.
59. Findlater, *Findlater's*, p. 252.
60. *Dublin Evening Mail*, 18 August 1914; Orr, *Field of Bones*, p. 25.
61. *Dublin Evening Mail*, 25 and 28 September 1914.
62. Novick, *Conceiving Revolution*, 84.
63. Hart, *The IRA at War*, p. 118–9.
64. Some 7 per cent of the population of the city joined up, compared with 2 per cent of the county. O'Flanagan, 'Dublin City in an Age of War and Revolution,' p. 44–5 and appendix 3. Dublin's recruitment level was exceeded only by Belfast and Derry. Dooley, *Irishmen or English Soldiers?*, p. 7.
65. Reservists were paid between 3s 6d and 7s a week and were liable for annual training camps as well as military duty for up to twelve years after being discharged.
66. See, for example, the case of Francis Fitzpatrick of the Paving Department, whose half pay was stopped in mid-1915 on the grounds that his family were not enduring any hardship. Dublin Corporation Minutes, 1915, p. 13; Dublin Corporation Reports, 1915, vol. 2, p. 279, 378.
67. Arthur Guinness, Commemorative Roll. The figure for officers includes a small number of cadets and warrant officers. Murray, 'The First World War and a Dublin distillery workforce.'
68. Irish Railway Record Society Archive, European War, General Correspondence, Part 1, file 2314; *Irish Times*, 18 February 1915.
69. Irish Railway Record Society Archive, European War, Recruitment, file 2600.
70. Dublin Corporation Reports, 1916, vol. 1, Report no. 67.
71. Daly, *Dublin*, p. 109–11; O'Flanagan, 'Dublin City in an Age of War and Revolution,' p. 36, 52.

72. O'Flanagan, 'Dublin City in an Age of War and Revolution,' p. 44–5.
73. Emmet Dalton served as an officer in the Royal Dublin Fusiliers during the First World War and was awarded the Military Cross. His younger brother Charlie joined the Irish Volunteers after the Easter Rising and became a member of the GHQ Intelligence Department. Sergeant William Malone was a reservist in the Royal Dublin Fusiliers and was killed at Mouse Trap Farm on 24 May 1915. A year later his brother Michael Malone, a lieutenant in the Irish Volunteers, was shot by British soldiers while defending Mount Street Bridge during the rising.
74. Andrews, *Dublin Made Me*, p. 44.
75. Irwin, *Betrayal in Ireland*, p. 8, 10, 17. The Irwins had a long association with the British army. The author's grandfather had been an NCO in the East Yorkshire Regiment and his brother served as an officer in the First World War. The maid, Rosie, was married 'out of the house' to a soldier as she was an orphan.

Chapter 3: 'Blood, horror, shrieks and groans' (pp 50–68)

1. O'Flanagan, 'Dublin City in an Age of War and Revolution,' p. 9.
2. Strachan, *The First World War*, p. 867–8.
3. Guinness managed to mitigate some of the worst aspects of the duty later in the war by reducing the specific gravity and thus the alcoholic strength of its stout. Dennison and MacDonagh, *Guinness*, p. 158–9.
4. *Freeman's Journal* and *Irish Times*, 30 April 1915; *Irish Independent*, 1 May 1915.
5. *Irish Independent*, 3 May 1915.
6. *Cork Free Press*, 1 May 1915, quoted in the *Irish Independent* of 1 May 1915.
7. O'Flanagan, 'Dublin City in an Age of War and Revolution,' p. 14–15; Murray, 'The First World War and a Dublin distillery workforce'; *Saothar*, 15, 1990.
8. Cody et al., *The Parliament of Labour*, p. 111.
9. Clarkson, *Labour and Nationalism in Ireland*, p. 253.
10. Yeates, *Lockout*, p. 282–3, 286.
11. Connolly, *Workers' Republic*, 12 June 1915.
12. Manifesto to the Electors of College Green, reprinted in the *Workers' Republic*.
13. Cody et al., *The Parliament of Labour*, p. 112.
14. *Irish Independent*, 12 and 14 June 1915; Mitchell, *Labour in Irish Politics*, p. 63–6; Cody et al., *The Parliament of Labour*, p. 111–13; O'Brien, *Forth the Banners Go*, p. 262–4.
15. *Dublin Evening Mail*, 15 September 1914.
16. Johnstone, *Orange, Green and Khaki*, p. 75–9; *Irish Independent*, 27 April 1915.
17. Johnstone, *Orange, Green and Khaki*, p. 75–9.
18. Dublin Corporation Minutes, 1915, p. 248.
19. Dublin Corporation Minutes, 1915, p. 410–15; Yeates, *Lockout*, p. 506–7.
20. *Irish Independent*, 21 July 1915.
21. Dublin Corporation Minutes, 1915, p. 416–17.
22. Johnston, *Home or Away*, p. 80. Mahon resumed command of the division shortly afterwards for its Balkan campaign.
23. Orr, *Field of Bones*, p. 123–32.

24. *Irish Independent*, 19 August 1915.
25. 'The Dubsters' was the title given, only half-jokingly, to an amalgamated battalion of Royal Munster Fusiliers and Royal Dublin Fusiliers at Gallipoli after their losses became too heavy to sustain separate units.
26. *Irish Independent*, 25 August 1915.
27. *Irish Independent*, 27 August 1915.
28. *Irish Independent*, 27 August 1915.
29. *Irish Independent*, 27 August 1915.
30. Dickinson, *The Dublin of Yesterday*, p. 69.
31. Dickinson, *The Dublin of Yesterday*, p. 71.
32. *Irish Independent*, 28 August 1915.
33. The first letter of condolence Cameron received was from the Catholic parish priest at Haddington Road church, indicating the strong cross-community support that still existed at this time for the war and the sense of mutual loss. Cameron Papers.
34. Tom Kettle, a former Irish Party MP and professor of national economics at University College, Dublin, had joined the British army in 1914 and was serving as a recruiting officer in 1915.
35. *Freeman's Journal*, 10 September 1915.
36. *Irish Independent*, 9 August 1915.
37. O'Brien, *Forth the Banners Go*, p. 264.
38. *Irish Worker*, 8 August 1914.
39. *Irish Independent*, 16 and 17 September 1915.
40. Maume, *The Long Gestation*, p. 223.
41. *Irish Worker*, 17 January 1914.
42. See above.
43. *Irish Independent*, 30 September to 2 October 1915. The Pillar survived the 1916 Rising only to fall prey to the fast-food restaurant plague that engulfed Dublin's premier street in more recent times. Bullet holes can still be seen below the McDonald's sign.
44. Tynan, *The Years of the Shadow*, p. 178.
45. *Irish Times*, 4 September 1915.
46. Orr, *Field of Bones*, p. 22.
47. The Belfast recruitment area included Cos. Antrim and Down. The Dublin recruitment area consisted of the city and county.
48. Murray, *Seán O'Casey*, p. 93.
49. Dublin Corporation Reports, 1915, vol. 1, p. 351–2.
50. Dublin Corporation Reports, vol. 2, p. 115–18.
51. Dublin Corporation Reports, vol. 1, p. 319, 916.
52. Dublin Corporation Minutes, 1915, p. 287, 311.
53. Dublin Corporation Reports, 1915, vol. 1, p. 975. The amounts paid in allowances for employees who joined the British army are not given separately but cannot have been large. See chap. 2 above.
54. O'Flanagan, 'Dublin City in an Age of War and Revolution,' p. 23.

55. *Irish Independent*, 28 September 1915.
56. *Irish Times and Irish Independent*, 24 to 30 September 1915; O'Flanagan, 'Dublin City in an Age of War and Revolution,' p. 23.
57. *Freeman's Journal*, 23 September 1915.
58. *Evening Standard*, 23 September 1915.
59. *Irish Independent*, 8 August 1915.
60. *Irish Independent*, 4 October 1915.
61. O'Flanagan, 'Dublin City in an Age of War and Revolution,' p. 125.

Chapter 4: 'Without the shedding of Blood' (pp 69–89)
1. Novick, *Conceiving Revolution*, p. 36.
2. Novick, *Conceiving Revolution*, p. 48; *Irish Independent* circulation figures for 1913 to 1915.
3. Greaves, *The Life and Times of James Connolly*, p. 297–8.
4. O'Riordan, 'Michael O'Leary, Kuno Meyer and Peadar Ó Laoghaire.' Ben Novick, in *Conceiving Revolution*, argues that the ability of anti-war propaganda to strike a deeper resonance with its audience than the more numerous and technically better-produced pro-British propaganda was an important factor in their success.
5. *Irish Independent*, 10 June 1915.
6. Ward, *Hanna Sheehy Skeffington*, p. 140–42. His father-in-law was David Sheehy. Tom Kettle was his brother-in-law; another brother-in-law, Francis Cruise O'Brien, was a prominent journalist in Dublin.
7. *Irish Independent*, 25 September 1914.
8. Valiulis, *Portrait of a Revolutionary*, p. 10–12.
9. Ó Lúing, *I Die in a Good Cause*, p. 35–6.
10. Valiulis, *Portrait of a Revolutionary*, p. 10–12.
11. Yeates, *Lockout*, p. 439. The fact that his father, Andrew Kettle, had been a leading figure in the Land League in the 1880s cut no ice with the Citizen Army men.
12. Newsinger, *Rebel City*, p. 120. Colonel Moore would adhere to the Redmondite Volunteers at the split but later joined the post-1916 independence movement. He would serve in the Free State Senate, become a founder-member of Fianna Fáil, and campaign against land annuities. He was a brother of the novelist George Moore.
13. Newsinger, *Rebel City*, p. 117–18. There was almost a social cachet to being in the Citizen Army. Its women members included Constance Markievicz, Dr Kathleen Lynn, her companion Madeleine ffrench-Mullen, the Abbey actor Helena Molony, and Nellie Gifford, whose sisters Grace and Muriel married the 1916 signatories Joseph Plunkett and Thomas MacDonagh, respectively. It also reflected the fact that, unlike the Volunteers, the Citizen Army admitted women to full membership.
14. *Irish Worker*, 3 October 1914.
15. Yeates, *Lockout*, chap. 41.
16. Ó Cathasaigh, *The Story of the Irish Citizen Army*, p. 52.

17. *Irish Independent*, 2 August 1915.

18. Dudley Edwards, *Patrick Pearse*, p. 235.

19. Pearse, *Political Writings and Speeches*, p. 137.

20. McGarry, *The Rising*, p. 92.

21. Quoted by Newsinger, *Rebel City*, p. 125.

22. *Workers' Republic*, 5 February 1916.

23. *Irish Independent*, 14 August 1915.

24. *Irish Independent*, 18 September 1915.

25. Ireland's Memorial Records. This compared with an average fatality rate for Ireland of 23 per cent. However, these figures are not directly comparable. For instance, they do not take account of reservists recalled on the outbreak of war, or recruits from Britain allocated to Irish regiments. Another factor affecting the figures is the lack of details on Irishmen who enlisted in the navy or air force.

26. Robbins, *Under the Starry Plough*, p. 45–53; Irwin, *Betrayal in Ireland*, p. 17–18; Valiulis, *Portrait of a Revolutionary*, p. 10–12.

27. Ben Novick, 'Gun running and the Great War,' in Gregory and Pašeta, *Ireland and the Great War*, p. 104–7. The Martini rifles would have been considered obsolescent but would have been at least as effective as the Mausers landed at Howth the previous year. The identification of E Company as the culprits is in *Frank Henderson's Easter Rising*, p. 35. Henderson is generally regarded as extremely reliable. The company commander was Captain Patrick Weafer, a native of Enniscorthy who was killed in action in the Imperial Hotel during the rising. O'Farrell, *Who's Who in the Irish War of Independence*.

28. Connolly to Peter Keeley, 25 February 1915, in Connolly, *Between Comrades*, p. 526; Woggon, 'Not merely a labour organisation.'

29. Theresa Moriarty, 'Work, warfare and wages: Industrial controls and Irish trade unionism in the First World War,' in Gregory and Pašeta, *Ireland and the Great War*, p. 73; Greaves, *The Life and Times of James Connolly*, p. 318. Former soldiers were liable for service for up to twelve years after their term of enlistment ended. Connolly's almost pathological hatred of the British army is one of the unexplored mysteries of his life.

30. Woggon, 'Not merely a labour organisation.'

31. Watson's stockbroker brother George was a spokesman for the Unionist business interests in Dublin and a strong critic of home rule, which added to the political undertones in the dispute.

32. Woggon, 'Not merely a labour organisation,' p. 45–9.

33. *Irish Independent*, 30 June 1916. In June 1916 William O'Brien had been allowed to travel under guard from Fron Goch, where he was detained after the Easter Rising, to London to attend an earlier unsuccessful mediation hearing into the dispute. Morrissey, *William O'Brien*, p. 108. The company faced another major dispute with the National Seamen's and Firemen's Union and the ITGWU in November 1916 when seamen, firemen, waggoners and other non-dockers secured 40s for a 60-hour week from Sir George Askwith. *Labour Gazette*, December 1916.

34. *Irish Independent*, 3 April 1916.
35. *Irish Independent*, 31 May 1916.
36. *Irish Times*, 14 and 31 May and 10 June 1916.
37. Wolfe, *Labour Supply and Regulation*, p. 99–147.
38. Theresa Moriarty, 'Work, warfare and wages: Industrial controls and Irish trade unionism in the First World War,' in Gregory and Pašeta, *Ireland and the Great War*, p. 79.
39. Morrissey, *William O'Brien*, p. 94.
40. Novick, *Conceiving Revolution*, p. 176. Redmond had latched on to an apocryphal report of a German officer captured with a map of Ireland, so detailed that it showed 'every farm in every parish.' The *Gael* was quick to point out that a map with so much detail would have to be at least at the scale of six inches to the mile and so would measure 150 feet by 80 feet, and it suggested that the Germans had disguised it as a groundsheet for two hundred men. That Redmond could be ridiculed so savagely showed that his stock was falling. Robbins, *Under the Starry Plough*, p. 62. Connolly was convinced that the real target of the raid was the union's own printing press.
41. See Kevin Nowlan, 'Tom Clarke, MacDermott and the IRB,' in Martin, *Leaders and Men of the Easter Rising*, p. 113; Ó Broin, *Revolutionary Underground*, chap. 9; Morrissey, *William O'Brien*, p. 134–8; Cody, *The Remarkable Patrick Daly*.
42. Dublin Corporation Reports, 1916, vol. 1, p. 52–3.
43. Light labouring jobs, such as night watchman, were often given to ex-soldiers invalided out or to older workers no longer fit for heavier duties.
44. Dublin Corporation Minutes, 24 January 1916, p. 127–9.
45. Dublin Corporation Minutes, 6 and 14 March 1916, p. 138, 149–158; Dublin Corporation Reports, 1916, vol. 1, p. 243–4. For the first time the war bonus was secured for most, but not all, of the non-permanent corporation workers.
46. Like other major housing projects, the Sheriff Street slum clearance proved politically and financially impossible before the advent of the Irish Free State.
47. Dublin Corporation Minutes, 6 March 1916, p. 145–6.
48. Dublin Corporation Minutes, 14 March 1916, p. 154. Further evidence of the softening of the constitutional nationalists towards the Volunteers came on 30 March 1916 when Alderman Patrick Corrigan, a UIL stalwart and slum landlord indicted in the 1914 Housing Commission report, presided at a public meeting in the Mansion House to protest at the deportation of Irish Volunteer organisers to Britain for making seditious speeches. Carden, *The Alderman*, p. 97.
49. *Irish Times* and *Irish Independent*, 18 March 1916. No provision seems to have been made for meeting the religious obligations of non-Catholics.
50. *Irish Times* and *Irish Independent*, 18 March 1916; Henderson, *Frank Henderson's Easter Rising*; Ó Lúing, *I Die in a Good Cause*, p. 75.
51. *Irish Times*, 18 March 1916.
52. *Irish Independent*, 18 March 1916; letter from Private Thomas Finn, C Company, 2nd Battalion, Royal Dublin Fusiliers, to Monica Roberts, 23 March 1916, Roberts Collection, vol. 2.

53. *Irish Times*, 13 February 1918; Roberts Collection, introduction.

54. See, for instance, correspondence from Sergeant Brooks, Private Kirwin (or Kirwan) and Private J. O'Halloran to Monica Roberts, Roberts Collection, vol. 2.

55. Monica Roberts to Private J. May, 10 July 1915, Roberts Collection, vol. 2.

56. Sergeant Brooks to Monica Roberts, December 1915, Roberts Collection, vol. 2.

57. Sergeant Brooks to Monica Roberts, 29 October 1915, Roberts Collection, vol. 2.

58. Private Edward Mordaunt, B Company, 2nd Battalion, Royal Dublin Fusiliers, to Monica Roberts, 18 July 1915, Roberts Collection, vol. 1.

59. Private Edward Mordaunt, B Company, 2nd Battalion, Royal Dublin Fusiliers, to Monica Roberts, 28 August 1915, Roberts Collection, vol. 1.

60. Private Joseph Clarke, 7th Platoon, B Company, 2nd Battalion, Royal Dublin Fusiliers, to Monica Roberts, 22 April 1916, Roberts Collection, vol. 1.

61. Private Edward Mordaunt, B Company, 2nd Battalion, Royal Dublin Fusiliers, to Monica Roberts, 28 August 1915, Roberts Collection, vol. 1.

62. Private Edward Mordaunt, B Company, 2nd Battalion, Royal Dublin Fusiliers, to Monica Roberts, 7 and 17 December 1915 and 25 January 1916, Roberts Collection, vol. 1.

63. Private Harry Loughlin, 20 August 1915, to Monica Roberts, Roberts Collection, vol. 1. By the end of the year he was in hospital at Alexandria with shrapnel wounds to his right hand and left leg.

64. Private Thomas Finn, 8 April 1916, and Sergeant Edward Heafey, 14 April 1916, to Monica Roberts, Roberts Collection, vol. 2.

65. *Irish Times*, 18 March 1916; Plunkett Dillon, *All in the Blood*, p. 169.

66. The *Irish Times* had begun publishing lists of past and present students of TCD and UCD who had served in the Crown forces. On St Patrick's Day eighty-six names were published; many of those mentioned had died or been seriously wounded and invalided out.

67. Robinson, *Memories*, p. 232.

68. Novick, *Conceiving Revolution*, p. 66.

69. Foy and Barton, *The Easter Rising*, p. 20–23; Ó Lúing, *I Die in a Good Cause*, p. 75.

70. Richard Mulcahy, television interview, 2 February 1966, quoted by Valiulis, *Portrait of a Revolutionary*, p. 6.

71. Valiulis, *Portrait of a Revolutionary*, p. 8–12.

72. Bureau of Military History, Witness Statements, WS 819, Liam Archer.

73. Bureau of Military History, Witness Statements, WS 284, Michael Staines.

74. James Connolly, 'Physical force in Irish politics', in *Socialism and Nationalism*, p. 53–7.

75. Plunkett Dillon, *All in the Blood*, p. 197–9; Robbins, *Under the Starry Plough*, p. 70–73.

76. Ó Lúing, *I Die in a Good Cause*, p. 77; Bureau of Military History, Witness Statements, WS 251, Richard Balfe.

77. Moran, *Staging the Easter Rising*, p. 15.

Chapter 5: 'A scene of greater splendour ... never before witnessed' (pp 90–114)

1. Smith passed the information to the IRB Military Council through the writer Liam O'Flaherty, a member of the Volunteers. It is generally accepted that the author of the forgery was Joseph Plunkett.

2. Carden, *The Alderman*, p. 97–9; *Irish Independent*, 20 April 1916. In contrast, the liberal unionist *Irish Times* omitted any reference to Kelly's speech in its report of the corporation's proceedings that day, as did the official minutes of the meeting.

3. The great majority of members of the IRB and of the Irish Volunteers knew nothing about the rising, and some leading members of both who did know were opposed to the project. Like MacNeill, they believed that armed resistance was justified, or likely to succeed, only if it was in response to attempts to introduce conscription.

4. Lynch had only been informed shortly beforehand, by Seán Mac Diarmada, a member of the Military Council and one of the prime movers in the rising.

5. Estimates of the number vary. Ó Lúing, *I Die in a Good Cause*, p. 76–9, says twenty to thirty; McGarry, *The Rising*, p. 235, says sixty. Ó Lúing spoke to participants, while McGarry uses witness statements from the Bureau of Military History.

6. Ó Lúing, *I Die in a Good Cause*, p. 91.

7. Robbins, *Under the Starry Plough*, p. 78; Bureau of Military History, Witness Statements, ws 1043, Joseph V. Lawless.

8. Henderson, *Frank Henderson's Easter Rising*, p. 33–5.

9. Robbins, *Under the Starry Plough*, p. 63–73; Bureau of Military History, Witness Statements, ws 819, Liam Archer.

10. When the British captured Liberty Hall they were puzzled to find that only the type for the second half of the Proclamation could be found. The reason was that lack of type meant that the top half had to be printed first and then the same type used again for the bottom half, though Brady's skill as a compositor made the document appear seamless. Devine and O'Riordan, *James Connolly, Liberty Hall and the 1916 Rising*, p. 43–7.

11. Murray, *Seán O'Casey*, p. 88. There was apparently one signatory of the Proclamation who was most reluctant to sign a document giving equality to women, but his identity remains a secret. It was not, however, Clarke himself: the old Fenian seems to have been infected by the general social radicalism of the city during his sojourn there. Clarke, *Revolutionary Woman*, p. 69.

12. Caulfield, *The Easter Rebellion*, p. 113–15.

13. *Irish Times*, 25 April 1916.

14. *Irish Times*, 25 April 1916.

15. Irwin, *Betrayal in Ireland*, p. 20–22.

16. She was the first of twenty-eight children (aged between two and sixteen) to be shot dead during the rising. Matthews, *Renegades*, p. 145–6.

17. Orr, *Field of Bones*, p. 195; *1916 Rebellion Handbook*, p. 56. The obituary of Browning in the *Irish Times* of 2 May 1916 devotes most space to his prowess as a

cricketer: 'no more brilliant exponent of the game has ever done duty for Dublin University, of which he was a graduate.'

18. Bureau of Military History, Witness Statements, ws 251, Richard Balfe.
19. Caulfield, *The Easter Rebellion*, p. 85–8.
20. Morrissey, *William O'Brien*, p. 99.
21. O'Casey, *Drums Under the Windows*, p. 272.
22. McGarry, *The Rising*, p. 146.
23. O'Brien, *Dear, Dirty Dublin*, p. 260; *Irish Times*, 7 August 1916; DMP Statistical Returns, 1919.
24. Stephens, *The Insurrection in Dublin*, p. 19–21; Foy and Barton, *The Easter Rising*, p. 59; DMP Report for 1916, 1919.
25. The headquarters of de Valera's battalion is usually given as Boland's Mills, which dominated the Grand Canal Docks and Ringsend Bridge; in fact it was the less imposing Boland's Bakery in Grand Canal Street.
26. Irwin, *Betrayal in Ireland*, p. 25–6.
27. Cottrell, *The War for Ireland*, p. 57, 62.
28. Townshend, *Easter 1916*, p. 189; Bureau of Military History, Witness Statements, ws 198, James Walsh.
29. *Catholic Bulletin*, December 1917, quoted by Foy and Barton, *The Easter Rising*, p. 80–81.
30. O'Brien, *Blood on the Streets*, p. 64–5.
31. *1916 Rebellion Handbook*, p. 280–81.
32. O'Brien, *Blood on the Streets*, p. 57–8; Foy and Barton, *The Easter Rising*, p. 78–9. Medical personnel from Sir Patrick Dun's Hospital continued to treat wounded soldiers, as well as circumstances permitted, throughout the rest of the fighting.
33. Townshend, *Easter 1916*, p. 181–4. Marlborough Barracks is now McKee Barracks; Richmond Barracks, Inchicore (later Keogh Barracks, later Keogh Square), was demolished in 1969 to make way for St Michael's Estate; the Royal Barracks became Collins Barracks (now part of the National Museum); Portobello Barracks is now Cathal Brugha Barracks.
34. Irish Railway Record Society Archive, GSWR, Sinn Féin Rebellion, file 2659.
35. Townshend, *Easter 1916*, p. 184.
36. Foy and Barton, *The Easter Rising*, p. 97–103; Caulfield, *The Easter Rebellion*, p. 76–9, 287–90.
37. Bureau of Military History, Witness Statements, ws 251, Richard Balfe; Caulfield, *The Easter Rebellion*, p. 215–19.
38. Foy and Barton, *The Easter Rising*, p. 117. Up to four hundred civilians found refuge there, mainly women and children.
39. One of the bakers who remained at work was among the civilians killed in the area.
40. Foy and Barton, *The Easter Rising*, p. 117.
41. Bureau of Military History, Witness Statements, ws 819, Liam Archer.
42. In contrast, the British army put a machine gun post on the roof of Jervis Street Hospital to strafe the GPO garrison.

43. Bureau of Military History, Witness Statements, ws 819, Liam Archer.

44. The original vehicles were imported in 1913 to combat mass pickets on the docks during the lock-out.

45. *1916 Rebellion Handbook*, p. 50–51, 269; Foy and Barton, *The Easter Rising*, p. 120, 189.

46. The officer commanding the Dublin University Officers' Training Corps, Major Harris, was conducting the field day with the Dublin Veterans' Corps in Kingstown when the rising began. He took the main contingent safely back to Beggars' Bush Barracks, while F. H. Browning led a smaller contingent towards the city—possibly against orders—with fatal consequences. *Irish Times*, 5 May 1916 and 7 August 1916. Many members of the OTC who had gone home for the Easter break reported for duty to the nearest military post. *1916 Rebellion Handbook*, p. 15–16; Dooney, 'Trinity College and the War.'

47. According to some accounts he was shot straight through the heart. Either way death appears to have been instantaneous.

48. Lyons, *The Enigma of Tom Kettle*, p. 293.

49. O'Brien, *Blood on the Streets*, p. 67–8. Among the clergymen was Father Thomas McNevin from Westland Row, who had gained some notoriety in the 1913 Lock-out as a prosecution witness against Dora Montefiore and Lucille Rand for 'kidnapping' strikers' children. Bureau of Military History, Witness Statements, ws 310, James Grace.

50. Caulfield, *The Easter Rebellion*, p. 124. Brosnan was on leave with his family in Dublin when the rising occurred. He immediately went to offer his services to the army. He disarmed a rebel outside Dublin Castle but was still wearing civilian clothes and so was mistaken for a rebel and shot. Several British soldiers with Irish regiments were also killed or injured.

51. *1916 Rebellion Handbook*, p. 49–53.

52. Foy and Barton, *The Easter Rising*, p. 187.

53. Foy and Barton, *The Easter Rising*, p. 184.

54. John J. Reynolds, 'The Four Courts and North King Street area in 1916,' *An tÓglach*, 15 and 29 May 1926, quoted by Foy and Barton, *The Easter Rising*, p. 116.

55. Foy and Barton, *The Easter Rising*, p. 209.

56. *1916 Rebellion Handbook*, p. 232–45; Geraghty and Whitehead, *The Dublin Fire Brigade*, p. 148.

57. *1916 Rebellion Handbook*, p. 280–81.

58. *1916 Rebellion Handbook*, p. 232–45.

59. *1916 Rebellion Handbook*, p. 232–45.

60. One of Father Eugene Sheehy's altar boys in Bruree had been Éamon de Valera, later commandant of the 3rd Battalion, holding the south-east quadrant of the city, who owed much of his early political as well as religious formation to the priest.

61. Ward, *Hanna Sheehy Skeffington*, p. 155.

62. Ward, *Hanna Sheehy Skeffington*, p. 155; Levenson and Natterstad, *Hanna Sheehy Skeffington*, p. 78.

63. *1916 Rebellion Handbook*; Shooting of Three Men in Portobello Barracks, Royal Commission of Inquiry, p. 215.

64. Shooting of Three Men in Portobello Barracks, Royal Commission of Inquiry, p. 215.

Chapter 6: 'These Sinn Feiners are a lot of murderers' (pp 115–26)

1. Yeates, *Lockout*, p. 577.
2. Irwin, *Betrayal in Ireland*, p. 32–4.
3. Letter to Monica Roberts, 14 June 1916, Roberts Collection. Of course soldiers who felt differently would hardly have confided such seditious thoughts to Monica Roberts.
4. Letter to Monica Roberts, 18 July 1917, Roberts Collection.
5. William de Comb to Monica Roberts, 25 July 1917, Roberts Collection.
6. Irwin, *Betrayal in Ireland*, p. 35.
7. Dalton, *With the Dublin Brigade*, p. 40–43.
8. O'Brien, *Dear, Dirty Dublin*, p. 269.
9. *Irish Independent*, 4 May 1916; O'Brien, *Dear, Dirty Dublin*, p. 263.
10. *Irish Independent*, 4 May 1916.
11. *Irish Times*, 11 May 1916.
12. Foy and Barton, *The Easter Rising*, p. 117; *Irish Independent* and *Irish Times*, 4 May 1916.
13. *Irish Times*, 15 May 1916.
14. Foy and Barton, *The Easter Rising*, p. 206.
15. Murphy always denied any prior knowledge of the editorial.
16. *Irish Times*, 5 May 1916.
17. Dangerfield, *The Damnable Question*, p. 213–17.
18. *Irish Independent* and *Irish Times*, 7 July 1916.
19. Dublin Corporation Minutes, 5 June 1916.
20. Geraghty and Whitehead, *The Dublin Fire Brigade*, p. 148; Foy and Barton, *The Easter Rising*, p. 210.
21. *Irish Times*, 15 June 1916.
22. When Arthur Lynch, MP for Clare, raised in the House of Commons the issue of compensation for wrongful imprisonment on behalf of one prominent Dubliner, Arthur Griffith, who was 'head of a lawful political association,' namely Sinn Féin, Griffith wrote an angry letter to the papers from Reading Prison denouncing Lynch's 'reprehensible' conduct. 'Your questions I regard as an insult in their suggestion that I dissociate myself in any way from the actions of my brother Irishmen now dead or in prison.'
23. Report of the Dublin Metropolitan Police for 1916, Parliamentary Papers, 1919; *Irish Independent*, 25 May, 4 August and 8 August 1916 and 24 March and 8 April 1917. The rate was reduced by 1s 6d to 10s 11d in the pound north of the Liffey and 10s 2d on the south side.
24. McManus, *Dublin*, p. 68–74; Finnan, *John Redmond and Irish Unity*, p. 152–3.
25. McManus, *Dublin*, p. 68–75; O'Brien, *Dear, Dirty Dublin*, p. 271–4; O'Flanagan, 'Dublin City in an Age of War and Revolution'; Dublin Metropolitan Police Report for 1916, Parliamentary Papers, 1919.

26.   Bureau of Military History, Witness Statements, ws 268, W. T. Cosgrave.
27.   Dublin Corporation Minutes, 10 May 1916; *Irish Times*, 11 May 1916.

Chapter 7: The 'calamity of rebellion' (pp 127–43)
1.   Cosgrave's motion remained on the order paper even though he was in prison.
2.   Dublin Corporation Minutes, 7 August 1916. The ETU comparators were craftsmen in the corporation's Stanley Street workshop.
3.   Jeffrey, *Ireland and the Great War*, p. 39; Fingall, *Seventy Years Young*, p. 348. Nor did Kitchener receive any credit for ordering the court-martial of Bowen-Colthurst for the murder of Francis Sheehy Skeffington, which began the day beforehand: that went to Major Vane.
4.   *Irish Times*, 12 June 1916.
5.   Dublin Corporation Minutes, 5 and 19 June 1916. The unsuccessful Unionist nominee was W. E. Taylor, a wholesale printer and stationer.
6.   Dangerfield, *The Damnable Question*, p. 195. Though committed to Broadmoor Criminal Lunatic Asylum in Berkshire, Bowen-Colthurst was released after twenty months and emigrated to Canada on a military pension.
7.   *Irish Times*, 13 and 16 May 1916; Dublin Corporation Minutes, 2 August 1916; Foy and Barton, *The Easter Rising*, p. 188.
8.   Dillon represented Mayo in the House of Commons.
9.   Lyons, *John Dillon*, p. 372–83.
10.   *Irish Independent*, 22 May 1916.
11.   *Irish Times*, 8 June 1915; Dublin Corporation Minutes, 3 July 1916.
12.   Dublin Corporation Minutes, 7 August 1916.
13.   O'Flanagan, 'Dublin City in an Age of War and Revolution,' p. 26.
14.   Allan was a former senior figure in the IRB who resigned all positions in the organisation in 1910 after serious policy differences with Tom Clarke; nevertheless he remained committed to old comrades in the organisation. John MacBride, later executed for his role in the Easter Rising, stayed in Allan's house on the night before the rising began. Allan later worked for Michael Collins, and his position in the corporation provided the latter with invaluable contacts and information.
15.   Dublin Corporation Minutes, 7 August 1916; *Irish Times*, 4 December 1917; *Irish Times*, 25 February 1919.
16.   O'Flanagan, 'Dublin City in an Age of War and Revolution,' p. 15.
17.   *Irish Times*, 7 July 1917.
18.   *Irish Times*, 27 October 1915.
19.   Dublin Corporation Reports, 1917, no. 202; O'Flanagan, 'Dublin City in an Age of War and Revolution,' p. 25.
20.   *Irish Times*, 1 February 1915 and 8 May 1915. In fact sailing under false colours became the rule, with German submarines flying Royal Navy ensigns when approaching potential victims and British 'Q ships' flying the colours of neutral countries as they hunted German submarines, leading to the notorious *Baralong* incident in August 1915, when a Q ship of that name, flying American colours, sank a German submarine and then shot all the survivors. *Irish Times*, 19 August 1915.

21. The *Irish Times*, 2 November 1917, cited the examples of a six-year-old vessel with a premium of £54,000, compared with £39,800 in 1914, and a fourteen-year-old vessel on which the premium had risen from £27,000 to £44,500.

22. The Dublin Corporation Electricity Supplies Committee, which was also battling with higher fuel prices, could increase prices for consumers or seek subsidies from the city. See chap. 2 above.

23. Dublin Corporation Minutes, 2 October 1916.

24. *Irish Independent*, 9 January 1917.

25. *Irish Times*, 26 October 1917

26. *Irish Times*, 26 March 1918, and *Irish Independent*, 26 March 1918.

27. Dublin Corporation Minutes, 7 August 1916. The corporation's representatives on the Pensions Committee consisted mainly of nationalist councillors, with one Unionist. Besides Mrs Williams, the committee included two hoteliers, a tobacconist, a cigar merchant and a builder. None appeared to have skills particularly requisite, but they may have seen membership as a valuable source of political patronage that would yield votes from servicemen and their families when the war was over.

28. *Irish Times*, 25 November 1916. Midwives earned between £23 and £24 per annum. Ó Móráin, *Irish Association of Directors of Nursing and Midwifery*, p. 20.

29. Walsh, *Anglican Women in Dublin*, p. 200.

30. Edith Cavell was the British matron of the Berkendael Medical Institute who was shot by the Germans for helping Allied soldiers escape.

31. Ó Móráin, *Irish Association of Directors of Nursing and Midwifery*, p. 27.

32. *Irish Times*, 8 and 19 August, 1 September and 1 November 1916; Minutes of Grand Lodge, 7 December 1916; Grand Lodge Annual Report, 1917. A doctor and former army officer, Geddes was the Unionist MP for Basingstoke and was Minister of National Service in 1917. His Dublin connection was a result of his appointment as professor of anatomy at the College of Surgeons from 1909 to 1913. He was probably recruited to the Freemasons through the Chief Medical Officer for Dublin and deputy grand master in Ireland, Sir Charles Cameron.

33. *Irish Independent*, 4 October 1916. Besides Lord Donoughmore as grand master, Sir William Goulding was a junior grand warden and Sir Maurice Dockrell a junior grand deacon in the Masons. Grand Lodge Annual Report, 1917.

34. *Irish Times*, 18 November 1916.

35. *Irish Independent*, 21 October 1916; *Irish Times*, 27 November 1916.

36. *Irish Independent*, 17 and 27 November and 19 December 1916; *Irish Times*, 12, 13, 15 and 18 December.

Chapter 8: 'Would anyone seriously suggest for a moment that Willie Cosgrave was a criminal?' (pp 144–63)

1. *Irish Times*, 3 and 6 July; *Irish Independent*, 3, 4 and 10 July.

2. Finnan, *John Redmond and Irish Unity*, p. 209–10. In fact it was a mine that sank the *Hampshire*.

3. *Irish Times*, 10 October 1916.

4. *Irish Independent*, 5 September 1916.

5. Dublin Corporation Minutes, 22 January 1917.

6. *Irish Independent*, 10 October 1916.

7. *Irish Times*, 9 September 1916.

8. *Irish Times*, 8 February 1917.

9. Details of the admittedly small sample are available at www.glasnevintrust.ie. I have excluded from the figures an English naval petty officer, Robert Glaister, shot in the 1916 Rising. The remainder are all from Dublin city and county.

10. Johnston, *Home or Away*, p. 214–15; Dungan, *They Shall Not Grow Old*, p. 38–9. That there were no references to the raid in the press could be due to military censorship; but the fact that an operation on such a scale, which would have virtually rearmed the Dublin Brigade, passed unremarked in rebel circles suggests that the number of weapons taken was relatively small.

11. Dublin Corporation Minutes, 4 September 1917; *Irish Independent*, 5 September 1917.

12. O'Flanagan, 'Dublin City in an Age of War and Revolution,' p. 46.

13. O'Flanagan, 'Dublin City in an Age of War and Revolution,' p. 51.

14. *Irish Times*, 3 July 1915. It was chaired by Patrick J. Leonard, president of the Dublin Chamber of Commerce.

15. Other members of the committee included Richard W. Booth, Arthur W. Spence, David Baird and Henry Dockrell.

16. Grigg, *Lloyd George*, p. 256; *Irish Times*, 8 August and 25 September 1915; O'Flanagan, 'Dublin City in an Age of War and Revolution,' p. 11–13. The other plants were established in Cork, Limerick and Galway.

17. Smellie would later provide a detailed account of the company's activities, *Ship Building and Repairing in Dublin*, 1901–1923 [1935], from which most of the following details are taken.

18. Sweeney, *Liffey Ships and Shipbuilding*, p. 78–82. In 1923 the *Helga* became the *Muirchú*, the Irish Free State's first (and only) naval vessel.

19. See, for example, letter from William O'Brien, secretary of Dublin United Trades Council and Labour League, to Dublin Corporation, 5 March 1917, and reports of a stormy meeting of the Ports and Docks Board, *Irish Times* and *Irish Independent*, 20 April 1917.

20. Fourteen vessels were built in British yards to this model and ten in Dublin. Sweeney, *Liffey Ships and Shipbuilding*, p. 107.

21. While £520 was subscribed to the Prince of Wales Fund by the end of the war, more than £1,500 was subscribed to war loans in early 1917 alone through a Post Office Savings Bank scheme.

22. Smellie, *Ship Building and Repairing in Dublin*, chap. 9.

23. *Labour Gazette*, Report on Employment of Women in Munitions Factories, February 1916.

24. *Weekly Irish Times*, 25 December 1916.

25. *Labour Gazette*, January 1916; *Irish Times*, 8 March 1917. Margaret Culhane was one of a growing band of middle-class women who sought careers as much out of necessity as choice. She turned to professional social work to support her two children after her husband, Frank, a solicitor, died.

26. *Irish Independent*, 12 February 1917.

27. Dublin Corporation Minutes, 9 October 1916.

28. Dublin Corporation Minutes, 9 October 1916 and 2 April 1917; Dublin Corporation Reports, 1920, no. 61.

29. Dublin Corporation Reports, 1917, no. 173, and 1918, no. 272. Mrs Smith was one of the few female members of the Corporation Inspectorate, starting off as a sanitary sub-officer in 1890 and progressing to full sanitary inspector in 1913. She was later appointed an inspector under the Shops Acts. Although at the top of the salary scale by then, she was paid £20 a year less than her male counterparts, until December 1920, when the councillors approved a pay parity increase. Dublin Corporation Reports, 1920, no. 8.

30. *Irish Independent*, 27 July 1918; Dublin Corporation Reports, 1918, no. 243.

31. It kept this basic format through a series of incarnations before its final closure in 1962. See Zimmermann, *The History of Dublin Cinemas*, p. 169–70.

32. Dublin Corporation Reports, 1920, no. 243. The cinema closed in 1919 and reopened under new management in 1921.

33. Collins, *The Cosgrave Legacy*, p. 12–13. Collins and Cosgrave family lore is wrong to imagine that Cosgrave was in the first wave of releases: like others convicted of serious offences, he had to wait until June.

34. Geraghty, *William Patrick Partridge and His Times*, p. 276–94.

35. Maguire, *The Civil Service and the Revolution in Ireland*, p. 35–7. McElligott took up a successful career in journalism, editing the *Statist*, and returned to Ireland in 1923 to take up the position of assistant secretary of the Department of Finance in the new Free State government. He succeeded Joseph Brennan as secretary in 1927 and retired in 1953, becoming governor of the Central Bank.

36. Hart, *Mick*, p. 38–9.

37. Hart, *Mick*, p. 115.

38. National Archives, CO 904/193/11a.

39. Dublin Corporation Reports, 1916, vol. 3; Dublin Corporation Minutes, 10 February and 19 and 23 June 1917; *Irish Times*, 15 April and 3 and 4 August 1919.

40. *Irish Independent*, 4 September 1917; *Irish Times*, 17 September 1917.

Chapter 9: 'The baby was then nine or ten days old, and the girl said that she would drown it' (pp 164–80)

1. *Irish Independent*, 24 January 1917.

2. Dublin Corporation Reports, 1917, no. 248; *Irish Times*, 1 July 1916.

3. *1916 Rebellion Handbook*, p. 27–8.

4. *Irish Independent*, 28 July 1917; Irish Railway Record Society Archive, GSWR, Sinn Féin Rebellion, file 2659; *Irish Times*, 12 December 1916 and 3 December 1917.

5. *Irish Times*, 1 January 1917.

6. *Irish Independent*, 6 June 1917.

7. *Irish Independent*, 30 March 1917; Finnan, *John Redmond and Irish Unity*, p. 152–3.

8. National Archives, CSORP/1918/5778, 25183–25271.

9. Maurice Headlam and Sir John J. Taylor (the latter knighted for his services in 1919) were both protégés of Walter Long, a former leader of the Unionist Party and MP for South County Dublin.
10. O'Halpin, *The Decline of the Union*, p. 209.
11. Memo by Sir William F. Byrne, Under-Secretary, 1916–18, National Archives, CSORP 25183–25271.
12. Mrs Mackenzie's business must have revived, as she was still trading in the mid-1920s.
13. *Irish Independent*, 9 February 1917; *Irish Times*, 9 February 1917.
14. The wealthiest widow was Nannie, wife of Michael O'Rahilly, who refused to take anything from the fund. Ironically, one of Lillie Connolly's minor benefactors was a Catholic priest.
15. Matthews, *Renegades*, p. 160–71.
16. Rigney, 'Military service and GSWR staff.'
17. Irish Railway Record Society Archive, GSWR, Sinn Féin Rebellion, file 2659.
18. Irish Railway Record Society Archive, GSWR, Sinn Féin Rebellion, file 2659.
19. Irish Railway Record Society Archive, GSWR, Sinn Féin Rebellion, file 2659, and DSER, Sinn Féin Rebellion, file 1404.
20. They were W. E. H. Lecky, the liberal Unionist and historian who wrote the landmark *History of Ireland in the Eighteenth Century*, and Edward Dowden, professor of English literature, an imperial Unionist who dismissed the Irish literary movement of Yeats and Lady Gregory as 'flapping green banners.' He declined to intensify his 'spiritual brogue' on their behalf.
21. *Irish Times*, 3 and 6 February 1917.
22. Plunkett was generally referred to as Count Plunkett after being made a Papal count in 1877.
23. *Irish Independent*, 6 February 1917.
24. *Irish Independent*, 6 February 1917; *Irish Times*, 7 February 1917.
25. *Irish Times*, 8 February 1917.
26. *Irish Independent*, 1 January and 10 February 1917.
27. *Irish Times*, 8 February 1917.
28. Lord Barmbrack would later be prosecuted for overcharging on 'war' bread but pleaded, successfully, that the law applied to retailers whereas he was a wholesale baker. *Irish Independent*, 18 October 1917.
29. *Irish Independent*, 12 February 1917. Russell was a former Ulster Unionist MP who had defected to the Liberals.
30. *Irish Times*, 8 March and 13 April 1917; *Irish Independent*, 20 October 1917.
31. *Irish Independent*, 27 March 1917.
32. *Weekly Irish Times*, 7 April 1917.

Chapter 10: 'The most destructive bird that could possibly be' (pp 181–201)
1. *Irish Times*, 23 January 1917.
2. *Irish Times*, 18 September 1916.
3. *Irish Times*, 17 February, 29 March, 25 September and 9 October 1916 and 13 November 1917.

4. *Irish Times*, 14 October 1917.

5. *Irish Times*, 20 September and 14 October 1917.

6. *Irish Times* and *Irish Independent*, 2 December 1916.

7. *Irish Times*, 6 March 1917.

8. *Irish Times* and *Irish Independent*, 5 February and 6 March 1917.

9. *Irish Times*, 11 July 1919; Meenan, *The Irish Economy*, p. 90–91.

10. It would be a persistent problem: boundary walls on railways were raised and barbed wire used as late as 1918 to deter gangs. Dublin Corporation Reports, 1918, no. 207.

11. O'Flanagan, 'Dublin City in an Age of War and Revolution,' p. 27, 48; *Irish Independent*, 13 January 1917.

12. The reference is to Cathedral Street, where the fire consumed Lawrence's toy shop.

13. *Irish Times* and *Irish Independent*, 7 February 1917; Dublin Corporation Reports, 1917, no. 266.

14. Dublin Corporation Reports, 1917, no. 267. A new scale of £150 to £200 a year was approved, with annual increments of £10. The Belfast rate was £156, plus a war bonus of £23 8s. The Dublin war bonus was only £13.

15. Sir Charles Cameron, The Quality of the Milk Used in Dublin, appendix to Dublin Corporation Reports, 1917, no. 122.

16. Dublin Corporation Reports, Pubic Health Reports, 1916–17.

17. See chap. 6 above.

18. *Irish Independent*, 9 October 1917.

19. *Irish Times*, 4 December 1917.

20. Flanagan, 'Dublin City in an Age of War and Revolution,' p. 25–6.

21. *Irish Independent*, 9 October 1917; *Irish Times*, 12 December 1917.

22. *Irish Independent* and *Irish Times*, 8 March 1917.

23. Quoted by Devine, *Organising History*, p. 90. Ironically, in later life O'Brien would become a virulent anti-communist.

24. Devine, *Organising History*, p. 68, 89–93. The figure may well have dropped to as low as 3,500 in early 1916.

25. Morrissey, *A Man Called Hughes*, p. 90.

26. *Irish Times*, 9 and 10 April 1917; *Irish Independent*, 10 April 1917.

27. *Irish Independent*, 10 April 1917.

28. *Irish Times*, 4, 9 and 13 April 1917.

29. *Irish Independent* and *Irish Times*, 20 April 1917.

30. *Irish Independent*, 30 April and 11 May 1917; Ó Lúing, *I Die in a Good Cause*, p. 120–23.

31. Morrissey, *William J. Walsh*, p. 300–22; Coleman, *County Longford and the Irish Revolution*, p. 62–4.

32. *Irish Times*, 11 and 13 June 1917.

33. Robbins, *Under the Starry Plough*, p. 151. He gives the date of his release as August 1916, but this is not possible. The details suggest it was June 1917, when all the convicted prisoners were released.

34. *Irish Times* and *Irish Independent*, 18, 19 and 20 June 1917; *Weekly Irish Times*, 23 June 1917.

35. *Irish Times*, 31 January 1910.

36. *Irish Times*, 10 and 26 June and 7 July 1917. A contest almost ensued nevertheless when at two minutes to the close of nominations a woman appeared with a male companion seeking to place her brother, Captain Charles Vincent Fox vc, on the ballot paper. She said he had recently escaped from a German prisoner-of-war camp and would soon be in a position to take up his duties if elected. However, representatives of the other parties were not prepared to take her word, and Hearn was duly declared elected unopposed.

37. McDowell, *The Irish Convention*, p. 103.

38. *Irish Independent*, 7 August 1917.

39. *Irish Times*, 13 August 1917.

40. Dublin Corporation Minutes, 9 September 1917.

41. Dublin Corporation Minutes, 8 October 1917.

42. *Irish Independent*, 9 October 1917.

Chapter 11: 'I die in a good cause' (pp 202–23)

1. One of his cousins was the American actor Gregory Peck.

2. Ó Lúing, *I Die in a Good Cause*, p. 140–41.

3. *Irish Times*, 4 September 1917.

4. Ó Lúing, *I Die in a Good Cause*, p. 157–64.

5. Ashe had a penchant for poetry and doggerel. In contrast to 'Let me carry your Cross for Ireland, Lord' he also penned the following item in his American Diary: 'And when I die don't bury me at all, But pitch my bones in alcohol, Put a bottle of boose [*sic*] at my head and feet, And then my bones, they will surely keep. My story is told and you'll agree, That this is what boose [*sic*] has done to me.' Mss 46,788, NLI. Ó Lúing, *I Die in a Good Cause*; O'Casey, *Inishfallen, Fare Thee Well*, p. 16.

6. *Irish Times*, 2 October 1917.

7. O'Casey, *Inishfallen, Fare Thee Well*, p. 16; Ó Lúing, *I Die in a Good Cause*, p. 174–82.

8. *Irish Times*, 6 November 1917.

9. Sir Bryan Mahon was later nominated to the Free State Senate by W. T. Cosgrave in recognition of the role he played during this difficult period. Cosgrave had been chairman of the Estates Committee. Bureau of Military History, Witness Statements, ws 268, W. T. Cosgrave.

10. *Irish Independent*, 1 and 4 October 1917; Ó Lúing, *I Die in a Good Cause*, p. 175–82.

11. After their release from Mountjoy, Thomas Ashe's fellow hunger-strikers visited the graveside and took a vow that if they were ever rearrested they would immediately go on hunger strike. One of them, Seán Treacy, decided he would never again go to prison. He was killed three years later resisting arrest in Talbot Street, Dublin.

12. *Irish Independent*, 12 January and 23 February 1918.

13. *Irish Times*, 20 April 1917.

14. Macardle, *The Irish Republic*, p. 232.
15. Laffan, *The Resurrection of Ireland*, p. 118.
16. *Irish Times*, 26 October 1917.
17. Andrews, *Dublin Made Me*, p. 99–100.
18. *Irish Times*, 26 October 1917.
19. *Irish Times*, 26 October 1917; Pádraig Yeates, 'Craft workers during the Irish revolution,' *Saothar*, 33.
20. Dublin Corporation Reports, 1917, no. 128.
21. Stokes, *Death in the Irish Sea*, p. 26.
22. Dublin Corporation Reports, 1917, no. 275.
23. *Irish Times*, 3 November 1917.
24. Dublin Corporation Reports, 1918, no. 13; Prunty, *Dublin Slums*, p. 328–33; Yeates, *Lockout*, p. 108.
25. The occupations are listed separately for first-class tenements and the rest. However, as there is no significant divergence between individuals within occupations, their earnings, and which class of tenement they inhabited, the totals have been combined.
26. See Mona Hearn, 'Life for domestic servants in Dublin,' in Luddy and Murphy, *Women Surviving*; McCaffrey, 'Jacob's women workers in the 1913 lock-out.'
27. *Labour Gazette*, May 1919.
28. *Irish Times*, 28 August and 11 December 1917.
29. Quoted by Johnstone, *Orange, Green and Khaki*, p. 290–91; *Irish Independent*, 27 August 1917; *Irish Times*, 1 September 1917.
30. *Irish Independent*, 6 January 1917.

Chapter 12: 'A coercionist, conscriptionist Lord Lieutenant' (pp 224–46)

1. *Irish Independent*, 25 January 1918.
2. *Irish Independent*, 26 January 1918.
3. *Irish Times* and *Irish Independent*, 6 April 1918. Gaisford St Lawrence was a frequent contributor to charities, across the religious divide: see, for example, the Society of St Vincent de Paul subscription lists.
4. Gilbert, *The Routledge Atlas of the First World War*, p. 79–80. Between 1914 and 1918 only one German submarine was sunk in the Irish Sea, out of a total of 178. *Irish Times*, 15 March 1918.
5. *Irish Independent*, 2 January 1918.
6. *Irish Independent*, 26 February 1918.
7. See chap. 6 above for the milk price controversy.
8. *Irish Independent*, 26 January 1918.
9. *Irish Times*, 6 February 1918.
10. Dalton, *With the Dublin Brigade*, p. 51–5.
11. *Irish Times*, 27 April 1918.
12. *Irish Times*, 5 February 1918.
13. *Irish Independent*, 5 February 1918; *Irish Times*, 9 February 1918.
14. See, for example, *Irish Times*, 9 February 1918.

15. *London Express*, 4 February 1918, editorial comment.

16. See chap. 9 above.

17. Devine, *Organising History*, p. 92.

18. Devine, *Organising History*. See also chap. 4 and 7 above. Cody et al., *The Parliament of Labour*, Theresa Moriarty, 'Work, warfare and wages: Industrial controls and Irish trade unionism in the First World War,' in Gregory and Pašeta, *Ireland and the Great War*. The British National Federation of Women Workers was heavily dependent for growth in membership on the munitions industry, and when the industry was wound down in 1919 its Irish membership collapsed fairly rapidly. *Irish Times* and *Irish Independent*, 5 and 6 November 1917; *Labour Gazette*.

19. *Labour Gazette*, January 1919.

20. *Irish Times* and *Irish Independent*, 31 October 1917.

21. Some 56 per cent of Irish recruits in 1918 joined the newly formed Royal Air Force. Jeffrey, *Ireland and the Great War*, p. 6.

22. *Irish Times*, 26 January 1918.

23. Adrian Gregory, 'You might as well recruit Germans,' in Gregory and Pašeta, *Ireland and the Great War*, p. 113–32.

24. Morrissey, *William O'Brien*, p. 146–7. O'Brien succeeded in sidelining his main rival, P. T. Daly, secretary of the ITUC, by proposing that the congress delegation consist of one delegate from Belfast, another from Cork, and himself as president.

25. John Redmond had died on 6 March 1918.

26. *Irish Independent* and *Irish Times*, 9 April 1918.

27. McDowell, *The Irish Convention*, p. 103. Many public bodies in the South, including the Dublin Trades Council, had refused to nominate delegates to the convention, although Northern trade union organisations did so.

28. *Irish Independent*, 19 April 1918.

29. Morrissey, *William O'Brien*, p. 147–8.

30. *Irish Independent*, 19 April 1918.

31. *Irish Times*, 22 April 1918.

32. *Irish Independent*, 24 April 1918.

33. The details of the night are well recorded by sources as varied as Taylor, *Michael Collins*, p. 70, Dwyer, *The Squad and the Intelligence Operations of Michael Collins*, p. 8–12, and Foy, *Michael Collins's Intelligence War*, p. 11–14; McMahon, *British Spies and Irish Rebels*, p. 24–5.

34. National Archives, CAB/24/59.

35. The 'advanced Sinn Feiner' editing the journal could have been Frank Gallagher or Cathal O'Shannon. Gallagher later joined the Sinn Féin publicity department, and O'Shannon was a veteran member of the IRB and the Labour Party. The journal changed its name from *Irish Opinion* to *Voice of Labour* in January 1918. It was financed by J. Malcolm Lyon, a British businessman who tried, unsuccessfully, to wean Irish Labour away from Sinn Féin. The Dublin link was E. A. Aston, a consultant engineer who came from a liberal Unionist background and was active in the Dublin Citizens' Association. Over time suspicions developed that British intelligence might be behind the funding operation.

36. National Archives, CAB/24/59.
37. The *Irish Independent* put the crowd at the Cullen funeral at five thousand and the DMP at two thousand. National Archives, CAB/24/59; *Irish Independent*, 3 June 1918; *Irish Times*, 15 June 1918.
38. *Irish Times*, 10 June 1918.
39. *Irish Independent*, 10 June 1918.
40. Denmark House was a former nursing home in Great Denmark Street that had been converted to offices for use by various groups of women workers.
41. See Jones, *These Obstreperous Lassies*, and Cullen Owens, *Louie Bennett*. Bennett would go on to become the first woman to be elected president of the ITUC and served two terms, 1932 and 1948. Helena Molony was elected president in 1937 and Helen Chenevix in 1951.
42. Matthews, *Renegades*, p. 218.
43. *Irish Independent*, 10 June 1918.
44. *Irish Independent* and *Irish Times*, 10 June 1918.
45. *Irish Times*, 4 June 1918.
46. See chap. 5 above.
47. The former director of intelligence for the Volunteers, Éamonn Duggan, was his solicitor. Duggan would later serve as a Sinn Féin MP and was one of the negotiators at the talks on the Anglo-Irish Treaty.
48. *Irish Times*, 4 June 1918; National Archives, CAB/24/59.
49. *Irish Independent*, 14 June 1918; and see Ó Broin, *Revolutionary Underground*, for Daly and Allan.
50. *Irish Independent*, 14 June 1918.

Chapter 13: 'The torpedo exploded in the middle of the Post Office, destroying the stairs, the only means of escape' (pp 247–69)

1. The ban on the Gaelic League surprised many observers; it was included by mistake for the Gaelic Athletic Association. The GAA thus escaped the ban.
2. *Irish Times* and *Irish Independent*, 4, 9, 10 and 23 July 1918.
3. An added cost was that Rathdown Rural District Union in south Co. Dublin availed of the reorganisation to close its workhouse and export the problem to Dublin.
4. O'Flanagan, 'Dublin City in an Age of War and Revolution,' p. 98–9.
5. Wolfe, *Labour Supply and Regulation*, chap. 13.
6. *Irish Times*, 4 to 7 September 12918.
7. *Irish Times*, 7 September 1918.
8. *Weekly Irish Times*, 16 November 1918.
9. Dublin Corporation Minutes, p. 502–4, 558–60.
10. *Irish Times*, 9 September 1918.
11. See McCracken, *MacBride's Brigade*, chap. 7.
12. *Irish Times*, 31 August 1918.
13. National Archives, CAB 24/70.
14. See chap. 8 above.
15. Cody et al., *The Parliament of Labour*, p. 121.

16. Mitchell, *Labour in Irish Politics*, p. 92–3; Morrissey, *William O'Brien*, p. 154–5; Cody et al., *The Parliament of Labour*, p. 111–21. For Louie Bennett see chap. 8 above, Fox, *Louie Bennett*, and Cullen Owens, *Louie Bennett*, p. 41–3. Neil O'Flanagan, in 'Dublin City in an Age of War and Revolution,' argues that the Daly-O'Brien split was the main reason for Labour's failure to dominate politics in Dublin after the Easter Rising.

17. *Irish Times*, 12 October 1918.

18. See chap. 4 above.

19. *Irish Times*, 12 October 1918; Stokes, *Death in the Irish Sea*, p. 46.

20. Higgins, 'The sinking of the RMS *Leinster* recalled.'

21. *Irish Independent*, 12 October 1918, and Michael Lee.

22. *Irish Times*, 12 October 1918.

23. Novick, *Conceiving Revolution*, p. 76–9.

24. Among the naval vessels to race to the scene and pick up survivors was the *Helga*, which had shelled Liberty Hall during the rising.

25. National Archives, CAB/24/70; Stokes, *Death in the Irish Sea*, p. 136. The sinking of the *Leinster* may have boosted recruitment, because Dublin's figures rose to 2,591 by the end of October.

26. See chap. 3 above.

27. See chap. 4 above.

28. National Society for the Prevention of Cruelty to Children, Annual Reports.

29. National Society for the Prevention of Cruelty to Children, Annual Report, 1919–1920.

30. Jane Leonard, 'Survivors,' in Horne, *Our War*.

31. Most offences under the Shops Acts involved employers failing to give employees their half day off.

32. *Irish Independent*, 21 December 1918; *Irish Times*, 27 February 1919.

33. *Irish Independent*, 16 December 1918.

34. *Labour Gazette*.

35. *Labour Gazette*.

36. O'Flanagan, 'Dublin City in an Age of War and Revolution,' p. 90–95; Raftery and O'Sullivan, *Suffer Little Children*, p. 69–72; Robbins, *Fools and Mad*, p. 183–95

37. Robbins, *Fools and Mad*, p. 183; Robbins, *Grangegorman*, p. 210–19.

38. *Irish Times*, 5 November 1917.

39. Dublin Corporation Reports, 1919, no. 194.

40. *Irish Times*, 18 September and 3 November 1914, 1 January, 31 March and 10 May 1915, 3 April 1916, 1 January and 28 May 1917, and 3 September 1919.

Chapter 14: 'You haven't got a republic yet, so get out of the way!' (pp 270–99)

1. Dublin Corporation, Quarterly Breviate Reports of Public Health Committee, 1913–1920.

2. *Irish Times*, 29 June and 9 July 1918.

3. In the week ending 3 July, 25 deaths out of 120 in Dublin were among children aged one to five years old and a further 15 were of children under twelve months,

according to the *Irish Independent*, 4 July 1918. The *Irish Times* of 6 July 1918 reported that there had been five deaths from influenza in the city for the same period (all of them adults).

4. *Irish Times*, 2 and 6 July 1918.
5. *Irish Times*, 20 July 1918. Other deaths were accounted for as follows: 31 from TB, 14 from heart disease and 12 from bronchitis.
6. *Irish Independent*, 21 November 1918.
7. Ó hÓgartaigh, *Kathleen Lynn*, p. 42.
8. *Irish Times*, 26 and 28 February 1918.
9. Dublin Corporation Reports, 1919, no. 254; *Irish Times*, 26 February 1919; *Irish Independent*, 27 March 1919.
10. *Irish Independent*, 27 March 1919. These figures exclude the deaths of those admitted to Dublin hospitals from places outside the capital.
11. Dublin Corporation Reports, 1919, no. 263, 265, 284.
12. See chap. 3 above.
13. Dublin Corporation Reports, 1921, no. 60; Annual Report of the Grand Lodge of Free and Accepted Masons, 1920.
14. Cameron Papers, Report of the Deputy Grand Secretary of the Grand Lodge of Ireland, 1920; *Irish Times*, 28 February 1921; Ó hÓgartaigh, *Kathleen Lynn*, p. 41; Freemasons Roll of Honour; Parkinson, *History of the Grand Lodge of Free and Accepted Masons of Ireland*, vol. 1.
15. Luddy, *Prostitution and Irish Society*, p. 186. Joseph O'Brien, *Dear, Dirty Dublin*, p. 116, argues that if stillbirths and premature births related to syphilis are included in death rates these would rank as one of the main causes of infant mortality, as well as leaving many children with serious medical conditions.
16. Yeates, *Lockout*, p. 53–4, 363–4.
17. Luddy, *Prostitution and Irish Society*, p. 165–72.
18. Yeates, *Lockout*, p. 502.
19. Weekly *Irish Times*, 23 October 1915.
20. Luddy, *Prostitution and Irish Society*. See chap. 5, and Johnston-Keogh, 'Dublin's Women Patrol and women's entry into policy.'
21. Luddy, *Prostitution and Irish Society*, p. 178.
22. Dublin Corporation Reports, 1918, no. 13. I use the term 'comparative deprivation' in the industrial relations sense, where the erosion of a differential in pay or conditions can cause resentment among the group adversely affected. This often manifests itself in various forms of negative behaviour.
23. Quoted by Dennison and MacDonagh, *Guinness*; see especially chap. 10 and 13.
24. Matthews, *Renegades*, p. 211–12.
25. Luddy, *Prostitution and Irish Society*, p. 191; Ó hÓgartaigh, *Kathleen Lynn*, p. 39.
26. Luddy, *Prostitution and Irish Society*, p. 204–5; Matthews, *Renegades*, p. 222.
27. For a detailed debate on the issues raised by the 1926 Interdepartmental Report see Howell, 'Venereal disease and the politics of prostitution in the Irish Free State,' Riordan, 'Venereal disease in the Irish Free State,' and Howell, 'The politics of prostitution and the politics of public health in the Irish Free State.'

28. *Irish Times*, 16 November 1918.

29. Lynch's peculiar political trajectory had seen him fight against the British Empire during the Boer War and subsequently be condemned to death for high treason, only to have the sentence commuted to a short prison sentence, then become Home Rule MP for Galway. After the First World War he continued his parliamentary career as a Labour MP for Battersea South.

30. Ryan, *Comrades*, p. 41, 42.

31. Bureau of Military History, Witness Statements, WS 1119, Joseph McDonagh; *Irish Times* and *Irish Independent*, 12 to 16 November 1918.

32. Richard Coleman had died on 12 December in Usk Prison in Monmouthshire. By coincidence, he had served under Thomas Ashe at Ashbourne in 1916.

33. *Irish Independent*, 13 November 1918. Cissie Cahalan was a shop worker and a member of the Irish Linen Drapers' Assistants' Association.

34. Ward, *Hanna Sheehy Skeffington*, p. 226.

35. *Irish Times*, 6 December 1918.

36. National Archives, CAB 24/70.

37. Mulholland, *The Politics and Relationships of Kathleen Lynn*, p. 63.

38. He would later serve briefly as first Commissioner of the Garda Síochána.

39. Originally opposed to the militarism of the Volunteers, Little would later take the anti-Treaty side in the Civil War and served in the Four Courts garrison. He subsequently edited *An Phoblacht*, the IRA newspaper, and served as a Fianna Fáil TD and as Minister for Posts and Telegraphs during the Second World War.

40. Bureau of Military History, Witness Statements, WS 660, Thomas Leahy.

41. Dublin Corporation Minutes, 18 October 1918, item no. 646.

42. *Irish Times*, 12 November 1918.

43. Dublin Corporation Minutes, 2 November 1919, item no. 666.

44. *Irish Independent*, 16 July 1918.

45. *Irish Times*, 3 December 1918.

46. *Irish Times*, 1 March 1919.

47. It would take another world war to resolve the chaos of the British coal industry through nationalisation. One permanent benefit from the coal shortage was government funding to extend the Cavan and Leitrim Light Railway into the Arigna Valley and open up its seams for the Dublin market.

48. McCamley, *Dublin Tramworkers*, p. 119.

49. *Irish Independent*, 25 March 1918; *Irish Times*, 27 and 28 February, 11 and 21 March and 8 April 1919.

50. *Irish Times*, 25 February 1918.

51. Mitchell, *Labour in Irish Politics*, p. 107–10. Even after it was amended, the Democratic Programme was considered 'communistic' by some senior members of the Dáil, including Piaras Béaslaí, Kevin O'Higgins and Cathal Brugha. Morrissey, *William O'Brien*, p. 162.

52. Dáil Éireann, Minutes of Proceedings, 21 January 1919, p. 22–4; Gaughan, *Thomas Johnson*, p. 157. At the same time central figures, such as Collins and Cosgrave, did

show statist tendencies, which came to characterise the approach of successive Irish governments to economic development. Collins believed that the development of mining and natural resources was the proper domain of the state, while Cosgrave was an advocate of the state as the sole provider of insurance policies and products for commercial and social purposes. Mitchell, *Revolutionary Government in Ireland*, p. 49.

Chapter 15: A flickering green light at the end of a long tunnel (pp 300–311)

1.   This is not to deny that that there were occasional clashes in Dublin city centre, usually outside Trinity College, between students and republicans, such as the highly publicised riot on VE Day involving a young Charles Haughey. See contemporaneous news reports, *Irish Times*, 1926–49; Wills, *That Neutral Island*, p. 170–72.
2.   The attitude of the unions to the company would change after the war, but that is another story.
3.   *Irish Independent*, 5 February 1919.

SELECT BIBLIOGRAPHY

The bibliography includes only sources cited in the text or the notes.

PRIMARY SOURCES

Ashe Papers, National Library of Ireland
Asquith Papers, Bodleian Library, Oxford
Cabinet Papers, National Archives (London)
Cameron Papers, Royal College of Surgeons in Ireland, Dublin
Chief Secretary's Office, National Archives, Dublin
Colonial Office Files
Dáil Éireann, Minutes of Proceedings, 1919–21
Dublin Chamber of Commerce, Annual Reports, 1913–18
Dublin Corporation, Minutes and Reports, 1911–22, Dublin City Archives
Dr William Walsh Laity Papers, Dublin Diocesan Archive
Dublin Metropolitan Police, Annual Reports and Statistical Returns, 1912–19
Dublin Trades Council Minutes, 1913–1928, Irish Labour History Society
Glasnevin Trust
Guinness Archive, Dublin
Ireland's Memorial Records, 1914–1918 (CD), Dublin: Eneclann, 2005
Irish Railway Records Society Archive, Dublin
Irish Transport and General Workers Union records, National Library of Ireland
Masonic Grand Lodge of Free and Accepted Masons, Ireland
National Society for the Prevention of Cruelty to Children, Annual Reports, 1911–24, National Library of Ireland
Report of the Departmental Committee into the Housing Conditions of the Working Classes in the City of Dublin, 1914, National Library of Ireland
Roberts Collection, Royal Dublin Fusiliers Association Archive, Dublin City Archives
Witness Statements, Bureau of Military History, Dublin

I NEWSPAPERS AND PERIODICALS
Catholic Bulletin
Dublin Evening Mail
Evening Telegraph
Freeman's Journal
Irish Independent

Irish Times
Labour Gazette (London)

II ARTICLES IN PERIODICALS, AND PAPERS DELIVERED AT SEMINARS AND CONFERENCES

Cody, Séamus, *The Remarkable Patrick Daly* (ILHS Monograph), Dublin: Irish Labour History Society, 1985.

Higgins, J. J. 'The sinking of the RMS Leinster recalled,' *Postal Worker*, November 1936.

Howell, Philip, 'The politics of prostitution and the politics of public health in the Irish Free State: A response to Susannah Riordan,' *Irish Historical Studies*, November 2007.

Howell, Philip, 'Venereal disease and the politics of prostitution in the Irish Free State,' *Irish Historical Studies*, May 2003.

Johnston-Keogh, John, 'Dublin's Women Patrol and women's entry into policy,' paper presented to Women's History Association of Ireland and Irish Labour History Society, Dublin, 22 and 23 October 2010.

McCaffrey, Patricia, 'Jacob's women workers in the 1913 lock-out,' *Saothar*, 16, 1991.

Maguire, Martin, 'The Dublin working class, 1870s–1930s: Economy, society, politics,' in Thomas Bartlett (ed.), *History and Environment*, Dublin: UCD Press, 1988.

Maguire, Martin, 'The organisation and activism of Dublin's Protestant working class, 1883–1935,' *Irish Historical Studies*, May 1994.

Maguire, Martin, 'A socio-economic analysis of the Dublin working class, 1870–1926,' *Irish Economic and Social History*, 20, 1993.

Murray, Peter, 'The First World War and a Dublin distillery workforce: Recruiting and redundancy at John Power, 1915–1917,' *Saothar*, 15, 1990.

O'Flanagan, Neil, 'Dublin City in an Age of War and Revolution, 1914–1924,' MA thesis, University College, Dublin, 1985.

O'Riordan, Manus, 'Connolly reassessed: The Irish and European context,' Paper presented at Dr Douglas Hyde Conference, Strokestown, 2001.

O'Riordan, Manus, 'Michael O'Leary, Kuno Meyer and Peadar Ó Laoghaire,' *Ballingeary Historical Society Journal*, 2005.

Rigney, Peter, 'Military service and GSWR staff, 1914–1923,' *Journal of the Irish Railway Record Society*, October 2006

Riordan, Susannah, 'Venereal disease in the Irish Free State: The politics of public health,' *Irish Historical Studies*, May 2007.

Woggon, Helga, 'Not merely a labour organisation: The ITGWU and the Dublin dock strike, 1915–16,' *Saothar*, 27, 2002.

Yeates, Pádraig, 'Craft workers during the Irish revolution,' *Saothar*, 33, 2008.

III BOOKS

Andrews, C. S., *Dublin Made Me: An Autobiography*, Dublin and Cork: Mercier, 1979.

Arthur Guinness, Son and Company Ltd, 'Commemorative Roll,' n.d.

Augusteijn, Joost, *From Public Defiance to Guerrilla Warfare: The Experience of Ordinary Volunteers in the Irish War of Independence, 1916–1921*, Dublin: Irish Academic Press, 1996.

Bartlett, Thomas (ed.), *History and Environment*, Dublin: UCD Press, 1988.

Bew, Paul, *Ideology and the Irish Question: Ulster Unionism and Irish Nationalism, 1912–1916*, Oxford: Clarendon Press, 1944.

Bolster, Evelyn, *The Knights of St Columbanus*, Dublin: Gill & Macmillan, 1979.

Carden, Sheila, *The Alderman: Alderman Tom Kelly (1868–1942) and Dublin Corporation*, Dublin: Dublin City Council, 2007.

Caulfield, Max, *The Easter Rebellion*, London and Worcester: Frederick Muller, 1964.

Clarke, Kathleen (Helen Litton, ed.), *Revolutionary Woman: Kathleen Clarke (1878–1972): An Autobiography*, Dublin: O'Brien Press, 1991.

Clarkson, J. Dunsmore, *Labour and Nationalism in Ireland*, New York: Columbia University Press, 1925, reprinted 1978.

Cody, Séamus, O'Dowd, John, and Rigney, Peter, *The Parliament of Labour: 100 Years of the Dublin Council of Trade Unions*, Dublin: Dublin Council of Trade Unions, 1986.

Coleman, Marie, *County Longford and the Irish Revolution, 1910–1923*, Dublin: Irish Academic Press, 2003.

Collins, Stephen, *The Cosgrave Legacy*, Dublin: Blackwater Press, 1996.

Connolly, James (Donal Nevin, ed.), *Between Comrades: Letters and Correspondence, 1889–1916*, Dublin: Gill & Macmillan, 2005.

Connolly, James (Desmond Ryan, ed.), *Socialism and Nationalism*, Dublin: Three Candles, 1948.

Connolly, James (Desmond Ryan, ed.), *The Workers' Republic*, Dublin: Three Candles, 1951.

Cottrell, Peter (ed.), *The War for Ireland, 1913–1923*, London: Osprey Publishing, 2009.

Cruise O'Brien, Conor (ed.), *The Shaping of Modern Ireland*, London: Routledge and Kegan Paul, 1960.

Cullen Owens, Rosemary, *Louie Bennett*, Cork: Cork University Press, 2001.

Dalton, Charles, *With the Dublin Brigade (1917–1921)*, London: Peter Davies, 1929.

Daly, Mary E., *Dublin, the Deposed Capital: A Social and Economic History, 1860–1914*, Cork: Cork University Press, 1984.

Dangerfield, George, *The Damnable Question: A Study in Anglo-Irish Relations*, London: Constable, 1977.

Dennison, S. R., and MacDonagh, Oliver, *Guinness, 1886–1939: From Incorporation to the Second World War*, Cork: Cork University Press, 1998.

Devine, Francis, *Organising History: A Centenary of SIPTU*, Dublin: Gill & Macmillan, 2009.

Devine, Francis, and O'Riordan, Manus, *James Connolly, Liberty Hall and the 1916 Rising*, Dublin: SIPTU, 2006.

Dickinson, Page L., *The Dublin of Yesterday*, London: Methuen, 1929.

Dooley, Thomas P., *Irishmen or English Soldiers?: The Times and World of a Southern Catholic Irish Man (1876–1916) Enlisting in the British Army During the First World War*, Liverpool: Liverpool University Press, 1995.

Dooney, Laura, 'Trinity College and the war,' in *Ireland and the First World War* (David Fitzpatrick, ed.), Dublin: Trinity History Workshop, 1986.

Dudley Edwards, Ruth, *Patrick Pearse: The Triumph of Failure*, London: Gollancz, 1977.

Dungan, Myles, *They Shall Not Grow Old: Irish Soldiers and the Great War*, Dublin: Four Courts Press, 1997.

Dwyer, T. Ryle, *The Squad and the Intelligence Operations of Michael Collins*, Cork: Mercier Press, 2005.

Ferriter, Diarmaid, *The Transformation of Ireland, 1900–2000*, London: Profile Books, 2004.

Findlater, Alex, *Findlater's: The Story of a Dublin Merchant Family, 1774–2001*, Dublin: A. and A. Farmar, 2001.

Fingall, Elizabeth Mary Margaret Burke Plunkett, Countess of, *Seventy Years Young: Memories of Elizabeth, Countess of Fingall* (as told to Pamela Hinkson), London: Collins, 1937; reprinted Dublin: Lilliput Press, 1995.

Finnan, Joseph P., *John Redmond and Irish Unity, 1912–1918*, Syracuse (NY): Syracuse University Press, 2004.

Fitzpatrick, David, *Harry Boland's Irish Revolution*, Cork: Cork University Press, 2003.

Ford, Alan, Milne, Kenneth, and McGuire, J. I., *As by Law Established: The Church of Ireland since the Reformation*, Dublin: Lilliput Press, 1995.

Fox, R. M., *The History of the Irish Citizen Army*, Dublin: James Duffy, 1943.

Fox, R. M., *Louie Bennett: Her Life and Times*, Dublin: Talbot Press [1958].

Foy, Michael T., *Michael Collins's Intelligence War: The Struggle between the British and the IRA, 1919–1921*, Stroud (Glos.): Sutton Publishing, 2006.

Foy, Michael, and Barton, Brian, *The Easter Rising*, Stroud (Glos.): Sutton Publishing, 1999.

Gaughan, J. Anthony, *Thomas Johnson, 1872–1963: First Leader of the Labour Party in Dáil Éireann*, Dublin: Kingdom Books, 1980.

Geraghty, Hugh, *William Patrick Partridge and His Times (1874–1917)*, Dublin: Curlew Books, 2003.

Geraghty, Tom, and Whitehead, Trevor, *The Dublin Fire Brigade: A History of the Brigade, the Fires and the Emergencies*, Dublin: Dublin City Council, 2004.

Gilbert, Martin, *The Routledge Atlas of the First World War*, London: Routledge, 1997.

Greaves, C. Desmond, *The Life and Times of James Connolly*, London: Lawrence and Wishart, 1961.

Gregory, Adrian, and Pašeta, Senia, *Ireland and the Great War: 'A war to unite us all'?* Manchester: Manchester University Press, 2002.

Grigg, John, *Lloyd George: From Peace to War, 1912–1916*, London: Harper-Collins, 1985.

Hart, Peter, *The IRA at War, 1916–1923*, Oxford: Oxford University Press, 2003.

Hart, Peter, *Mick: The Real Michael Collins*, London: Macmillan, 2005.

Henderson, Frank (Michael Hopkinson, ed.), *Frank Henderson's Easter Rising: Recollections of a Dublin Volunteer*, Cork: Cork University Press, 1998.

Hill, Jacqueline R., *From Patriots to Unionists: Dublin Civic Politics and Irish Protestant Patriotism, 1660–1840*, Oxford: Oxford University Press, 1997.

Horne, John, *Our War: Ireland and the Great War*, Dublin: Royal Irish Academy, 2008.

Irwin, Wilmot, *Betrayal in Ireland: An Eye-witness Record of the Tragic and Terrible Years of Revolution and Civil War in Ireland, 1916–24*, Belfast: Northern Whig [1966].

Jeffrey, Keith, *Ireland and the Great War*, Cambridge: Cambridge University Press, 2000.

Johnston, Kevin, *Home or Away: The Great War and the Irish Revolution*, Dublin: Gill & Macmillan, 2010.

Johnstone, Tom, *Orange, Green and Khaki: The Story of the Irish Regiments in the Great War, 1914–18*, Dublin: Gill & Macmillan, 1992.

Jones, Mary, *These Obstreperous Lassies: A History of the Irish Women Workers' Union*, Dublin: Gill & Macmillan, 1988.

Keane, Maureen, *Ishbel: Lady Aberdeen in Ireland*, Newtownards: Colourpoint Books, 1999.

Laffan, Michael, *The Resurrection of Ireland: The Sinn Féin Party, 1916–1923*, Cambridge: Cambridge University Press, 1999.

Levenson, Leah, and Natterstad, Jerry H., *Hanna Sheehy Skeffington: Irish Feminist*, Syracuse (NY): Syracuse University Press, 1986.

Luddy, Maria, *Prostitution and Irish Society, 1800–1940*, Cambridge: Cambridge University Press, 2007.

Luddy, Maria, and Murphy, Clíona (eds.), *Women Surviving: Studies in Irish Women's History in the 19th and 20th Centuries*, Dublin: Poolbeg Press, 1990.

Lyons, J. B., *The Enigma of Tom Kettle: Irish Patriot, Essayist, Poet, British Soldier*, Dublin: Glendale Press, 1983.

Lyons, F. S. L., *John Dillon: A Biography*, London: Routledge and Kegan Paul, 1968.

Macardle, Dorothy, *The Irish Republic: A Documented Chronicle of the Anglo-Irish Conflict and the Partitioning of Ireland, with a Detailed Account of the Period 1916–1923*, Dublin: Irish Press, 1951.

McCamley, Bill, *Dublin Tramworkers, 1872–1945*, Dublin: Labour History Workshop, 2008.

McCartney, Donal, *UCD: A National Idea: The History of University College, Dublin*, Dublin: Gill & Macmillan, 1999.

McCracken, Donal P., *MacBride's Brigade: Irish Commandos in the Anglo-Boer War*, Dublin: Four Courts Press, 1999.

McDowell, R. B., *Crisis and Decline: The Fate of Southern Unionists*, Dublin: Lilliput Press, 1997.

McDowell, R. B., *The Irish Convention, 1917–1918*, London: Routledge and Kegan Paul, 1970.

McGarry, Fearghal, *The Rising: Ireland, Easter 1916*, Oxford: Oxford University Press, 2010.

McMahon, Paul, *British Spies and Irish Rebels: British Intelligence, 1916–1945*, Woodbridge (Suffolk): Boydell Press, 2008.

McManus, Ruth, *Dublin, 1910–1940: Shaping the City and Suburbs*, Dublin: Four Courts Press, 2002.

Maguire, Martin, *The Civil Service and the Revolution in Ireland, 1912–1938: 'Shaking the blood-stained hand of Mr Collins,'* Manchester: Manchester University Press, 2008.

Martin, F. X. (ed.), *The Howth Gun-Running and the Kilcoole Gun-Running*, Dublin: Browne and Nolan, 1964.

Martin, F. X. (ed.), *The Irish Volunteers, 1913–1915: Recollections and Documents*, Dublin: James Duffy, 1963.

Martin, F. X., *Leaders and Men of the Easter Rising*, London: Methuen, 1967.

Matthews, Ann, *Renegades: Irish Republican Women, 1900–1922*, Cork: Mercier Press, 2010.

Maume, Patrick, *D. P. Moran*, Dundalk: Dundalgan Press, 1995.

Maume, Patrick, *The Long Gestation: Irish Nationalist Life, 1891–1918*, Dublin: Gill & Macmillan, 1999.

Meenan, James, *The Irish Economy since 1922*, Liverpool: Liverpool University Press, 1970.

Mitchell, Arthur, *Labour in Irish Politics*, Dublin: Irish University Press, 1974.

Mitchell, Arthur, *Revolutionary Government in Ireland: Dáil Éireann, 1919–22*, Dublin, Gill & Macmillan, 1995.

Montefiore, Dora B., *From a Victorian to a Modern*, London: E. Archer, 1917.

Moran, James, *Staging the Easter Rising: 1916 as Theatre*, Cork: Cork University Press, 2005.

Morrissey, Thomas J., *'A Man Called Hughes': The Life and Times of Seamus Hughes, 1881–1943*, Dublin: Veritas, 1991.

Morrissey, Thomas J., Introduction to Lambert McKenna, *The Social Teachings of James Connolly*, Dublin: Veritas, 1991.

Morrissey, Thomas J., *William J. Walsh, Archbishop of Dublin, 1841–1921: No Uncertain Voice*, Dublin: Four Courts Press, 2000.

Morrissey, Thomas J., *William O'Brien, 1881–1968: Socialist, Republican, Dáil Deputy, Editor and Trade Union Leader*, Dublin: Four Courts Press, 2007.

Mulholland, Marie, *The Politics and Relationships of Kathleen Lynn*, Dublin: Woodfield Press, 2002.

Murray, Christopher, *Seán O'Casey: Writer at Work: A Biography*, Dublin: Gill & Macmillan, 2004.

Newsinger, John, *Rebel City: Larkin, Connolly and the Dublin Labour Movement*, London: Merlin Press, 2004.

Novick, Ben, *Conceiving Revolution: Irish Nationalist Propaganda During the First World War*, Dublin: Four Courts Press, 2001.

O'Brien, Joseph V., *Dear, Dirty Dublin: A City in Distress, 1899–1916*, Berkeley: University of California Press, 1982.

O'Brien, Paul, *Blood on the Streets: 1916 and the Battle for Mount Street Bridge*, Cork: Mercier Press, 2008.

O'Brien, William X. (as told to Edward MacLysaght), *Forth the Banners Go: Reminiscences of William O'Brien*, Dublin: Three Candles, 1969.

Ó Broin, Leon, *Revolutionary Underground: The Story of the Irish Republican Brotherhood, 1858–1924*, Dublin: Gill & Macmillan, 1976.

O'Casey, Seán, *Drums Under the Windows*, London: Macmillan, 1945; reprinted London: Pan Books, 1973.

O'Casey, Seán, *Inishfallen, Fare Thee Well*, London: Macmillan 1949; reprinted London: Pan Books, 1973.

O Cathasaigh, P. [Seán O'Casey], *The Story of the Irish Citizen Army*, Dublin and London: Maunsel, 1919.

O'Farrell, Padraic, *Who's Who in the Irish War of Independence, 1916–1921*, Dublin: Mercier [1980].

O'Halpin, Eunan, *The Decline of the Union: British Government in Ireland, 1982–1920*, Dublin: Gill & Macmillan, 1997.

Ó hÓgartaigh, Margaret, *Kathleen Lynn: Irishwoman, Patriot, Doctor*, Dublin: Irish Academic Press, 2006.

Ó Lúing, Seán, *I Die in a Good Cause: A Study of Thomas Ashe, Idealist and Revolutionary*, Tralee: Kerryman, 1970.

Ó Maitiú, Séamas, *W. and R. Jacob: Celebrating 150 Years of Irish Biscuit Making*, Dublin: Woodfield Press, 2001.

O'Malley, Ernie, *On Another Man's Wound*, London: Four Square Books, 1961.

Ó Móráin, Pádraig, *Irish Association of Directors of Nursing and Midwifery, 1902–2004*, Dublin: IADNM, 2004.

Orr, Philip, *Field of Bones: An Irish Division at Gallipoli*, Dublin: Lilliput Press, 2007.

Parkinson, Richard, *History of the Grand Lodge of Free and Accepted Masons of Ireland*, Dublin: Lodge of Research, 1957.

Pašeta, Senia, *Before the Revolution: Nationalism, Social Change and Ireland's Catholic Elite*, Cork: Cork University Press, 1999.

Pearse, Patrick, *Political Writings and Speeches*, Dublin: Talbot Press, 1962.

Plunkett Dillon, Geraldine (Honor Ó Brolcháin, ed.), *All in the Blood: A Memoir of the Plunkett Family, the 1916 Rising and the War of Independence*, Dublin: A. and A. Farmar, 2006.

Prunty, Jacinta, *Dublin Slums, 1800–1925: A Study in Urban Geography*, Dublin: Irish Academic Press, 1998.

Raftery, Mary, and O'Sullivan, Eoin, *Suffer the Little Children: The Inside Story of Ireland's Industrial Schools*, Dublin: New Island Books, 1999.

Robbins, Frank, *Under the Starry Plough: Recollections of the Irish Citizen Army*, Dublin: Academy Press, 1977.

Robbins, Joseph, *Fools and Mad: A History of the Insane in Ireland*, Dublin: Institute of Public Administration, 1986.

Robbins, Joseph, *Grangegorman: Psychiatric Care in Dublin since 1815*, Dublin: Institute of Public Administration, 1992.

Robinson, Henry Augustus, *Memories, Wise and Otherwise*, London: Cassell, 1923.

Ryan, Annie, *Comrades: Inside the War of Independence*, Dublin: Liberties Press, 2007.

Smellie, John, *Ship Building and Repairing in Dublin: A Record of Work Carried Out by the Dublin Dockyard Company, 1901–1923*, Glasgow: McCorquodale and Company [1935].

Stephens, James, *The Insurrection in Dublin*, Dublin and London: Maunsel, 1916; reprinted Dublin: Scepter Books, 1965.

Stokes, Roy, *Death in the Irish Sea: The Sinking of the RMS Leinster*, Cork: Collins Press, 1998.

Strachan, Hew, *The First World War, vol. 1: To Arms*, Oxford: Oxford University Press, 2001.

Sweeney, Patrick, *Liffey Ships and Shipbuilding*, Dublin: Mercier Press, 2010.

Taylor, Rex, *Michael Collins*, London: Four Square Books, 1961.

Tierney, Michael (F. X. Martin, ed.), *Eoin MacNeill: Scholar and Man of Action, 1867–1945*, Oxford: Clarendon Press, 1980.

Townshend, Charles, *Easter 1916: The Irish Rebellion*, London: Allen Lane, 2005.

Tynan, Katharine, *The Years of the Shadow*, Boston: Houghton Mifflin, 1919.

Valiulis, Maryann Gialanella, *Portrait of a Revolutionary: General Richard Mulcahy and the Founding of the Irish Free State*, Dublin: Irish Academic Press, 1992.

Walsh, Oonagh, *Anglican Women in Dublin: Philanthropy, Politics and Education in the Early Twentieth Century*, Dublin: UCD Press, 2005.

Ward, Margaret, *Hanna Sheehy Skeffington: A Life*, Dublin: Attic Press, 1997.

Weekly Irish Times, *Sinn Fein Rebellion Handbook: Easter, 1916*, Dublin: Weekly Irish Times, 1917; reprinted as *1916 Rebellion Handbook*, Dublin: Mourne River Press, 1998.

Wills, Clair, *That Neutral Island: A Cultural History of Ireland During the Second World War*, London: Faber and Faber, 2007.

Wolfe, Humbert, *Labour Supply and Regulation*, Oxford: Clarendon Press, 1923.

Yeates, Pádraig, *Lockout: Dublin, 1913*, Dublin: Gill & Macmillan, 2000.

Zimmermann, Marc, *The History of Dublin Cinemas*, Dublin: Nonsuch, 2007.

INDEX